Sustainable Development Goals Series

The Sustainable Development Goals Series is Springer Nature's inaugural cross-imprint book series that addresses and supports the United Nations' seventeen Sustainable Development Goals. The series fosters comprehensive research focused on these global targets and endeavours to address some of society's greatest grand challenges. The SDGs are inherently multidisciplinary, and they bring people working across different fields together and working towards a common goal. In this spirit, the Sustainable Development Goals series is the first at Springer Nature to publish books under both the Springer and Palgrave Macmillan imprints, bringing the strengths of our imprints together.

The Sustainable Development Goals Series is organized into eighteen subseries: one subseries based around each of the seventeen respective Sustainable Development Goals, and an eighteenth subseries, "Connecting the Goals," which serves as a home for volumes addressing multiple goals or studying the SDGs as a whole. Each subseries is guided by an expert Subseries Advisor with years or decades of experience studying and addressing core components of their respective Goal.

The SDG Series has a remit as broad as the SDGs themselves, and contributions are welcome from scientists, academics, policymakers, and researchers working in fields related to any of the seventeen goals. If you are interested in contributing a monograph or curated volume to the series, please contact the Publishers: Zachary Romano [Springer; zachary.romano@springer.com] and Rachael Ballard [Palgrave Macmillan; rachael.ballard@palgrave.com].

More information about this series at
http://www.palgrave.com/gp/series/15486

Ashwanee Budoo-Scholtz ·
Emma Charlene Lubaale
Editors

Violence Against Women and Criminal Justice in Africa: Volume II

Sexual Violence and Vulnerability

palgrave
macmillan

Editors
Ashwanee Budoo-Scholtz
Faculty of Law
Centre for Human Rights
University of Pretoria
Hatfield, Pretoria, South Africa

Emma Charlene Lubaale
Faculty of Law
Rhodes University
Grahamstown/Makhanda, South Africa

ISSN 2523-3084 ISSN 2523-3092 (electronic)
Sustainable Development Goals Series
ISBN 978-3-030-75952-0 ISBN 978-3-030-75953-7 (eBook)
https://doi.org/10.1007/978-3-030-75953-7

This Palgrave Macmillan imprint is published by the registered company Springer Nature Switzerland AG
The registered company address is: Gewerbestrasse 11, 6330 Cham, Switzerland

To,

Every woman survivor of violence who is denied justice.

Foreword

Violence against women and girls is perhaps one of the most critical issues dominating discussions on the agendas of states across the African continent. This scourge is neither new nor unique to the African continent. Over the past few decades, however, it has become an increasingly public issue across states in Africa. The pervasiveness of violence against women and girls has seen some states label the scourge a national crisis warranting immediate redress. It can be considered as one of the main challenges to the realisation of women's rights in Africa.

Criminal justice systems in Africa have a fundamental role to play in the eradication of violence against women. Disheartening, however, progress has been extremely slow as far as holding perpetrators of such violence to account is concerned. A significant number of cases, if at all reported, hardly make it through the criminal justice system. All considered, it is indisputable that violence against women and girls on the African continent has reached alarming levels. It is equally irrefutable that criminal justice responses are generally wanting. But equally undeniable is the fact that most African states have made multiple reforms to national laws. Many have also committed themselves to international obligations by way of ratification of treaties relevant to addressing the scourge of violence against women and girls. Even so, these strides have not generally translated into better criminal accountability across justice systems in Africa. The challenges and prospects of criminal justice for women and girls in Africa, despite these reforms, have hardly been the subject of scholarly discussion.

The two edited volumes of this publication fill in this scholarly gap. They echo the provisions of article 4 of the Protocol to the African Charter on Human and Peoples' Rights (Maputo Protocol) that requires States parties to adopt and enforce laws, including punishing perpetrators, to ensure the elimination of violence against women. The contributions present a comprehensive and rigorous overview of the salient features and major developments in Africa's criminal justice systems in as far as justice for women is concerned, while also focussing on vulnerable women. It offers a unique insight into the practical challenges of advancing justice for women in cases of violence in the different regions in Africa.

As someone who has been engaged on women's rights on the continent, including on the issue of violence against women, I believe that the publication of these two volumes is timely and that the recommendations therein, if implemented, can ensure more accountability for violence against women in the criminal justice systems of African countries.

Yaoundé, Cameroon

Commissioner Lucy Asuagbor
African Commission on Human and Peoples' Rights'
Outgoing Special Rapporteur on the Rights of Women in Africa

Acknowledgments

The editors wish to express their appreciation to all authors for their patience and dedication in this process, with them having to work with close deadlines. The chapters in this volume could not have been finalised without the independent reviewers' insightful comments. Special thanks go to the editorial team at Palgrave Macmillan, especially to Naveen Dass and Josephine Taylor, in ensuring that the publication was on time. Emma thanks the Research Office of Rhodes University for funding her trip to Pretoria from Grahamstown so that she can have working sessions on the book with Ashwanee. Ashwanee is grateful to the financial support of the Centre for Human Rights, Faculty of Law, University of Pretoria, for assisting her in securing an editorial assistant, Janet Gbam, whose work is also acknowledged.

Contents

Notes on Contributors

Pierre T. Bata is a Doctor of International Law from the Catholic University of Central Africa (UCAC). He is currently a teacher at UCAC and coordinator of bachelor's degrees in legal and political science from the same institution. His work relates generally to issues related to International Human Rights Law, the law of armed conflict, the law of humanitarian action, the law of peace. He conducts in-depth research on the issue of sexual abuse and violence in Africa.

Ashwanee Budoo-Scholtz is the programme manager of the Master's in Human Rights and Democratisation in Africa at the Centre for Human Rights, Faculty of Law, University of Pretoria. She holds a doctorate and master's degree in law from the University of Pretoria and a bachelor's degree in law from the University of Mauritius. Her research, teaching and training areas are the African human rights system, with a focus on women's and girls' rights. She was previously a project coordinator of the Women's Rights of the Centre for Human Rights. In this role, she worked with and supported the research and standard-setting functions of the African Commission on Human and Peoples' Rights' Special Rapporteur on the Rights of Women in Africa (for example the general comment on child marriage adopted by the African Commission and the African Committee of Experts on the Rights and Welfare of the Child, the African Commission's report on child marriage and state reporting workshops). Dr. Budoo-Scholtz is a member of the Editorial Committee of the African Human Rights Yearbook and the Global Campus Human Rights Preparedness. She has a proven track record in conducting research, with publications in peer-reviewed journals and chapters in books.

Barbara L. Can is a lawyer and member of the Network of Public Interest Lawyers. She holds a Bachelor's degree in Law from Makerere University and a Post Graduate Diploma in Legal Practice and Legal Aid from the Law Development Centre, Kampala. She is a researcher with an interest in disability rights, girls' and women's rights, children's rights, legislative drafting and advocacy.

Christine Dowuona-Hammond is an Associate Professor at the School of Law, University of Ghana and the Managing Partner of Hammond Law Company, a Legal Consultancy firm in Ghana which specializes in Legal Research, Policy Analysis and Reform and Development Consultancy. Her areas of specialization and research interests include Contract Law and Negotiation; Commercial Law; Gender and Development; Consumer Law and Policy and the Law of Succession. She has been Legal Consultant to the Economic Community of West African States (ECOWAS) and consulted widely for international organisations including Carnegie Foundation, the World Bank, UNDP, DANIDA, UNICEF and GIZ.

Zaynab Essack is a research psychologist and senior research specialist at the Human and Social Development Programme at the Human Sciences Research Council. She obtained a Ph.D. in Psychology from the University of KwaZulu-Natal (2015) on the topic: An empirical study of standards of prevention in South African HIV vaccine trials: Norms, perspectives, and practices. Zaynab's current research interests include the sexual and reproductive well-being of adolescents and young women and developing and evaluating interventions to address current social issues in high-poverty and high HIV-prevalence communities. She is also interested in issues of race, inequality and identity. She is a member of the HSRC Research Ethics Committee.

Jackline N. Hakim holds an LLB from the University of the Gambia, an LLM in Human Rights and Democratisation in Africa from the University of Pretoria. She is currently a human rights researcher on children's right in South Sudan and Ethiopia.

Ama F. Hammond is Senior Lecturer at the University of Ghana School of Law, where she teaches the laws of Contract, Equity, and Succession, among other subjects, and coordinates the School's graduate programme. She is also the Deputy Editor of the University of Ghana Law Journal. Her research interests include legal pluralism, law and colonialism and the law of succession. Her publications have tended to focus on issues relating to law and society, emphasizing how law affects social change and policy, and how societal processes also influence law. She has worked as a Consultant and undertaken various research projects commissioned by national and international organizations in the areas of Contract law, Traditional Governance, Peace and Governance, Children's Rights, and Property Rights, among others. She served as a member of the Law Reform Commission of Ghana, and a member of the Joint Steering Committee of the Ascertainment of Customary Law Project (ACLP). Ama Hammond holds a Ph.D. in law from the University of British Columbia, Vancouver, Canada; a Master of Laws degree from Harvard Law School, Massachusetts, USA; a Bachelor of Laws degree from the University of Ghana; and a Bachelor of Arts degree from the University of Cape Coast, Ghana.

Adetokunbo Johnson holds a Doctor of Philosophy in Human Rights (D.Phil.) from the Faculty of Law, University of Pretoria. In her thesis, 'The voiceless woman: Countering dominant narratives concerning disabled women in Nigeria' she asked whether law and specifically the human rights framework can speak to the lived realities and experiences of the disabled woman in Nigeria. She holds a Master of Philosophy (M.Phil.) in Multidisciplinary Human Rights from the University of Pretoria; a Master of Arts (M.A.) in Human Rights from the University of Kent, Canterbury, United Kingdom and Bachelor of Science (B.Sc.) from Babcock University, Ogun State, Nigeria. She is a human rights researcher, advocate and scholar. Her research interests include a broad range of issues related to human rights, women's rights, disability rights and intersectionality.

Charlotte Kabaseke is an advocate of the Courts of Judicature of Uganda. Charlotte obtained a Bachelor of Laws Degree (LLB) from Uganda Christian University and Postgraduate Diploma in Legal Practice from the Law Development Centre, Kampala, following which she obtained a Master of Laws Degree (LLM) from Makerere University, Kampala, Uganda. She is a UN Fellow, having attended the United Nations (UN) International Law Fellowship Programme in July 2019. She is also an alumnus of the Hague Academy of International Law having attended the Summer course on Public International Law in July 2019. Charlotte worked as a Legal Assistant (Advocate) at the Justice Centres Uganda, a legal aid service provider. She was appointed Lecturer of Laws at Bishop Stuart University, Mbarara, Uganda and later became an acting Dean of the Faculty of Law in the same institution. At the same time, she practiced as an advocate with Nakuya and Co. Advocates, Kampala, Uganda. Charlotte recently obtained a PhD from the Research Institute of Environmental Law at the School of Law, Wuhan University, Wuhan, China. Charlotte's research is focused on the intersectionality between Gender and Environment in East Africa. Her research interests include among others, environmental law and policy, human rights law, Gender and the Law, Family law and Criminal law. She has previously researched on refugee rights in Uganda, sexual violence against women as well as child trafficking in Uganda.

Charity O. Kaniye-Ebeku is a Doctoral Candidate at University of Nicosia, Cyprus. She obtained her Bachelor of Laws (LLB) from the University of Huddersfield UK, Master of Laws (LLM) from Liverpool John Moores University UK and BL Nigerian Law School. Currently, she is a Law Lecturer at the University of Port Harcourt, Nigeria. She has keen interest on issues regarding the human rights of women and children. She has attended a lot of learned conferences locally and internationally and has productive papers published in academic journals.

She is a member of some professional bodies such as the Nigerian Bar Association (NBA), International Bar Association (IBA), Chartered Institute of Arbitrators (CIArb) UK, Nigeria Branch, Nigerian Association of Law Teachers (NALT), Ikwerre Daughters Lawyers Association where she is the current Vice Chairperson and African Women Lawyers Association (AWLA) where she is presently holding the position of an Assistant Coordinator, Rivers State branch, Nigeria.

Barbara Kitui works with a government justice reform programme, the Justice Law and Order Sector, Ministry of Justice and Constitutional Affairs in Uganda. She previously worked with the Foundation for Human Rights Initiative (non-governmental organization) specializing in access to justice and legal empowerment for deprived, marginalized and vulnerable persons. While in private practice, she specialized in commercial, family and land law. She holds a Master of Laws in Human Rights and Democratisation in Africa, University of Pretoria; Diploma in Legal Practice, Law Development Centre; and a Bachelor of Laws Degree, Makerere University.

Annette Lansink holds law degrees from universities in South Africa and the Netherlands. She is the former Dean of the School of Law at the University of Venda and has extensive experience in higher education and contributed to the transformation of the university in numerous leadership roles. Her research interests are in the areas of public international law, human rights and gender. She was Rapporteur on women and migration for the global International Law Association's Committee on Feminism and International Law. Consistent with her multi-disciplinary approach, she has in recent years again focussed her attention on Africanisation of legal education and epistemologies of the South. Given the breadth of her interests, she has published nationally and internationally in both scholarly journals and the popular media and delivered papers in many countries, institutions and fora, including the United Nations.

Arudi Laurah is a human rights defender drawn towards issues of women, gender and sexual minorities. To fulfil this vision the endeavour is governed by principles that exhibit the creation and documentation of authentic information, the zeal for social justice through advocacy, the quest for the realisation of equity, the explicit inclusion and protection of all persons and the accountability of state parties to international and regional obligations that they have acceded to. She holds an M.Phil. (Human rights and Democratisation in Africa) from the University of Pretoria and Bachelor of Arts in Humanities and Social Sciences from Kent University.

Emma Charlene Lubaale is an associate professor at the Faculty of Law of Rhodes University. She has previously taught law at the University of Venda. Prior to this, she taught and researched law in the capacity of a post-doctoral research fellow at the University of Pretoria's Institute of International and Comparative Law in Africa. She holds a doctorate and master's degree in law from the University of Pretoria; a bachelor's degree in Law from Makerere University and a post-graduate diploma in legal practice from Uganda's Law Development Centre. She recently concluded her studies towards a post-graduate diploma in Higher Education at the University of Kwazulu Natal. Her current areas of interest are criminal law in the domestic perspective, international criminal law, international human rights law, women and children's rights. She is currently a member of the Organisation of Women in Science for the Developing World, a member at the South African Young Academy of Science and is a rated researcher by the National Research Foundation (NRF) of South Africa. In January 2020, was appointed by the NRF to serve on the NRF Standing Panel for the Humanities and Social Sciences (HSS) from 2020 to 2023. She has served as a law reviewer for publishers including Springer Nature, the Pretoria University Law Press, the Journal *of Sexual Aggression, Speculum Juris, De Jure, South African Crime Quarterly* and *Journal of Law, Society and Development*.

Simangele D. Mavundla obtained her Ph.D. Candidate in Law at the University of KwaZulu-Natal. She has a master's degree in Law (LLM) from the University of Pretoria and a Bachelor's degree in law with Honours (LLB) from the University of Eswatini. She is a socio-legal Researcher and Lecturer. Her areas of interest in research are Gender and Law, Human Rights, HIV, Social Security, youth and policy development. She is also an advocate of the High Court of Eswatini.

Linda Mushoriwa is a post-doctoral research fellow at the University of Johannesburg, affiliated to the South African Research Chair in International Law. She obtained her Ph.D. degree from the University of KwaZulu Natal.

Pachalo Mwenelupembe is a lawyer based in Malawi. She is a graduate of both the University of Malawi and the University of Pretoria, through the Centre for Human Rights, where she obtained her LLB (Hons) and a LLM in Sexual and Reproductive rights respectively. In 2020, she founded PACHALAW, a legal advisory, consulting, litigation and research hub that works on human rights issues with a focus on women's rights, gender and other related disciplines of law. She is a proud mother to Seirra-Alice and Untwampoki.

Satang Nabaneh recently completed her doctoral studies at the Centre for Human Rights, Faculty of Law, University of Pretoria and was a PhD Fellow at the Centre on Law and Transformation, Norway. She holds a Master of Laws (LLM) in Human Rights and Democratisation in Africa from the University of Pretoria and Bachelor of Laws (LLB) from the University of The Gambia. She is an experienced scholar with demonstrated track record, scientific research, qualitative policy analysis and writings of over 30 publications including books, book chapters, journal articles, reports and advocacy materials. Her research interests include a broad range of issues related to human rights, women's rights, democracy and constitutionalism.

Josephine Ndagire is a Lecturer at the School of Law, Makerere University. Dr. Ndagire worked with a number of local and international organizations, most recently, as Head of Training at the International Nuremberg Principles Academy (Germany), Director of Legal Services at the Foundation for Human Rights Initiative (Uganda) and as a Senior Researcher at the Max Planck Institute for Foreign and International Criminal Law (Germany). Her publications include a book titled *National Redress for "Gendered" International Crimes: Uganda, Germany and the International Criminal System*', Verlag Dr. Kovac, Hamburg, 2015. She also conceptualised and co-published *Cooperation Between Civil Society Actors and Judicial Mechanisms During Prosecution of*

Conflict-Related Sexual Violence: Guiding Principles and Recommendations, International Nuremberg Principles Academy, April 2017. She holds a Doctor of Juridical Science (SJD) degree from Emory University (US), a Master of Laws (LLM) degree from the University of Notre Dame (US) and a Bachelor of Laws degree from Makerere University.

Esther Njieassam holds an LLB from the University of Buea in Cameroon, an LLM and LLD from North West University. Her research interests are: Human Rights, Social Justice, Environmental Law and Labour Law. Currently, she is a post-doctoral research fellow at the Faculty of Law of the University of Johannesburg.

Taiwo Odumosu is a doctoral candidate at the University of Nicosia, Cyprus. He holds a Master of Laws degree from the Olabisi Onabanjo University, Ago Iwoye, Ogun State, Nigeria (2005) and a Bachelor of Laws (LL. B) degree in 1998 from Ogun State University, Ago Iwoye, Nigeria. He was called to the Nigerian Bar in 2000. Odumosu teaches Law at the Department of Public Law of the Olabisi Onabanjo University, Ago Iwoye, Nigeria with research interest in Health and Medical Law, Public International Law, International Environmental Law, Law of Evidence, Administrative Law and Law, Popular Participation in Politics and Education Law. He is widely travelled and has attended and presented papers in both local and international conferences including Law and Social Transformations, Lancaster University, UK (2019), Sustainability Leadership at the Yale University, Connecticut, UK (2016). He was an associate editor on the Editorial Board of the Nigeria Weekly Law Report (NWLR). He is the Secretary to the Board of OOU Law Clinic and a Staff Clinician. He has led student clinicians to various law clinic events and currently heads the Street Law and Community Service Unit of the OOU Law Clinic. Odumosu belongs to several professional bodies amongst which are the Nigerian Bar Association, the National Association of Law Teachers, American Health Lawyers Association, Network of University Legal Aid Institution (NULAI), Clinical Legal Education Organisation (CLEO), etc. He is a creative writer, author and reviewer.

Iyabode Ogunniran is an associate professor at the Department of Public Law, Faculty of Law, University of Lagos. She holds a doctorate and master's degree from the same University. Her areas of research interest include Child Law, Constitutional Law and Criminal Justice. Dr. Ogunniran was a pioneer lecturer of Gender and the Law when the course was mounted in the Faculty in 2009 and has extensively published in reputable national and international journals in that area on issues such as *Gender and the Constitution, Gender Justice and Domestic Violence*. She was the Lagos Coordinator of the National Baseline Survey on Child Protection Issues with UNILAG/NBS/UNICEFF. She co-authored a book on *Child Justice Under the Child Rights Law of Lagos State*. Dr. Ogunniran was the recipient of the 2016 UNILAG Research Fair, Faculty Best Researcher Award. She is the co-coordinator of the Anti Human Trafficking Legal Hub (Lagos). She is a reviewer for the *Commonwealth Law Bulletin*, *UNILAG Journal of Humanities* and *UNILAG Sociological Review*.

Patricia A. P'Odong holds a Master's of Laws in Human Rights and Democratisation in Africa from the University of Pretoria. She is enrolled as a practicing advocate of the Courts of Judicature in Uganda. She is currently an assistant lecturer at the School of Law, Makerere University, and the Head of Clinical Legal Education in the Public Interest Law Clinic (PILAC), School of Law, Makerere University. She is also a Programme Officer for the Disability Law and Rights Centre, School of Law Makerere University. Ms. Atim's professional and research interest is mainly in human rights law, family law, children's rights, gender and the law, disability rights and clinical legal education.

Ellah T. M. Siang'andu teaches Criminal law, International law and Gender Discrimination at the School of Law, University of Zambia (Zambia). She holds a Doctor of Laws degree from the University of South Africa (South Africa), a Master of Laws, Public International Law, from the University of Nottingham (United Kingdom) and a Bachelor of Laws degree from the University of Hull (United Kingdom). She is a research fellow at the Southern African Institute for Policy and Research (SAIPAR) and also a Post-Doctoral Fellow under the Norwegian Programme for Capacity Development in Higher Education and

Research for Development (NORHED)/University of Zambia, where she has been working on a project focusing on women in prison with children.

Professor Ann Strode is Academic Leader of Socio-Legal Studies at the School of Law, University of KwaZulu-Natal, South Africa. She teaches constitutional and human rights law to second year LLB and Legal Studies (non LLB) students. Strode is well-established author having produced more than 40 peer reviewed publications. She has a keen research interest in HIV as a human rights issue. She has undertaken among others; a qualitative study into issues such as the forced or coerced sterilization of women living with HIV and critiquing legal approaches to HIV in the sub-Saharan region. She also writes in the area of research participants' rights. Her PhD dealt with the legal complexities of the participation of children in health research. She has published widely on the ethical-legal complexities of adolescent HIV prevention research. She is a Member of the Social Sciences and Health Research Ethics Committee, University of KwaZulu-Natal.

Abbreviations

1951 Convention	UN Convention Relating to the Status of Refugees and Exiles
ACHPR	African Charter on Human and Peoples' Rights
ACHPR Guidelines	African Commission on Human and Peoples' Rights' Guidelines on Combating Sexual Violence and Its Consequences in Africa
ACJA	Administration of Criminal Justice Act Nigeria
African Charter	African Charter on Human and Peoples' Rights
African Child Charter	African Charter on the Rights and Welfare of the Child
African Commission	African Commission on Human and Peoples' Rights
African Court	African Court on Human and Peoples' Rights
AIDS	Acquired Immunodeficiency Syndrome
ANC	Antenatal Care
ART	Antiretroviral Treatment
AU	African Union

Basic Principles	United Nations Basic Principles and Guidelines on the Right to a Remedy and Reparation for Victims of Gross Violations of International Human Rights Law and Serious Violations of International Humanitarian Law
BOR	Bill of Rights
BPfA	Beijing Declaration and Platform for Action
CALs	Coalition of African Lesbians
CAR	Central African Republic
CBHI	National Community Based Health Insurance
CDOs	Community Development Officers
CEDAW	United Nations Convention on the Elimination of all forms of Discrimination Against Women
CEDAW Committee	Committee on the Elimination of Discrimination Against Women
CEDOVIP	Center for Domestic Violence Prevention Uganda
CERD	Convention Against all forms of Racial Discrimination
CGE	Commission for Gender Equality
Comprehensive Strategy	United Nations Comprehensive Strategy on Assistance and Support to Victims of Sexual Exploitation and Abuse by UN Staff and Associate Personnel
CRC	United Nations Convention on the Rights of the Child
CRPD	United Nations Convention on the Rights of Persons with Disabilities
CRPD Committee	Committee on the Rights of Persons with Disabilities
CRSV	Conflict Related Sexual Violence
CSOs	Civil Society Organisations
Declaration	Declaration of Basic Principles of Justice for Victims of Crime and Abuse of Power
DEVAW	United Nations Declaration on the Elimination of Violence Against Women
DGAL	Directorate of Government Analytical Laboratories Uganda
DGIE	Directorate General of Immigration and Emigration

Disability Rights Protocol	Protocol to the African Charter on Human and Peoples' Rights on the Rights of Persons with Disabilities in Africa
DOVVSU	Domestic Violence and Victim Support Unit Uganda
DRC	Democratic Republic of Congo
DSW	Department of Social Welfare Uganda
EAC	East African Community
EU	European Union
FCT	Federal Capital Territory Nigeria
FGM	Female Genital Mutilation
GBV	Gender Based Violence
GBV Act	Anti-Gender Based Violence Act Zambia
HIV	Human Immunodeficiency Virus
HIV+	Human Immunodeficiency Virus Positive
HRBA	Human Rights-Based Approach
HRC	Human Rights Council
HREA	Human Rights Education Act Uganda
HSM	Holy Spirit Movement
ICAO	International Civil Aviation Organization
ICC	International Criminal Court
ICC Act	International Criminal Court Act Uganda
ICCPR	International Covenant on Civil and Political Rights
ICESCR	International Covenant on Economic Social and Cultural Rights
ICJ	International Commission of Jurists
ICPD, POA	International Conference on Population and Development, Programme of Action
ICRMW	International Convention on the Protection of the Rights of all Migrant Workers and Members of their Families
ICTR	International Criminal Tribunal for Rwanda
ICTY	International Criminal Tribunal for Yugoslavia
IDPs	Internally Displaced Persons
IPV	Intimate Partner Violence
IRC	International Rescue Committee
ISIL	Islamic State in Iraq and Levant
JLOS	Justice Law and Order Sector

JTF	Joint Task Force
Juba Agreement	Juba Peace Agreement on Accountability and Reconciliation
LAB	Legal Aid Board
LACVAW	Legislative Advocacy Coalition on Violence Against Women
LBQ	Lesbians, Bisexuals and Queer
LGBTIQ+	Lesbians, Gays, Bisexuals, Transgender, Intersex and Queer
LRA	Lord's Resistance Army
Maputo Protocol	Protocol to the African Charter on Human and Peoples' Rights on the Rights of Women in Africa
MGCSP	Ministry of Gender, Children and Social Protection Uganda
MIDIMAR	Ministry of Disaster Management and Refugees
MINUSCA	United Nations Multidimensional Integrated Stabilisation Mission in the Central African Republic
MMDAs	Metropolitan, Municipal and District Assemblies Uganda
MMR	Maternal Mortality Rate
MNJTF	Multinational Joint Task Force
MONUC	United Nations Organisation Mission in the Democratic Republic of Congo
MONUSCO	United Nations Organisation Stabilisation Mission in the Democratic Republic of Congo
MOUs	Memorandum of Understandings
Nairobi Declaration	Nairobi Declaration on Women's and Girls' Right to a Remedy and Reparation
NAP	National Plan of Action
NATO	North Atlantic Treaty Organisation Agreement
NCADV	National Coalition Against Domestic Violence
NCCEMD	National Committee for Confidential Enquiry into Maternal Deaths
NEMA	National Emergency Management Agency Nigeria
NGOs	Non-Governmental Organisations
NHIS	National Health Insurance Scheme
NHRIs	National Human Rights Institutions

Niamey Guidelines	African Commission on Human and Peoples' Rights' Guidelines on Combating Sexual Violence and Its Consequences in Africa
NPA	National Prosecutions Authority
NPOAA	Domestic Violence National Policy and Plan of Action
NTJP	National Transitional Justice Policy Uganda
OAU	Organisation of African Unity
ODPP	Office of the Directorate of Public Prosecutions
OIOS	United Nations Office of International Oversight Services
PLH	People Living with Human Immunodeficiency Virus
PNC	Postnatal Care
RECs	Regional Economic Communities
Review Committee	Trust Fund Review Committee
Rome Statute	Rome Statute of the International Criminal Court
SADC	Southern African Development Community
SADC Gender Protocol	Southern African Development Community Protocol on Gender and Development
SDGs	Sustainable Development Goals
SDP IV	Fourth Sector Development Plan
SEA	Sexual Exploitation and Abuse
SER	Socio-Economic Rights
SOB	Sexual Offences Bill Uganda
SODV Act	Sexual Offences and Domestic Violence Eswatini
SOFAs	Status of Force Agreements
SOGIE	Sexual Orientation, Gender Identity and Expression
SRHR	Sexual and Reproductive Health Rights
SSA	Sub-Saharan Africa
STIs	Sexually Transmitted Infections
SVAWG	Sexual Violence Against Women and Girls
TCCs	Troop Contributing Countries
TFV	Trust Fund for Victims
TIA	Trial on Indictment Act Uganda
Trust Fund	Trust Fund in Support of Victims of Sexual Exploitation and Abuse
UDHR	Universal Declaration of Human Rights

UHRC	Uganda Human Rights Commission
UN	United Nations
UNCAT	United Nations Convention Against Torture
UNCHR	United Nations Commission on Refugees
UNSC	United Nations Security Council
UWONET	Uganda Women's Network
VAW	Violence Against Women
VAWG	Violence Against Women and Girls
VRA	Victims' Right Advocate
WAJU	Women and Juvenile Unit Uganda
WHO	World Health Organisation
WLH	Women Living with Human Immunodeficiency Virus
ZCS	Zambia Correctional Service
ZPS	Zambia Police Service

List of Figures

Chapter 6

Part I

Introduction

1

Introduction

Ashwanee Budoo-Scholtz and Emma Charlene Lubaale

1 Sexual Violence, Women in Situations of Vulnerability and Criminal Justice

This book is part of a two Volume series focusing on violence against women and criminal justice in Africa. While Volume I focuses on the legislation and its limitations, the current Volume (Volume II) is dedicated to sexual violence and women who are in situations of vulnerability. Since the introduction to the first Volume has already provided a comprehensive overview of violence against women and girls in Africa, and the critical role of criminal justice in combatting the same, the introduction to the current Volume is specific to sexual violence and women in situations of vulnerability.

A. Budoo-Scholtz (✉)
Centre for Human Rights, Faculty of Law, University of Pretoria, Pretoria, South Africa

E. C. Lubaale
Faculty of Law, University of Rhodes, Grahamstown, South Africa

A. Budoo-Scholtz and E. C. Lubaale (eds.), *Violence Against Women and Criminal Justice in Africa: Volume II*, Sustainable Development Goals Series,
https://doi.org/10.1007/978-3-030-75953-7_1

Several global and regional human rights instruments expressly prohibit sexual violence while requiring States to ensure that their criminal justice systems are responsive to the issue. Some of them at the United Nations (UN) level are General Recommendation No. 19 of the Committee on the Elimination of Discrimination Against Women (CEDAW Committee),[1] the Declaration on the Elimination of All Forms of Discrimination Against Women 1993 and General Recommendation No. 35 of the CEDAW Committee,[2] updating its General Recommendation No. 19. In addition to these legal documents, Target 5.2 of Sustainable Development Goals 2030 (SDGs) aims to '[e]liminate all forms of violence against all women and girls in the public and private spheres, including trafficking and sexual and other types of exploitation'.[3] SDG 16 further focuses on inclusive societies and access to justice for all while promoting and enforcing 'non-discriminatory laws and policies for sustainable development'.[4]

At the regional level, paragraphs 37 and 51 of Agenda 2063 envisage an Africa free from all forms of gender-based violence and discrimination without expressly mentioning sexual violence.[5] However, the Protocol to the African Charter on Human and Peoples' Rights on the Rights of Women in Africa (Maputo Protocol) expressly provides for the protection of women from sexual violence.[6] It further imposes an obligation on states to ensure that their criminal justice systems are responsive to sexual violence by enacting and enforcing laws 'to prohibit all forms of violence against women including unwanted or forced sex whether the violence takes place in private or public'.[7] States also have the obligation

---

[1] CEDAW Committee, *General Recommendation No. 19 on violence against women* (1992).

[2] CEDAW Committee, *General Recommendation No. 35 on gender-based violence against women, updating general recommendation No.19* (2017).

[3] Website of the UN Department of Economic and Social Affairs 'Sustainable development', https://sdgs.un.org/goals/goal5.

[4] Target 16.b of the SDGs.

[5] African Union Commission, Agenda 2063 (2015), https://au.int/sites/default/files/documents/36204-doc-agenda2063_popular_version_en.pdf.

[6] Maputo Protocol, article 1(j).

[7] Maputo Protocol, article 4(2)(a).

to adopt measures to 'ensure the prevention, punishment and eradication of all forms of violence against women'[8] and to 'punish perpetrators of violence against women'.[9] Therefore, States parties to the Maputo Protocol have to ensure that survivors of sexual violence have access to the criminal justice system in the country.

The intersectionality theory[10] has led the international community to put more emphasis on specific measures to identify and protect women who face entrenched vulnerabilities. One can note this from the differences in the provisions of the Convention on the Elimination of All Forms of Discrimination Against Women (CEDAW) as compared to the Maputo Protocol. Despite emphasising on the elimination of discrimination against women, the CEDAW, a document drafted adopted in 1979 only mentions rural women as women in situations of vulnerability.[11] The Maputo Protocol, a document adopted in 2003, expressly protects: the girl child[12]; women in armed conflicts, including refugee and asylum-seeking women[13]; women living with Human Immunodeficiency Virus and Acquired Immunodeficiency Syndrome (HIV/AIDS)[14]; widows[15]; elderly women[16]; women with disabilities[17]; and women in distress.[18] This might have been the result of the emphasis that the international human rights community has been putting on women living in different

[8] Maputo Protocol, article 4(2)(c).

[9] Maputo Protocol, article 4(2)(e).

[10] First advanced to demonstrate how black women face multidimensional vulnerabilities as compared to black men or to white women: Kimberlé Crenshaw, 'Demarginalizing the intersection of race and sex: A black feminist critique of antidiscrimination doctrine, feminist theory and antiracist politics', 1 *University of Chicago Legal Forum* (1989): 139–167; For a more detailed on intersectionality, see Sylvia Tamale, *Decolonization and Afro-feminism* (2020): 64–80.

[11] CEDAW, article 14.

[12] Maputo Protocol, article 6(b).

[13] Maputo Protocol, article 11.

[14] Maputo Protocol, article 14.

[15] Maputo Protocol, article 20.

[16] Maputo Protocol, article 22.

[17] Maputo Protocol, article 23.

[18] Maputo Protocol, article 24.

situations of vulnerability.[19] The Maputo Protocol thus recognises these vulnerable situations as per the Leave No One Behind Principle of the SDGs[20] and, in some instances expressly requires States to ensure that women living in situations of vulnerability have access to justice in instances of violence.[21]

2 Overview of Chapters and Main Findings

The chapters in this Volume focus on access to justice for women who are survivors of sexual violence (Section Two), and for those who are in situations of vulnerability (Section Three). Some of them are case studies from different countries in Africa namely, Uganda, Ghana, Nigeria, Zambia, Malawi, Democratic Republic of Congo, Central African Republic and Eswatini. This Volume is a snapshot of the situation on the ground and does not claim to cover the multiplicity of issues that women who are survivors of sexual violence, and in situations of vulnerability face in accessing criminal justice. For instance, it does not cover all countries on the continent and some categories of women living in situations of vulnerability such as older women, the girl child, indigent widows, indigenous women, women living in detention and women engaged in sex work, amongst others. Nevertheless, the authors have provided a comprehensive and holistic overview of the topic they explored thereby giving the reader an insight on the position of women who are survivors of sexual violence and those in situations of vulnerability *vis-à-vis* the criminal justice system.

[19] See for instance the General Recommendations of the CEDAW Committee focusing on women living in situations of vulnerability such as women and AIDS, unpaid women workers in rural and urban family enterprises, disabled women, women migrant workers, older women, women in conflict situations, the gender-related dimensions of refugee status, asylum, nationality and statelessness of women, rural women and trafficked women and children, https://www.ohchr.org/en/hrbodies/cedaw/pages/recommendations.aspx.

[20] Website of the United Nations https://unsdg.un.org/2030-agenda/universal-values/leave-no-one-behind.

[21] *Supra* notes 13 to 18.

Kabaseke and Kitui analyse the challenges and prospects of the criminal justice system in Uganda in ensuring access to justice for female victims of sexual violence. They highlight the challenges that female victims of sexual violence face in accessing justice and make both legal and non-legal recommendations in the form of the following to ensure a better response of the criminal justice system to female victims of sexual violence. Some of them are amendment to the Penal Code Act, recognition of the rights of sexual violence victims, breaking gender stereotypes, adoption of a human rights approach in criminal justice, the need for specialised competence and specialised units, sensitisation of traditional and customary practices, ensuring reparations, compensation and restitution, and psychological support.

Dowuona-Hammond and Hammond present sexual violence in Ghana as a product of patriarchy and power imbalances. Hence, they contend that the mere adoption of laws is not sufficient to end impunity for sexual violence in Ghana and that there is a need for a more focused and purposeful adaptation of the criminal justice system to guarantee greater access to justice for victims. This includes the conscious provision of more sustainable support systems for victims of sexual violence that could contribute significantly to achieving improved outcomes in Ghana.

Siang'andu presents women survivors of sexual violence in Zambia as being overlooked by criminal justice. According to her, the fact that the law imposes high standards to prove sexual violence negatively affect women survivors of sexual violence, and acts as an impediment for women to access the justice system. She presents such high standards as discrimination against women and recommends law reforms that account for lived experiences of women as victims of rape and defilement.

Considering marital rape as a private issue, Uganda does not expressly criminalise the same. P'Odong and Can trace the origins of such non-criminalisation by highlighting that they are colonial laws that need to be reviewed in line with recent developments. Although there has been some judicial activism in cases of marital rape, they contend that for purposes of consistency and efficient protection of the rights of women, marital rape has to be expressly criminalised in Uganda.

Acknowledging that survivors of sexual violence in conflict-ridden areas face challenges to access criminal justice, Ogunniran focuses on strengthening legal responses in such situations. She does so by undertaking a case study of North-East Nigeria which is home to the Boko Haram insurgency and analyses whether the proposed Crimes Against Humanity, War Crimes, Genocide and Related Offences Bill 2012 will ensure more accountability for sexual violence during conflicts. She suggests adjustments to this Bill for effective prosecution of the insurgents and proffers holistic responses that accommodate survivors and communities.

Ndagire demonstrates the lack of reparations for victims of conflict-related sexual violence in Uganda by focusing on the conflict in Northern Uganda. She contends that while the National Transitional Justice Policy was adopted in 2019, it only lays the foundation for a reparation programme for war victims and fails to distinguish reparation and development programmes. She inspires herself from international instruments to make a case for an 'effective remedy' for victims/survivors of conflict-related sexual violence. She further states that reparations should not only be proportional to the gravity of the harm suffered, but also appropriate.

The police are the custodians of the laws and a pillar of criminal justice. Yet in some instances they are the ones that violate such laws without the government ensuring accountability. This is the contention of Mwenelupembe who assesses the incorporation of human rights in the fight against police sexual violence in Malawi. Despite criminal laws that protect women from sexual violence at the hands of police in Malawi, including the consideration of sexual violence by police officers as an aggravating factor, the practice is still prevalent. She contends that a human rights approach can be effectively employed to prevent and reduce police sexual violence.

Mushoriwa, Njieassam and Thibaut bring to the fore the dilemma where the protectors become the violators. They do so by undertaking a case study of UN peacekeeping missions in the Democratic Republic of Congo and Central African Republic. They highlight acts of sexual abuse and exploitation committed by members of the peacekeeping missions and assess the measures implemented by the UN in response to the problem. They conclude that the UN needs to review its accountability framework for peacekeeping forces to eradicate the culture of impunity amongst its peacekeepers to be in line with its commitment to the zero-tolerance policy on sexual abuse and exploitation.

Section Three of this Volume focuses on women in situations of vulnerability to assess whether the criminal justice system in Africa takes into account intersectionality in its responses. It starts with a chapter by Johnson and Nabaneh who assess the limits to achieve criminal accountability for violence against women with disabilities in Africa. Their analysis exposes the limits of criminal justice responses that refuse to acknowledge that interactions and intersections exist between gender and disability. It further reveals the importance of developing an intersectional lens to achieve significant criminal accountability, particularly for women with disabilities in Africa.

Hakim, Lansink and Lubaale present criminal accountability to address violations of the right to maternal health care of migrant and refugee women in South Africa and Uganda. They contend that the non-realisation of maternal health of migrant and refugee women leads to violence against women that necessitate the protection of the criminal justice system. They highlight the failure of national statutes and policy measures to adequately incorporate a human rights-based approach in both countries. Their chapter concludes that the two countries have made significant strides in the advancement of maternal healthcare for migrant and refugee women. It however underscores that more can be done to end the abuse of maternal healthcare rights of refugee and migrant women. In addition to invoking a rights-based approach, criminal accountability constitutes another measure Uganda and South Africa should embark on to bring an end to this abuse as it sends a clear message to culprits that these abuses are intolerable and will attract punishment.

Still in the context of refugee women, Kaniye Ebeku and Odumosu study the challenges that refugee women and girls survivors of violence face in accessing justice. They recommend States to consolidate their actions and take essential steps needed to guarantee the protection of refugee women and girls against violence, on a non-discriminatory basis, ranging from civil and political rights to economic, social and cultural rights, which are their entitlements under international law.

Mavundla, Strode and Essack analyse the challenges that women living with HIV in Eswatini face in accessing the criminal justice system. They conclude that women living with HIV are distrusting of such systems and find them ineffective. They recommend the government of Eswatini to adopt steps, including the implementation of laws and to include women living with HIV in the adoption of programmes on violence against women.

The last chapter of this Volume discusses the very important issue of women forming part of sexual minorities. Maina discusses the plight of Lesbians, Bisexuals and Queer women in Africa who are survivors of violence to access criminal justice. The chapter deduces that the discourse on diversity and inclusion is taking root and is significant for the expansion and adoption of a more inclusive purposive interpretation of laws. It further concludes that the patriarchal effect has limited the realisation of rights for all woman in society, and that laws are living documents and should reflect current social dynamics and realities.

References

African Union, 2003, Protocol to the African Charter on Human and Peoples' Rights on the Rights of Women in Africa.

African Union Commission, 2015, 'Agenda 2063', https://au.int/sites/default/files/documents/36204-doc-agenda2063_popular_version_en.pdf.

CEDAW Committee, 1992, *General Recommendation No. 19 on violence against women.*

CEDAW Committee, 2017, *General Recommendation No. 35 on gender-based violence against women, updating general recommendation No.19.*

Convention on the Elimination of all forms of Discrimination Against Women.

Kimberlé Crenshaw, 1989, 'Demarginalizing the intersection of race and sex: A black feminist critique of antidiscrimination doctrine, feminist theory and antiracist politics' 1 *University of Chicago Legal Forum.*

Sustainable Development Goals 2030.

Sylvia Tamale, 2020, *Decolonization and Afro-feminism.*

Website of the United Nations Department of Economic and Social Affairs, 'Sustainable development' https://sdgs.un.org/goals/goal5.

Part II

Sexual Violence Against Women and Girls and Criminal Justice

2

Responding to Sexual Violence, Protecting Survivors and Ending Impunity in Ghana

Christine Dowuona-Hammond and Ama F. Hammond

1 Introduction

Violence against women is a complicated and multidimensional phenomenon, which affects survivors in debilitative and destructive ways: physically, sexually, mentally, socially, psychologically and emotionally. It is internationally recognised as a form of discrimination against women, which impairs and nullifies their enjoyment of human

[1] Committee on the Elimination of Discrimination against Women, *General Recommendation No 19 on Violence against women* (1992), U.N. Doc. A/47/38, (1993): 1, reprinted in Compilation of General Comments and General Recommendations Adopted by Human Rights Treaty Bodies, U.N. Doc. HRI/GEN/1/Rev.6 (2003): 243, General Comment 7.

C. Dowuona-Hammond (✉) · A. F. Hammond
School of Law, University of Ghana, Accra, Ghana
e-mail: cdowuona-hammond@ug.edu.gh

A. F. Hammond
e-mail: afhammond@ug.edu.gh

A. Budoo-Scholtz and E. C. Lubaale (eds.), *Violence Against Women and Criminal Justice in Africa: Volume II*, Sustainable Development Goals Series,
https://doi.org/10.1007/978-3-030-75953-7_2

rights and fundamental freedoms.[1] The perpetration of violence targeted at women and girls, 'cuts across divisions of income, class, age, status and culture'.[2] Globally, it is recognised that violence against women is embedded in the entrenched power imbalances between men and women. Moreover, the low social and economic status of women operates both as a cause and consequence of violence against women.[3] In view of the debilitating impact of sexual violence, and the inextricability of such violence from the socioeconomic fortunes of women, the subject continues to be a topic of choice, and in fact, of necessity, in most progressive societies. Accordingly, this chapter seeks to critically assess the incidence of sexual violence against women in Ghana by analysing the relevant literature, including the findings of various studies on the subject. This is followed by an analytical description of the current legal and institutional framework for addressing sexual violence against women, pointing out the gaps in this framework. Lastly, this chapter makes recommendations for improving the impact of the existing legal, institutional and policy framework. Specifically, it suggests that a more focused and purposeful adaptation of the criminal justice system to guarantee greater access to justice for victims and the conscious provision of more sustainable support systems for victims of sexual violence could contribute significantly to achieving improved outcomes in Ghana. Essentially, this chapter argues that a more holistic and all-inclusive approach, which confronts the cultures of violence by re-examining the ways in which violence is condoned and tolerated by contemporary and institutional attitudes, which protect perpetrators and implicitly endorse impunity, is required to contend with violence against women.

---

[2] United Nations Department of Economic and Social Affairs, *The World's Women, 2015: Trends and Statistics*, (2015): 139.

[3] United Nations, *Beijing Declaration and Platform of Action, adopted at the Fourth World Conference on Wome*n (October 27, 1995), https://www.refworld.org/docid/3dde04324.html.

2 Understanding the Concept and Triggers of Sexual Violence Against Women in Ghana

In this section we discuss the incidence of violence against women generally, and focus on the cultural, political, economic and legal factors that engender such violence. Among many factors, we discuss the culture of patriarchy, fuelled by deeply entrenched social norms; the prevalence of economic policies that impoverish women; religious dictates that socialise women into accepting passive and subservient stations in life, and the poor enforcement of state laws, which results in the removal of expected legal protections for women. It should be noted that while we recognise that males also experience sexual violence, or violence generally, women are disproportionately victims of violence. Thus, our discussion focuses primarily on the effect of violence against women.[4]

The United Nations (UN) Declaration on the Elimination of Violence against Women defines violence against women as:

> ...any act of gender-based violence that results in, or is likely to result in, physical, sexual or psychological harm or suffering to women, including threats of such acts, coercion or arbitrary deprivation of liberty, whether occurring in public or in private life.[5]

Ghana's Domestic Violence Act of 2007 (Act 732), provides as yet, perhaps, the most comprehensive definition of sexual violence in domestic legislation, in recognising it as an abuse of the right to bodily

---

[4] World Health Organisation, 'Violence against Women' last modified November 29, 2017, https://www.who.int/news-room/fact-sheets/detail/violence-against-women.

[5] United Nations, *Declaration on the Elimination of Violence against Women*, (December 20, 1993), article 1, UN Doc A/RES/48/104; Other definitions can be found in the African Union, *Protocol to the African Charter on Human and Peoples' Rights on the Rights of Women in Africa*, July 11, 2003, (Maputo Protocol); United Nations, United Nations, *Beijing Declaration and Platform of Action*, adopted at the Fourth World Conference on Women, (27 October 1995), https://www.refworld.org/docid/3dde04324.html; *Beijing Declaration, supra* note 3, Paragraph 118.

integrity, sexual autonomy and human dignity.[6] Specifically, the Act defines sexual abuse as:

> the forceful engagement of another person in a sexual contact which includes sexual conduct that abuses, humiliates or degrades the other person or otherwise violates another person's sexual integrity or a sexual contact by a person aware of being infected with human immunodeficiency virus (HIV) or any other sexually transmitted disease with another person without that other person being given prior information of the infection.[7]

According to a UN report, domestic violence, which includes sexual, physical, emotional and emotional abuse, is a 'global epidemic' which affects women in all countries regardless of class, education, income, ethnicity, culture and age.[8] Several factors contribute to violence against women.

2.1 Cultural Factors

The cultural factors that account for the incidence of violence against women include social norms that promote cultural definitions of appropriate sex roles and gender-specific socialisation.[9] They also consist of norms and practices that advance notions of the family being under male control, and customs of marriage, like the dowry system, that commodify women.[10] More importantly though, in our opinion, are those traditional customs and norms that encourage belief in the inherent superiority of males, a phenomenon we loosely refer to as patriarchy. Violence against women in Ghana occurs largely within the context of patriarchal relations which perpetuate and reinforce a system of female

---

[6] Domestic Violence Act, 2007 (Act 732), Sect. 1(b)(ii).

[7] *Ibid.*, Sect. 1(b)(ii).

[8] UNICEF, *Domestic Violence Against Women and Girls*, Innocenti Digest, no. 6 (June 6, 2000): 2, http://www.unicef-irc.org/publications/pdf/digest6e.pdf.

[9] UNICEF, *supra* note 8, 7.

[10] *Ibid.*

subordination and male domination.[11] Patriarchy is an enduring system of inequality where ideas about life are conceptualised from the perspective of power, hierarchy, sex, subordination, domination and exclusion.[12] It creates violence, condones it and nurtures it. Harcourt, an academic, maintains that, '[t]he widespread of violence against women, whether physical, sexual or psychological, has its roots in patriarchal power structures, ideas and practices'.[13] Thus, violence against women has a 'strong cultural component'[14]; its 'legitimacy' is embedded in a system that rests on harmful, retrogressive and offensive ideas about masculinity and femininity, and which are themselves grounded in uninformed, mythical and dishonest social constructions.

In patriarchal societies, women are conscientised to believe that men have power over them; that men belong to a socially privileged class, and wield moral authority; that the real and perceived biological differences between men and women place men in a superior position—all aimed at excluding women from spaces of power. So deeply entrenched are these inequitable socio-cultural norms that women have arguably internalised 'the idea of their own inferiority',[15] thus making them, on average, more likely than men to condone domestic violence.[16] The subordinate position of women in society, coupled with socio-cultural practices and socialisation processes, render women disproportionately vulnerable to violence at all levels, albeit with significant rural–urban differences.[17]

---

[11] Akosua Adomako-Ampofo, 'Controlling and Punishing Women: Violence against Ghanaian Women', 56(20) *Review of African Political Economy* (1993): 102–111.

[12] Aldo Facio, 'What is Patriarchy?' translated by Michael Solis, (2013) http://learnwhr.org/wp-content/uploads/D-Facio-What-is-Patriarchy.pdf; See also, Loreen Maseno and Susan M. Kilonzo, 'Engendering Development: Demystifying Patriarchy and its Effects on Women in Rural Kenya', 3(2) *International Journal of Sociology and Anthropology*, (2011): 45–55, 46.

[13] Wendy Harcourt, *Body Politics in Development: Critical Debates in Gender and Development* (2013): 95.

[14] *Ibid.*

[15] Gerda Lerner, *The Creation of Patriarchy*, (1986): 218.

[16] Institute of Development Studies, Ghana Statistical Services and Associates, *Domestic Violence in Ghana: Incidence, Attitudes, Determinants and Consequences*, (2016): 23.1% of women and 13.8% of men consider wife-beating acceptable; 65.3% of women and 56.2% of men agree that women are to blame for rape if they wore revealing clothes.

[17] *Ibid.*

2.2 Religious Factors

Perhaps, in Africa, one of the greatest obstacles in protecting women from violence is the risk of challenge to religious laws and dictates, which promote the subjugation of women and the culture of violence against women.[18] Religion as conceptualised and practised in some societies, Ghana being no exception, encourages violence against women. Inevitably, religion becomes a weapon used to keep women in submission. It is our opinion that, the fact of religion being a precursor of violence against women is true of those religions that set low standards for women, prevent them from exercising their natural abilities and enjoying their freedoms. Rakoczy, a theologian, takes issue with those religions that presume the 'maleness' of God, and argues that, '[p]atriarchy is interwoven in the Christian tradition in distinct and pervasive ways'.[19] In support, she cites various passages from the bible and maintains that the images of God in Scripture are overwhelmingly male.[20] It is arguable that religions that emphasise the servile role of women and consider them faithful disciples if they live accordingly, contribute to gender-based violence. Similarly, Girard, a historian, boldly asserts that, '[v]iolence and the sacred are inseparable'.[21] Religion does have the tendency to reduce women to subservient positions and to act on their conscience to accept less than they deserve, thus mentally conditioning them to accept violence, a faithful ally of subordination.

2.3 Economic Factors

Women's economic dependence on men is a cause of sexual violence against women, especially by those closely related to the women. An interesting fact about gender violence is that much of the violence

[18] UNICEF, *supra* note 8, 7.

[19] Susan Rakoczy, 'Religion and Violence: The Suffering of Women', 8(61) *Agenda: Empowering Women for Gender Equity: Religion & Spirituality* (2004): 29–35, 31, https://doi.org/10.1080/10130950.2004.9676037.

[20] *Ibid*.

[21] Rene Girard, 'Violence and the Sacred', translation by Patrick Gregory, (1977), https://www.jstor.org/stable/2906898?seq=1.

experienced by women occur within the context of intimate relationships, often meted out by partners in marital, non-marital, co-residential and non-residential unions, both formal and informal.[22] Multi-country studies conducted on violence against women by World Health Organization (WHO) have found that at least 60% of women who reported incidents of physical or sexual violence or both, at some point in their lives, had been abused by a partner.[23] These studies showed that in Ghana, about 20% of ever-partnered women aged 15–49 years had experienced intimate partner physical and/or sexual violence at least once in their lifetime.[24] Not only are women abused by intimate partners, a significant percentage of sexual offences in Ghana is committed by persons known to or related to the victims/survivors, including family members, acquaintances and authority figures such as teachers, pastors and neighbours.[25] Such assaults are often perpetrated in the context of 'normal' activities such as socialising, helping a neighbour, interacting with a teacher or pastor. Unfortunately, it is in these situations that victims/survivors are more likely to be blamed, re-victimised and least supported.

It is unsurprising that women are abused by people with whom they have intimate relationships and as well as family members, acquaintances and authority figures. Being victims of societies in which gender is a potential determinant of wealth, women are arguably, more likely to find themselves at the mercy of their abusers because of their financial vulnerability. Such financial vulnerability is part of the broader concept

---

[22] UN, *supra* note 2, 150; Eric Y Tenkorang et al., 'Factors Influencing Domestic and Marital Violence Against Women in Ghana', 28 *Journal of Family Violence* (2013): 771–781.

[23] World Health Organization, *World Health Report: Make Every Mother and Child Count* (2005); UN, *supra* note 2,150.

[24] United Nations Statistics Division from Demographic and Health Surveys (DHS) and Reproductive Health Surveys (RHS) (ICF International, 2014) cited as the source by UN, *supra* note 2*:* 146, Fig. 6.5.

[25] Of the total number of cases reported between 2013 and 2018 on sexual offences (rape, attempted rape, defilement, indecent assault and incest), 24% to 31% were allegedly perpetrated by family members and members of households. With regard to cases of defilement—sexual assault of minors—reported in the five-year period (2013–2018), between 24 and 39% of alleged perpetrators were close family members and members of the victim's household. See the Domestic Violence and Victim Support Unit (DOVVSU), Annual Report (Accra, 2013–2018).

of the feminisation of poverty which refers to 'the process in which deep-seated and multidimensional cultural, social, and structural factors cause and exacerbate poverty among women and girls'.[26] It is important to note that, disparities in the labour market which manifest themselves in limited access to cash and credit, wage gaps between men and women, sometimes in the same line of employment, and which also confine women to lower paid jobs, contribute to the comparative financial insecurity of women, making them almost perpetual dependants and prone to mistreatment.[27] Such disparities are forms of gender-based violence and are termed as economic violence against women. There is no doubt that, '[p]overty marginalizes women, undermines their autonomy, and creates a cycle of dependence that nurtures violence'.[28]

A study conducted by Apatinga and Tenkorang shows that a lack of income and access to resources makes women vulnerable and exposes them to sexual violence.[29] Women are still prone to abuse when there are no economic opportunities for their husbands, the study reveals. Financial constraints remain a major source of friction in many marriages and promote violence.

2.4 Legal Factors

Discriminatory laws, including customary laws regarding inheritance and property rights, the lukewarm enforcement of the laws on maintenance after divorce, as well as those on child custody, expose the inequalities in our societies. More specifically, they expose how these problems affect the lives of women, their independence, their livelihood and self-worth.

---

[26] Cassandra L Melo, 'The Feminization of Poverty: A Brief Analysis of Gender Issues and Poverty among Women and Girls', 1(1) *The Canadian Journal of Critical Nursing Discourse* (2019): 73–81, 73.

[27] Esteban Ortiz-Ospina, 'Economic Inequality by Gender', *OurWorldInData.org* (2018) https://ourworldindata.org/economic-inequality-by-gender; See also, Gervin A Apatinga and Eric Y Tenkorang, 'Determinants of Sexual Violence Against Married Women: Qualitative Evidence from Ghana', *Sexual Abuse* (2020): 14.

[28] *Ibid.*, 3.

[29] *Ibid.*, 10.

Some scholars have argued that laws are sometimes designed to keep women subordinated and to control their sexuality.[30] In our opinion though, the failure of the police to enforce enacted legislation, but rather advocating for traditional customary laws, tends to work to the disadvantage of women. Fenrich and Higgins, legal academics, confirm that even where women understand their rights and have the resources to pursue their claims, they often encounter significant impediments from law enforcement agents.[31] Notions of the family being private and beyond the control of the state promote violence against women. They encourage the perpetual abuse of women who cannot depend on state structures for protection against ill-treatment. Also, in communities where customary laws are deeply entrenched, state law enforcement agents, especially those in rural areas, are often reluctant to enforce state law and apply sanctions when it is violated because these same officials are often also charged by their traditional communities with the responsibility of upholding customary laws.[32]

Relying on the constitutional prohibition of discrimination on grounds of gender,[33] women's rights organisations have progressively pursued an agenda for the incremental reform of Ghana's criminal laws to outlaw specific forms of violence against women and girls and impose more severe penalties for sexual offences. In the ensuing section, we review the existing legal and institutional framework which addresses sexual violence against women and girls in Ghana. We also highlight the gaps and deficiencies, which have hampered the achievement of real and tangible protection for victims of sexual violence.

---

30 Lynne Henderson, 'Law's Patriarchy', *Scholarly Works*, Paper 876 (1991): 412 http://scholars.law.unlv.edu/facpub/876.

31 Jeanmarie Fenrich and Tracy Higgins, 'Promise Unfulfilled: Law, Culture and Women's Inheritance Rights in Ghana', 25 *Fordham International Law Journal*, (2001): 334.

32 Edward Kutsoati and Randall Morck, 'Family Ties, Inheritance Rights, and Successful Poverty Alleviation: Evidence from Ghana', NBER Working Paper No. 18080 (May 2012): 15.

33 The Constitution of the Republic of Ghana, 1992, article 17(2).

3 Legal and Institutional Frameworks and Gaps in Addressing Sexual Violence Against Women in Ghana

This section elaborates on the legal and institutional framework for the protection of women from sexual violence. We discuss the international legal dimensions of the issue and analyse the domestic legal and institutional framework, while highlighting the gaps at the domestic level and the implications for the protection of women and girls from sexual violence.

3.1 International Legal Framework

Perhaps, the most pervasive of the international legal instruments which has in many ways revolutionised the way women's rights are perceived the world over is the Convention on the Elimination of All Forms of Discrimination Against Women (CEDAW), which Ghana ratified on 2 February 1986. This Convention was instrumental and groundbreaking from its inception because it provided, arguably, for the very first time, the definition of discrimination against women.[34] Article 2 of the CEDAW requires state parties to condemn discrimination against women in all forms and take appropriate measures to embody the principle of equality in their constitutions and laws, and to modify or abolish existing laws, regulations, customs and practices which discriminate against women, among other requirements.

The Declaration on the Elimination of Violence Against Women was adopted by the UN General Assembly in 1993 to complement the CEDAW. This Declaration makes some important statements. First, it defines 'violence against Women'.[35] It further defines sexual violence as a type of violence against women.[36] It defines violence to include:

---

[34] United Nations, *Convention on the Elimination of All Forms of Discrimination against Women*, G.A. Res. 34/180, U.N. GAOR 34th Sess., Supp. No. 46 AT 193, U.N. Doc. A/34/46 (September 3, 1981), article 1.

[35] *Declaration on the Elimination of Violence Against Women*, article 1.

[36] *Ibid.*, article 2.

> …physical, sexual, psychological violence occurring in the family including battering, sexual abuse of female children in the household, dowry-related violence, marital rape, female genital mutilation and other traditional practices harmful to women, non-spousal violence and violence related to exploitation.

It also includes these forms of violence occurring within the general community, at work and in places of learning, or perpetrated and condoned by the state, as well as trafficking in women and forced prostitution.[37] In addition, it reaffirms women's right to basic human rights and liberties.[38]

On a regional level, Ghana is a party to the African Charter on Human and Peoples' Rights, which was adopted in 1981. The African Union adopted the Protocol to the African Charter on Human and Peoples' Rights on the Rights of Women in Africa (Maputo Protocol) in 2003. Ghana ratified this protocol in 2007. The Maputo Protocol also provides a definition of 'violence against women'. It defines it as[39]:

> …all acts perpetrated against women which cause or could cause them physical, sexual, psychological, and economic harm, including the threat to take such acts; or to undertake the imposition of arbitrary restrictions on or deprivation of fundamental freedoms in private or public life in peace time and during situations of armed conflicts or of war.

For the purposes of preventing violence against women, articles 2, 3, 4 and 5 of the Maputo Protocol are instructive. Article 2 deals extensively with discrimination against women. Article 3 protects the dignity of women. Article 4 protects the right to life, integrity and security of women. States are, among others, encouraged to respect the life and dignity of women and take steps to protect women from cruel, inhuman and degrading punishment and treatment. Article 5 further sanctions

[37] *Ibid.*, article 2.

[38] *Ibid.*, article 3.

[39] Maputo Protocol, article 1.

all forms of harmful practices which affect women and are contrary to recognised international standards, including Female Genital Mutilation (FGM).

3.2 Domestic Legal Framework

Ghana has committed itself, globally and regionally, to protect women from sexual violence.[40] In this regard, the past two decades have seen some promising legislative and policy reforms aimed at expanding and enhancing the state's response to violence against women. At the very basic level, every Ghanaian is entitled to a certain bundle of rights guaranteed in the 1992 Constitution.[41] For instance, the Constitution guarantees the right to human dignity. Article 15(1) states categorically that, '[t]he dignity of all persons shall be inviolable'. Additionally, the Constitution states that 'a person shall not be discriminated against on grounds of *gender*, race, colour, ethnic origin, religion, creed or social or economic status'.[42] It is important to note that the Constitution also guarantees cultural rights. Specifically, it secures the right of every person to enjoy, practice, profess, maintain and promote any culture, language, tradition or religion.[43] Nevertheless, all customary practices which dehumanise or are injurious to the physical and mental well-being of a person are prohibited.[44]

Relying on the constitutional prohibition of discrimination on grounds of gender,[45] the country's criminal laws have been incrementally reformed to outlaw specific forms of violence against women and girls and impose more severe penalties for sexual offences. These include: modifications in the legal definitions and penalties for sexual offences

40 See for example a Ghanaian report on the CEDAW, https://www.un.org/womenwatch/daw/cedaw/cedaw36/statements/CEDAW%20STATEMENT%20Ghana.pdf.

41 Constitution, article 12.

42 *Ibid.*, article 17(2).

43 *Ibid.*, article 26(1).

44 *Ibid.*, article 26(2).

45 *Ibid.*, article 17(2).

aimed at casting the net wider to punish a wider range of offences, especially those involving minors; the removal of the marital exception to rape; the enactment of the Domestic Violence Act, 2007 (Act 32) and a Domestic Violence National Policy and Plan of Action—2009–2019 (NPOAA) to guide the implementation of the Act and the enactment of the Human Trafficking Act, 2005 (Act 694).

3.2.1 The Criminal Offences Act

The Criminal Offences Act, 1960 (Act 29) (as amended) provides a fairly robust framework for addressing violence against women and girls, prohibits rape, defilement, indecent assault, incest and unnatural carnal knowledge, seduction or prostitution and compulsion of marriage. The increasing incidence of sexual assaults was highlighted in Ghana during the 1990s via increased media attention and women's rights activism, as a public issue requiring urgent legislative reform.[46] Strident calls for more severe penalties for rape and other sexual offences were made in Parliament by some female Members of Parliament,[47] and the increasing media attention given to reports of violence against women made the issue more visible. This triggered the first significant attempt to reform the law on sexual offences in Ghana in 1993, via the Criminal Code (Amendment) Act (Act 458), which made changes to the provisions of Act 29 relating to sexual offences, particularly, rape and defilement.

Subsequent years of advocacy and activism by key women's rights organisations and civil society organisations (CSOs) resulted in the enactment of laws prohibiting and criminalising traditional practices considered harmful to women, such as widowhood rights, FGM, forced marriages and child abuse.[48] More extensive reforms were subsequently made to the law on sexual offences in 1998 via the Criminal Code Amendment Act, (Act 554). The Act increased the age of criminal and

[46] Mensa-Bonsu, 'Regulating Sexual Self-Expression through Criminal Legislation: The Case for Reform', in *Mobilising the Law for Ghana's Future: Appraising to Revolutionise* edited by Christine Dowuona-Hammond, Ama F. Hammond and Raymond A. Atuguba, (2020):2- 42.

[47] Republic of Ghana, Parliamentary Debates, Parliament, July 14, 1994, 1226.

[48] Criminal Offences Act, 1960 (Act 29) as amended.

sexual responsibility[49]; revised the provisions on sexual offences; specifically enacted the offence of indecent assault[50]; prohibited customary or ritual servitude, *trokosi,* a practice involving the enslavement of young girls by shrines to atone for offences committed by family members[51]; doubled the mandatory minimum sentence for rape[52]; invalidated marriages contracted by compulsion or duress[53]; and imposed more severe punishments for incest and child prostitution.[54] Significantly, Act 554 introduced an age limit into the definition of the offence of rape, redefining it as the 'carnal knowledge of a female of sixteen years or above without her consent', and increased the punishment to a minimum term of five years and maximum term of twenty years.[55]

It is noted that Ghana's law on rape is limited to the requirement of proof of penile penetration as an essential element. In view of the enhanced penalty for rape in the current law, it may be appropriate for the statutory definition of rape to be expanded to take into account other forms of sexual assault and invasions of bodily integrity suffered by women and girls, which are not covered by the current definition.[56] In particular, it is suggested that the offence be redefined to include the intentional penetration of other body parts, such as the anus and mouth.

It is noted further that sexual violations of the body of a person which fall short of vaginal penetration are currently classified under Ghana's criminal law as 'indecent assault', which is a misdemeanour subject to a minimum imprisonment term of six months and maximum term of

---

[49] Criminal Offences Act, 1960 (Act 29) as amended by Sect. 4 of Act 554, Sect. 26.

[50] Criminal Offences Act, 1960 (Act 29) as amended by Sect. 11 of Act 554, Sect. 103.

[51] Criminal Offences Act, 1960 (Act 29) as amended, Sect. 314A.

[52] Criminal Offences Act, 1960 (Act 29) as amended by Sect. 11 of Act 554, Sect. 97.

[53] Criminal Offences Act, 1960 (Act 29) as amended by Sect. 11 of Act 554, Sect. 100; See Children's Act, 1998 (Act 560), Sects. 14 and 15.

[54] Sections 105–108 of the Criminal Offences Act, 1960 (Act 29) as amended by Sect. 11 of Act 554, Sects. 105–108.

[55] Criminal Offences Act, 1960 (Act 29), Sects. 97 and 98.

[56] United Nations Economic & Social Affairs Division for the Advancement of Women, *Handbook for Legislation on Violence against Women* (2009): 26; Sylvia Walby et al., 'Law and the Criminal Justice System' in *Stopping Rape: Towards a Comprehensive Policy* (2015), 120–121.

three years.[57] For one thing, the existing penalty for the offence of indecent assault does not adequately reflect the severity of the acts which constitute the offence. Also, lumping together all acts which fall short of vaginal penetration under the category of 'indecent assault' does not take into account the fact that some of these acts, especially when perpetrated against minors, could cause grievous permanent damage, warranting much more severe punishment. The current state of the law on indecent assault could result in serious sex offenders and paedophiles being treated leniently, thus encouraging impunity. The penalty for indecent assault should be reviewed upwards, and should be dependent on the gravity of the act.

The requirement of corroboration of evidence also acts as a significant impediment, not only to the progression of sexual offence cases through the criminal justice system, but also to convictions.[58] Even though Ghana's criminal procedure and evidence rules do not require corroboration to sustain a finding of fact or verdict, unless expressly required by statute,[59] in practice, the courts do require and rely heavily on corroboration in assessing the weight and credibility of evidence, especially in sexual offence cases.[60] In sexual offence cases in particular, independent evidence in the form of medical reports and evidence given by medical officers is almost always required to corroborate the evidence of the victim/survivor and to support a finding that sexual assault has occurred.[61] Problems with obtaining medical reports for submission as corroborative evidence are well-known and rampant. Most victims cannot afford the costs of obtaining medical reports and tend to drop the case as soon as they are confronted with such costs. Studies have

---

57 Criminal Offences Act, 1960 (Act 29), Sect. 103(2).

58 Laura Mitchell, 'Service Users' Perceptions of the Domestic Violence and Victims' Support Unit, Ghana Police Service,' last modified 2011, https://static1.squarespace.com/static/536c4ee8e4b0b60bc6ca7c74/t/5437f188e4b05ef245bd6a2a/1412952456336/Perceptions+of+the+Domestic+Violence+and+Victim%27s+Support+Unit+Ghana+Police+Service+2012+Laura+Mitchelll+June+2012.pdf.

59 Evidence Act, 1975 (NRCD 323), Sect. 7(3).

60 SA Brobbey, *Essentials of the Ghana Law of Evidence,* (2014), 85.

61 *Hanson v. The Republic* [1975] 1 GLR 477; J. Ofori-Boateng, *The Ghana Law of Evidence*, 2nd ed (2000), 52; *Commissioner of Police v. Sem* [1962] 2 GLR 77, *State v. Ohene -Kesson and Mensah* [1961] GLR 708, 714; P.K. Twumasi, *Criminal Law in Ghana* (1985), 284.

ascertained that the costs associated with obtaining medical reports and getting medical officers to give expert evidence in support of the victim's case, are major deterring factors for victims/survivors and account for the cessation of a good number of sexual offence cases.[62]

The introduction of the age limit of 16 years in Ghana's current definition of rape is also problematic. The distinction created by the age limitation means that sexual assaults committed on girls aged below 16 years are prosecuted as 'defilement' and not rape, which creates the absurdity of 'treating physically violent sexual assaults on minors on the same level as notional violence on a minor'.[63] Further, experience has shown that definitions of rape founded on proof of lack of consent tend to expose the survivor to secondary victimisation in placing the burden on the prosecution to prove beyond reasonable doubt that the victim/survivor did not consent to the assault. To address this, some countries have developed definitions of rape which rely on the existence of certain circumstances, rather than a requirement to demonstrate a lack of consent.[64] Such an approach minimises secondary victimisation of the survivor in judicial proceedings by enacting a definition of sexual assault that either necessitates the existence of 'unequivocal and voluntary agreement' and requires proof by the accused person of steps taken to ascertain whether the complainant/survivor was consenting; or requires proof that the act took place in 'coercive circumstances' and includes a broad range of circumstances that can be described as 'coercive'.[65]

Moreover, the Criminal Offences Act, 1960 (Act 29) accommodates what came to be described as 'marital rape', a relic of the common

---

[62] *Ibid.*

[63] *Supra* 41.

[64] For example, the definition of rape under Namibia's Combating of Rape Act (2000) requires the existence of certain 'coercive circumstances', instead of proof of lack of consent. A similar definition has been adopted in the Lesotho Sexual Offences Act (2003). Canada's Criminal Code contains a positive consent standard which states: 'consent' means, for the purposes of this section, the voluntary agreement of the complainant to engage in the sexual activity in question; UN Division for the Advancement of Women, *Handbook for Legislation on Violence against Women 2009*, 27.

[65] United Nations Economic & Social Affairs Division for the Advancement of Women, *Handbook for Legislation on Violence against Women 2009* (2010).

law, persisted in Ghana's laws for far too long.[66] This controversial exemption enacted in Sect. 42(g) of Act 29, stipulated in essence that the consent given by a woman to marriage, and by extension, to sexual relations with her husband, could not be revoked except by divorce or dissolution of the marriage. In addition to being discriminatory of women, this provision fully exempted patently criminal conduct—rape and sexual assault—within an institution which promises safety, protection and security.[67] For years, the marital rape exemption was considered a blot on the landscape of Ghana's criminal law, described as 'a cultural tool of domination and humiliation for husbands to use against their wives'.[68] An initial attempt to repeal Sect. 42(g) of Act 29 in the draft Domestic Violence Bill, generated quite an uproar and strong opposition among Ghana's lawmakers and sections of the public.[69] The provision undoing the marital rape exemption was eventually removed from the Bill to preserve its chances of being enacted into law.[70] Eventually, the marital rape exemption was excised from the Criminal Offences Act by the statute law revision process instituted to revise, compile and publish the consolidated laws of Ghana as of 1 January 1999.[71]

[66] Nancy Kaymar Stafford, 'Permission for Domestic Violence: Marital Rape in Ghanaian Marriages', '*Women's Rights Law Reporter* 63 (2007): 64–65.

[67] United Nations, *Convention on the Elimination of All Forms of Discrimination against Women*, G.A. Res. 34/180, U.N. GAOR 34th Sess., Supp. No. 46 AT 193, U.N. Doc. A/34/46 (September 3, 1981).

[68] Nancy Kaymar Stafford, 'Permission for Domestic Violence: Marital Rape in Ghanaian Marriages', 29(63) *Women's Rights Law Reporter* (2007): 67.

[69] See, I.K. Gyasi, 'Domestic Violence Bill – Specified Offences (2)',' *Ghanaian Chronicle*, December 11, 2006, https://allafrica.com/stories/200612111567.html; Stephen A. Quaye, Moses O Amponsah and Ernest P Asare, 'Domestic Violence Bill', *Ghanaian Chronicle*, September 13, 2005.

[70] Sadia Hodžić, 'Unsettling Power: Domestic Violence, Gender Politics and Struggles over Sovereignty in Ghana',74(3) *Ethnos: Journal of Anthropology* (2009): 331–360.

[71] Laws of Ghana (Revised Edition) Act, 1998 (Act 562). In the process of revising and compiling the laws of Ghana, the Statute Law Revision Commissioner excluded Sect. 42(g), which gave life to the notorious marital rape exemption, from the Criminal Offences Act, (Act 29).

3.2.2 The Domestic Violence Act

The Domestic Violence Act, 2007 (Act 732) was passed to address, among many issues, intimate partner violence. In accordance with the relevant international laws earlier discussed, this Act defines domestic violence to include sexual abuse.[72] The Act further makes it a crime for a person to engage in domestic violence. The penalty for contravention is a maximum fine of five hundred penalty units or a term of imprisonment of not more than two years or both.[73] The Court may, in addition, ask the perpetrator to pay compensation to the victim.[74] The Act also provides that violence in the domestic setting cannot be justified by consent. Other provisions provide for police assistance and help. In this regard, a police officer shall respond to a request by a person for assistance from domestic violence and shall offer the protection that the circumstances of the case or the person who made the report requires, even when the person reporting is not the victim of the domestic violence.[75]

A large proportion of Ghana's Domestic Violence Act is focused on legal interventions and medical services, consisting of police and court interventions. Comparatively, it has been noted that the legislation does not place sufficient focus on shelter facilities for the protection of survivors of domestic violence.[76] Interestingly, the Act makes provision for the establishment of a Domestic Violence Fund,[77] which is to be applied towards:

[72] See Sect. 1 of Act 732; Sexual abuse is defined under the Act to include 'forceful engagement of another person in a sexual contact which includes sexual conduct that abuses, humiliates or degrades the other person or otherwise violates another's sexual integrity or sexual contact by a person aware of being infected with human immunodeficiency virus (HIV) or any other sexually transmitted disease with another person without the other person being given prior information of the infection.'.

[73] *Ibid.*, Sect. 3(2).

[74] *Ibid.*, Sect. 3(3).

[75] *Ibid.*, sub-Sect. 6–10.

[76] Centre for Gender Studies and Advocacy (CEGENSA), 'Beyond Domestic Violence Laws: Women's Experiences and Perception of Protection Services in Ghana',' last modified April 2016, http://cegensa.ug.edu.gh/sites/cegensa.ug.edu.gh/files/Beyond%20Domestic.pdf.

[77] Act 732, Sects. 29–34.

> ...the construction of reception shelters for victims of domestic violence in regions and districts; and for training and capacity building of persons connected with the provision of shelter, rehabilitation and reintegration.[78]

Funding for the shelters is expected to come from voluntary contributions as well as money approved by Parliament or the Minister of Finance. The fund has however not been established since the passing of the Act in 2007, and no state-funded shelters have been established to date.[79] The provision of shelter and other protective facilities is an integral part of the state's response to gender-based violence. Creating more shelters with both public and private funding would be a significant step towards improving the state's response to domestic violence in Ghana.

3.2.3 Human Trafficking Act

Related to the Domestic Violence Act is the Human Trafficking Act, 2005 (Act 694). This Act is the main piece of legislation which outlaws the sexual exploitation of women. It defines human trafficking to include induced prostitution and other forms of sexual exploitation. It also establishes a fund to support victims.[80] However, the Act does not provide an explicit guarantee that victims of trafficking will not be prosecuted for any illegal acts that are a direct consequence of their trafficking. We propose the introduction of such a provision to ensure that women who find themselves in such vulnerable positions are protected by the law in order to forestall a cycle of abuse.

3.2.4 Children's Act

The Children's Act, 1998 (Act 560) is an important piece of legislation. It states that the welfare of the child, including the girl-child, shall always

[78] Act 732, Sect. 31.

[79] *Supra.*

[80] Act 694, Sect. 1.

be the paramount consideration in all matters involving children.[81] The Act charges parents with the responsibility of ensuring that they protect their child from neglect, discrimination, violence, abuse, exposure to physical and moral hazards and oppression.[82] In addition, any person who has information about an incidence of child abuse is mandated to make a report of such to the Department of Social Welfare (DSW)[83] and if investigations by the Department reveal that 'a child has been abused or is in need of immediate care and protection' the Department 'shall direct a probation officer or social welfare officer accompanied by the police to remove the child to a place of safety'.[84] Among other provisions, it establishes the minimum age of marriage as eighteen years and goes further to say that no person shall force a child to be betrothed, be the subject matter of a dowry transaction or be married, thus complementing the relevant provisions of Act 29 on compulsion of marriage.

With regard to the protection of children, Part One of the Children's Act, 1998 (Act 560), lists certain basic rights to which all children are entitled.[85] Nevertheless, the list does not include the right to protection against sexual abuse and exploitation. Accordingly, it is proposed that the list of protections stated in the Act be expanded to include the protection of children from sexual abuse and exploitation. This will ensure further protection of children, including the girl-child, from 'all forms of sexual abuse such as procuring or allowing a child to be procured for commercial sexual exploitation'; 'encouraging, inducing or forcing a child to be used for the sexual gratification of another person'; and 'using a child in or deliberately exposing a child to sexual activities or pornography'.

Furthermore, the definition of a child in need of care and protection in Sect. 18 of Act 560 does not include a child at risk of sexual abuse. However, it is important that such children are regarded as being in need of care and protection so that they can benefit from the allocated state resources and interventions. Consequently, we propose that the statutory definition of the circumstances where a child may be in need of care and

[81] Act 560, Sect. 2 on welfare principle.

[82] *Ibid.,* Sect. 6(3)(a).

[83] *Ibid.,* Sect. 17.

[84] *Ibid.,* Sect. 19.

[85] See the Children's Act, 1998 (Act 560) sub-Sects. 3–14.

protection should include a child who has experienced or is at risk of all forms of violence, abuse, and exploitation. In other words, the existing definition in the Act should be expanded to include explicitly a child who has been sexually harassed, abused or is likely to be exposed to sexual abuse and exploitation including prostitution and pornography. This will go a long way to protect children, including girls, from further sexual abuse and strengthen the legislative framework for protecting girls from violence.

Again, to protect children from abuse, certain persons with criminal convictions, especially those that are child-related, must be prohibited from working in an environment that brings them into direct contact with children. Act 560 does not have such a provision. Firstly, we suggest an amendment requiring that all persons proposing to work with children must undergo criminal record checks. Secondly, we recommend that persons with criminal convictions should be prohibited from working with children. More specifically, such persons should include those who have been convicted of a felony for child abuse or neglect; physical assault, battery, or a drug-related offence; spousal abuse; a crime against children including child pornography; or a crime involving violence, including rape, sexual assault and murder.

The Children's Amendment Act, 2016 (Act 937) was promulgated to make further provisions in respect of foster care, adoption and related matters. Nevertheless, this Act includes limited guidance on the criteria for adoptive and foster parents. It is important that the Act provides extended guidelines to make sure that children grow up in the best environment possible, free of discrimination, violence and sexual abuse. Consequently, the Act must be amended to exclude specifically from eligibility, a person who has been convicted of a child-related offence, or is suspected on reasonable ground, of having committed such an offence or a related offence.

To be effective, laws addressing sexual violence must be multidisciplinary. In addition to prescribing adequate punishment of offenders, they must address issues of prevention, protection, survivor empowerment and support (health, economic, social, psychological), promote institutional coordination of responsibilities and make provision for practical emergency procedures and responses.[86] The Domestic Violence Act, 2007 is perhaps the best example of multidisciplinary legislation in Ghana. The Act was accompanied by a National Domestic Violence Policy and Plan of Action to implement the Domestic Violence Act 2009–2019 (NPOAA), which created an expansive and comprehensive framework for implementation of the Act, focused on strategies for prevention, protection and provision of support for victim–survivors. This framework is founded on the pillars of protection of victims, provision of targeted services, prevention of violence and perpetrator accountability or prosecution.

3.3 Institutional Framework and Their Gaps

Fundamentally, the institutional framework for addressing sexual violence against women and girls in Ghana comprises various government ministries, such as the Ministry of Gender, Children and Social Protection (MGCSP), the Ministry of Interior, the Ministry of Health, the Ministry of Justice, the Police Service, the Judicial Service, the Metropolitan, Municipal and District Assemblies (MMDAs) and CSOs. The MGCSP is the central management agency responsible for policy formulation and oversight and coordination of all matters relating to the implementation of the Domestic Violence Act, 2007 (Act 732) and other statutes and policies relating to children and women. In that capacity, the Ministry has developed policies such as the National Domestic Violence Policy and the National Plan of Action to Implement the Domestic Violence Act, 2007 (Act 732) (2009–2019), and the Child and Family Welfare Policy. This Ministry also houses the DSW. The Ministry of Interior under the Human Trafficking Act, 2015 (Act 694) is responsible for dealing with human trafficking issues. The Police Service, the Judicial Service and the Immigration Service and other related law enforcement bodies are tasked to implement laws which protect women and children. A review of the Domestic Violence Act, 2007 (Act 732) shows that express references are made to the police and their duties stipulated.

---

[86] *Ibid.*

The Human Trafficking Act (Act 694) also assigns specific responsibilities to the Immigration and the Police Service. The Ministry of Justice, headed by the Attorney General, is responsible for promoting respect for the rule of law and human rights, equality of access to justice and equal treatment of all persons before the law.

The quality of response of Ghana's criminal justice system to sexual violence, in terms of holding sexual offenders accountable and protecting survivors or victims of sexual violence, depends to a large extent on the level of training and interventionist skills, availability of shelter facilities and coordinated delivery of other support services to assist survivors of violence.[87] Legislative and policy reforms made in the recent past have been focused on intensifying criminal prosecution of offenders; establishing a framework centred on victim protection; and enhancing the training and orientation of law enforcement professionals. However, problems with the design of response institutions and limited inter-agency coordination continue to hamper the achievement of improved outcomes for victims of sexual violence.

The National Policy and Plan of Action (NPPOA) recognises domestic violence as multidimensional issue, and as a social, legal, health, educational, economic and human rights problem. The Policy creates a comprehensive framework for an integrated and coordinated approach to the provision of support to victims which involves the Police Service, hospitals, DSW, courts and non-governmental organisations (NGOs). The Plan is designed to facilitate coordination at the community, district, regional and national levels and identifies various actors at these levels, to be facilitated by inter-agency and intra-agency protocols to promote effective coordination, information sharing and improved case management. The strategies outlined in the NPPOA focus on prevention through advocacy and awareness-raising, training for service providers, provision of services to meet victims/survivors' needs including the provision of shelter services.

Overall, Ghana's legal framework on sexual violence goes beyond the criminalisation of violence and addresses issues of protection by

[87] United States Department of State, 'Ghana 2018 Rights Report', in *Country Reports on Human Rights Practices for 2018* (Bureau of Democracy, Human Rights and Labour, 2018) www.state.gov/wp-content/uploads/2019/03/Ghana-2018.pdf.

making provision for protective orders (civil protection and occupation orders) to be issued by Gender-Based Violence courts for the benefit of victims/survivors.[88] The Domestic Violence Act enables a court to make an order to remove the perpetrator from a home shared with the survivor while still being responsible for the upkeep of the home.[89] The court also has the power to refer parties for counselling and the DSW is empowered to appoint probation officers to monitor and report back to the court.[90]

The DSW is charged with the role of ensuring rehabilitation and reintegration of victims of domestic violence and sexual violence back into their families and is specifically responsible for the preparation of social enquiry reports in domestic violence cases. Significantly, the DSW is responsible for the running of homes for children and youth in need of care and protection, the operation of state-run domestic violence shelters and the development of standards for the running of private shelters. The fact that no state-run domestic violence shelters have been established since 2009 reflects the lack of prioritisation accorded to the Policy and Plan of Action for protection of victims/survivors of domestic violence and sexual violence in Ghana. The impact and influence of the DSW have been minimal due to perennial budgetary constraints and logistical problems.

Medical officers and health workers are empowered by the Domestic Violence Act (Sect. 6(3)) to file complaints of domestic violence or sexual violence on behalf of victims/survivors. Even though the Act guarantees the provision of free medical care for victims/survivors, this is not available to victims/survivors of sexual violence in practice. Indeed, the Domestic Violence Management Board has not yet clarified the scope of the state-provided free medical treatment promised in the Domestic Violence Act and Regulations. The proposed standardisation of medical fees to be charged by medical officers for the provision of services and the negotiation between the Domestic Violence Management Board and the National Health Insurance Scheme, though elaborately outlined in the

[88] Act 732, Sects. 11–19, 21 & 22.

[89] Act 732, Sect. 17(1)(c).

[90] Act 732, Sect. 17(1).

NPPOA, have not taken place.[91] As a result, victims of sexual violence continue to fall through the cracks and drop out of the criminal justice system on account of their inability to pay for medical reports and treatment, and this has been shown to contribute significantly to the high attrition rates and low conviction rates seen in sexual violence cases.[92]

A specialised unit of the Ghana Police Service was first established in 1998, as the Women and Juvenile Unit (WAJU), to address the rising number of cases of violence against women and children and research trends of crimes against women and children. The name of the Unit was changed to the Domestic Violence and Victim Support Unit (DOVVSU) in 2004, and its role expanded to, among other responsibilities, protect the rights and promoting the welfare of children and women by preventing and prosecuting offences committed against them in the domestic domain and within the community. The establishment of the Specialised Unit of the Police Service and the expansion of its geographical reach in the country has contributed to making domestic violence a more visible public issue and enhanced access to the justice system for survivors of gender-based violence.[93] The impact of the DOVVSU in delivering quality services and support to victims of gender-based violence and domestic violence has however, been stifled by capacity constraints; logistical challenges and lack of inter-agency support and coordination.[94] The Unit has not benefited from sustained training of staff; the progression of cases in the courts has remained slow; and critical support services such as counselling emergency shelters, legal advice and medical services are still lacking. Personnel do not have adequate specialised training in investigative and prosecutorial skills to provide targeted support to victims of sexual violence. This contributes to the high attrition rates of sexual violence cases within the criminal justice system and the low conviction rates recorded in the courts. It has been

---

91 Dr Angela Dwamena-Aboagye (Executive Director, Ark Foundation), in an interview with the authors, June 19, 2020.

92 *Ibid.*

93 ActionAid, 'Fighting Domestic Violence in Ghana: How DOVVSU Set-ups Provide Safe Spaces for Survivors,' https://ghana.actionaid.org/sites/ghana/files/publications/DOVVSU%20AAG%20book%20Print%20-%20Final%20Approved.pdf.

94 Mitchell, *supra* note 89.

noted, however, that DOVVSU personnel exhibit much motivation and professionalism in their work despite heavy workloads and lack of logistical support.[95]

In terms of providing support for victims, state agencies rely heavily on NGOs and CSOs for the provision of shelter facilities, counselling and rehabilitation services.[96] State facilities for the protection of survivors of sexual violence are simply non-existent,[97] resulting in victims being returned to their homes in cases deemed to be relatively less severe. The DOVVSU and the DSW routinely refer cases to NGOs to identify temporary shelters for victims.[98] In many respects, the Ark Foundation complements the role of the DOVVSU and the DSW and the Police Service, but on an informal basis.

3.3.1 Gender-Based Violence Courts

As part of its attempts to improve access to justice and enhance institutional capacity to deliver standardised services to survivors of gender-based violence, the Judicial Service of Ghana established the Gender-Based Violence Courts (GBV courts) as specialised courts with a mandate to improve and streamline the handling and prosecution of gender-based violence and sexual violence cases. A GBV court has the status of a Circuit Court, which has original jurisdiction in all criminal matters other than treason, offences triable on indictment and offences punishable by death and life imprisonment.[99] Domestic violence cases as well as sexual offences (indecent assault, defilement and incest, though not rape) fall within the jurisdiction of the GBV courts.

---

[95] *Ibid.*

[96] Dr Angela Dwamena-Aboagye (Executive Director, Ark Foundation), in an interview with the authors, June 19, 2020.

[97] See Centre for Gender Studies and Advocacy (CEGENSA), 'Providing Better Protection for Victims of Domestic Violence in Ghana' 5, http://cegensa.ug.edu.gh/sites/cegensa.ug.edu.gh/files/Policy%20Brief-Domestic%20Violence.pdf.

[98] The only state owned and operated shelter facility is dedicated to child victims of trafficking in Ghana.

[99] Courts Act, 1993 (Act 459) Sect. 43.

The specialised courts are manned by specially trained judges, even though not necessarily trained court administrative staff. GBV courts are equipped with child-friendly facilities in the form of special waiting rooms, separate testifying room with CCTV equipment and intermediaries to ensure that adult and child victims/survivors can testify without feeling intimidated by the presence of the accused person in the same room.[100] This is a critical component of the support given to survivors and witnesses during court hearings. To protect the privacy of survivors and witnesses, the GBV courts empty the court of all persons, save those whose presence is mandatory and hold cases in camera, using blinds or curtains and closing all doors to prevent eavesdropping. Extensive guidelines have been developed to govern the operations of the gender-based violence courts to ensure that survivors of sexual violence, especially children, are treated fairly, with dignity and respect.[101]

Operated efficiently, the GBV courts could significantly reduce attrition rates and improve conviction rates for sexual offences. Currently, however, there are real factors which impede the experience of survivors of sexual violence in accessing justice which need to be addressed.

To begin with, prosecution of sexual violence cases is generally acknowledged as being sub-standard, and indeed act as significant contributory factors to low conviction rates in gender-based violence cases and high attrition rates.[102] Experience of the GBV courts shows that there is an urgent need to reorient the prosecution of gender-based violence and sexual offence cases from being police-driven to lawyer-driven.[103] Police prosecutors generally do not have the requisite training or legal knowledge for effective prosecution of sexual violence cases and are often handicapped by such lack of training, sensitisation and knowledge. One judge who had handled a GBV court for three years strongly recommended that to improve conviction rates, Police Prosecutors would have to be replaced by State Attorneys from the Attorney General's

[100] Judicial Service of Ghana, *Operational Guidelines, Child-Friendly Gender-Based Violence Courts in Ghana*, (2019).

[101] *Supra* note 133.

[102] Her Ladyship, Justice Abena Oppong Adzin- Doku (Justice of High Court), in an interview with the authors, June 2020.

[103] *Ibid.*

Department in gender-based violence and sexual offence cases.[104] This would involve the training of State Attorneys as special prosecutors to effectively progress sexual violence cases through the criminal justice system and reduce attrition. The use of specially trained state prosecutors who are lawyers would help to keep survivors within the criminal justice system and provide higher quality prosecution and contribute to improve conviction rates. Handling of sexual offence cases by specially trained prosecutors would shorten the travel time from reporting of the Police to court judgement and also help reduce secondary victimisation and trauma suffered by victim/survivors during the process.[105]

Even though the Domestic Violence Regulations prescribes modalities for the provision of free medical treatment for victims of domestic violence, this is not yet a reality for survivors. Victims are required to pay between 250 cedis (about USD 43) and 800 cedis (about 136 UDS)[106] for medical officers to sign medical reports for submission as evidence in court. Prosecutors routinely refuse to proceed with the case without medical reports to corroborate admitted evidence, and the courts will hardly convict without corroboration. Even though the DOVVSU and a number of NGOs have trained a few medical officers, who are willing to give evidence, sign medical reports and provide other assistance to survivors of gender-based violence, they are too few to make a difference.

The GBV courts have been established in Accra, Kumasi, Tema, Koforidua and Sunyani to hear cases relating to family and sexual violence.[107] Thus, a good proportion of sexual violence cases continue to be tried in regular courts by judges with minimal gender-specific training

---

[104] *Ibid.*

[105] Maastoera Sadan, Lulama Dikweni, and Shaamela Cassiem, *Pilot assessment: The Sexual Offences Court in Wynberg and Cape Town and Related Service,* (2001), http://www.endvawnow.org/uploads/browser/files/assessment_sexual_offences_courts_sa.pdf; *supra* note 89, 120–121.

[106] That is: $44 -$140 per the official exchange rate provided by the Bank of Ghana, last modified November 19, 2020, See: https://www.bog.gov.gh/treasury-and-the-markets/daily-interbank-fx-rates/.

[107] Judicial Service of Ghana, 'Children Before the Courts in Ghana: Towards Child-Friendly Justice', (2018), 18.

and many courts outside Accra do not have the physical space to accommodate child-friendly waiting rooms or testifying rooms as required.[108] Most court staff who interact with victims and witnesses in gender-based violence cases are not trained in how to deal with survivors and witnesses of sexual offences. Ghana must aim to establish GBV courts in each of the 16 regions of the country, and training for judges and court administration staff must be scaled up considerably. Protocols to facilitate and coordinate referrals to professionals free of charge for survivors are not being implemented as part of an integrated response to sexual violence. Judges of GBV courts noted that there should be psychologists attached to police stations and the courts, who can be called upon to provide survivors with needed services.[109] In the absence of such protocols, judges are compelled to rely on their personal acquaintances for the provision of critical services to victims/survivors where this is possible.[110]

With regard to sentencing, it is noted that the Criminal Offences Act (Act 29) prescribes minimum and maximum sentences for most of the sexual offences: defilement (term of imprisonment of not less than seven years and not more than 25 years); indecent assault (minimum imprisonment term of six months and maximum term of three years); rape (minimum of five years, maximum of 25 years); and incest (minimum of three years and maximum of five years' imprisonment). Guidelines for sentencing in rape, defilement, indecent assault and incest cases make provision for aggravating and mitigating factors to be considered by the judge. Aggravating factors appropriately include long duration, large age difference between perpetrator and victim, younger aged and vulnerable victim, excessive violence, greater injury (physical or psychological), violation of safe place, family, position of trust and transmission of disease. The prescription of minimum and maximum terms significantly reduces the judges' discretion in sentencing and keeps sentences within the pre-determined range established by law. This is a positive impact of the law which has helped to eliminate the practice of some judges in the past, of giving strangely lenient sentences for sexual offences.

---

[108] Her Ladyship, Justice Abena Oppong Adzin-Doku (Justice of the High Court of Ghana), in an interview with the authors, June 2020.

[109] *Ibid.*

[110] *Ibid.*

4 Improving Ghana's Response to Sexual Violence

The realities confronting survivors of gender-based crimes and sexual offences in Ghana in accessing justice illustrate the need for a more targeted and purposeful adaptation of the criminal justice system to protect survivors from secondary victimisation, achieve higher rates of convictions and provide targeted support for survivors of such crimes. Specific measures are required to improve outcomes at every stage of the criminal justice process: investigation, prosecution, trial, conviction and sentencing. The chapter recognises that significant progress has been made in constructing a comprehensive legislative infrastructure for combatting violence against women in Ghana. However, there is the need for a more targeted implementation plan to make the criminal justice system more accessible in the real sense, to women and girls in Ghana. To address the scourge of sexual violence against women, a comprehensive legislative and policy approach is required which not only criminalises all forms of violence against women, but ensures the effective prosecution and punishment of offenders, contributes to the prevention of such violence and empowers, supports and protects survivors.

Ghana's prospects for improving its response to sexual violence are quite promising in view of the comprehensive legal infrastructure which is already in place. The NPPOA for the implementation of the Domestic Violence Act formulated in 2009, provides an elaborate framework for the delivery of critical support services to survivors of gender-based violence. The Policy has however seen very little corresponding action to translate its objectives into reality. The Plan of Action must be progressively and systematically implemented to make justice more accessible in the real sense, to women and girls who survive sexual violence in Ghana. More attention must be paid to ensuring smooth and effective inter-agency collaboration to guarantee access to survivors of sexual offences. Effective and smooth collaboration between the Police, the DSW, the courts and health care providers, is critical to guaranteeing the protection of victim survivors.

Ultimately, the state has a responsibility to provide a broad range of protective services that are integrated, well-coordinated and accessible to victims/survivors of sexual offences. Protection and support of survivors/victims of sexual violence must include legal actions, provision of information, general support services, assistance in complaints, encouraging reporting, specialist support services, shelters, telephone lines, rehabilitation services, protection and support for child witnesses, encouraging reporting of sexual offences by professionals.

For a start, medical and legal linkages must be established to enhance the delivery of protective services in sexual violence cases. The guidelines outlined in the Domestic Violence NPPOA must be implemented to ensure that public healthcare facilities provide victims/survivors with the required range of treatment options after sexual violence. This must be integrated into the National Healthcare Policy to ensure that all public healthcare facilities provide victims/survivors with post-sexual assault care services free of charge and must be covered under the national health insurance scheme as a basic healthcare need. Special inter-agency protocols and standardised referral guidelines must be developed and implemented to enhance coordination between the health sector, the Police Service and the judicial service/courts to ensure that services are integrated by cross-referrals between these stakeholders sectors.[111] Inter-agency and intra-agency protocols must be rigorously implemented to facilitate and coordinate victim referrals to professionals free of charge as part of an integrated response to sexual violence. There should be psychologists attached to police stations and the courts, who can be called upon to provide survivors with the entire range of healthcare interventions, including clinical treatment, psychological support, counselling and therapy. Budgetary provisions must be made for the delivery of these services and special inter-agency protocols and standardised referral guidelines must be developed and implemented to enhance coordination between the health sector, the Police Service and the judicial

[111] Nduku Kilonzo et al., 'Sexual Violence Legislation in Sub-Saharan Africa: The Need for Strengthened Medico-legal Linkages', 17(34) *Reproductive Health Matters,* (November 2009): 10–19.

service/courts, to ensure that services are integrated by cross-referrals between these stakeholder sectors.[112]

As noted earlier, studies assessing the performance of the Unit have noted that in spite of the formidable logistical constraints affecting the work of the DOVVSU, officials are highly motivated, dedicated and committed to protecting women's rights; and users of the service are generally satisfied with the limited services received.[113] Thus, personnel of the Unit can be easily motivated through training and incentivised to further enhance their performance in responding to domestic violence and sexual offences. The infrastructure of the DOVVSU must be expanded to enable the Unit to offer logistical resources to encourage reporting and enhance the experience of victims who report cases of sexual violence. The Unit must be equipped with designated offices to guarantee victims' privacy when reporting cases involving sexual violence. In particular, there must be protocols for providing victims/survivors of sexual violence with counselling services or legal services free of charge. Overall, the DOVVSU must be better resourced to enhance its delivery of support and protective services to victims/survivors of sexual violence.

The National Gender Policy, launched by the Ministry of Gender and Social Protection in May 2015 to streamline Ghana's development effort in Gender Equality and Women Empowerment, described gender budgeting as a means improve women's economic opportunities by way of engendering macro-economic and trade policies so that the basic and strategic needs of both men and women are addressed.[114] It is noted that under the National Domestic Violence Policy, the Ministry of Finance and Economic Planning is required to ensure resource mobilisation and adequate budgetary allocations for domestic violence programmes; actively engage with development partners to mobilise extra budgetary resources in support of domestic violence programmes and facilitate the re-allocation of resources to support programmes on domestic violence. Competing government priorities and lack of political will are major

[112] *Ibid.*

[113] Mitchell, *supra* note 89.

[114] The Ministry of Gender and Social Protection, 'National Gender Policy: Mainstreaming Gender Equality and Women's Empowerment into Ghana's Development Efforts (Accra, 2015), 15–21.

challenges facing gender equality and women's empowerment, and by extension, hamper the state's response to sexual violence.[115] More effort must be made towards accelerating the implementation of the gender-responsive budgeting initiative that the government had agreed to undertake, to translate the objectives of these policies into reality.

5 Conclusion

Ghana has made significant strides in establishing a comprehensive legal and institutional framework for enhancing its response to sexual violence. This chapter sought to critically assess the response of Ghana's legal and institutional framework to the incidence of sexual violence against women and girls; it highlighted the achievements of the framework and noted the deficiencies and gaps, which have limited its impact. It has argued for a more focused and purposeful adaptation of the rules of criminal procedure to guarantee greater access to justice for victims and the conscious provision of more sustainable support systems for victims of sexual violence to improve their experience and quality of interaction with the criminal justice system. The chapter advocates a more holistic and all-inclusive approach to be adopted in the implementation of the applicable laws and for a more rigorous inter-agency collaboration to deliver support services to victims of sexual offences. More innovative measures must be adopted as part of the state's commitment to the prevention of sexual violence. These must be focused on awareness-raising and education; enhanced training of law enforcement professionals; preventive intervention and treatment programmes with greater participation from and engagement with the private sector and the media. Ultimately, responding to sexual violence should entail not only criminalising violence against women, but also ensuring the effective prosecution and punishment of offenders, and delivering tangible support and protection to victims/survivors of sexual violence.

---

[115] *Ibid.*

Acknowledgments The authors acknowledge the research assistance of Akua Prempeh Owusu-Boakye and Prosper Batariwah

References

ActionAid Ghana, 2020, 'Fighting Domestic Violence in Ghana: How DOVVSU Set-ups Provide Safe spaces for Survivors.' https://ghana.actionaid.org/sites/ghana/files/publications/DOVVSU%20AAG%20book%20Print%20-%20Final%20Approved.pdf.

African Union, 2003, Protocol to the African Charter on Human and Peoples' Rights on the Rights of Women in Africa, https://www.refworld.org/docid/3f4b139d4.html.

Akosua Adomako-Ampofo, 1993, 'Controlling and Punishing Women: Violence against Ghanaian Women', *Review of African Political Economy* 20(56), 102–111.

Alda Facio, 2013, 'What is Patriarchy?', Translated from Spanish by Michael Solis, http://learnwhr.org/wp-content/uploads/D-Facio-What-isPatriarchy.pdf.

Bonnie S Fisher et al, 2003, 'Reporting Sexual Victimization to The Police and Others: Results from a National-Level Study of College Women', *Criminal Justice and Behaviour.*

Cassandra L Melo, 2019, 'The Feminization of Poverty: A Brief Analysis of Gender Issues and Poverty among Women and Girls', 1(1) *The Canadian Journal of Critical Nursing Discourse.*

Cassia Spohn and Katharine Tellis, 2012, 'The Criminal Justice System's Response to Sexual Violence', 18(2) *Violence Against Women.*

Centre for Gender Studies and Advocacy, 'Providing Better Protection for Victims of Domestic Violence in Ghana', http://cegensa.ug.edu.gh/sites/cegensa.ug.edu.gh/files/Policy%20Brief-Domestic%20Violence.pdf.

Centre for Gender Studies and Advocacy, 2016. 'Beyond Domestic Violence Laws: Women's Experiences and Perception of Protection Services in Ghana', http://cegensa.ug.edu.gh/sites/cegensa.ug.edu.gh/files/Beyond%20Domestic.pdf.

Clare McGlynn, 2011, 'Feminism, Rape and the Search for Justice', 31(4) *Oxford Journal of Legal Studies.*

Commissioner of Police v. Sem [1962] 2 GLR 77.
Cynthia Cockburn, 2004, 'The Continuum of Violence: A Gender Perspective on War and Peace', in *Sites of Violence: Gender and Conflict Zones,* edited by W. Giles and J. Hyndman (2004): 1–38.
Dorcas Coker-Appiah and Kathy Cusack, 1999, Breaking the Silence and Challenging the Myth of Violence Against Women and Children in Ghana: Report of a National Study on Violence (Accra-North: Gender Studies & Human Rights Documentation Centre).
Dzodzi Tsikata, 2001, *Gender Training in Ghana: Politics, Issues and Tools.*
E Adu-Gyamfi, 2014, 'Challenges Undermining Domestic Violence Victims' Access to Justice in Mampong Municipality of Ghana', *Journal of Law, Policy and Globalization* 27, 75–90.
Edward Kutsoati and Randall Morck, 2012, 'Family Ties, Inheritance Rights, and Successful Poverty Alleviation: Evidence from Ghana', NBER Working Paper No. 18080.
Eric Y Tenkorang et al, 2013, 'Factors Influencing Domestic and Marital Violence Against Women in Ghana', *Journal of Family Violence.*
Esteban Ortiz-Ospina, 2018, 'Economic Inequality by Gender', https://ourworldindata.org/economic-inequality-by-gender.
Fitnat NA Adjetey, 1995, 'Reclaiming the African Woman's Individuality: The Struggle Between Women's Reproductive Autonomy and African Society and Culture', *American University Law Review* 44(1), 1351.
Francis D Boateng and Lee D Heeuk, 2014, 'Willingness to Report Sexual Offenses to the Police in Ghana', *Victims and Offenders* 9, 436–454.
Gerda Lerner, 1986, *The Creation of Patriarchy.*
Gervin A Apatinga, and Tenkorang Eric Y, 2020, 'Determinants of Sexual Violence Against Married Women: Qualitative Evidence from Ghana', *Sexual Abuse* 3.
H Khelghat-Doost, and S Sibly, 2020, 'The Impact of Patriarchy on Women's Political Participation', 10(3) *International Journal of Academic Research in Business and Social Sciences.*
Hanson v. The Republic [1975] 1 GLR 477.
Hazel M McFerson,, 2020, 'Poverty Among Women in Sub-Saharan Africa: A Review of Selected Issues', 11(4) *Journal of International Women's Studies.*
Henrietta Mensa-Bonsu, 2020, 'Regulating Sexual Self-Expression through Criminal Legislation: The Case for Reform' in *Mobilising the Law for Ghana's Future: Appraising to Revolutionise* edited by Christine Dowuona-Hammond, Ama F. Hammond and Raymond A. Atuguba.

IK Gyasi, 2006, 'Domestic Violence Bill – Specified Offences (2)', *Ghanaian Chronicle*, https://allafrica.com/stories/200612111567.html.

Institute of Development Studies, 2016, Ghana Statistical Services and Associates, *Domestic Violence in Ghana: Incidence, Attitudes, Determinants and Consequences.*

ISSER, Ipsos MORI, International Centre for Research on Women (ICRW) and NUI Galway. (2019) 'Economic and Social Costs of Violence Against Women in Ghana: Summary Report' https://www.ipsos.com/sites/default/files/ct/publication/documents/2019-07/economic-social-costs-violence-women-girls-ghana-2019.pdf.

J Ofori-Boateng, 2000, *The Ghana Law of Evidence*, 2nd ed.

Janice Du Mont and Myhr Terri, 2000, 'So Few Convictions: The Role of Client-Relate Characteristics in the Legal Processing of Sexual Assaults', 6 *Violence Against Women* (2000).

Jeanmarie Fenrich and Tracy Higgins, 2001, 'Promise Unfulfilled: Law, Culture and Women's Inheritance Rights in Ghana', 25 *Fordham International Law Journal* 259.

Johan Galtung, 1960, *Peace by Peaceful Means: Peace and Conflict, Development and Civilization.*

Judicial Service of Ghana, 2018, 'Children Before the Courts in Ghana: Towards Child-Friendly Justice'.

Judicial Service of Ghana, 2019, 'Operational Guidelines, Child-Friendly Gender-Based Violence Courts in Ghana'.

Kieran M Kennedy, 2019, 'The Relationship of Victim Injury to the Progression of Sexual Crimes through the Criminal Justice System', 19 *Journal of Forensic and Legal Medicine*.

Kilonzo *et al*, 2009, 'Sexual Violence Legislation in Sub-Saharan Africa: The Need for Strengthened Medico-legal Linkages', 17(34) *Reproductive Health Matters.*

Laura Mitchell, 2011, *Service Users' Perceptions of the Domestic Violence and Victims' Support Unit, Ghana Police Service,* https://static1.squarespace.com/static/536c4ee8e4b0b60bc6ca7c74/t/5437f188e4b05ef245bd6a2a/1412952456336/Perceptions+of+the+Domestic+Violence+and+Victim%27s+Support+Unit+Ghana+Police+Service+2012+Laura+Mitchelll+June+2012.pdf.

Lesotho Sexual Offences Act (2003).

Loreen Maseno, and Susan M. Kilonzo, 2011, 'Engendering Development: Demystifying Patriarchy and its Effects on Women in Rural Kenya', 3(2) *International Journal of Sociology and Anthropology.*

Lynne Henderson, 1991 'Law's Patriarchy', *Scholarly Works,* 876 http://scholars.law.unlv.edu/facpub/876.
Maastoera Sadan, Lulama Dikweni, and Shaamela Cassiem, 2001, *Pilot assessment: The Sexual Offences Court in Wynberg and Cape Town and Related Service,* http://www.endvawnow.org/uploads/browser/files/assessment_sexual_offences_courts_sa.pdf.
Margaret Ivy Amoakohene, 2004, 'Violence Against Women in Ghana: A Look at Women's Perceptions and Review of Policy and Social Responses', *Social Science & Medicine* 59, no. 11, 2372–2385.
Namibia Combating of Rape Act (2000).
Nancy Chi Cantalupo et al, 2004, 'Domestic Violence in Ghana: The Open Secret,' 7 *Georgetown Journal of Gender and Law* 531–597.
Nancy Kaymar Stafford, 2007, 'Permission for Domestic Violence: Marital Rape in Ghanaian Marriages', 63 *Women's Rights Law Reporter.*
PK Twumasi, 1985, *Criminal Law in Ghana.*
Rene Girard, 1977, *Violence and the Sacred.* translated by Patrick Gregory.
Richard B Felson and Pare Paul-Phillipe, 2007, 'Does the Criminal Justice System Treat Domestic Violence and Sexual Assault Offenders Leniently?' 24(3) *Justice Quarterly* 435–459.
Romi Sigsworth, Lisa Vetten, Rachel Jewkins, and Nicola Christofides, 2009, 'Policing Rape in South Africa in Gender: Empowering Women for Gender Equity', 82 *Gender and the Legal System.*
Rosemary Ofei-Aboagye, 1994, 'Domestic Violence in Ghana: An Initial Step', 4(1) *Columbia Journal Gender Law.*
SA Brobbey, 2014, *Essentials of the Ghana Law of Evidence.*
Sadia Hodžić, 2009, 'Unsettling Power: Domestic Violence, Gender Politics and Struggles over Sovereignty in Ghana', 74(3) *Ethnos: Journal of Anthropology,* 331–360.
State v. Ohene -Kesson and Mensah [1961] GLR 708, 714.
Stephen A Quaye, Moses O. Amponsah and Ernest P. Asare, 2005, 'Domestic Violence Bill', *Ghanaian Chronicle*
Susan Rakoczy, 2004, 'Religion and Violence: The Suffering of Women', 8(61) *Agenda: Empowering Women for Gender Equity,* Doi:https://doi.org/10.1080/10130950.2004.9676037.
Sylvia Walby *et al,* 2015, 'Law and the Criminal Justice System' in *Stopping Rape: Towards a Comprehensive Policy.*
The Constitution of the Republic of Ghana, 1992.

The Ministry of Gender and Social Protection, 2015, 'National Gender Policy: Mainstreaming Gender Equality and Women's Empowerment into Ghana's Development Efforts'.
The Republic of Ghana Children's Act, 1998 (Act 560).
The Republic of Ghana Courts Act, 1993 (Act 459).
The Republic of Ghana Criminal Code (Amendment) Act, 1993(Act 458).
The Republic of Ghana Criminal Code (Amendment) Act, 1998 (Act 554).
The Republic of Ghana Criminal Offences Act, 1960 (Act 29).
The Republic of Ghana Domestic Violence Act, 2007 (Act 732).
The Republic of Ghana Evidence Act, 1975 (NRCD 323).
The Republic of Ghana Human Trafficking Act, 2005 (Act 694).
The Republic of Ghana Laws of Ghana (Revised Edition) Act, 1998 (Act 562).
The Republic of Ghana, Parliamentary Debates, Parliament, July 14, 1994, 1226.
UN Division for the Advancement of Women, 2009, *Handbook for Legislation on Violence against Women.*
United Nations Children's Fund, 2000, *Domestic Violence Against Women and Girls*, Innocenti Digest, no. 6 http://www.unicef-irc.org/publications/pdf/digest6e.pdf.
United Nations Department of Economic and Social Affairs, 2015, *The World's Women, 2015: Trends and Statistics.*
United Nations Economic & Social Affairs Division for the Advancement of Women, 2010, *Handbook for Legislation on Violence against Women 2009.*
United Nations Statistics Division from Demographic and Health Surveys (DHS) and Reproductive Health Surveys (RHS) (ICF International, 2014) cited as the source by United Nations Department of Economic and Social Affairs, 2015 The *World's Women, 2015: Trends and Statistics.*
United Nations, 1981, Convention on the Elimination of All Forms of Discrimination against Women, G.A. Res. 34/180, U.N. GAOR 34th Sess., Supp. No. 46 AT 193, U.N. Doc. A/34/46
United Nations, 1992, The Committee on the Elimination of Discrimination against Women, General Recommendation 19, Violence against women, U.N. Doc. A/47/38 at 1 (1993), reprinted in Compilation of General Comments and General Recommendations Adopted by Human Rights Treaty Bodies, U.N. Doc. HRI/GEN/1/Rev.6 at 243 (2003), General Comment 7.
United Nations, 1993, Declaration on the Elimination of Violence against Women, UN Doc A/RES/48/104, December 20, 1993.

United Nations, 1995, Beijing Declaration and Platform of Action, adopted at the Fourth World Conference on Women, October 27, 1995, https://www.refworld.org/docid/3dde04324.html.

United Nations, Beijing Declaration and Platform of Action, adopted at the Fourth World Conference on Women, October 27, 1995. https://www.refworld.org/docid/3dde04324.html.

United States Department of State, 2018, 'Ghana 2018 Rights Report', in *Country Reports on Human Rights Practices for 2018* www.state.gov/wp-content/uploads/2019/03/Ghana-2018.pdf.

Wendy Harcourt, 2013, *Body Politics in Development: Critical Debates in Gender and Development*.

World Health Organisation, 'Violence against Women', https://www.who.int/news-room/fact-sheets/detail/violence-against-women.

World Health Organization, 2005, *World Health Report: Make Every Mother and Child Count.*

3

Access to Justice for Female Victims of Sexual Violence in Uganda

Charlotte Kabaseke and Barbara Kitui

1 Background

Violence against women and girls (VAWG) is a global concern[1] with one in three women being affected by violence.[2] Approximately 35% of

---

[1] * Advocate, Courts of Judicature of Uganda;.
** Ministry of Justice and Constitutional Affairs, Uganda;.
United Nations General Assembly Resolution 48/104, *Declaration on the Elimination of Violence against Women* 20 December 20, 1993, article 1. Violence against women is defined as: '…any act of gender-based violence that results in, or is likely to result in, physical, sexual or psychological harm or suffering to women, including threats of such acts, coercion or arbitrary deprivation of liberty, whether occurring in public or private life…' See UNICEF, *Violence against children*, May 25, 2020, https://data.unicef.org/topic/child-protection/violence/. Violence against girls is described as that which: '…takes many forms, including physical, sexual, and emotional abuse, and may involve neglect or deprivation. Violence occurs in many settings, including the home, school, community and over the internet. Similarly, a wide range of perpetrators commit violence against children, such as family members, intimate partners, teachers, neighbours, strangers and other children. Such violence not only inflicts harm, pain and humiliation on children; it also kills…'.

[2] World Bank, 'The World Bank Gender-Based Violence (Violence Against Women and Girl', May 25, 2020, https://www.worldbank.org/en/topic/socialdevelopment/brief/violence-against-women-and-girls: Violence implies physical and or sexual violence meted by intimate partners or otherwise.

C. Kabaseke (✉)
Courts of Judicature, Uganda Christian University, Mukono, Uganda

B. Kitui
Ministry of Justice and Constitutional Affairs, Kampala, Uganda

A. Budoo-Scholtz and E. C. Lubaale (eds.), *Violence Against Women and Criminal Justice in Africa: Volume II*, Sustainable Development Goals Series,
https://doi.org/10.1007/978-3-030-75953-7_3

women across the globe have reported acts of physical/sexual violence against them, with 7% of women having been sexually assaulted by non-intimate partners and 38% of women-related murders being attributed to intimate partners.[3] Moreover, 200 million women have undergone female genital mutilation.[4] According to the United Nations (UN) Women, in 2018, the world average of physical and sexual violence stood at 17.8%.[5] Physical and sexual violence against women and girls was reported at 6.1% Europe and North America, 11.8% in Latin America, 23.0% Central and Southern Asia and 34.7% in Oceania excluding Australia and New Zealand.[6] In order to address VAWG concerns, several interventions have been made by international agencies including the UN. For example, the World Bank Group developed strategies aimed at strengthening interventions geared at minimising VAWG by focusing on improving human endowments including: health, education and social protection[7]; removing constraints for more and better jobs[8]; removing barriers to women's ownership of and control over assets[9]; and enhancing women's voices and agency and engaging men and boys.[10]

In Africa, it is estimated that 21.5% of women and girls in sub-Saharan Africa experience physical and sexual violence while the percentage is at 12.3% in North Africa and Western Asia.[11] It is reported that one out two women have encountered 'either physical and/or sexual intimate partner violence or sexual violence by a non-partner at some point in their lifetime'.[12] For the year 2013, 'African women and girls

[3] *Ibid* 1., violence implies physical and or sexual violence meted by intimate partners or otherwise.

[4] World Bank, *supra* note 2.

[5] United Nations Women, *Progress of the World's Women 2019–2020: Families in a changing world* (2019) 180.

[6] *Ibid.*

[7] World Bank, *World Bank Group Gender Strategy: Gender Equality, Poverty Reduction and Inclusive Growth (FY16-23)* (2015) 31–41.

[8] *Ibid.*, 41–51.

[9] *Ibid.*, 52–55.

[10] *Ibid.*, 56–59.

[11] United Nations Women, *supra* note 5.

[12] African Union, United Nations Human Rights Office of the High Commissioner and UN Women, *Women's Rights in Africa* (2016): 11, http://www.ohchr.org/Documents/Issues/Women/WRGS/WomensRightsinAfrica_singlepages.pdf.

accounted for 62% (179,000) of all global deaths from preventable causes related to pregnancy and childbirth…'[13] which is certainly a form of emotional and psychological violence against African women and girls.

This situation persists, despite the fact that several countries across the globe, including Uganda, have ratified international instruments to safeguard women from all forms of violence including the Convention on the Elimination of All Forms of Discrimination against Women (CEDAW)[14] and the Protocol to the African Charter on Human and Peoples' Rights on the Rights of Women (Maputo Protocol).[15] In addition, numerous steps have been taken within the African continent to safeguard women and girls from sexual violence. For example, 2000–2020 was declared as 'African Women's Decade'.[16]

Uganda is not an exception to this global crisis of VAWG. In 2019, a total of 1528 women were raped compared to 1,580 in 2018. Out of the 1,528 rapes, 688 suspects were arraigned, 20 convicted, 6 acquitted, 15 discharged and 647 pending trial.[17] A total of 13,682 cases of defilement were reported in 2019 with 13,441 female and 241 male victims.[18] Out of the 13,682 cases, 126 children were defiled.[19] Incidences of defilement were highest in East Kyoga, Elgon 922 (with Mbale District recording 317 cases) and Kamuli 274 cases.[20] The age groups defiled between 0–8 years, 9–14 years and 15–17 years were 1,026, 2,100 and 10,556, respectively.[21] The 15–17 years age group accounted for the highest because some societies assume that girls this age are ready for marriage[22]

---

13 *Ibid.*

14 United Nations, *The Convention on the Elimination of All Forms of Discrimination against Women* adopted on December 18, 1979 and came into force on September 3, 1981.

15 African Union, *The Protocol to the African Charter on Human and Peoples' Rights on the Rights of Women* adopted on July 11, 2003 and came into force in November 2005.

16 United Nations *Women Africa*, 15 June 2020, https://www.unwomen.org/en/where-we-are/africa.

17 Uganda Police Force, *The Annual Crime Report 2019* (2019): 16.

18 *Ibid.*, 14.

19 *Ibid.*

20 *Ibid.*

21 *Ibid.*

22 *Ibid.*

despite the fact that the laws of Uganda prohibit child marriage.[23] In 2019, the perpetrators of defilement included 84 parents, 249 guardians, 113 primary school teachers, 64 secondary school teachers and 390 HIV-positive persons.[24] Out of 13,682 defilements, 5,889 suspects were arrested and forwarded to court for trial with 1,006 convictions secured and 4,353 pending trial.[25] In relation to domestic violence, 2019 had 13,693 cases reported to police in comparison to 13,916 cases in 2018. Only 1,390 were taken to court, 359 convicted, 21 acquitted, 288 dismissed, 722 'pending in court' and 5,039 ongoing investigations.[26] Although there is no information on collated sexual violence against women and girls (SVAWG) annual conviction rates, the number of convictions secured as indicated above is glaringly lower than it should be.

Despite the existence of 18 institutions directly involved in the adjudication and dispensation of justice in Uganda,[27] sexual violence persists. These institutions unlike several other African countries provide access to justice through a sector wide approach. Currently, the Justice Law and Order Sector finalised its Fourth Sector Development Plan (SDP IV) and is set to commence a new programme under the third National Development Plan.[28] The SDP IV guides the Justice Law and Order Sector (JLOS) interventions on access to justice, and sexual violence against

---

23 Children (Amendment) Act 2016, Sect. 42A(1) protects children from violence including child marriages.

24 *Ibid.*, 14.

25 *Ibid.*, 14.

26 *Ibid.*, 17. There is a dearth of information relating to annual conviction rates. Information on convictions for specific crimes commitment was obtainable from Uganda Police Reports.

27 Justice Law and Order Sector (JLOS), *Fourth Sector Development Plan 2017–2020* (2017) 12–13. JLOS institutions are: Ministry of Justice and Constitutional Affairs, the Judiciary, Ministry of Internal Affairs (Community Service, Directorate of Government Analytical Laboratories, Directorate of Non-Governmental Organisations and Small Arms and Light Weapons), Ministry of Gender, Labour and Social Development, Ministry of Local Government, Office of the Director of Public Prosecutions, Judicial Service Commission, Uganda Human Rights Commission, Uganda Law Reform Commission, Uganda Police Force, Uganda Prison Service, Directorate of Citizenship and Immigration Control, Uganda Registration Services Bureau, Tax Appeals Tribunal, Law Development Centre, National Identification and Registration Authority, Uganda Law Society and the Centre for Arbitration and Dispute Resolution.

28 *Ibid.*, JLOS, *Fourth Sector Development Plan 2017–2020*. The new programme will situate justice law and order institutions under the Governance and Security Programme.

women and girls remains top on the agenda. There are also specific interventions to address justice for children concerns, including violence against girls.[29] It is reported that in Uganda, gender-based violence costs some specific sectors like health Uganda Shillings (UGX) 18.3 billion, UGX19.5 billon for police and UGX12.7 billion for local councils[30] which approximates to United States Dollars (USD) 4.94 million, USD 5.27 million and USD 3.43 million, respectively.[31]

Scholarly works of feminism on SVAWG note that rape depicts societal culture of male supremacy over women and girls.[32] They propound that rape is a mechanism of demeaning women and leaving them frightened.[33] They argue that rape is more or less about 'power-gender dynamic' than acts of criminality.[34] Other scholars expound that rape represents a domineering sexual scheme.[35] The aim of rapists is the 'objectification' of their victims.[36] The authors of this chapter agree that the objectification and humiliation of women is wrong and must stop because any form of VAWG is detrimental to one's life.

Though the concept of VWAG broadly includes sexual abuse and exploitation, child sacrifice, child labour and forced labour, child marriage, child and women trafficking, institutional abuse, female genital mutilation and any other form of physical or emotional abuse[37] and domestic violence,[38] for purposes of this chapter, VWAG is interpreted

29 *Ibid.*, 49 & 37.

30 United Nations Population Fund, 'Evaluation of UNFPA support to the prevention, response to and elimination of gender-based violence and harmful practices 2012–2017: Uganda Case Study' (2018) 8–9.

31 31 One United States Dollar is equivalent to Uganda Shilling 3697. Exchange Rates US Dollar (USD) to Ugandan Shilling (UGX) exchange rate history, September 24, 2020, https://www.exchangerates.org.uk/USD-UGX-exchange-rate-history.html.

32 Andrew Lawrence Spivak, *Sexual Violence; Beyond the feminist-evolutionary debate* (2011):35.

33 *Ibid.*

34 *Ibid.*, 36.

35 Ann J Cahill, 'Sexual Violence and Objectification', in *Theorising Sexual Violence* J Rene Heberle and Victoria Grace (eds) (2009): 19.

36 *Ibid.*, 24.

37 Children (Amendment) Act, *supra* note 24.

38 Domestic Violence Act 2010, Sect. 2 defines domestic violence to include mental or physical harm, harassment, verbal and psychological abuse, economic abuse and sexual abuse. See

within the context of sexual violence and specifically rape and defilement. This chapter seeks to assess how access to justice can be enhanced for female victims of sexual violence in Uganda. This is addressed by assessing the sufficiency of existing legislative framework on sexual violence, unearthing the legal and non-legal challenges faced by women and girls in accessing justice, and providing prospects that are aimed at enhancing access to justice for women and girls in Uganda.

2 Recognition of Access to Justice for Women Victims of Sexual Violence: A Legal Analysis

International human rights law has several provisions to ensure access to justice for women victims of sexual violence throughout the entire criminal justice system. Article 2 of the CEDAW provides for non-discrimination against women and requires states parties to ensure that they have in place adequate measures to ensure equality between men and women. The connection between gender equality and access to justice is that the existing gender inequalities between men and women which result from the patriarchal society regard women and girls as second-class citizens hence exacerbating violence against women and girls. The inequalities are also reflected in the justice system, and the bias against girls and women victims of sexual violence start right from the stage of reporting at the police station which discourages women from pursuing the case further. Article 3 requires states parties to have in place measures to ensure that women enjoy their fundamental rights and freedoms equally with the men. Article 15(1) is more relevant to this chapter and provides that women and men are equal before the law and should enjoy equal protection of the law. Impliedly, women are entitled to access to justice equally with the men. Although not directly linked to access to justice, article 11 of the CEDAW places an obligation upon states parties to guard against discrimination against women and

UNICEF *Uganda Violence Against Children Survey: Findings from a National Survey, 2015* (2015).

promote equality within employment spheres. Paragraph 17 of General Recommendation 19 of the Committee on the Elimination of Discrimination Against Women (CEDAW Committee),[39] in further elaborating on article 11, recognises that sexual violence against women impairs their employment.

Article 12 of CEDAW requires states to ensure non-discrimination against women in the delivery of health services. Paragraph 19 of General Recommendation 19 further recognises that violence against women places women at a health risk. In addition, article 16 of the CEDAW requires States parties to eliminate discrimination against women in the marriage and family sphere. In light of this, paragraph 23 of General Recommendation 19 of the CEDAW Recommendation recognises that women suffer rape and other forms of sexual assault within the family setting. Paragraph 24(b) of General Recommendation 19 places an obligation upon states to ensure that they adopt laws that ensure adequate protection of women against rape, assault and gender-based violence among others. Paragraphs 24(i) and (t) which are most relevant to this chapter place an obligation on states to ensure that, '[e]ffective complaints procedures and remedies, including compensation, should be provided', and that states responses must include:

> ...penal sanctions, civil remedies compensatory provisions to protect women against all kinds of violence, including, inter alia, violence and abuse in the family, sexual assault and sexual harassment in the workplace.

These robust provisions notwithstanding, sexual violence against women and specifically rape remain prevalent as elaborated in the preceding paragraphs of this chapter. Although the General Recommendations of the CEDAW Committee endeavour to strengthen CEDAW provisions especially in relation to sexual violence, General Recommendations are still non-legally binding and States are not bound by these provisions. This position still leaves women largely vulnerable. Despite

---

[39] CEDAW *General Recommendation no. 19 on Violence Against Women*, Adopted by the CEDAW Committee on the Elimination of Discrimination Against Women, Eleventh session (1992), September 28, 2020 https://tbinternet.ohchr.org/Treaties/CEDAW/Shared%20Documents/1_Global/INT_CEDAW_GEC_3731_E.pdf.

the fact that the CEDAW entirely on protecting women, it lacks express provisions on women's access to justice in criminal matters and does not create state obligations in terms of access of justice.

Article 5 of the African Charter on Human and Peoples' Rights (ACHPR) provides for 'the right to redress for victims of torture and other cruel, inhuman or degrading punishment or treatment'. In interpreting this article, the African Commission on Human and Peoples' Rights (African Commission) stated that states parties are required to adopt measures aimed to address barriers against justice for acts of sexual and gender-based violence which may amount to torture and other ill-treatment.[40] Additionally, article 7 promotes access to justice and recognises every individual's right to have their cause heard. This article is, however, in favour of accused persons as opposed to victims of crime. Further, article 8 of the Protocol to the Maputo Protocol provides that states parties should take appropriate action and adopt measures to ensure that women enjoy access to judicial and legal services effectively.

In addition, existing discriminatory laws and practices should be reformed in order to protect women's rights. Article 8(d) requires states parties to equip law enforcement organs at all levels to enable them to effectively interpret and enforce gender equality rights. This provision implies that all state organs in the criminal justice system, including the police, courts of law, prosecution office and the defence counsel need to be equipped both physically and with appropriate knowledge on how to handle cases involving sexual violence against women. Unfortunately, this has not been the case in Uganda, as is discussed in the next section of this paper. In addition, the Maputo Protocol requires states to 'prohibit, prevent and punish all forms of violence against women including unwanted or forced sex whether the violence takes place in private or public'.[41] In achieving this, states parties shall adopt and implement appropriate measures to prohibit any exploitation or degradation of women. Furthermore, article 3(4) provides that:

---

40 African Commission on Human and Peoples' Rights, *General comment No. 4 on the African Charter on Human and Peoples' Rights: the right to redress for victims of torture and other cruel, inhuman or degrading punishment or treatment (article 5)* (2017), paragraphs 57–61.

41 Maputo Protocol, article 4(2)(a).

> State parties 'shall also adopt and implement appropriate measures to ensure the protection of every woman's right to respect for her dignity and protection of women from all forms of violence, particularly sexual and verbal violence.[42]

Moreover, the Maputo Protocol requires States parties to 'punish the perpetrators of violence against women and implement programmes for the rehabilitation of women victims'.[43] Despite the existence of these robust provisions at the African regional level, the region is still marred with cultural and stereotypical beliefs that discriminate against women. As a result, during rape trials, myths about rape, which are not in favour of women are evoked leaving victims at a disadvantage of accessing justice. A case in point is *Uganda v Lt. Col. Galungbe,*[44] where Justice Kityo stated as follows:

> ...She truthfully admitted of having previously had another sexual experience with another man as her boyfriend ... Being a girl of loose morals ... constitutes a possible defence to the charge.

Article 1(a) of the Declaration of Basic Principles of Justice for Victims of Crime and Abuse of Power (Declaration)[45] defines victims among others as:

> ...persons who, individually or collectively, have suffered harm, including physical or mental injury, emotional suffering, economic loss or substantial impairment of their fundamental rights, through acts or omissions that are in violation of criminal laws operative within member states, including those laws proscribing criminal abuse of power.

The Declaration *inter alia* provides for the need for victims to have access to justice and fair treatment, restitution, compensation and assistance, including material medical and psychological assistance (article

[42] Maputo Protocol, article 3(4).

[43] Maputo Protocol, article 4(2)(e).

[44] Criminal Session Case no.30 of 1989 (Unreported).

[45] General Assembly Resolution 40/43 of November 29, 1985.

8–13). The criminal justice system in many countries unfortunately puts emphasis on the rights of the suspects and offenders and not the victims of crime. This is also the case of the Ugandan law on rape that do not provide such protection to its victims. The needs of the victims as well as their rights are therefore not upheld. Article 4 of the Declaration provides that victims should be treated with compassion and dignity. It has, however, been noted that victims continue to be humiliated in the courts of law due to, among other factors, myths and mind-sets about sexual violence, as well as culture and stigmatisation.[46] The International Commission of Jurists (ICJ) has noted that the application of the law of women's access to justice is still marred with gender stereotypes and assumptions.[47] A case in point is the case of *Uganda v Tumwesigye,*[48] where the trial judge stated that, 'the doctor found that the hymen had been ruptured a year ago. Therefore … it could not be said that it was the accused that had ruptured the hymen'. With such biases still being reflected in the courts of law, one of the major institutions for delivery of justice, access to justice for women victims of sexual violence against women will remain a far cry. It is therefore necessary that these biases be done away with.[49] Article 6 of the Declaration further requires that views of the victim should be considered at the different stages of the trial. It further provides that cases should be disposed of expeditiously. Unfortunately, victims in the criminal justice system continue to be passive participants in the courts of law unless they are called upon as witnesses.[50] In addition, the criminal justice system does not dispose of cases expeditiously and victims have in some cases lost interest in their cases. Despite the robust legal provisions advanced by the Declaration, it

---

[46] Charlotte Kabaseke, 'Justice for Rape Victims In Uganda: Definitional Crises and Errors of Justice in Prosecuting Rape Cases' in Uganda' in *Women and Minority Rights Law in Africa: Reimaging Equality and Addressing Discrimination* edited by Michael Addaney (2019): 79.

[47] 'Sexual Violence Against Women: Eradicating Harmful Gender Stereotypes and Assumptions in Law and Practice,' International Commission of Jurists 2015, http://www.icj.org/icjaddresses-harmful-gender-stereotypes-and-assumptions.

[48] *Uganda v Tumwesigye* Criminal Session case no. 40 of 1990 (Unreported) (Uganda).

[49] Charlotte Kabaseke, *supra* note 46, 83.

[50] Matthew Hall, *The Relationship between Victims and Prosecutors: Defending Victims' Rights? Criminal Law Review* (2010): 31–45.

is general to all victims of crime and not specific to women. Furthermore, it is only a Declaration and not a legally binding document.

The Rome statute of the International Criminal Court (ICC)[51] did well in trying to mainstream gender into international humanitarian law as well as criminal law. In article 7, it recognises rape and sexual violence of comparable gravity as crimes against humanity. Further, in article 8, rape and 'sexual violence also constitutes a grave breach of the Geneva Conventions' and are listed among war crimes. These provisions, while a step in the right direction, were not deemed to be enough for achieving access to justice of women victims through involving them fully in the trial.[52] As a result, the ICC rules of evidence were enacted to strengthen the already existing provisions especially concerning the protection of victims.[53] The rules prohibit the attack of victims based on, among others, their past sexual history during trial. Most relevant to this chapter, the rules provide for the victim's full participation in the trial whether they are witnesses or not. This has enhanced the practice of women's voices being heard during the trial.[54] It is, however, unfortunate that in criminal trials, victims remain passive participants. Similarly, for victims of sexual violence, they can be invited as witnesses in their own. Prosecution can, however, choose not to invite them as witnesses. Further, the relationship between the prosecution and victims is purely for evidence and this does not accord full involvement of victims. This is an obstacle to access justice for rape victims.[55]

Similarly, having noted the vulnerability of women to sexual violence during situations of armed conflict, the Security Council pointed out the role of the criminal justice system in ensuring the protection of women and girls during situations of armed conflict. Security Council Resolution 1325 (2000) on Women, Peace and Security provides that

---

[51] Adopted at a diplomatic conference in Rome, Italy on July 17, 1998, entered into force on July 1, 2002.

[52] Niamh Reilly, *Seeking Gender Justice in Post-Conflict Transitions: towards a Transformative Women's Human Rights Approach* 3(2) *International Journal of Law in Context* (2007): 155–172 at 161–162.

[53] International Criminal Court, *ICC Rules of Procedure and Evidence* (The Hague: ICC 2013).

[54] Niamh Reilly, *supra* note 52, 161–162.

[55] Matthew Hall, *supra* note 50, 31–45.

the judicial systems should put in place special measures to ensure that women and girls are protected from sexual violence and that their human rights are protected during trial. Furthermore, states are called upon to ensure that during sexual violence trials, the special needs of women should be considered. This applies to all the different organs of the criminal justice system.

Moreover, UN Security Council Resolution 65/228 (2002) (Strengthening Crime Prevention and Criminal Justice), while underscoring the implication of sexual violence during times of armed conflict, called upon member states to ensure the prosecution of sexual violence cases and to ensure proper investigation, equality before the law as well as the punishment of all perpetrators. In addition to being non-legally binding, the resolutions are specific to women in armed conflict and hence women who suffer sexual violence out of conflict may not invoke protection under the resolutions.

The CEDAW Committee has, while expounding on the right to access to justice for women, pointed out that it involves 'justiciability, availability, accessibility, good quality and accountability of justice systems, and the provision of remedies for victims'.[56] Justiciability enables women to have access to justice without any barrier and also for women to be empowered to claim all their rights including the right to access to justice as provide under the CEDAW. Some of the non-justiciable barriers that hinder women's access to justice include among others gender stereotypes and discrimination against women, which have also been reflected in the criminal justice system.[57] For example, in the Zimbabwean case of *Pedisizai Musumhiri v State of Zimbabwe*,[58] the honourable Judge stated that:

> … the conduct of rape victims generally falls short of the standard that society has so relentlessly crafted in terms of expected behaviour and its ideal victim. She must scream - very loudly. She must show evidence of

---

[56] Committee on the Elimination of Discrimination against Women (CEDAW Committee), *General Recommendation No. 33 on women's access to justice* (2015) (CEDAW/C/GC/33).

[57] CEDAW Committee, *supra* note 56, paragraph 8.

[58] (2014) HH 404–14 (Zimbabwe).

physical resistance. She must be battered and bruised if she is a genuine victim.

Availability and accessibility requires that the justice system including courts of law and police should be available to all people whether in the urban or rural areas.[59] The courts should also be physically accessible and filing court documents should be affordable.[60] It has been observed that many sexual violence victims are unable to report cases or attend court proceedings because the police and courts of law are long distances away.[61] Mobile courts would be a good interim measure to ensure accessibility of courts.[62] In addition, legal aid clinics where women are able to access free legal advice would go a long way in aiding women in accessing criminal justice. At the moment, Uganda has in place some legal aid service providers like the Uganda Association of Women for Lawyers (FIDA). However, it specifically offers legal aid services for women only situated in Kampala, the Capital City with just one other country office. It is therefore not sufficient to offer services across the country. With respect to good quality and accountable justice systems, the justice system should be gender sensitive, based on international standards.[63]

At the domestic level, article 28 of the Constitution of the Republic of Uganda 1995 provides for the right to a fair hearing. It lays down the different rights of accused persons. There is no similar provision on victims' rights. Although the Constitution can be hailed for being gender sensitive, it lacks provisions on women's access to justice. In addition, the Penal Code Act of Uganda,[64] the major law on the protection of women and girls from sexual violence in Uganda provides for the maximum punishment for rape which is death. It has, however, been noted that the maximum death sentence is rarely issued. Cases in point include *Uganda*

---

59 United Nations Office on Drugs and Crime (UNDOC), Handbook on GENDER DIMENSIONS of criminal justice responses to terrorism (2019) 173.

60 *Ibid.*

61 *Ibid.*

62 *Ibid.*

63 *Ibid.*, 175.

64 Penal Code Act, Chapter 120, Laws of Uganda 2000, Sect. 124.

v Akute Stephen[65] in which the accused was found guilty of rape but was only sentenced to 7 years imprisonment. Similarly, in *Uganda v Rwendeire Hussein*[66] the accused was sentenced to 12 strokes of the cane. The lack of provisions on a minimum sentence which gives discretion to the Judges to issue minimum sentences of their choice leaves punishment for the offenders seemingly unfair in many cases. This not only continues to facilitate continued violence against women, it also complicates adequate access to justice for women.[67] In addition, the Penal Code Act categorises the offence of rape as an offence against morality as opposed to being an offence against the person.[68] Impliedly, the justice system places more emphasis on the sexual and immoral aspect of the offence as opposed to the violent nature of the offence. The gravity of the offence is not appreciated, and this continues to make access to justice for women victims of sexual violence even more difficult.[69]

Currently, Uganda has developed the Sexual Offences Bill 2019 (SOB)[70] which seeks to address the short falls outlined above. According to Sect. 1 of the explanatory memorandum, The SOB seeks to, among others:

> …enact a specific law on sexual offences for the effectual prevention of sexual violence; to enhance punishment of sexual offenders; to provide for the protection of victims during sexual offences trials.

Sections 2 and 3 of the SOB provide for the offence of rape and introduce the offence of aggravated rape. The punishment for the offence of rape has been reduced to life imprisonment. Hopefully, this will encourage judicial officers to sentence offenders to harsher sentences than they have been doing. Section 3 of the SOB also introduces gang rape, marital rape and rape by persons in positions of authority. This further strengthens the offence of rape, thereby further protecting women from

---

65 Criminal case no.8 of 2008 (Unreported) (Uganda).

66 Criminal case no. 263/1994 (Unreported) (Uganda).

67 Charlotte Kabaseke, *supra* note 46, 84.

68 Penal Code Act of Uganda, Division III, Chapter XIV and Division IV, Chapter XVIII.

69 Charlotte Kabaseke, *supra* note 46, 84–85.

70 Bill no. 32 of 2019.

rape and sexual abuse generally. Although these provisions alone may not be entirely sufficient to protect women against sexual abuse, they will go a long way in providing some depth and enhancing the law on women's protection from sexual abuse. Promising as the provisions are, the Sexual Offences Bill has not yet been signed into law.

Uganda adopted the International Criminal Court Act in 2010[71] which criminalises war crimes and crimes against humanity as outlined in Sects. 9 and 10 of the ICC statute (Sects. 9 and 10). Rape is one of these crimes (articles 7 and 8 of the Rome Statute of the ICC 2011). This is an indicator that Uganda is putting effort to curb sexual violence against women in Uganda. However, the country still faces many challenges in ensuring that female victims of sexual violence have access to criminal justice.

3 Access to Justice Concerns for Female Victims

This part examines the procedural and institutional concerns in dealing with SVAWG in Uganda. It focuses on the pre-trial, trial and post-trial issues that negatively impact on females as victims. It also analyses JLOS' institutional gaps that limit access to justice for women and girls in Uganda.[72]

At the point of entry into the formal justice system, police structures are literally open to the public. There is no room for privacy. There are usually several people at the police station to report all kinds of cases. When a person mentions that they are a victim of sexual violence, it can

[71] Act no. 11 of 2010.

[72] Through the author's work with JLOS, in-depth insights were obtained in relation to SWAG and emerging concerns.

easily attract everyone's attention.[73] The recording of the case is sometimes not comfortable as the manner in which the victims are required to narrate their story is sometimes humiliating to them.[74] From the onset of recording sexual violence cases, little or no attention is given to the psychological needs of victims and sometimes witnesses. There is no provision for psychosocial officers to attend to the emotional and psychological needs of victims.[75] More attention is spent on building the criminal case, forwarding the file to Office of the Directorate of Public Prosecution (ODPP) for sanctioning.[76] It is opined that the absence of psychological support to victims and witnesses may compromise the general well-being of the victim, quality of their testimony and impede their ability to obtain holistic justice—which is beyond securing a conviction and may include emotional, psychological healing.

Sometimes there are delays in reporting cases by the victims,[77] preparing files for sanctioning, and cause-listing, arresting the accused

---

[73] This is a daily occurrence in Uganda when interfacing with police to obtain assistance, every case is reported openly at the counter and owing to the limited space and lack of privacy; the environment may be intimidating to victims of sexual violence. United Nations High Commissioner for Refugees, *Monthly protection update Sexual and Gender Based Violence (SGBV)*, September 26, 2020, https://reliefweb.int/sites/reliefweb.int/files/resources/72932.pdf. There is stigma associated with reporting GBV cases.

[74] These concerns were raised in Kapchorwa District where a monitoring and evaluation of the SGBV court session was conducted in 2018. The sessions were conducted by the Judiciary in conjunction with the Office of the Directorate of Public Prosecution (DPP), Uganda Police Force, Uganda Prisons Service, Uganda Law Society (defence counsel), Directorate of Government Analytical Laboratories and Probation officers. See Human Rights Watch, *Sexual Violence: Uganda Police Should Support Victims, Not Blame Them*, June 22, 2020, https://www.hrw.org/news/2020/02/18/sexual-violence-uganda-police-should-support-victims-not-blame-them.

[75] United Nations High Commissioner for Refugees *Ibid* Note 40. There is stigma associated with reporting GBV cases.

[76] Psychosocial support is a major challenge in Uganda's criminal justice system. This concern extends to prosecutors, judicial officers and all court actors who are sometimes traumatised after holding sessions. New Vision, *Gruesome Evidence Affecting Mental Health of Judges*, September 19, 2020, https://www.newvision.co.ug/news/1527393/gruesome-evidence-affecting-mental-health-judges. Honourable Justice Duncan Gaswaga raised concerns about the need for counselling, psychosocial support after handling traumatising criminal cases which leave them with 'hallucinations when you get back home….all these cases are stressful'. This raises concerns as to victims' stress levels which are unattended during the course of justice.

[77] The stigma associated with SVAWG makes them shy away from reporting to the responsible authorities.

person and investigations.[78] At times the delays arise from logistical challenges[79] and ignorance by the victims of their rights and duties in ensuring they report to police at the earliest opportune moment. Often times, some victims and witnesses lose interest in their cases either because they have received 'compensation'[80] for the harm caused—compensation is illegal for sexual violence cases—or sometimes because the victim has moved on with their life and are not desirous of opening scars which they may not have disclosed in their new relationship.[81]

Another concern with delayed prosecution of perpetrators of sexual violence is that when perpetrators are remanded beyond the mandatory period, they apply for bail and secure their release from incarceration.[82] Subsequently, some take advantage of porous borders and flee the country when they hear that there is an ongoing sexual and gender-based violence court session.[83] As a result, the court has to issue summons and

---

[78] New Vision, *Increase Police budget to ease GBV investigations – activists*, September 24, 2020, https://www.newvision.co.ug/news/1491089/increase-police-budget-ease-gbv-investigations-activists.

[79] *Ibid.* See United Nations Africa Renewal *Uganda: Violence against women unabated despite laws and policies*, 26 September 2020, https://www.un.org/africarenewal/news/uganda-violence-against-women-unabated-despite-laws-and-policies.

[80] Save the Children *Ending Impunity: Getting Children Justice for Sexual Violence*, June 22, 2020, https://uganda.savethechildren.net/news/ending-impunity-getting-children-justice-sexual-violence. Sometimes perpetrators pay illegal sums of money or articles as compensation to the girl's family in order to escape prosecution. Other times, they propose marriage to their victims and pay families dowry.

[81] This was particularly raised in Sironko and Mbale districts which borders Kenya. Some of the.

victims were married and did not wish to continue with the defilement cases. This was during the monitoring and evaluation of the SGBV sessions in 2018.

[82] Article 23(6)(c) of the Constitution of the Republic of Uganda provides for the right to mandatory bail if a person has committed a case triable before the High Court and is remanded for 360 days before their case is committed to the High Court regardless of the offence committed and gravity.

[83] During the JLOS SGBV special session in Sironko district in 2018, some accused persons who were released on bail fled the country when the session commenced. Securing their arrest became another cost for the state which was not budgeted for hence justice for the victim in that case remained uncertain.

commence the process of re-arresting which costs the state a lot of money and injustice to the victims of sexual violence.[84]

While handling forensics, some police officers take samples from the victim of sexual violence without following up accused persons and taking their sample—as a reagent against the sample.[85] Consequently, such errors pose challenges for prosecution when they adduce evidence that indeed the victim was raped by a person who is before court but cannot link the forensic evidence to the accused. This situation frustrates several prosecutors because at the point of trial, forensics cannot be reconstructed to directly pin the accused person. The general management of scenes of crime also remains a constant challenge in the criminal justice system.[86] Several people do not respect scenes of crime and are sometimes oblivious to the fact that the evidence gathered at the scene could incriminate them.[87]

The functionality of the Directorate of Government Analytical Laboratories (DGAL) in promoting access to justice for female victims of sexual violence has been met with serious challenges. Limited funding hinders the equipping and tooling of DGAL which stalls optimal operations in the various regions—Mbale, Mbarara and Moroto districts.[88] Moreover, DGAL official have low salary scales despite their immense workload.[89] As a result of their limited numbers and equipment, access to justice is delayed when scientific methods to verify sexual offences cannot be effectively harnessed. Nevertheless, officers at DGAL continue providing expert witnesses testimonies. It can be argued that use of

[84] During the prosecution of criminal cases, when an accused person is released on bail and the case is rescheduled for hearing while one is on bail and cannot be found, summons are issued by Court to the police to ensure that the accused person is brought to court.

[85] This concern was raised during a monitoring visit to the Police in Mbale during the SGBV court sessions in 2018. It was also raised by the Directorate of Government Analytical Laboratory during a monitoring visit on October 23, 2019.

[86] United Nations Africa Renewal *Ibid* Note 46. Police have limited investigative skills coupled with financial constraints.

[87] In most televised scene of crimes, people gather around the scene of crime which may sometimes pause challenges in evidence gathering.

[88] Parliament of Uganda, *Report of the Committee on Defence and Internal Affairs on the Oversight visit to the Regional Forensic Analytical Government Laboratories in Eastern Uganda, Mbale* (2018) 4–5.

[89] *Ibid.*, 7.

technology would address concerns of traveling across the country to provide evidence. Until DGAL concerns are holistically addressed, justice in sexual violence for women may be negatively affected. Storage for exhibits in Uganda's police cells is challenging.[90] The management of exhibits by police officers and the absence of exhibit stores leaves the evidence compromised and sometimes at the risk of damage. Consequently, when a case is cause-listed, some exhibits may be ruined or totally destroyed and perpetrators cannot be pinned for offences committed.[91]

The absence of witness protection legislation leaves numerous female victims of sexual violence vulnerable.[92] Oftentimes victims fear to report, attend trials or adduce evidence that incriminates perpetrators because of the harm they inflict on witnesses after the trial.[93] Even though state prosecutors encourage them to speak, they sometimes raise concerns over guarantees of personal safety. As a result, some sexual offenders are released without trial.[94] Witness protection legislation may greatly contribute to enabling victims and witnesses speak up for justice.

---

[90] This is a widespread concern and an observation in most police stations in Uganda. Exhibits are even kept outside and exposed to rain and sun which can impact on the quality of evidence adduced during trial. Currently in the new Justice Centres (Justice Centres are physical collectively constructed structures for justice institutions involved in adjudication including police, court, prosecution) constructed by JLOS, special attention is being made to include exhibit stores at police.

[91] This is the general observation of police stations. With ongoing Justice Law and Order Sector constructions under the Fourth Strategic Development Plan (which may stretch into subsequent strategic plans), provision has been made for exhibit stores in the new constructions.

[92] ODPP relies on Witness Protection Guidelines to provide safety for witnesses though this is nonbinding on the State, Uganda Human Rights Commission and Office of the High Commissioner for Human Rights *Witness Protection Guidelines* (2019) https://dpp.go.ug/index.php/component/jdownloads/send/51-odpp-handbook/84-witness-protection-guidelines. Another set of guidelines is the Office of the Directorate of Public Prosecution *Victims' Rights and Empowerment Guidelines* (2019) https://dpp.go.ug/index.php/component/jdownloads/send/51-odpp-handbook/83-victims-rights-and-empowerment-guidelines.

[93] Post SGBV sessions meeting and review of the SGBV project held on May 13, 2019 at Kabira Country Club, Kampala Uganda. This was raised as one of the concerns which necessitated the enactment of witness protection legislation in Uganda.

[94] Mike J Chibita, *Investigation and Prosecution of Sexual and Gender-Based Crimes: Ensuring access to justice for victims of sexual and gender-based crimes at the national level: The Uganda experience* (2015) *Fourteenth Session of the Assembly of State Parties International Criminal Court* 3, https://asp.icc-cpi.int/iccdocs/asp_docs/ASP14/ASP14-PD-COMP-PL1-Chibita-ENG.pdf.

During trial there are some procedures that remain challenging to under-age girls who are victims of sexual violence. According to the law, the evidence of a child has to be corroborated after a *voire dire*—a trial within a trial—has been conducted. In the case of *Uganda v Ngaswireki & Another*,[95] Lady Justice Margaret Mutonyi held that in instances where children are victims of crime, they have a right to be heard and their evidence should not be distrusted or disregarded because they are children. It was further held, concerning a child who can understand the proceedings, that: 'he should be allowed to have their testimony tested by cross examination to avoid the requirement of the particular fact especially where the child is the sole identifying witness'. The concern about dogmatically treating children's evidence with caution is that it puts to question the testimony of a child and is premised on the fact that a child may not be telling the truth—and yet children more often than not tell more truths. This injustice against children necessitates legislative review for girl victims of sexual violence to obtain holistic justice – dispensing with the dogmatic rule applicable to children's evidence.

Although probation officers are meant to help children through the justice system as victims, witnesses and children in conflict with the law, their limited numbers negatively impact on the quality of justice for children. It often leaves the children alone throughout the trial without any psychosocial support. Consequently, the children become traumatised, fearful and unable to effectively present their cases throughout the trial.[96] There are some defence counsels who engage in theatrics[97] while cross-examining victims or witnesses of sexual violence. Sometimes this intimidates the victims and causes them to shy away from the trial or

---

[95] *Uganda v Ngaswireki & Another*, HCCA 2 of 2017. See also comprehensive discussion by Lubaale on the need to visit the rules on corroboration in relation to children's evidence. Emma Charlene Lubaale 'Admissibility of evidence presented by children in sex abuse prosecutions in Uganda: The case for reforms' 5 *African Journal of Law and Criminology* (2015): 1–15.

[96] In districts like Sironko where victim assessment reports were provided for trials, it helped in the prosecution of the cases and determining the mindset of the parties involved for the judicial officers to put into consideration when determining his cases. This was evidenced during the SGBV special session of 2018.

[97] For example, in one of the SGBV sessions, defense counsel was pacing up and down the court, flipping his pen and intently staring the victim (girl) in the eye at a very close range as he cross examined her on issues relating to how the perpetrator defiled her—this left the girl terrified.

provide distorted evidence—yet often times after sexual violence, one may not be as coherent as expected by the court because of associated trauma.[98] As officers of court, defence counsel should remain committed to dispensing justice and not just getting criminals off the hook. This does not imply that the presumption of innocence does not apply in sexual offences, but the truth should be pursued.

From the commencement of criminal proceedings, some victims and witnesses are ignorant of their rights and processes. The lack of information disempowers some victims of SGBV to advocate for justice in court. Sometimes all their concerns are not well-articulated and the judiciary has to juggle ensuring that the victim does not grossly face injustice because of their ignorance while ensuring that a fair trial is conducted.[99] Information even before one is a victim of sexual violence is important so that women in particular know how to proceed with their cases in the eventuality that they become witnesses or victims.[100]

From the above discussions, post-trial stage concerns relate to compensation for victims of sexual violence,[101] psychological recovery, witness protection for victims and witnesses of crime. Another concern is reintegration of perpetrators into the community after serving their offences. How are they reintegrated? Is the community safe and ready to receive them? Relatedly are concerns about reintegration of the victim or witnesses into the community. Are there cultural concerns that may need attention in order to safeguard the victims? How can local leaders or peer influencers at grassroots ensure that victims and witnesses are embraced

[98] This was a particular concern with the private lawyers in the Mbale court who were cross-examining witnesses and victims without special consideration to the challenges encountered. They were pacing in the room while cross-examining the child in a very intimidating manner. It was recommended that gender sensitive defence counsel is engaged in order for victims and witnesses to feel safe when sharing their ordeal so that evidence does not have to be extracted by humiliating victims.

[99] This was experienced by many courts during the 2019 sexual and gender-based violence court session.

[100] This can be attained through legal empowerment. In Uganda, the Constitution mandates the Judicial Service Commission to disseminate legal information to the public. Currently Uganda does not have a witness protection law

[101] Is the compensation adequate to restore the victim? Is it commensurate to the perpetrator's earnings? Can compensation be paid for life in instances of wealthy perpetrators in instances where the harm is grave and the victim may need support for life?

and accepted in society without facing stigma? Without addressing these post-trial concerns, victims and witnesses may continue experiencing partial justice. There is therefore a need to improve women's access to justice in sexual violence cases.

4 Prospects for Improving women's Access to Justice in Sexual Violence Cases and Situations

4.1 Amendment to the Penal Code Act

The Penal Code Act of Uganda needs to be amended so that the offence of rape can be recognised as an offence against the person rather than an offence against morality.[102] This would put rape in its right perspective.[103] Emphasising the violent nature of rape would help a great deal in changing societal attitudes as well as court and police attitudes towards the crime. The amendment can follow the Canadian example by redefining the offence of rape as 'Sexual Assault', and accompanying it with the three levels of punishment depending on the gravity: simple sexual assault carrying punishment of ten years; sexual assault 'involving a weapon, bodily harm or threats to a third party', carrying a punishment of up to 14 years imprisonment; and 'aggravated sexual assault which involves wounding, maiming, disfiguring or endangering life', carrying life imprisonment.[104] The Canadian example is relevant to the Ugandan context especially for purposes of ensuring that stricter sentences are passed since as has been noted, the Ugandan courts have been observed as rarely passing maximum sentence. This chapter recommends that the death penalty as the maximum punishment for the offence of rape and defilement be revised since as observed, the courts rarely pass it. In

[102] Uganda has in place the Sexual Offence Bill no. 32 of 2019, which proposes some reforms to the rape law in the Penal Code. It has been passed by Parliament and awaits presidential assent.

[103] Sylvia Tamale, *Rape Law and The violation of women in Uganda: A critical perspective* (1) 2 *Uganda Law Society Review* (1992): 195–211.

[104] Carol Smart, *Feminism and the power of Law* (1989).

addition, a minimum punishment should be set in order to reduce the discretion that the judicial officers exercise over minimum punishment in sexual offence. The minimum punishment would go a long way in encouraging judges to convict sexual offenders since as noted earlier, most of them are reluctant to pass maximum sentence and instead issue offenders to unfairly low sentences.[105]

4.2 Recognition of the Rights of Sexual Violence Victims

The rights of victims of sexual violence should be recognised. Emphasis has always been placed on the rights of defendants.[106] For instance, the Constitution of the Republic of Uganda[107] only emphasises on the rights of suspects/detainees/accused persons. However, the general rights in the Bill of Rights,[108] such as the rights to equality, dignity, privacy and specifically the right to freedom from all forms of violence do include victims in the ambit of their protection. As indicated above in court judgments, reliance on the rights to dignity and privacy of victims giving evidence in court have served to justify placing a limitation on the rights of the accused, thereby carving out an allowance for the victim and the witnesses, such as testifying in camera. It is recommended that the rights of female victims be included in the rape/sexual offences law of Uganda including the right to confidentiality, privacy, respect for dignity, protection from publicity about the offence and the right to receive Post Exposure Prophylaxis. Nevertheless, it is not easy to protect the rights of women survivors of violence since lawyers must know more than the laws and be aware of the local welfare or police bureaucrats, who often

---

105 Charlotte Kabaseke, *Sexual Violence Against Women: A Critical Analysis on the Rape in Uganda* (Master of Laws dissertation) (2012) 95–96.

106 International Commission of Jurists, *Sexual Violence Against Women: Eradicating Harmful Gender Stereotypes and Assumptions in Law and Practice* (2015) 8, 9, 10, http://www.icj.org/icj addresses-harmful-gender-stereotypes-and-assumptions.

107 Constitution of the Republic of Uganda, article 28.

108 The Universal Declaration of Human Rights (1948), the International Covenant on Civil and Political Rights (1966) and the International Covenant on Economic, Social and Cultural Rights (1966).

run circles around uninformed clients, denying them their legal rights through technicalities.[109]

4.3 Breaking Gender Stereotypes

Most criminal justice systems were developed by men and are marred with gender stereotypes at different stages, including the case reporting stage at the police station, the investigation stage, the trial and post-trial stages. Gender mainstreaming into the criminal justice system has been advanced as a strategy to ensure an accountable justice system which respects rule of law and human rights. This can be done by pointing out the difference between the impact of law, policies, practices as well as plans and programmes on men and women.[110] This will ensure that experiences of both men and women are captured and proper solutions are arrived in ensuring that sexual violence victims access justice. Gender mainstreaming also minimises gender inequalities and ensures an effective criminal justice system.[111]

4.4 Adoption of Human Rights Based Approach in Criminal Justice

Adopting a human rights based approach as well as a victim centred approach has been advanced as a reliable measure for enhancing access to justice for women victims of sexual violence.[112] In achieving this, states are required to establish criminal justice systems which treat victims with dignity throughout the whole process.[113] The victim centred approach is guided by, among others, 'doing no harm' principle which places emphasis on the well-being, empowerment and safety of victims, placing

---

[109] Charlotte Kabaseke, *supra* note 105, 95 and 96.

[110] UNDOC, *supra* note 59, 175.16.

[111] *Ibid.*, 17.

[112] United Nations General Assembly resolution 65/228, annex, principles 13 (a), 15 and 16.

[113] UNODC, *Strengthening Crime Prevention and Criminal Justice Responses to Violence against Women* (2014) 34.

these as key factors which criminal justice responses to sexual and gender-based violence need to advance.[114] The criminal justice system should restore privacy of women and girls which is eroded by acts of sexual violence. In a bid to realise all this, the criminal justice system needs to ensure that the risks of the survivors are minimised as much as possible especially as they cooperate with the investigators, prosecutors and adjudicators.[115]

4.5 Need for Specialised Competence to Handle Sexual Violence Related Crimes

It has been observed that there is lack of specialised competence to investigate, prosecute and adjudicate sexual violence matters. This could be attributed to the fact that sexual offences are provided by penal laws just like any other offence. There is a need for the personnel in the criminal justice system to be sensitised and trained in handling sexual violence cases.[116] Training should include interviewing of the survivors during investigations and examination of survivors in courts. The different personnel in the criminal justice system also need to be trained on how to respond to the specific vulnerabilities and needs of the sexual violence survivors.[117]

4.6 Specialised Units for Handling Sexual Violence Related Crimes

It is also important to establish specialised units for handling sexual violence cases at the different criminal justice levels. A specialised unit for handling the reporting of sexual violence cases at police and special courts for handling cases of sexual violence would go a long way in ensuring victims' confidence in the justice system. This also ensures

---

[114] Ibid., 155.

[115] *Ibid.*, 176.

[116] *Ibid.*, 157.

[117] *Ibid.*, 175.

a coordinated approach in providing accountability.[118] Sexual violence cases are heard in open court and victims of sexual violence give testimony in open court. This practice discourages women and girls from reporting cases because they go through double trauma after the experience of sexual violence. Specialised units would therefore go a long way in building girls and women's confidence and hence a step in realising their access to justice.[119]

4.7 Traditional and Customary Processes for Handling Sexual Violence Crimes

Traditional and customary processes have also been advanced as a mechanism to achieve access to justice for victims of gender-based violence. They have been credited for being expeditious, for promoting and delivering decisions that are legitimately accepted at community level and for offering redress and accountability. While a great strategy, the processes have been critiqued for being marred with gender discrimination and for potentially advancing violence against women further and violating women's rights.[120] It has therefore been recommended that their contribution to the justice system should be enhanced by gender sensitive systems especially informed by international human rights law standards.[121] For instance, transitional justice mechanisms employed by the Government of Uganda to address the violations perpetrated by the Lord's Army in Northern Uganda during the 20 years' insurgency promoted reconciliation through forgiveness of the offenders and traditional reparations. These mechanisms were, however, critiqued for not considering the gravity of sexual and gender-based violence related harms. The mechanisms have, however, been enhanced by adopting the Acholi Gender Principles as well as appointing a minister responsible for gender issues and women's access to justice.[122] Whereas the traditional

---

[118] *Ibid.*

[119] Charlotte Kabaseke 2012, *supra* note 105, 99.

[120] UNDOC, *supra* note 59, 198.

[121] OHCHR A/HRC/27/21, paragraph 36.

[122] UNDOC, supra note 59, 198–199.

and customary mechanism for girls and women's access to justice has had many pitfalls, they have contributed to access to justice for women victims of sexual violence. For example, cases are heard and determined in a timely manner. In order for these processes to be employed, however, there is need for 'victim consent, risk assessment and safety measures as well as acceptance of violence as wrongful act'.[123]

4.8 Reparations, Compensation and Restitution

Whereas reparations, compensation and restitution have not been common among criminal law remedies, it has been advanced as vital remedy in sexual cases. The Declaration of Basic Principles of Justice for Victims of Crime and Abuse of Power[124] provides for restitution and compensation as remedies for victims of criminal offence. This is because the victims suffer irreparable damage and reparations, compensation and restitution can go a long way in aiding them to get rehabilitated in terms of catering for their health needs.[125] While it is generally not possible to restore rape victims to their original situation, compensation may help in reducing the victim's economic distress after the rape experience. Compensation would include costs required for legal expert assistance, medicine and medical services as well as psychological and social services.[126] It should be imperative for reparation processes to include crimes of sexual violence and the needs of survivors as a key point of focus and ensure that all women who have been subjected to violence, including rape, have access to redress in the form of access to justice; and to reparations including 'compensation, rehabilitation, satisfaction and guarantees of non-repetition'. Although victims are the proximate cause in all criminal proceedings, they secure little, if any, recognition. It is further proposed that if the offender is not able to pay the compensation, the victim should have access to a Victim's Compensation Fund to

---

123 *Ibid.*

124 Declaration of Basic Principles of Justice, articles 8–13.

125 Charlotte Kabaseke, *supra* note 105, 97.

126 *Ibid.*

be set up by the state.[127] The SOB brings on board victim's compensation. It is hoped that the Bill will soon be assented to by the president so that victims can benefit.

4.9 Psychosocial Support for Female Victims

It is proposed that psychosocial support is provided for female victims of VAWG. As stated earlier, there are no psychosocial services available to female victims from the time they interface with the criminal justice system to the time they obtain justice—which is securing a conviction against the accused person. Without psychosocial services particularly for victims, justice cannot be said to be done holistically. It is imperative that Government increases the number of probation officers and assigns them to provide services to female victims. Government can also liaise with non-state actors who can render these services to those in need. It is also important that these services extend to the supply side of the justice system—courts, prosecution, police and defence counsel—so that they are able to deliver enhanced justice to female victims.

5 Conclusion

This chapter presented the statistics relating to VAWG globally, regionally and nationally. It analysed international, regional and domestic legal provisions on access to justice by women victims of sexual violence. It discussed concerns negatively impacting the pursuit of justice by female victims as discussed in part three. Legal recommendations were proposed in the form of recognition of victims' rights and the adoption of a human rights approach. Non-legal recommendations comprised the establishment of specialised units and courts for handling sexual violence cases, education for all concerned stakeholders on sexual violence, reparations and compensation for rape victims, and psychosocial support needs to be provided for female victims throughout their interface with the justice

[127] Lillian Tibatemwa-Ekirikubinsa, *Sexual Assaults and Offences Against Morality* (2005).

system. This would go a long way in ensuring that there is a clear appreciation of the uniqueness of sexual offences and would ensure disposal of cases in a timely manner and with the privacy they deserve.

References

African Commission on Human and Peoples' Rights, 2017, *General comment No. 4 on the African Charter on Human and Peoples' Rights: the right to redress for victims of torture and other cruel, inhuman or degrading punishment or treatment.*

African Union, United Nations Human Rights Office of the High Commissioner and UN Women, 2016, *Women's Rights in Africa*, http://www.ohchr.org/Documents/Issues/Women/WRGS/WomensRightsinAfrica_singlepages.pdf.

Andrew Lawrence Spivak, 2011, *Sexual Violence; Beyond the feminist-evolutionary debate.*

Ann J Cahill, 2009, 'Sexual Violence and Objectification', in *Theorising Sexual Violence*, edited by J Rene Heberle and Victoria Grace.

Carol Smart, 1989 *Feminism and the power of Law.* (1989).

CEDAW Committee, 2015, General Recommendation No. 33 on women's access to justice (CEDAW/C/GC/33).

CEDAW, 1992, General Recommendation no. 19 on Violence Against Women, Adopted by the CEDAW Committee on the Elimination of Discrimination Against Women, Eleventh session https://tbinternet.ohchr.org/Treaties/CEDAW/Shared%20Documents/1_Global/INT_CEDAW_GEC_3731_E.pdf.

Charlotte Kabaseke, 2012, *Sexual Violence Against Women: A Critical Analysis on the Rape in Uganda* (Master of Laws dissertation).

Charlotte Kabaseke, 2019, 'Justice for Rape Victims In Uganda: Definitional Crises and Errors of Justice in Prosecuting Rape Cases' in *Women and Minority Rights Law in Africa: Reimaging Equality and Addressing Discrimination,* edited by Michael Addaney.

Children (Amendment) Act 2016, Uganda.

Constitution of the Republic of Uganda (1995).

Convention on the Elimination of All Forms of Discrimination against Women (1979).

Domestic Violence Act 2010, Uganda.

Exchange Rates *US Dollar (USD) to Ugandan Shilling (UGX) exchange rate history*, https://www.exchangerates.org.uk/USD-UGX-exchange-rate-history.html.

General Assembly, 1985, Declaration of Basic Principles of Justice for Victims of Crime and Abuse of Power, Resolution 40/43 of November 29, 1985.

General Assembly, 1993, Declaration on the Elimination of Violence against Women.

Human Rights Watch, *Sexual Violence: Uganda Police Should Support Victims, Not Blame Them*, https://www.hrw.org/news/2020/02/18/sexual-violence-uganda-police-should-support-victims-not-blame-them.

International Commission of Jurists, 2015, 'Sexual Violence Against Women: Eradicating Harmful Gender Stereotypes and Assumptions in Law and Practice', http://www.icj.org/icjaddresses-harmful-gender-stereotypes-and-assumptions.

International Commission of Jurists, 2015, *Sexual Violence Against Women: Eradicating Harmful Gender Stereotypes and Assumptions in Law and Practice,* http://www.icj.org/icjaddresses-harmful-gender-stereotypes-and-assumptions.

International Covenant on Civil and Political Rights (1966).

International Covenant on Economic, Social and Cultural Rights (1966).

International Criminal Court Act no. 11 of 2010 (Uganda).

International Criminal Court, *ICC Rules of Procedure and Evidence* (2013).

International Criminal Court, *Rome Statute of the ICC* (2011).

Justice Law and Order Sector, 2017, *Fourth Sector Development Plan 2017–2020.*

Lillian Tibatemwa-Ekirikubinza, 2005, *Sexual Assaults and Offences Against Morality.*

Lubaale Emma Charlene, 2015, 'Admissibility of evidence presented by children in sex abuse prosecutions in Uganda: The case for reforms' 5 *African Journal of Law and Criminology.*

Matthew Hall, 2010, The Relationship between Victims and Prosecutors: Defending Victims' Rights? *Criminal Law Review.*

Mike J Chibita, 2015, Investigation and Prosecution of Sexual and Gender-Based Crimes: Ensuring access to justice for victims of sexual and gender-based crimes at the national level: The Uganda experience, Fourteenth Session of the Assembly of State Parties International Criminal

Court, https://asp.icc-cpi.int/iccdocs/asp_docs/ASP14/ASP14-PD-COMP-PL1-Chibita-ENG.pdf.

New Vision *Gruesome Evidence Affecting Mental Health of Judges*, https://www.newvision.co.ug/news/1527393/gruesome-evidence-affecting-mental-health-judges.

New Vision *Increase Police budget to ease GBV investigations – activists*, https://www.newvision.co.ug/news/1491089/increase-police-budget-ease-gbv-investigations-activists.

Niamh Reilly, 2007, 'Seeking Gender Justice in Post-Conflict Transitions: towards a Transformative Women's Human Rights Approach' (3)2 *International Journal of Law in Context*.

Office of the Directorate of Public Prosecution, 2019, *Victims' Rights and Empowerment Guidelines,* https://dpp.go.ug/index.php/component/jdownloads/send/51-odpp-handbook/83-victims-rights-and-empowerment-guidelines.

Parliament of Uganda, 2018, *Report of the Committee on Defence and Internal Affairs on the Oversight visit to the Regional Forensic Analytical Government Laboratories in Eastern Uganda, Mbale.*

Pedisizai Musumbiri v State of Zimbabwe (2014) HH 404–14 (Zimbabwe).

Penal Code Act, Chapter 120, Laws of Uganda 2000 (Uganda).

Protocol to the African Charter on Human and Peoples' Rights on the Rights of Women in Africa (2003).

Rome Statute of the International Criminal Court (Adopted at a diplomatic conference in Rome, Italy on July 17, 1998, entered into force on July 1, 2002).

Save the Children, *Ending Impunity: Getting Children Justice for Sexual Violence*, https://uganda.savethechildren.net/news/ending-impunity-getting-children-justice.

Sexual Offence Bill no. 32 of 2019 (Uganda).

Sylvia Tamale, 1992, 'Rape Law and the violation of women in Uganda: A critical perspective' 1(2) *Uganda Law Society Review*.

Uganda Human Rights Commission and Office of the High Commissioner for Human Rights, 2019, *Witness Protection Guidelines* https://dpp.go.ug/index.php/component/jdownloads/send/51-odpp-handbook/84-witness-protection-guidelines.

Uganda Police Force, *The Annual Crime Report 2019* (2019).

Uganda v Akute Stephen Criminal case no.8 of 2008 (Unreported) (Uganda).

Uganda V Lt. Col. Galungbe Criminal Session Case no.30 of 1989 (Unreported).

Uganda v Ngaswireki & Another, HCCA 2 of 2017.

Uganda v Rwendeire Hussein Criminal case no. 263/1994 (Unreported) (Uganda).

Uganda v Tumwesigye Criminal Session case no. 40 of 1990 (Unreported) (Uganda).

Uganda Vs Ngaswireki & Another HCCA 2 of 2017.

UN Security Council Resolution 1325 (2000) (Women, Peace and Security).

UN Security Council Resolution 65/228 (2002) (Strengthening Crime Prevention and 'Criminal Justice).

UNICEF, 2015, 'Uganda Violence Against Children Survey: Findings from a National Survey, *2015*.

UNICEF, *Violence against children*, https://data.unicef.org/topic/child-protection/violence/.

United Nations Africa Renewal *Uganda: Violence against women unabated despite laws and policies*, https://www.un.org/africarenewal/news/uganda-violence-against-women-unabated-despite-laws-and-policies.

United Nations General Assembly Resolution 48/104 *Declaration on the Elimination of Violence against Women* December 20, 1993.

United Nations General Assembly resolution 65/228, annex, principles.

United Nations High Commissioner for Refugees, *Monthly protection update Sexual and Gender Based Violence,* https://reliefweb.int/sites/reliefweb.int/files/resources/72932.pdf.

United Nations Human Rights Council, 2014, *Report of the Human Rights Council on its twenty-seventh session,* A/HRC/27/21, https://www.ohchr.org/EN/HRBodies/HRC/RegularSessions/Session27/Documents/A.

United Nations Office on Drugs and Crime, 2019, *Handbook on Gender Dimensions of criminal justice responses to terrorism.*

United Nations Population Fund, 2018, *Evaluation of UNFPA support to the prevention, response to and elimination of gender-based violence and harmful practices 2012–2017: Uganda Case Study.*

United Nations *Women Africa*, https://www.unwomen.org/en/where-we-are/africa.

United Nations Women, 2019, *Progress of the World's Women 2019–2020: Families in a changing world*

Universal Declaration of Human Rights (1948).

UNODC, 2014, *Strengthening Crime Prevention and Criminal Justice Responses to Violence against Women.*

World Bank *The World Bank Gender-Based Violence (Violence Against Women and Girls)*, https://www.worldbank.org/en/topic/socialdevelopment/brief/violence-against-women-and-girls.

World Bank, 2015, *World Bank Group Gender Strategy: Gender Equality, Poverty Reduction and Inclusive Growth (FY16–23).*

4

Women as Survivors of Sexual Violence in Zambia: The Unheard Voices

Ellah T. M. Siang'andu

1 Introduction

Despite extensive amendments to the Penal Code[1] in 2005[2] and in 2011[3] as a response to sexual violence against women, such cases continue to rise in Zambia. The two amendment Acts amend the principal Act, the Penal Code,[4] by introducing a number of new provisions for the purposes of enhancing the law on sexual violence. This chapter seeks to critically assess Zambia's national legal framework for women as

[1] Penal Code, Chapter 87 of the Laws of Zambia.

[2] Penal Code (Amendment) Act No. 15 of 2005.

[3] Penal Code (Amendment) Act No. 2 of 2011.

[4] Penal Code, *supra* note 1.

E. T. M. Siang'andu (✉)
School of Law, University of Zambia, Lusaka, Zambia

A. Budoo-Scholtz and E. C. Lubaale (eds.), *Violence Against Women and Criminal Justice in Africa: Volume II*, Sustainable Development Goals Series,
https://doi.org/10.1007/978-3-030-75953-7_4

survivors of sexual violence. The term woman is used throughout this chapter to refer to persons of a female gender, including girls.[5]

Sexual violence can affect both women and men. However, women and girls are particularly the most negatively impacted.[6] On this basis, for the purposes of this chapter, violence is defined as that 'which is directed against a woman because she is a woman or that affects women disproportionately'.[7] Sexual violence can occur within a family or among strangers.[8] In Zambia, with the exception of the conduct of marital rape, most sexual violence related offences are criminalised under the Penal Code.

Adopting a doctrinal approach, the chapter strives to address the following questions: How have courts addressed sexual violence offences? How have courts defined the elements of the sexual violence related offences? what has been the effect of the definitions of the offences on women as victims of sexual violence in Zambia? What have been the assumptions or misconceptions underlying the prosecution of sexual violence offences in Zambia?

Using the feminist theories, the chapter seeks to question the objectivity of the law on sexual violence in Zambia. It is informed by feminist perspectives on sexuality and dominance. It is premised on the idea of locating women's rights by understanding that the subordination of women is due to the fact they are valued less than men.[9] Tong argues that the 'male's attempts to control the female body and the construction of female sexuality to serve male needs' has resulted in the oppression

[5] The Protocol to the African Charter on Human and Peoples' Rights on the Rights of Women in Africa also known as the Maputo Protocol was adopted in 2003 but only came into force in 2005 hereinafter The Maputo Protocol, article 1(k).

[6] The National Legal Aid Clinic for Women, *Government of the Republic of Zambia* United Nations Joint Programme on Gender Based Violence, A Compilation of Judgments from the Local Courts, United Nations Zambia, (2012): 7.

[7] CEDAW Committee, *General Recommendation No 19 on Violence Against Women* (1992) UN Doc A/47/38, paragraph 6.

[8] United Nations *Declaration on the Elimination of All Forms of Violence Against Women* (1993): article 2.

[9] Jo Bridgeman and Susan Millns, *Feminist Perspectives on Law, Law's Engagement with the Female Body* (2008): 69.

of women.[10] Based on Marxism, MacKinnon argues that as a consequence of the construction of women's sexuality in male terms, women are alienated.[11] Tong further explains the position that:

> male violence against women is normalised and legitimised in sexual practices through the assumption that when it comes to sex, men are by nature aggressive and dominant, whereas women are by nature passive and submissive. Because male dominance and female submission are the norm in something as fundamental as sexuality, they become the norm in other contexts as well. Women will always remain subordinate to men unless sexuality is reconceived and reconstructed.[12]

MacKinnon in applying her analysis to law contends that laws are gendered because they are presented as being neutral and objective, when in fact they represent the male perspective.[13] Accordingly, the law is gendered because it is formulated from a male perspective without taking into account women's standpoint. MacKinnon concludes that the 'social power of men over women' extends through the laws that purport to protect women.[14] The criminal laws on rape and defilement in Zambia are used to illustrate the notion the laws adopted to protect women in fact end up negatively affecting them as demonstrated below.

This chapter illustrates how the Zambian criminal law responds to sexual violence against women. It demonstrates how it fails to distinguish the circumstances in which it occurs and consequently, highlights the gender blindness of the criminal law on sexual violence. The chapter begins by considering the notion of sexual violence under global, regional and national levels. It then proceeds to consider the national legal framework on protecting women as survivors of sexual violence. The main object is to illustrate the gaps in the national legal framework on sexual

---

[10] Rosemarie Tong, *Feminist Thought: A Comprehensive Introduction* (1989): 72.

[11] Catharine A MacKinnon, 'Feminism, Marxism, Methods and the State: An Agenda for Theory', 7 *Signs* (1981–1982): 515.

[12] Tong, *supra* note 10, 72.

[13] Catharine A MacKinnon, *Toward a Feminist Theory of the State* (1989): 248.

[14] Ibid., 241–245.

violence. This is done by examining in depth the law and practice on the treatment of victims of sexual violence in Zambia.

2 Sexual Violence in Zambia

Women in Zambia experience sexual violence and the law needs to ensure that it addresses their suffering as survivors of sexual violence. Sexual violence refers to the use of sexual contact by a person to another against his or her will.[15] It involves acts such as forced penetration of the vagina and/or anus by either a penis or other objects. It also includes touching of the perineum including the vagina, penis, or anus or other objects, or the placing of the mouth or tongue on a person's perineum, and conducting sexual acts with animals.[16] In Zambia, the Penal Code criminalises majority of offences that constitute sexual violence. However, the Penal Code does not use the term 'sexual violence' but adopts the term 'offences against morality'.[17] These include rape,[18] indecent assault,[19] defilement of child,[20] 'defilement of imbecile or person with mental illness',[21] indecent practices between persons of the same sex,[22] incest,[23] abortion,[24] sexual harassment,[25] 'procuring child or other person for prostitution',[26] sale or trafficking in children,[27] harmful cultural practices,[28] and child pornography[29]

[15] CMV Clarkson and Keating, *Criminal Law, Text and Materials* (2003): 600.

[16] Ibid.

[17] Set out in Chapter XV of the Penal Code Chapter 87 of the Laws of Zambia.

[18] Penal Code, section 132.

[19] Penal Code, as amended by Act No. 15 of 2005, section 137.

[20] *Supra* note 2.

[21] Penal Code, section 139.

[22] Ibid., section 158(1).

[23] Ibid., section 159.

[24] Ibid., section 152.

[25] Ibid., section 137A.

[26] Ibid., section 140.

[27] Ibid., section 143.

[28] Ibid., section 157.

[29] Ibid., section 177.

among others. This chapter, however, focuses only on the sexual violence offences of rape and defilement. The use of the phrase offences against morality suggests that sexual violence related offences are criminalised by the state on the basis that they are immoral. However, it is time Zambia shifted from the perception of regarding sexual violence crimes as offences against morality, to viewing them for what they really are, that is offences against personal dignity and sexual autonomy of the complainant.[30] Referring to them as sexual violence offences will reflect the heinous nature of the offences that ought to be prohibited at all costs. Besides, not everything that is immoral is actually prohibited.

Despite the existence of criminal laws that prohibit sexual violence, the level of convictions is way lower than the number of reported cases.[31] This is due to several reasons including 'bias against the victims', 'endemic problems of the criminal justice system', 'discrimination and other inadequacies under the customary law'.[32] Consequently, these challenges have led to a failure to investigate, prosecute and punish these offenses.[33] This negatively affects survivors of sexual violence who have little recourse to the criminal justice system. At the same time, the possibility of offenders committing similar offences again would be high on the basis of alleged offender escaping without punishment. Criminal justice is a 'system of practices and institutions vested with the responsibility to maintain social control, deterring and mitigating crime and punishing those who violate criminal law'.[34] In order to ensure efficacy and success in the criminal justice system, there are many institutions that are involved, each vested with specific roles and jurisdiction. The five crucial institutions include the judiciary, the Zambia Police Service (ZPS), National Prosecutions Authority (NPA), the Legal Aid Board (LAB) and the Zambia Correctional Service (ZCS).[35]

---

30 Simon E Kulusika, *Criminal law in Zambia, Doctrine Theory and Practice* (2020): 145.

31 Ibid., 219.

32 Human Rights Watch, 'Suffering in Silence: The Links Between Human Rights Abuses and HIV Transmission to Girls in Zambia' (2002): 54.

33 Ibid.

34 Zambia Institute of Advanced Legal Education, 'Reference Training Manual for Paralegals Level 1 in Zambia', Book 1 (2019): 23.

35 Ibid.

The laws are sometimes futile due to the existence of strict procedures adopted for prosecuting such offences. Munalula[36] notes the possibility of encountering bias in the manner courts handle family and sexual violence matters before them. The contention is that these are areas where laws may make direct reference to women, thus establishing different standards about the manner parties may prosecute or litigate the case. This implies that women may be subjected to strict requirements for the prosecution of sexual violence offences that may often disadvantage them as survivors of sexual violence.[37] Prosecution of sexual violence related offences often calls for scrutiny of the character and the motivation of the survivor.[38] For example, the requirement of corroboration of the act and identification of the accused person in sexual violence related offences[39] as a condition for securing a conviction of the offences makes it challenging to ensure justice for women as survivors. Unlike other offences, the prosecution of sexual offences takes into account factors that do not form part of the elements of the offences. Some of them are time taken in reporting the sexual violence offence to the ZPS, the appearance of the victim, the need to demonstrate proof of resistance and the application of force. The contention is that the law on sexual violence in Zambia fails to provide adequate protection for survivors of sexual violence. The law is biased towards protecting perpetrators over the survivors of sexual violence. It is imperative for the law to balance the rights of both perpetrators[40] and the victims during sexual violence trials.

[36] Mulela M Munalula, *Women Gender Discrimination and the Law Cases and Materials* (2005): 201.

[37] Ibid., 201.

[38] Bernadette Malunga, 'The Rule of Corroboration in Sexual Offences and Women's Access to Justice in Malawi', *Zambia Law Journal* 46 (2015): 121.

[39] *The People v Thomas Monroe* (HPS/45/2011).

[40] Rights of the accused persons are guaranteed under the Constitution, Chapter one of the Laws of Zambia, article 18.

3 Global and Regional Legal Framework on Sexual Violence

Zambia is a state party to global[41] and regional[42] instruments that seek to protect women as survivors of sexual violence. Zambia is obliged to ensure women are protected from sexual violence regardless of where and how it occurs. It is obliged to ensure that measures exist to effectively address the predicaments of women as survivors of sexual violence. Violence against women refers to:

> ... an act of gender-based violence that results in, or is likely to results in physical, sexual or psychological harm or suffering to women, including threats of such acts, coercion, or arbitrary deprivations of liberty, whether occurring in private or public life.[43]

Thus, the United Nations Declaration on the Elimination of Violence against Women (DEVAW) defines violence against women as including 'all forms of gender-based violence', including physical, sexual and psychological regardless of the context or setting they may occur.

At the regional level, Zambia is a state party to the Protocol to the African Charter on Human and Peoples' Rights on the Rights of Women in Africa (Maputo Protocol). The Maputo Protocol which was adopted on July 11, 2003 and entered into force on November 25, 2005 recognises sexual harm as a category of violence that can be perpetrated against women.[44] State parties are under an obligation to 'enact and enforce laws that prohibit all forms of violence against women' including 'unwanted or forced sexual intercourse' regardless of whether it takes place in private or public.[45] In addition, state parties are obliged 'to adopt appropriate and effective measures to identify the causes and consequences of sexual

[41] *The United Nations Declaration on the Elimination of Violence Against Women* (DEVAW) of 1993.

[42] Protocol to the African Charter on Human and Peoples' Rights on the Rights of Women in Africa 2003; the Gender and Development Declaration of the Southern African Development Community.

[43] DEVAW 1993, article 1.

[44] Maputo Protocol, article 1.

[45] Maputo Protocol, article 4(2).

violence against women'[46]; to punish offenders of sexual violence against women; and to provide 'rehabilitation programmes for women survivors of violence'.[47]

In 1997 Zambia signed the Gender and Development Protocol of the Southern African Development Community (SADC Gender Protocol), in which the state pledged to 'take urgent measures to prevent and deal with the increasing levels of violence against women and children'.[48]

The Addendum to the SADC Protocol on Gender and Development[49] catergorises violence as including physical, emotional, economic, sexual and psychological violence.[50]

4 National Legal Framework on Sexual Violence

Different national legislation prohibit sexual violence in Zambia.[51] Similar to the international standards addressed above, at the national level, the Anti-Gender Based Violence Act[52] (GBV Act) recognises sexual violence as a form of gender-based violence regardless of whether it occurs in public or private life.[53] It was enacted in order to protect survivors of gender-based violence.[54] The GBV Act refers to sexual violence as:

---

46 Maputo Protocol, article 4(2)(c).

47 Ibid.

48 Southern African Development Community, *Gender and Development: A Declaration by Heads of State or Government of the Southern African Development Community*, par. H(ix), September 8, 1997.

49 The Prevention, Eradication of Violence Against Women and Children: An Addendum to the 1997 Protocol on Gender and Development by SADC Heads of States or Governments 1998 (SADC Addendum on Violence).

50 SADC Addendum on Violence 1998, article 5.

51 The Penal Code, Anti-Gender Based Violence Act No. 1 of 2011, Criminal and Procedure Code, Chapter 88 of the Laws of Zambia, Education Act No. 23 of 2015 & Gender Equity and Equality Act No 22 of 2015.

52 GBV Act, section 3.

53 Ibid.

54 Ibid., section 1.

> ...the engagement if another person in sexual conduct, whether married or not, which includes sexual conduct that abuses, humiliates or degrades the other person or otherwise violates another person's sexual integrity, or sexual conduct by a person aware of being infected with HIV or any other sexually transmitted infection with another person without that other person being given prior information of the infection.[55]

Gender means 'female or male and the role that individuals play in society by virtue of their sex or status'.[56] A victim seeking protection from sexual harm such as rape or defilement can apply to a court for a protection order 'to prevent either the respondent, an associated respondent, or both, from further committing acts which constitute gender-based violence against the victim'.[57] The court may issue a protection order to 'prohibit a respondent from committing an act of gender-based violence personally'; or 'against an applicant or a relation or associate of the applicant'.[58] A protection order may:

> ...prohibit the respondent or an associated respondent, or both, from physically sexually assaulting or using physical force against the applicant or any relation, friend, a legal representative or any other person associated with the applicant; forcibly confining or detaining the applicant or any relation or friend of the applicant; depriving the applicant access to adequate food, water, clothing, shelter or rest; (d) forcing the applicant to engage in any sexual contact, whether married or not; engaging in any sexual conduct that abuses, humiliates or degrades the complainant or otherwise violates the applicant's integrity, whether married or not.[59]

The GBV Act also makes provision for the occupation order that can be issued by the subordinate court.[60] The occupation order is ideal for

---

[55] GBV Act, section 3.

[56] Ibid.

[57] GBV Act, section 10(1).

[58] GBV Act, section 13.

[59] GBV Act, section 14.

[60] GBV Act, section 20 (1).

parties that live under the same household. It is an order that is issued by the court requiring 'a respondent to vacate the matrimonial home or other home which the respondent shares with the applicant and to continue to pay rent, mortgage payment' and maintenance to the applicant.[61] It is thus ideal for parties that are in a relationship. The GBV Act makes provision of shelters for victims.[62] However, shelter for victims is not readily available countrywide apart from Lusaka and Ndola.[63]

Despite the above measures, the GBV Act does not establish criminal offences. It needs to be used with the other written Zambian laws, that address the substantial criminal laws and procedure on sexual violence related offences in Zambia.[64] Moreover, the GBV Act has been described as ineffective due to the rising numbers of gender-based violence cases. This is despite the establishment of the fast-track courts on the matter in Kabwe and Lusaka which were launched in 2016 in an effort to enhance the hearing of gender-based violence cases.[65] Clearly, the two courts are not accessible to every woman who experiences sexual violence in Zambia. Neither have the courts constituted a deterrence against gender-based violence cases nor are they accessible country wide.

One of the main reasons for the ineffectiveness of the GBV Act can be the lack of consideration for the socio-economic conditions of women that experience sexual harm. The levels of inequalities between women and men in Zambia are generally high. The only way to address this problem is to ensure that lived experiences of women are reflected in the GBV Act and law in general. There is also a low awareness of the existence of protective orders under the GBV Act.[66] They are very few women who are aware of the provision of protection orders for victims of domestic and gender violence under the GBV Act.[67] Consequently, survivors of GBV continue to be victimised by their perpetrators. The next section considers the law on rape and defilement. It considers the

---

61 Ibid.

62 GBV Act, section 24.

63 See the GBV issue paper.

64 Penal Code, Criminal and Procedure Act Chapter 88 of the Laws of Zambia.

65 Zambia Institute of Advanced Legal Education, *supra* note 40, 163.

66 Ibid.

67 Ibid.

definitions of the offences as provided under the Penal Code. It evaluates the effect of the different elements that constitute the offences and their implications on women as survivors of such crimes.

4.1 The Law on Rape

In Zambia, the crime of rape refers to non-consensual sexual intercourse that can only be committed by a man against a woman or a girl.[68] It is defined as follows:

> Any person who has unlawful carnal knowledge of a woman or girl, without her consent, or with her consent, if the consent is obtained by force or by means of threats or intimidation of any kind, or by fear of bodily harm, or by means of false representations as to the nature of the act, or, in the case of a married woman, by personating her husband, is guilty of the felony termed rape.[69]

A person convicted of rape may be imprisoned 'for a period of not less than 15 years and may be liable to imprisonment for life'.[70] Based on the definition of rape, the Penal Code establishes three categories that provide for circumstances under which the offence of rape can be deemed to have been committed. Firstly, where any person has 'unlawful carnal knowledge of a woman or girl without her consent'. Secondly, having carnal knowledge with a woman or girl with her consent but where it is obtained by 'force, threats, intimidation, fear of bodily harm, by means of false representation as to the nature of the act, or by personating the woman or girls husband or partner'. And thirdly, where a woman or girl 'revokes her consent to sexual intercourse during the act'. The three categories thus constitute bases on which criminal liability for the rape can be established.

The elements of the offence of rape are thus as follows: sexual intercourse (carnal knowledge), the absence of consent, intention to commit

---

[68] Penal Code, section 132.

[69] Penal Code, section 132.

[70] Penal Code, section 133.

rape or reckless as nature of consent.[71] In order to establish criminal liability for rape, all the elements of the offence must be established by the prosecution beyond reasonable doubt. Sexual intercourse is proved by proving vaginal penetration with a penis.[72] The use of fingers or other objects does not constitute rape: it would be regarded as indecent assault.[73] Consent must be freely given by the victim and one should not be coerced into consenting. In addition, corroboration of both the commission of the offence and the identity of the offender is required in order to eliminate twin dangers of false complaint and false implication.[74] During the trial, it must be demonstrated by the complainant, that is the survivor that, the act actually occurred, meaning that there was penetration and the accused had the intention to commit the offence. Rape is proved by the absence of consent on the part of the woman. The evidence of the victim requires corroboration in form of medical evidence for it to be accepted. This is in addition to the humiliation and trauma of describing the actual events as they happened and includes naming of body parts that form the basis of the rape trial. The notion of absence of consent has been constructed from a male perspective as it requires consideration of circumstances that is bias to the man's perspective—that is the manner the man honestly believed the situation to have been. On this basis, Smart argues that '[i]n practice it would seem that consent is assumed and the raped women must prove non-consent'.[75]

The criminal laws on rape fail to envisage a situation where the complainant or victim gives up resisting the act of rape and gives in to the act. The law is instead narrow and makes it difficult to secure a conviction for the offence of rape. The law on rape fails to accord the victim of rape sufficient protection to combat the sexual offence both during trial and after. In rape cases the complainant, that is the victim, is obliged to prove that she did not consent to the sexual intercourse by availing the court medical evidence illustrating external bruises as evidence for

---

[71] Penal Code, section 132.

[72] R v. Yohani Mporokoso (1939) 2 NRLR 152.

[73] Penal Code, section 137.

[74] *The People v Thomas Monroe* (HPS/45/2011).

[75] Carol Smart, *Feminism and the Power of Law Pathologizing Female Sexuality in a Phallocentric Culture* (1989): 28–32, 33.

the lack of consent.[76] As argued by Munalula, the criticism of rape trials is that the survivors are obliged to prove that they did not consent by means of medical proof of injury sustained during the commission of the sexual offence.[77] In addition, there are other requirements such as the need to report the rape allegations as soon as it occurs. The current laws on rape are unrealistic as it does not account for women that live in rural areas where they need to walk miles to access police stations and hospitals.

The mental elements which must be proved in the offence of rape are intention, knowledge and recklessness.[78] This means either the perpetrator must intend to have sexual intercourse without consent; or that he must know that the woman or girl is not consenting; or he must be reckless as to whether she is consenting.[79]

The existing definition of rape in Zambia is gendered as it only recognises men as offenders. The definition of rape is restrictive as it only recognises survivors of rape as those who are penetrated by a penis vaginally only. Penetration orally or anally would be deemed to constitute an offence of indecent assault.[80] The law on rape thus excludes the female perpetrator–male victim paradigm. Particularly, cases where the male survivors are 'forced to penetrate' female perpetrators. However, it is imperative to do away with such a definition of rape as it can be committed against any person regardless of their sex. Both women and men are in need of protection against the conduct of rape. Historically, this definition of rape was never based on the respect of women's autonomy as victims of heinous of rape but as a representation of a woman as quasi-property of their father and husband.[81] This means that historically the rape of a woman was perceived not as the violation of a woman's body but as the violation of the proprietary rights of fathers and husbands, and the possible embarrassment that such a conduct can cause upon a family.

---

[76] Munalula 2005, *supra* note 36, 132.

[77] Ibid.,132, 151.

[78] Simon E Kulusika, *Criminal Law in Zambia Doctrine Theory and Practice* (2020): 223.

[79] Ibid.

[80] Penal Code, section 137.

[81] William Wilson, *Criminal Law*, 5th edition (2014): 328.

Therefore, under Zambian law, rape is committed by a man against a woman or a girl. A female is incapable of committing rape but may, however, be charged and prosecuted for indecent assault.[82] The law on rape fails to envisage circumstances whereby a woman can be deemed to have 'raped' a man. Similarly, a man cannot be prosecuted for having non-consensual sexual intercourse with his wife without her consent. This implies that marital rape is not prohibited under criminal law. As contended by Munalula,[83] this has wider implications as it means that married women are not protected from unwanted pregnancy and they are at risk of acquiring sexual related diseases such as Human Immunodeficiency Virus (HIV) and Acquired Immunity Deficiency Syndrome (AIDS). It is to be noted that women are more at risk of contracting HIV/AIDS than men.[84] This is further worsened by the fact that abortion is illegal and any person found guilty could be sentenced to up to fourteen years' imprisonment.[85]

Section 152 of the Penal Code clearly prohibits abortion inclusive of circumstances where the pregnancy is as a result of martial rape. Such women are excluded from possibilities of seeking to terminate a pregnancy which is as a result of 'marital rape' as the definition of rape automatically excludes married women. The Termination of Pregnancy Act[86] permits abortion where a woman is unable to endure the pregnancy on the basis of strict conditions as stipulated by the law. Accordingly, the person shall not be guilty of abortion when pregnancy is terminated upon recommendation by three registered medical practitioners, and among them one medical practitioner needs to be a specialist in the

[82] Penal Code, section 137.

[83] Margaret M Munalula, 'Regulating to Liberate Zambia's Population Policy Through the Reproductive Rights Lens,' *Zambia Law Journal* (2013): 95.

[84] Karen Stefiszyn, 'The African Regional Response to Gender-Based Violence' (17–49) in *Gender-Based Violence in Africa, Perspectives from the Continent*, Centre for Human Rights University of Pretoria Law Press (2013): 18.

[85] Penal Code, section 152.

[86] Termination of Pregnancy Act, Chapter 304 of the Laws of Zambia, sections 3 & 6.

branch of medicine in which the patient's condition is based.[87] Termination thus only allowed on health grounds.[88] However, termination is not permitted on the grounds of rape.

While the penalty for rape is severe, the construction of the law is not without flaws. The narrow definition of rape under Zambian criminal law is reflective of the expected passive role of women when it comes to sexuality. Women are not expected to rape or initiate sexual intercourse. This implies that criminal law is merely a reflection of the expectations of women in a patriarchal society. There is need for Zambia to amend this outdated provision and develop the law based on reality and the challenges faced by society today. It is essential for criminal law to be neutral and applied to both women and men equally. Gender neutrality within rape would entail the law recognising that both women and men can be rape victims and perpetrators.[89] Gender neutrality within rape would thus involve expanding the definition of rape in the Penal Code to incorporate male victims and female perpetrators. A broad definition of rape that is more inclusive has an ability to afford protection and prevention of harm at an equal basis. Hence, criminal law will be able to extend protection to male survivors as well as acknowledging that males can also be survivors of rape.

4.2 The Law on Defilement

Contrary to the narrow definition of rape, defilement is defined as 'unlawful sexual intercourse by a man or woman with a child under the age of sixteen years'.[90] The term defilement is used in the laws of Zambia to mean carnal knowledge of a child below the age of 16 years. The law prohibits unlawful sexual intercourse with a child below the age of 16, even if the parents or guardians of such a child were

---

[87] Termination of Pregnancy Act, sections 3.

[88] Ibid.

[89] Philip NS Rumney, 'In Defence of Gender Neutrality Within Rape', 6(1) *Seattle Journal for Social Justice* (2007): 481.

[90] Penal Code Chapter 87 of the Laws of Zambia as amended by Act No. 15 of 2005, Section 138.

to consent. The wording of the provision, however, implies that lawful sexual intercourse with a child below the age of 16 could be permitted under certain circumstances where the child is married under customary law. This is argued on the premise that criminal law does not prohibit child marriages.

Defilement is a crime that must be prosecuted in the courts of law. The law assumes that a child below the age of 16 years is incapable of consenting to any sexual activity.[91] This means that even if a child agrees to take part in a sexual act, the agreement would not be officially accepted. A 'child' is defined as a 'person below the age of sixteen years'.[92] The current definition of the child under the Penal Code is contrary to the definition of the child as provided in the Republic's Constitution[93] and under the Convention on the Rights of the Child (CRC) which is 18 years.[94]

It is thus necessary to align the definition of the child in the Penal Code to 18 years which is the acceptable age in international law in order to enhance the protection of children generally. Based on the definition of the offence of defilement of the child, the elements are as follows: the age of the victim, proof of both physical and medical confirming the occurrence of the sexual act on the child by the accused person; and finally, corroboration of the act and identity of the accused person. The law seeks to protect children from defilement by inferring that a child is incapable of validly consenting to sexual intercourse.

However, the law on defilement is more biased towards the offender than the survivors. This is reflected by the 2011 amendment to the Penal Code to reintroduce a proviso which allows for a defence of reasonable belief by the perpetrator that the child was above the age of 16 years.[95] The Penal Code was amended by insertion of the proviso that:

> provided that it shall be a defence for a person charged with an offence under this section to show that the person had reasonable cause to believe,

---

[91] Penal Code, section 137(2).

[92] Penal Code, section 131A.

[93] Constitution (Amendment) Act No. 2 of 2016, article 266.

[94] Convention on the Rights of the Child, article 2.

[95] Penal Code (Amendment) Act No. 3 of 2011, section 138(1).

and that the child against whom the offence was committed was of, or above the age of 16.[96]

The reintroduction of the proviso is a setback to protecting children especially in a country like Zambia where the offence of defilement is predominant.[97] Cases on defilement have continued to rise. Provision of a defence that the child looks older than 16 is a drawback for protection of children against the horrendous offence of defilement. There is no clear justification for the reintroduction of the 'reasonable cause to believe' defence apart from the need to ensure and recognise the power of a man over a woman.

Hence the country is failing to protect the survivors of defilement, majority of whom are girls below the age of 16 years old. It is necessary to conduct further research to determine the effect of the reintroduction of the proviso on girls as survivors of defilement. Especially that defilement cases mostly involve children who should not be engaging in sexual activities by virtue of them being children. It is thus clear that the law that is intended to protect children in fact ends up oppressing them, thereby reducing the chances of ensuring equality between women and men. The law can only effectively protect offenders and victims of sexual violence if both female and male perspectives were taken into account. While the law makes provision for protection of children from sexual exploitation, more needs to be done to enhance their protection. As it is, most child defilement cases where the victim is below 16 years are not reported as their parents prefer monetary gain than having perpetrators prosecuted.[98] Moreover, in many cases, it is difficult to establish the age of the child since they were not registered. The government needs to adopt measures to ensure that birth registration is done for every new-born child to, among others, know the actual age of children in defilement cases. Despite birth registration being compulsory,[99] masses of Zambia's population that live in rural areas are unable to register the birth of their children due to inaccessibility. As such many children do

[96] The same proviso was repealed by the Amendment Act No. 15 of 2005.

[97] Simon E Kulusika, *Criminal Law in Zambia Doctrine Theory and Practice* (2020): 154.

[98] Zambia Institute of Advanced Legal Education, *supra* note 40, 164.

[99] Births and Deaths Registration Act, Chapter 51 of the Laws of Zambia.

not have birth records or birth certificates. This is a challenge since in most defilement cases, official documents such as birth record or certificate are required to prove the actual age of a child. Such non-registration also leads to disadvantages for the girl since she is vulnerable to child marriages as her actual age will remain unknown. Therefore, children in marriages who are being defiled might not have a remedy due to the non-existence of official documents recording their birth.

5 Conclusion and Way Forward

This chapter has demonstrated that despite criminal law prohibiting sexual violence related offences particularly rape and defilement, the law can still be enhanced to ensure adequate protection of both offender and complainant during trial. While both the offences of rape and defilement are prohibited under the Zambian legal system, the offences are subjected to common cultural myths and stereotypes.[100] The effect of these assumptions has been the continued stereotypical beliefs about what constitutes suitable female and male sexual behaviour.

Offences of rape and defilement have far-reaching consequences on the victims including unwanted pregnancy, forced sexual intercourse, contraction of sexually transmitted diseases such as HIV/AIDS, pain, suffering, mental torture and aggregated damages.[101] Others include dropping out of school, doomed to a life of poverty, without hope, child marriages, forced to become responsible parents at such tender ages, missing out on childhood and violations of individual anatomy. There is need for the state to strengthen its policy and laws in enhancing protection of women against sexual violence, particularly rape and defilement.

---

[100] Mary W Stewart, SA Dobbin & SI Gatowski 'Definitions of Rape: Victims, Police and Prosecutors', 4 *Feminist Legal Studies* (1996):160.

[101] Rosaria Mashita Katakwe (A minor suing by her Guardian and next friend Petronella Mwamba and Edward Hakasenke, Woodlands 'A' Basic School, Ministry of Education, Attorney General High Court for Zambia 2006/HP/0327).

Institutions vested with the responsibility of combating sexual violence such as the Victim Support Unit of the ZPS vested with the responsibility of handling sexual violence offences must be expanded and trained to handle defilement and rape cases effectively. While the Republican Constitution guarantees protecting for the accused person by guaranteeing a fair trial, no rights are accorded to survivors.[102] It is necessary for the law to strike a balance between the rights accorded to survivors and perpetrators in sexual offence cases in order to ensure both parties are adequately protected. It is also necessary for the law to refrain from adding extra elements in establishing criminal liability such as the law of defilement where the perpetrator can be exonerated if he believes the child was over 16 years. Moreover, the tenancy to blame women for rape must come to an end. The notion that women lie about being raped must also be eliminated. The government needs to engage in sensitisation campaigns to eliminate the following myths about rape: women ask for it, women are not careful enough, women should never follow strangers, no means yes, women provoke it, women are accomplices and women should never go out without a protector.[103] The law on rape and defilement needs to be revised and amended to ensure all practices and customs that discriminate against women are repealed. Most importantly, empirical research must be conducted prior to the amended of the sexual violence laws on rape and defilement in order to ensure that the lived realities of women are reflected and accounted for. Furthermore, the government needs to criminalise marital rape since as long as marital rape remains unacknowledged as a criminal offence, a category of women remains unprotected against sexual violence in Zambia.

[102] Article 18 of the Constitution, Chapter One of the Laws of Zambia.

[103] Jo Bridgeman and Susan Millns *Feminist Perspectives on Law Law's Engagement with the Female Body*, London, Sweet & Maxwell (1998), 391.

References

Anti-Gender Based Violence Act No 1 of 2011.

Births and Deaths Registration Act, Chapter 51 of the Laws of Zambia.

Bridgeman Jo and Millns Susan, 2008, *Feminist Perspectives on Law, Law's Engagement with the Female Body.*

C Smart, 1989, *Feminism and the Power of Law Pathologizing Female Sexuality in a Phallocentric Culture.*

Committee on the Elimination of Discrimination Against Womw, 1992, *General Recommendation No 19 on Violence against Women* UN Doc A/47/38.

Clarkson and Kneating, 2003, *Criminal Law, Text and Materials.*

Constitution (Amendment) Act No. 2 of 2016.

Constitution of Zambia.

Convention on the Rights of the Child.

Criminal and Procedure Code, Chapter 88 of the Laws of Zambia.

Education Act No. 23 of 2015.

Education Amendments Act No. 23 of 2011.

Gender Equity and Equality Act No 22 of 2015.

Human Rights Watch, 2002, Suffering in Silence, The Links between Human Rights Abuses and HIV Transmission to Girls in Zambia.

Karen Stefiszyn, 2013, The African Regional Response to Gender-Based Violence in *Gender-Based Violence in Africa, Perspectives from the Continent.*

Malunga Bernadette, 2015, 'The Rule of Corroboration in Sexual Offences and Women's Access to Justice in Malawi', 46 *Zambia Law Journal.*

MaxKinnon CA, (1981–1982), 'Feminism, Marxism, Methods and the State: An Agenda for Theory', 7 *Signs.*

MaxKinnon CA, 1989, *Toward a Feminist Theory of the State.*

Munalula Margaret, 2005, *Women, Gender Discrimination and the Law Cases and Materials.*

Munalula Margaret, 2013, 'Regulating to Liberate Zambia's Population Policy Through the Reproductive Rights Lens', *Zambia Law Journal.*

MW Stewart, SA Dobbin and SI Gatowski, 1996, 'Definitions of Rape: Victims, Police and Prosecutors' 4 *Feminist Legal Studies.*

Penal Code (Amendment) Act No. 15 of 2005.

Penal Code (Amendment) Act No. 2 of 2011.

Penal Code Chapter 87 of the Laws of Zambia.

Philip NS Rumney, 2007, 'In Defence of Gender Neutrality within Rape', 6(1) *Seattle Journal for Social Justice*.

Prevention, Eradication of Violence Against Women and Children: An Addendum to the 1997 Declaration on Gender and Development by SADC Heads of States or Governments 1998.

Protocol to the African Charter on Human and Peoples' Rights on the Rights of Women in Africa 2003.

R Tong, 1989, *Feminist Thought: A Comprehensive Introduction.*

R v. Yohani Mporokoso (1939) 2 NRLR 152.

Rosaria Mashita Katakwe, *A Minor Suing by Her Guardian and Next Friend Petronella Mwamba and Edward Hakasenke, Woodlands 'A' Basic School, Ministry of Education, Attorney General High Court for Zambia,* 2006/HP/0327.

Simon E Kulusika, 2020, *Criminal Law in Zambia Doctrine Theory and Practice.*

Southern African Development Community, 1997, *Gender and Development: A Declaration by Heads of State or Government of the Southern African Development Community.*

Termination of Pregnancy Act, Chapter 304 of the Laws of Zambia.

The National Legal Aid Clinic for Women, 2012, 'Government of the Republic of Zambia' United Nations Joint Programme on Gender Based Violence, A Compilation of Judgments from the Local Courts.

The People v Thomas Monroe (HPS/45/2011).

UN, 1993, *Declaration on the Elimination of all forms of Violence Against Women.*

W Wilson, 2014, *Criminal Law.*

Zambia Institute of Advanced Legal Education, 2019, 'Reference Training Manual for Paralegals Level 1 in Zambia'.

5

Combating Marital Rape: The Law and the Criminal Justice System in Uganda

Patricia A. P'Odong and Barbara L. Can

1 Background

A study by United Nations (UN) Women reveals that up to 70% of 'women have experienced physical and/or sexual violence from an intimate partner in their lifetime'.[1] According to data from the National Coalition Against Domestic Violence (NCADV), between 10 and 14%

[1] UN WOMEN, 'Facts and Figures: Ending Violence Against Women', https://www.unwomen.org/en/what-we-do/ending-violence-against-women/facts-and-figures.

[2] Erika W Smith, '5 Statistics That'll Change How You Think About Marital Rape', 2019, https://www.refinery29.com/en-us/marital-rape-in-relationships-statistics.

P. A. P'Odong (✉)
School of Law, Makerere University, Kampala, Uganda

B. L. Can
Network for Public Interest Lawyers (NETPIL), Makerere University, Kampala, Uganda

A. Budoo-Scholtz and E. C. Lubaale (eds.), *Violence Against Women and Criminal Justice in Africa: Volume II*, Sustainable Development Goals Series,
https://doi.org/10.1007/978-3-030-75953-7_5

of married women experience marital rape during the duration of marriage.[2] Smith also observes that forced sex 'committed by husbands or ex-husbands were four times more common among women who had ever been married', than rapes committed by strangers.[3] Rape is 'associated with a range of gynecological and reproductive health problems', including HIV and other sexually transmitted infections (STIs), unwanted pregnancy, vaginal bleeding or infection, fibroids, decreased sexual desire, genital irritation, pain during inter-course, chronic pelvic pain and urinary tract infections.[4]

In contemporary times, rape may be defined as any person having unlawful sexual intercourse, using any object without the consent of the victim/survivor and intruding any part of the body. In *The Prosecutor V Jean-Paul Akayesu*[5] case, while considering the 'extent to which acts of sexual violence constitute crimes against humanity under article 3(g) of its Statute',[6] the International Criminal Tribunal for Rwanda (ICTR) broadened the meaning of rape. It noted that while rape has been historically defined in national jurisdictions as non-consensual sexual intercourse, 'variations on the form of rape may include acts which involve the insertion of objects and/or the use of bodily orifices not considered to be intrinsically sexual'. The Tribunal stated that:

> Rape is a form of aggression and that the central elements of the crime of rape cannot be captured in a mechanical description of objects and

---

[3] Ibid.

[4] Akina Mama Wa Afrika, 'Uganda Baseline Study Report' (2017): 11, https://www.akinamamawaafrika.org/wp-content/uploads/2019/10/AMwA-Baseline-report-FINAL-1.pdf; Also see Iryna Zablotska et al., 'Alcohol Use, Intimate Partner Violence, Sexual Coercion and HIV Among Women Aged 15–24 in Rakai, Uganda', in 13 *AIDS Behav* (2009): 225–233, 230, https://link.springer.com/content/pdf/10.1007/s10461-007-9333-5.pdf; https://www.hrw.org/legacy/campaigns/women/aids/factsheet.html.

[5] *The Prosecutor v. Jean-Paul Akayesu (Trial Judgement)*, ICTR-96-4-T, International Criminal Tribunal for Rwanda (ICTR), September 2, 1998, https://www.refworld.org/cases,ICTR,40278fbb4.html.

[6] Statute of the International Tribunal for Rwanda, article 3 states that the International Tribunal for Rwanda shall have the power to prosecute persons responsible for the following crimes when committed as part of a widespread or systematic attack against any civilian population on national, political, ethnic, racial or religious grounds: (g) rape https://unictr.irmct.org/sites/unictr.org/files/legal-library/100131_Statute_en_fr_0.pdf.

> body parts...Rape is a physical invasion of a sexual nature, committed on a person under circumstances which are coercive...Further, that coercive circumstances need not be evidenced by a show of physical force. Threats, intimidation, extortion and other forms of duress which prey on fear or desperation may constitute coercion, and coercion may be inherent in certain circumstances...[7]

As for marital rape, it is non-consensual sex in which the perpetrator is the victim's spouse.[8] Although marital rape is a common occurrence in Uganda, our cultural and social norms do not recognise marital rape as a problem and victims often conceal it.[9] Causes of marital rape include: insensitivity to one's sexual feelings; superiority complex and patriarchal norms that makes men superior; and sexual deprivation of a husband by his wife due to suspicions of infidelity.[10] In other cases, perpetrators of marital rape, rape their victims to show anger and to reinforce power, dominance and control over their wives.[11]

Despite there being rampant incidents, in many countries, similar to Uganda, marital rape is either not criminalised, or is criminalised but enforcement remains a problem.[12] Notably, the criminalisation of marital rape in some countries has been through the removal of statutory exemptions from the definitions of rape in existing statutes, judicial decisions, and inclusion of provisions in the law that expressly prohibit

---

[7] *Supra* note 5, paragraph 597–598.

[8] Zahara Nampewo, 'Till Violence Do us Part: A Critical Analysis of the Legal Regime on Cruelty as a Ground for Divorce in Uganda', in *The Politics of Putting Asunder; Divorce, Law and the Family in Uganda*, edited by Nassali Maria (2016): 142.

[9] Prima Kwagala, Advocate and Executive Director, Probono-Women Initiative, confirmed that although she has a number of women who seek divorce following indecencies of marital rape they prefer not to term the incidences as marital rapespeak, June 12, 2020.

[10] Beatrice Nakibuuka, 'Marital Rape, the Plague Silently Afflicting Women', *The Daily Monitor*, March 19, 2016, https://www.monitor.co.ug/Magazines/Full-Woman/Marital-rape-the-plague-silently-afflicting-women/689842-3122730-d0kl8y/index.html.

[11] Website of Indiana Coalition Against Sexual Assault, https://www.rainn.org/pdf-files-and-other-documents/Public-Policy/Issues/Marital_Rape.pdf.

[12] Patience Akumu, 'The Phenomenon on Marital Rape', *The Observer Newspaper*, May 26, 2010, https://observer.ug/lifestyle/73-people-society/8645-the-phenomenon-of-marital-rape.

marriage as a defence to rape or enacting statutes which expressly criminalise marital rape. Some of them are South Africa,[13] Namibia,[14] Zimbabwe[15] and Rwanda.[16]

Borrowing a leaf from these countries, it is our contention in this chapter that Uganda needs to criminalise marital rape. The discussion in this chapter revolves around the existing legal framework, progressive judicial activism and the gaps that need to be filled, especially under the law, in the fight against marital rape.

2 Tracing Marital Rape in Common Law

Uganda became a British protectorate in 1894 and as such mainly applies English common law. The 1902 Order in Council had a reception clause which stated that all applicable laws in the United Kingdom would be applicable in Uganda at that time.[17] Common Law is still applicable in Uganda as part of the Reception of English Law, preserved in section 14 of the 1966 Judicature Act.

In common law, marital rape was considered impossible since spouses were entitled to conjugal rights as a legal implication of marriage. This was shown by Sir Matthew Hale (1609–1676), in his legal treatise *History*

[13] The Criminal Law (Sexual Offences and Related Matters) Amendment Act, 2007, provides for sexual offences section and illegalises marital rape. Section 56 provides that it is no defence for any accused person charged with a sexual offence to contend that a marital or other relationship exists or existed between him or her and the complainant.

[14] The Combating of Rape Act of 2000, section 2(3) provides that rape within marriage or other relationship is specifically prohibited.

[15] Criminal Law Codification and Reform Act, section 68(a) which states unequivocally that the fact that a victim of rape was the spouse of the person accused of rape does not suffice as a defence.

[16] Law No.59 of 2008 (Criminalize Marital Rape) states that it is forbidden to make sex with one's spouse without their consent.

[17] J. Oloka-Onyango, 'An Overview of the Legal System in Uganda', Presentation at the China-Africa Legal Forum, November 25, 2015, https://www.researchgate.net/publication/341776281_AN_OVERVIEW_OF_THE_LEGAL_SYSTEM_IN_UGANDA.

of the Pleas of the Crown (posthumously, 1736), where he stated that[18] 'the husband cannot be guilty of' raping his own wife since the consent given to the husband during the marriage is a contract and hence the wife cannot withdraw the consent during the marriage.

The rationale behind this was emphasised in R V Clarke[19] where the wife obtained a 'judicial separation order stating she was no longer bound to live with her husband'. Two weeks after the order was issued the wife was allegedly raped by her husband. Although it was held that when the wife had been given a separation order, 'the consent to intercourse was effectively revoked', court noted as follows:

> The position was that the wife, by process of law, namely, by marriage, had given consent to the husband to exercise the marital right during such time as ordinary relations created by marriage contract subsisted between them...[20]

The later cases still relied on Hale's proposition. In *R v Miller*,[21] the defendant's wife had left him in 1952 and petitioned for divorce the following year. The defendant had sexual intercourse with the wife against her will prior to hearing of the petition. He was charged with rape and assault occasioning actual bodily harm. The defendant's defence was the marital consent exemption to rape. Lynskey J still held that the husband had no case to answer on a charge of rape since the marriage still existed at the time of the rape.

This decision was followed by *R v O'Brien*,[22] in which Park J ruled that 'a decree nisi effectively terminated a marriage and revoked the wife's implied consent to marital intercourse'. Hence subsequent intercourse by

---

18 Hale's pronouncement was accepted as an enduring principle of the common law as evidenced by the first edition of Archbold, *A Summary of the Law Relative to Pleading and Evidence in Criminal Cases* (1822), which simply stated: 'A husband also cannot be guilty of a rape upon his wife'.

19 *R v Clarke* [1949] 2 ALLER 448.

20 Ibid., paragraph 449.

21 *R v Miller* [1954] 2 QB 282; *R v* Kowalski (1987) 86 Cr App R 339; *R v Sharples* [1990] Crim LR 198 and *R v J* [1991] 1 ALL ER 759.

22 *R v O'Brien* [1974] 3 ALLER 663.

the husband without her consent constituted rape. There was a similar holding in *R v Steele*[23] where court held that:

> …where a husband and wife are living apart and the husband has made an undertaking to the court not to molest the wife, then that is in effect equivalent to the granting of an injunction and eliminates the wife's implied consent to sexual intercourse.

The effect of these decisions was that rape could only be after the marriage had been terminated and not during the marriage.

However, in the cases presented towards the late twentieth century, courts were more unwilling to rely on the marital exemption in rape. This led to two applauded decisions by the House of Lords in *R V R*[24] where the court determined that it is possible for a husband to rape his wife. In this case, the appellant and the wife had matrimonial difficulties and the wife left the matrimonial home. She had informed the appellant about her intention to petition for divorce. However, she had not started any legal proceedings before the incident took place. While she was at her parent's home, the appellant forced his way there and attempted to have sexual intercourse with her against her will. The question which the judge had to decide was 'whether in those circumstances, despite her refusal in fact to consent to sexual intercourse, the wife must be deemed by the fact of marriage to have consented'. The husband had contended that by the marital rape exemption under common law, it was not possible for a husband to rape his wife. Dismissing the appeal, the husband was sentenced to three years' imprisonment for the attempted rape and 18 months' imprisonment concurrent for the assault. Lord Keith stated that:

> The common law is capable of evolving in the light of changing social, economic and cultural developments. Hale's proposition reflected the state of affairs in these respects at the time it was enunciated. Since then the status of women, and particularly of married women, has changed out of all recognition in various ways which are very familiar and upon

---

[23] *R v Steele* [1976] 65 CRIM LR 188.

[24] *R v R* [1991] UKHL 599, 61612; paragraphs B-D, https://www.iclr.co.uk/wp-content/uploads/media/vote/1971-1995/RvR_ac1992-1-599.pdf.

> which it is unnecessary to go into detail. Apart from property matters and the availability of matrimonial remedies, one of the most important changes is that marriage is in modern times regarded as a partnership of equals and no longer one in which the wife must be the subservient chattel of the husband. Hale's proposition involves that by marriage a wife gives her irrevocable consent to sexual intercourse with her husband under all circumstances and irrespective of the state of her health or how she happens to be feeling at the time. In modern times any reasonable person must regard that conception as quite unacceptable...

Similarly, in *R v C (Rape: Marital Exemption)*,[25] there were nine counts in an indictment against a husband and a co-accused 'for various offences of a sexual nature against an estranged wife'. One of these was of rape as a principal. Simon Brown J, while using common law as the basis„ took the 'radical' step of holding that Hale's proposition was 'no longer the law and that the whole concept of a marital exemption in rape was misconceived'.[26]

Equally, in *People V Liberta*,[27] the wife claimed that the husband raped her. The Defendant moved to dismiss the charge under New York Penal Law on marital exemption. The trial court granted Defendant's motion and dismissed the indictment based on the marital exemption. The Appellate Division reversed the decision of the trial court and recommended the case for trial. The Court of Appeals affirmed the judgment of the Appellate Division, finding section 130.35 was unconstitutional due to the marital exemption provision and stated that 'marital rape exemption denies married women equal protection of the laws' and that a 'married women has the same right to control her body as does an unmarried woman'.

As stated, by the 1902 Order in Council, Uganda adopted British statutory laws and the common law system.[28] As a result, many of

[25] *R v C* [1991] 1 All ER 755.

[26] Ibid., paragraph 758.

[27] *People v. Liberta* 90 A.D. 2d 681, https://www.law.cornell.edu/women-and-justice/resource/people_v_liberta.

[28] The Uganda Order in Council, 1902, https://books.google.com/books/about/The_Uganda_Order_in_Council.html?id=YkDlNAEACAAJ.

Uganda's domestic laws date back to the colonial era, hence the relevance of the common law jurisprudence and appreciating the legislative developments to-date, which is not reflected in the Ugandan law.

3 The State of Marital Rape in Uganda: A Hidden Crime

The 2009 Uganda's State Report to the Committee on the Elimination of Discrimination Against Women (CEDAW Committee) revealed that a combination of socio-economic, cultural and legal barriers that fuel the high rates of violence against women in Uganda.[29] Rape, including marital rape, battery, assault, defilement and female genital mutilation (FGM) continue to be forms of violence experienced by Ugandan women.[30] According to the Uganda Police Force, 1,528 cases of rape were reported in 2019 and 1,580 cases in 2018. A total of 1,531 women were victims of rape. 688 suspects of rape were charged in Court, 20 were convicted, 6 were acquitted and 15 discharged while 647 were still awaiting trial.[31] Unfortunately, many women do not report rape cases where the perpetrators are their husbands.[32] As a result, statistics on marital rape are therefore not disaggregated and are not specifically represented. Over the years, the government has taken laudable steps to uphold women's rights in both the public and private sphere. In so doing, Uganda has ratified a number of global and regional instruments, as well as adopted policies that protect women against all forms of violence and sexual abuse, even within marriage, as analysed below.

---

[29] Ministry of Gender, Labour and Social Development, Combined 4th, 5th, 6th and 7th Periodic Report on the Implementation of CEDAW in Uganda (2009), 128, https://www2.ohchr.org/english/bodies/cedaw/docs/AdvanceVersions/CEDAW-C-UGA-7.pdf.

[30] Organisation for Economic Co-operation and Development Development Centre, 'Social Institutions & Gender Index', https://www.genderindex.org/wp-content/uploads/files/datasheets/2019/UG.pdf.

[31] Uganda Police 'Annual Crime Report 2019' (2019): 16, https://www.upf.go.ug/wp-content/uploads/2020/04/Annual-Crime-Report-2019-Public.pdf?x45801.

[32] Indiana Coalition Against Sexual Assault, *supra* note 11.

3.1 Global Laws

The UN Universal Declaration of Human Rights 1945 (UDHR), UN Convention Against Torture (UNCAT)[33] and International Covenant on Civil and Political Rights (ICCPR)[34] guarantee equality of men and women[35] and freedom from torture, inhumane or degrading treatment.[36] In addition, article 16 of the Convention on the Elimination of All Forms of Discrimination against Women (CEDAW)[37] requires states parties to take all appropriate measures to eliminate discrimination against women in all aspects of life.[38] Men and women should have equal rights and responsibilities in all matters relating to marriage and family relations.[39] The CEDAW Committee and other treaty bodies such as the Committee Against Torture and the Human Rights Committee have recognised that violence against women which includes marital rape can breach 'fundamental rights to life, liberty and security of person, non-discrimination and freedom from torture'.[40]

The UN Declaration on the Elimination of Violence Against Women (DEVAW) further expressly recognises violence against women as including marital rape.[41] The Beijing Platform for Action declares that 'violence against women constitutes a violation of basic human rights and is an obstacle to the achievement of the objectives of equality,

---

33 Accession by Uganda on the November 3, 1986.

34 Accession by Uganda on the July 21, 1995.

35 UDHR, article 1: All human beings are born free and equal in dignity and rights. They are endowed with reason and conscience and should act towards one another in a spirit of brotherhood (Also see article 26 of the ICCPR).

36 UDHR, article 5: No one shall be subjected to torture or to cruel, inhuman or degrading treatment or punishment. (See also ICCPR, article 7).

37 Adopted and opened for signature, ratification and accession by General Assembly resolution 34/180 of 18 December 1979. Uganda ratified the Convention in 1985.

38 CEDAW, articles 1 and 2 on discrimination against women.

39 CEDAW, article 16.

40 Melanie Randall and Vasanthi Venkatesh, *Symposium on the International Legal Obligation to Criminalise Marital Rape Criminalising Sexual Violence Against Women in Intimate Relationships: State Obligations Under Human Rights Law* (2015), https://core.ac.uk/download/pdf/42550941.pdf.

41 DEVAW, articles 1 and 2.

development and peace'.[42] Unfortunately both the DEVAW and Beijing Platform of Action 'lack binding legal authority and are merely strong statements of principle to the international community'.[43]

3.2 Regional Laws

The African Charter on Human and Peoples' Rights (ACHPR)[44] recognises the right to equal protection of the law for both men and women[45] and freedom from inhuman and degrading treatment.[46] The ACHPR further requires states to 'eliminate every form of discrimination against women' and also to ensure the 'protection of the rights of women as stipulated in international declarations and conventions'.[47]

The Protocol to the ACHPR on the Rights of Women in Africa (Maputo Protocol)[48] defines violence against women to mean 'all acts perpetrated against women' which cause or could cause them, among others, sexual harm, including the threat to take such acts.[49] Article 3(4) is specific on sexual violence. It places an obligation on states parties to adopt measures to ensure respect for women's dignity and 'protection from all forms of violence particularly, sexual and verbal violence'. Article 4 protects the right to life, integrity and security of the person. The Maputo Protocol also binds states parties to ensure that women and men enjoy equal rights in marriage.[50]

Although Uganda is yet to ratify the Protocol to the ACHPR on the Rights of Persons with Disabilities (Disability Rights Protocol) in

---

42 Ibid.

43 Akina Mama Wa Afrika, *supra* note 4, 14.

44 Adopted June 27, 1981, OAU Doc. CAB/LEG/67/3 rev. 5, 21 I.L.M. 58 (1982), entered into force October 21, 1986. Ratified by Uganda on the March 27, 1986.

45 African Charter, articles 3 and 19.

46 African Charter, article 5.

47 African Charter, article 18(3).

48 Adopted in July 2003 and came into force on the November 25, 2005. Ratified by Uganda on July 22, 2010.

49 Maputo Protocol, article 1(j).

50 Maputo Protocol, article 6.

Uganda,[51] the Protocol, under article 27, obliges states parties to ensure that 'women with disabilities are protected from sexual and gender based violence and are provided with rehabilitation and psychosocial support against sexual and gender based violence'.[52]

Uganda is also party to several other instruments for the promotion of gender equality in Africa such as the African Union Gender Policy,[53] Solemn Declaration on Gender Equality,[54] the Protocol on the Suppression of Sexual Violence of the International Conference on the Great Lakes Region (ICGLR)[55] and the Goma Declaration[56] on Eradicating Sexual Violence and Ending Impunity in the Great Lakes Region, June 2008.[57] These regional undertakings demonstrate Uganda's commitment to combat all forms of violence against women, including marital rape.

3.3 Domestic Laws

3.3.1 The 1995 Constitution

At the national level, the Constitution of the Republic of Uganda guarantees equality under the law regardless of sex or gender.[58] Article 22 guarantees the right to life and article 24 calls for respect for human

[51] Adopted on January 29, 2018.

[52] Disability Rights Protocol, article 7(j).

[53] The desired effect and impact of this Policy is to offer opportunities for empowerment of women, guarantee their protection against violence and rape, as well as ensure their participation in public and economic life.

[54] It was adopted by the AU Assembly in 2004, calling for member states' continual action towards achieving gender equality and reinforcing their commitment to international and regional women's rights instruments. In addition to calling for wider ratification of the Protocol to the African Charter on Human and Peoples' Rights on the Rights of Women in Africa, it also addresses state responsibility for tackling violence against women and gender-based discrimination.

[55] One of the objectives of the Protocol is to provide protection for women and children against the impunity of sexual violence in the specific context of the Great Lakes region.

[56] It recommends that member states allocate funds from the national budget to projects related to the prevention of SGBV and assistance to survivors, strengthening on institutions working on SGBV.

[57] Akina Mama Wa Afrika, *supra* note 4, 14.

[58] The Constitution, article 21.

dignity and protection from torture and inhumane treatment. Women are to be accorded the full respect and dignity as men, and any form of torture or degrading treatment or punishment to them amounts to breach of this article.[59] The Constitution further protects the right to privacy under article 27 and article 31 guarantees equality of both men and women in marriage and during its dissolution.

Article 32 mandates the state to make laws in favour of marginalised groups on the basis of gender. Article 33 further provides that women are to be accorded 'equal dignity of the person with men'. 'Women shall have the right to affirmative action for the purpose of redressing the imbalances created by history, tradition or custom'.[60] 'Laws, cultures, customs or traditions which are against the dignity, welfare or interest of women or which undermine their status', are prohibited by the Constitution.[61] The Constitution is therefore, through the above articles, alive to the various inequalities such as sexual violence and marital rape that are mainly faced by women given the patriarchal setup of most societies in Uganda.[62]

3.3.2 The Penal Code Act Cap 120

Section 123 of the Penal Code Act provides for the offence of rape and stipulates the following:

> Any person who has unlawful carnal knowledge of a woman or girl, without her consent, or with her consent, if the consent is obtained by force or by means of threats or intimidation of any kind or by fear of bodily harm, or by means of false representations as to the nature of the act, or in the case of a married woman, by personating her husband, commits the felony termed rape.

However, from the wording in this section, the law envisages a situation of rape of a married woman only by a man who is not her husband and

---

[59] Under article 44, this right is a non-derogable right.

[60] Constitution, article 33(5).

[61] Constitution, article 32(2).

[62] Constitution, article 2(2): The Constitution is the supreme law in Uganda.

does not see boys or men as possible victims of rape.[63] This is a narrow interpretation of rape compared to how it was defined in the *Prosecutor V Akayesu.*[64]

3.3.3 The Domestic Violence Act 2010

The Domestic Violence Act addresses all forms of violence including sexual violence but does not specifically mention marital rape. Under Section 2 of the Act, domestic violence includes the act or omission 'of a perpetrator which causes physical, emotional, psychological and sexual abuse to the victim'. The Act further defines sexual abuse as 'any conduct of a sexual nature that abuses, humiliates, degrades or otherwise violates the dignity of another person'.[65] This can be given a wider interpretation to include marital rape as rape as a form of sexual abuse committed within the domestic sphere.

3.3.4 The Prevention and Prohibition of Torture Act 2012

Under the Prevention and Prohibition of Torture Act, 'physical torture may include rape and sexual abuse, including the insertion of foreign bodies into the sexual organs or rectum or electrical torture of the genitals'.[66] This provision can also benefit from wide interpretation to include marital rape.

Evidently, the existing progressive legal and policy framework present fertile ground for protecting women against marital rape as a form of sexual violence. However, Uganda does not have a consolidated law

---

[63] Zahara, *supra* note 8, 144.

[64] *The Prosecutor v. Jean-Paul Akayesu, supra* note 5.

[65] Domestic Violence Act 2010, section 2.

[66] In addition to the above, there are several policies specifically addressing Gender-Based Violence (GBV). One is the National Policy on the Elimination of GBV in Uganda and its Action Plan which was launched in 2016 and is consistent with the Uganda Gender Policy 2007. Others include the National Action Plan on Women 2008 and very specific to Violence Against Women is the National Referral Pathway for Prevention and Response to Gender-Based Violence Cases in Uganda 2013. The National Policy Guidelines and Service Standards for Reproductive Health Services also clearly stipulate the range of services that should be offered to survivors of GBV.

expressly criminalising marital rape. The various advocacy efforts to enact such law led to the tabling of the Marriage and Divorce Bill 2009, which came under immense pressure and failed to be passed by Parliament. It was subsequently renamed the Marriage Bill 2017.[67]

The Sexual Offences Bill 2019[68] also consolidates sexual offences. Its object is to enact a specific law on sexual offences for the effective prevention of sexual violence. The Bill, however, does not expressly prohibit marital rape but criminalises rape under Clause 2.

The challenges in passing of Bills that govern sexual relations in Uganda was rights decried by Watera as follows:

> ...people just do not understand the notion of marital rape...The gravity of offenses also remains barely knowable because victims often do not report and research in this arena is limited... The little that exists is not tailored to an African or Ugandan setting, where norms and values are at different ends of the spectrum. These, factors have led to limited understanding of marital rape or even acknowledging its existence.

Although these bills are still shelved in Parliament,[69] they provide a ray of hope that marital rape will soon be expressly outlawed in Uganda's laws. Commendable, however, is the high level of judicial activism as demonstrated in progressive jurisprudence being delivered by the Courts in combating marital rape and upholding women's rights.[70]

---

[67] Clause 17 provides that Conjugal rights are the right of sexual intercourse between a husband and wife and that a spouse may deny the other spouse the right to sexual intercourse on reasonable grounds which may include: poor health; surgery that affects the capacity to engage in sexual intercourse; child birth; or reasonable fear that engaging in sexual intercourse is likely to cause physical or psychological injury or harm.

[68] The Bill was tabled for the first reading in parliament on November 26, 2019.

[69] The Marriage Bill has been shelved since 2013 and is under negative criticism by various stakeholders especially the men who do not want to change the status quo they are enjoying.

[70] Winnie B Watera, 'Comment: Marital Rape Controversy-Prejudices Hinder Progress on a Law That Could Improve the Lives of Women', *The Independent*, November 28, 2016. https://www.independent.co.ug/comment-marital-rape-controversy/.

4 Judicial Activism and the Enforcement of Women's Rights

There are a number of celebrated decisions adopted after the promulgation of the 1995 Constitution that seek to uplift the status of women in the society in conformity with the Constitution. Some of them are reviewed below.

In *Uganda Association of Women Lawyers & Others versus Attorney General*,[71] the petitioners sought the court to declare that section 4(1), 4(2), 5, 21, 22, 23, 24 and 26 of the Divorce Act, Cap. 249 are inconsistent with articles 21(1), 21(2), 31(1), 33(1) and 33(6) of the Constitution on the grounds that the said sections discriminated on the grounds of gender. The petitioners contended that the grounds of divorce as listed are not available to both sexes and that the compensation for adultery, costs against a co-respondent, alimony and settlement are not equal for both sexes. Court noted that the Divorce Act had 'archaic' contents that negates 'the concept of equality', that is a fundamental value of the Constitution. This decision strongly clarified the notion of equality between both men and women in the family realm.

In *Mifumi (U) Ltd & Ors versus AG*[72] the petitioner's contention was that men treat women as their property since men pay bride price for them. They claimed that this 'perpetuates inequality between men and women' which is prohibited by articles 21(1) and 21(2) of the Constitution. The Court, however, held that 'payment of bride price in customary marriage is overrated by the appellants as a significant factor in the promotion of inequality and violence against women'. The Court stated that 'there are many more husbands who give bride price but who do not use it as a justification for inflicting violence and abuse on their wives'. The Court held that although there might be some husbands who use bride price as an excuse for violence against their wife, this is merely a pretext and not the actual reason for such behaviour. Hence, this cannot constitute sufficient justification for 'denying the enjoyment and practice of the custom to people who cherish it as is provided for under

[71] Constitutional Petition No. 2 of 2003.

[72] Constitutional Appeal No: 02 of 2014.

article 37 of the Constitution'. However, laudably in this decision, the Court annulled the practice of return of bride price upon dissolution of a marriage.

The issue of marital rape was specifically considered in *Uganda V Yiga Hamidu & ORS.*[73] A1 (Hamidu Yiga) visited the complainant's home and there appeared to have been a full agreement that the two would wed on Sunday 12 August 2001. However, it was decided that the couple would wed only after they had tested on three separate occasions for human immunodeficiency virus (HIV). Before the testing for HIV had been duly carried out, A1 went to the complainant's home to collect her but she and members of her family refused. A1 then went ahead and hired some men to apprehend the complainant and deliver her to his home and this was done. While at his home, A1 forcefully had sexual intercourse with the complainant as the two men held her hands and legs. In his evidence A1 agreed that on 13 August 2001, he had sexual intercourse with the complainant and stated that he did so as her husband because the two were husband and wife. Musoke Kibuuka J stated the following:

> Even if it was true that A1 and the complainant had been customarily or otherwise truly married and were, therefore husband and wife still the facts and circumstances of this case would render the accused guilty of rape. Section 117 of the Penal Code Act (now section 123 of the Penal Code Act) does not make any exception to a married person… It clearly appears to me that the existence of a valid marriage between an accused and complainant or an honest belief that a valid marriage between the two does/can exist in Uganda, no longer constitute a good defence against a charge of rape after the promulgation of the Constitution of the Republic of Uganda, 1995… The presumption of consent, even in marriage is wiped out by the provisions of the Constitution as husband and wife enjoy equal rights in marriage. …[74]

[73] Criminal Session Case 005 of 2002.

[74] Ibid., 8.

Furthermore, in *Uganda V Lomoe Nakoupuet*,[75] the court condemned the cultural practice of raping girls in Karamoja region as a practice preceding a marriage ceremony. In this case, the victim was raped and forced by her parents and brothers to enter into an arranged marriage without her full and free consent.

In the case of *Uganda V Byaruhanga*,[76] the judge observed that rape can also be attributed to the manner in which marriage negotiations were held in Uganda. The practice is known as 'okunegura' or 'okwetika' which involves the kidnapping of the girl. They held this practice as 'unconstitutional, illegal and abominable' and one that has no place in modern society.

The above decisions confirm the fact that Ugandan courts have commendably risen up to the challenge, and adjudicated on the protection of the rights of women as enshrined in the Uganda's domestic laws, and global and regional treaties to which Uganda is party. It is clear from the analysed decisions that any perpetrator of marital rape will most probably not walk out the courts scot-free. However, since statute law is not expressly clear on marital rape, it is still up to the discretion of the judge to conclude whether or not there was marital rape and whether it is a crime.

5 What Do Survivors of Marital Rape Have to Say? Testimonies

There are several impacts of marital rape, be it on the individual, on the family or on society at large. Women who have been sexually abused by their partners experience 'pain, humiliation and distress, with accompanying physical, emotional and psychological harm'.[77] 'Children in households where marital rape occurs often suffer from the psychological effects of witnessing violence, and such violence can undermine

[75] Criminal Case No. 109 of 2016.

[76] Criminal Session No. 361 of 2013.

[77] Indiana Coalition Against Sexual Assault, *supra* note 11.

the ability of their mothers to care for them'.[78] Studies indicate that women are traumatised more by 'a rape at the hands of a spouse as they feel violated by someone with whom they share their lives, homes and possibly children', in addition to 'violation of their bodies: they are faced with a betrayal of trust and intimacy'.[79] Marital rape victims are also more likely to experience multiple rape incidents as most continue to live with the perpetrators due to fear of more violence, loss of financial security and false hope that the spouse shall change.[80]

A housewife and mother of two shared the experience of being raped by husband as follows:

> It was only two months after I had delivered… I got complications after three weeks. … my husband was persistently demanding for sex. After a week, he said he was tired of waiting and forcefully had sex with me. It was so painful that I got bruised and bled. He raped me for three consecutive nights but I could not tell anyone about my problem. I felt betrayed by the man I trusted for a husband and I lived in fear when he came home.[81]

Sometimes, the partners were so forceful that they ruptured the sexual organs of the victims. This is the case of Tina who describes the pain and injuries she suffered from her first sexual intercourse after traditionally marrying her husband at the age of 16.[82]

In many instances, husbands under the influence of alcohol force their wives into sex. Akanyo narrated the following on how her partner had subjected her to physical and sexual abuse a few weeks into the relationship:

---

78 Ibid.

79 Ibid.

80 Ibid.

81 Beatrice Nakibuuka, 'Marital Rape, the Plague Silently Afflicting Women', *The Daily Monitor*, March 19, 2016, https://www.monitor.co.ug/Magazines/Full-Woman/Marital-rape-the-plague-silently-afflicting-women/689842-3122730-d0kl8y/index.html.

82 Esther Nanfuka et al., 'Leaving a Violent Child Marriage: Experiences of Adult Survivors in Uganda', *Social Sciences* (2020), file:///C:/Users/DELL/Downloads/Leaving%20a%20Violent%20Child%20Marriage.pdf.

> After a few weeks of staying together he started beating me whenever he came back home drunk. He would force me to have sex any time and even worse when he was drunk. He beat me for many days consecutively...[83]

Lack of financial independence forces majority of the victims to stay in the marriage or even go back to the perpetrators after leaving. Ageno, who eventually left the marriage after fifteen years, narrates her misery as follows:

> I was only 14 years old, life in marriage was not easy but I had nothing to do until I gave birth. ... My husband would even force me into having sex with him... I went back to my aunt, but the situation was even worse, so I decided to come back to my husband.[84]

Getting testimonies from victims of marital rape is close to impossible as majority of the victims do not report cases of marital rape and are not even aware that the law criminalises marital rape. This presents a great need for expressly criminalising marital rape in the Ugandan Penal laws and sensitising people about the various laws protecting their rights in marriage.

6 Challenges Faced by Victims of Marital Rape in Accessing Criminal Justice

There are a number of challenges that inhibit the proper identification and handling of marital rape cases in Uganda. Some of them are discussed below.

83 Ibid.

84 Ibid.

6.1 None or Under Reporting

There is considerable evidence that victims of marital rape are hesitant to share their experiences as compared to those raped by strangers due to various factors like: loyalty to husband; privacy of family matters; and 'unwillingness to accept their own victimisation as it is emotionally painful to acknowledge that one is being betrayed by the person one depends upon for love and support'.[85] Social support or jobs skills could assist women to leave marriages and since many women do not have access to such, they cannot acknowledge such rapes.[86] In addition, there are the perceptions that a woman's role in marriage is to care for her husband's sexual needs at all times among others. There is also uncertainty regarding what constitutes consensual sexual relations, ambiguity regarding what constitutes 'force'.[87] Moreover, many women feel guilt and consider themselves responsible for the abuse, and have 'no words to describe their experience'. Many marital rape survivors 'have expressed the belief that they are obligated by their marriage vows to submit to all sexual acts, and therefore these acts are not considered rape, regardless of the nature of the sexual experience'.[88]

6.2 Inadequate Funding and Staff Capacity

Poor funding for programmes and sectors that are geared towards combating violence against women also remains a huge challenge. It is reported that in 2016 and 2017 the Ministry of Gender, Labour and Social Development budgeted to spend UGX 1.68 billion (USD 450,000) on violence against women programmes, large support from

[85] Patricia Mahoney and Linda M Williams, 'Sexual Assault in Marriage: Prevalence, Consequences, and Treatment of Wife Rape', *Family Research Laboratory* (2007), http://www.ncdsv.org/images/nnfr_partnerviolence_a20-yearliteraturereviewandsynthesis.pdf.

[86] Ibid.

[87] Ibid.

[88] Ibid.

donor agencies.[89] This is coupled with limited human resource to effectively implement the laws and prosecute perpetrators. According to Ministry of Gender, Labour and Social Development's Ministerial Policy Statement for Financial Year 2016/2017, for that period, the 'Directorate of Gender and Women Affairs had only 10 staff members, a fraction of the workforce required'. As for the Child and Family Protection Unit of the Uganda Police Force, they have only 645 police officers to cover 112 districts. This is a challenge as the police has to respond to the numerous reported cases.[90] Police also lack the requisite skills and financial support to adequately investigate cases related to marital rape and violence against women.

6.3 Access to Justice

Access to justice is limited by 'an inadequate number of critical facilities' such as shelters 'where victims can be accommodated, receive counseling and other support before returning home'. There is also an absence of specialised courts where it would be safe for women to report their cases.[91] This is compounded by the high cost of litigation, corruption in the justice system, inaccessible court premises, inaccessible legal presentation and limited access to legal aid services.[92] As a result, may people resort to Local Council Courts and family structures to resolve these disputes. Nevertheless, in many instances, these structures may have no jurisdiction to handle the matter, no sufficient legal knowledge and are bedeviled by patriarchal and cultural biases.[93] The laws on violence

---

[89] Mutayati, 'Uganda: Violence Against Women Unabated Despite Laws and Policies', https://www.un.org/africarenewal/news/uganda-violence-against-women-unabated-despite-laws-and-policies.

[90] Ibid.

[91] Ibid.

[92] The HiiL 'Innovating Justice: Justice Needs in Uganda 2016 Report on Access to Justice'. https://www.hiil.org/wp-content/uploads/2018/07/Uganda-Mini-Folder_2016.pdf; Legal Aid Service Providers Network (LAPSNET), 'The Status of Access to Justice for Poor, Marginalised and Vulnerable People of Uganda' (2017). http://www.laspnet.org/joomla-pages/reports/research-reports/377-access-to-justice-for-the-poor-marginalised-and-vulnerable-people-of-uganda/file.

[93] Ibid.

against women has also been criticised for its failure to address the pre-existing difficulties such as costs associated with the complaint process that inhibit women in particular from accessing justice. The absence of National Legal Aid Policy and legislation does not help since most of the victims are potentially persons that require legal assistance.[94]

6.4 Limited Knowledge of the Law and Negative Attitudes Towards Reporting Cases of Domestic Violence

A report by Center for Domestic Violence Prevention (CEDOVIP) states that 'duty bearers at local level who are responsible for the protection and promotion of violence free communities, and implementation of gender related laws and policies' have 'limited knowledge on even the existing relevant laws and policies'. They also have negative attitudes towards gender-based violence. A baseline survey by the Domestic Violence Coalition revealed that 'more than 50% of duty bearers (police, community activists, health workers, and local council officials) believed that at least one reason was sufficient justification for beating one's wife'. The survey also demonstrated that awareness of the Domestic Violence Act ranged from 18% among health workers to 43% among the police.[95]

Uganda Women's Network (UWONET) states that at community level, people have limited awareness of the existing policies and laws on gender-based violence 'as well as their rights and responsibilities'. In an assessment on gender-based violence in Busoga region, only 44.1% police officers had basic knowledge about the topic, while health officers had only 8.1%, Community Development Officers (CDOs) were at 36.4% and 11.2% for Local Councilors. Only 4.3% of health officers knew ways of addressing gender-based violence survivors, while this was 14.6% among the CDO's and 8.4% among the Local councilors.[96] Besides the law, there is also limited knowledge of judicial decisions

94 Ibid.

95 Akina Mama Wa Afrika, *supra* note 4, 16.

96 Ibid.

about marital rape even if most of Uganda's information on marital rape largely lies in Uganda's judicial decisions than polices and laws.

6.5 Lack of Express Provision

The lack of an express provision criminalising marital rape as is the case in South Africa, Rwanda or Zimbabwe among others may pose a major challenge in the fight against marital rape. Existing laws such as the Penal Code (Amendment) Act 2007, the Domestic Violence Act 2010 address key aspects of marital rape while none of them expressly criminalises marital rape.[97] The effective enforcement of the laws in force is also lacking. For instance, Despite being passed in 2009, the Domestic Violence Act is not yet a functional or fully appreciated by actors within the criminal justice system. As such, victims of marital rape may fall through the cracks, unless saved by judicial activism.

6.6 Limited Public Awareness

Sensitisation of masses about these laws have been left to the goodwill of civil society organisations 'who have established community groups and mechanisms by which citizens and local leaders can push for accountability on violence against women cases'. However, civil society organisations' 'work is limited to certain parts of the country where projects are implemented and does not cover the entire country'.[98]

---

[97] Mutayati, *supra* note 89.

[98] Akina Mama Wa Afrika, *supra* note 4, 16.

6.7 Limited Research and Testimonies/Statistics on Marital Rape

While carrying out our research, we approached a number of women organisations and lawyers. However, they could not avail us with information concerning marital rape as it was scanty and few women actually opened up about it or even knew they were victims of marital rape.

7 Way Forward and Recommendations

7.1 Legislative Reform and Express Criminalisation of Marital Rape

Borrowing a leaf from countries such as South Africa, Namibia and Rwanda, Uganda must pass a law to expressly criminalise marital rape. Moreover, the enactment of the Marriage Bill 2017 and the Sexual Offences Bill is long over dues. The sentiments expressed below, speaks volumes of Uganda's dilemma:

> While some men are arguing that preventing forced sex with their wives is not part of African values, women have thrown their weight behind the bill, arguing that the inclusion of this crime in the law books would go a long way in reducing abuse of women in marriages.[99]

Therefore, Uganda must prevail over cultural dictates to enhance protection of women's rights.

7.2 Address Patriarchy

Marital rape in Uganda stems from patriarchal cultural practices and results into gender inequalities and unjust treatment of women. There is thus a need to sensitise the citizens on equality of men and women and

[99] Christine Wanjala, 'Marital Rape: Is It a Crime or a Conjugal Right?', *Monitor Newspaper*, March 16, 2013.

the laws that address patriarchy. Women need to be empowered to access justice in cases of abuse so as they are able to report the perpetrators.

7.3 Judicial Activism

As demonstrated in the above cases, in the absence of explicit law, judicial activism should be encouraged. Judges should be more pragmatic and progressive to shift from the patriarchal cultural beliefs and mindsets. They need to breathe life into the various progressive laws and policies that seek to protect women from sexual violence and read into marital rape. Judges should have regard to article 273(1) of the Constitution that requires existing laws to be construed or interpreted with such modifications, adaptations, qualifications and expectations as may be necessary to bring it into conformity with the Constitution.

7.4 Enhance Access to Justice

Government must address the challenges that inhibit access to justice as well as pass the National Legal Aid Bill[100] and Policy. This will buttress the access to legal aid services for many women who are indigent, and hindered from accessing justice due to the cost implication. It will also strengthen the capacity of legal aid service providers to broaden their reach and provide the much desired services. Other Justice, Law and Order Sector must also be adequately financed and with sufficient personnel to execute their mandate in an expeditious manner. As we know, 'Justice delayed is Justice denied'.[101]

7.5 Sensitisation Campaigns

The government needs to be involved in sensitisation campaigns focused on marital rape. Such campaigns can focus on what amounts to marital

[100] Parliament granted Hon. Komakech Lyandro leave to introduce a private member's Bill entitled 'The National Legal Aid Bill' 2018 on September 25, 2020.

[101] Constitution, article 126.

rape, the procedure one should undertake when raped or where to report to cases of rape. The government, with the support of civil society organisations, needs to create shelters and support groups to rehabilitate women who have undergone marital rape.

8 Conclusion

This paper reveals that the vice of marital rape still persists unabated in Uganda's society. This is as a result of negative cultural practices and beliefs, fear for stigma, financial insecurity and failure by victims/ survivors to report such cases or even acknowledge them as marital rape. Although there is no explicit statutory law prohibiting marital rape, various other laws, through judicial activism, have been interpreted to create a pool of progressive jurisprudence on the protection of women's rights in the field of marital rape. Therefore, it is argued that with the effective implementation of the recommendations made, Uganda will achieve additional strides and consolidate its gains in promoting, fulfilling, protecting and realising the rights of women to be protected from all forms of sexual violence and freedom from inhuman, cruel and degrading treatment. However, for purposes of consistency and efficient protection of the rights of women, marital rape has to be expressly criminalised in Uganda.

References

Akina Mama Wa Afrika, 2017, 'Uganda Baseline Study Report', https://www.akinamamawaafrika.org/wp-content/uploads/2019/10/AMwA-Baseline-report-FINAL-1.pdf.

Akumu Patience, May 26, 2010, 'The Phenomenon on Marital Rape', https://observer.ug/lifestyle/73-people-society/8645-the-phenomenon-of-marital-rape.

Beatrice Nakibuuka, March 19, 2019, 'Marital Rape, the Plague Silently Afflicting Women', *The Daily Monitor*, https://www.monitor.co.ug/Mag

azines/Full-Woman/Marital-rape-the-plague-silently-afflicting-women/689842-3122730-d0kl8y/index.html.

Brenda W Watera, November 28, 2016, 'Comment: Marital Rape Controversy-Prejudices Hinder Progress on a Law That Could Improve the Lives of Women', *The Independent*, https://www.independent.co.ug/comment-marital-rape-controversy/.

CEDAW Committee, 2009, 'Consideration of Report Submitted by States Parties Under Article 18 of the Convention on the Elimination of Discrimination Against Women: Uganda', https://www2.ohchr.org/english/bodies/cedaw/docs/AdvanceVersions/CEDAW-C-UGA-7.pdf.

Committee on the Elimination of Discrimination Against Women, 1992, *General Recommendation 19*, UN Doc.A/47/38.

Convention on the Elimination of all forms of Discrimination Against Women.

Criminal Justice and Public Order Act 1994.

Erika W Smith, 2019, '5 Statistics That'll Change How You Think About Marital Rape', https://www.refinery29.com/en-us/marital-rape-in-relationships-statistics.

Esther Nanfuka et al., 2020, 'Leaving a Violent Child Marriage: Experiences of Adult Survivors in Uganda'.

Human Rights Watch, 2003, 'Domestic Violence and Women's Vulnerability to HIV in Uganda', https://www.hrw.org/report/2003/08/13/just-die-quietly/domestic-violence-and-womens-vulnerability-hiv-uganda.

Indiana Coalition Against Sexual Assault, https://www.rainn.org/pdf-files-and-other-documents/Public-Policy/Issues/Marital_Rape.pdf.

International Covenant on Civil and Political Rights, 1966.

J Oloka-Onyango, 2015, 'An Overview of the Legal System in Uganda', Presentation at the China-Africa.

Legal Aid Service Providers Network, 2017, 'The Status of Access to Justice for Poor, Marginalised and Vulnerable People of Uganda', http://www.laspnet.org/joomla-pages/reports/research-reports/377-access-to-justice-for-the-poor-marginalised-and-vulnerable-people-of-uganda/file.

Legal Forum, November 25, 2015, https://www.researchgate.net/publication/341776281_AN_OVERVIEW_OF_THE_LEGAL_SYSTEM_IN_UGANDA.

Melanie Randall and VasanthiVenkatesh, 2015, *Symposium on the International Legal Obligation to Criminalise Marital Rape Criminalisng Sexual Violence against Women in Intimate Relationships: State Obligations under Human Rights Law*.

Mifumi (U) Ltd & Ors V AG, Constitutional Appeal No: 02 Of 2014.

Ministry of Gender, Labour and Social Development, 2009, 'Combined 4th, 5th, 6th & 7th Periodic'.
Murithi Koome, March 28, 2020, *Prosecuting Marital Rape in Kenya.*
Mutayati, 'Uganda: Violence Against Women Unabated Despite Laws and Policies', https://www.un.org/africarenewal/news/uganda-violence-against-women-unabated-despite-laws-and-policies.
Namibia, Domestic Violence, Including Protection, Services and Recourse Available to Victims (August 2010), https://www.refworld.org/docid/4e437a202.html.
OECD Development Centre, *Social Institutions & Gender Index*, https://www.genderindex.org/wp-content/uploads/files/datasheets/2019/UG.pdf.
Patricia Mahoney and Linda M Williams, 2007, 'Sexual Assault in Marriage: Prevalence, Consequences, and Treatment of Wife Rape', *Family Research Laboratory*, http://www.ncdsv.org/images/nnfr_partnerviolence_a20-yearliteraturereviewandsynthesis.pdf.
People v. Liberta 90 A.D. 2d 681.
R v C (Rape: Marital Exemption) (1991).
R V Clarke [1949] 2 ALLER 448.
R V J [1991] 1 ALL ER 759.
R V Kowalski (1987) 86 Cr App R 339.
R v Miller [1954] 2 QB 282.
R v O'Brien [1974] 3 ALLER 663.
R V Sharples [1990] Crim LR 198.
R v Steele [1976] 65 CRIM LR 188.
Ravi K Thiara and Gill Hague, 2011, 'Bride-Price, Poverty and Domestic Violence in Uganda', 34(6) *Women's Studies International Forum*, http://preventgbvafrica.org/wp-content/uploads/2013/10/Bride-Price-Poverty1.pdf.
Ravi K Thiara and Gill Hague, n.d., 'Bride-Price, Poverty and Domestic Violence in Uganda', http://preventgbvafrica.org/wp-content/uploads/2013/10/Bride-Price-Poverty1.pdf.
Sasha Hart, 2014, *Rape, Marriage, and Rights*, https://www.opendemocracy.net/5050/sasha-hart/rape-marriage-and-rights.
Sexual Offences Act 2003.
The African Charter on Human and Peoples' Rights.
The Combatting of Rape Act, Namibia, No.8 of 2000.
The Constitution of the Republic of Uganda, 1995 (As amended).
The Criminal Law (Sexual Offences and Related Matters) Amendment Act, 2007 of South Africa.
The Domestic Violence Act, 2010.

The HiiL, 2016, 'Innovating Justice: Justice Needs in Uganda 2016 Report on Access to Justice', https://www.hiil.org/wp-content/uploads/2018/07/Uganda-Mini-Folder_2016.pdf.

The Marriage Bill, 2017.

The Penal Code Act, Cap.120.

The Prevention and Prohibition of Torture Act, 2012.

The Prosecutor v. Jean-Paul Akayesu (Trial Judgement), ICTR-96–4-T, International Criminal Tribunal for Rwanda (ICTR), September 2, 1998, https://www.refworld.org/cases,ICTR,40278fbb4.html.

The Protocol to the African Charter on Human and Peoples' Rights on the Rights of Women in Africa 2003.

The Protocol to the African Charter on Human and Peoples' Rights on the Rights of Persons with Disabilities in Africa.

The Sexual Offences Bill, 2019.

Uganda Association of Women Lawyers & ORS V AG Constitutional Petition No 2 Of 2003.

Uganda Police, 2009, 'Annual Crime Report 2019', https://www.upf.go.ug/wp-content/uploads/2020/04/Annual-Crime-Report-2019-Public.pdf?x45801.

Uganda V Byaruhanga, Criminal Session No. 361 of 2013.

Uganda V Lomoe Nakoupuet Criminal Case No. 109 of 2016.

Uganda V Yiga Hamidu & ORS Criminal Session Case 005 of 2002.

UN Security Council, November 9, 1994, Statute of the International Tribunal for Rwanda.

UN Women, 'Facts and Figures: Ending Violence Against Women', https://www.unwomen.org/en/what-we-do/ending-violence-against-women/facts-and-figures.

United Nations Convention Against Torture.

United Nations, 1993, *Declaration on the Elimination of Violence Against Women.*

Universal Declaration of Human Rights, 1948.

Wanjala Christine, March 16, 2013, 'Marital Rape: Is It a Crime or a Conjugal right?!' *Daily Monitor Newspaper*.

Zablotska Iryna et al., 2009, 'Alcohol Use, Intimate Partner Violence, Sexual Coercion and HIV Among Women Aged 15–24 in Rakai, Uganda', 13 *AIDS Behav*, https://link.springer.com/content/pdf/10.1007/s10461-007-9333-5.pdf.

Zahara Nampewo, 2016, 'Till Violence Do Us Part: A Critical Analysis of the Legal Regime on Cruelty as a Ground for Divorce in Uganda', in *The Politics of Putting Asunder; Divorce, Law and the Family in Uganda*, edited by Maria Nassali.

6

Accountability for Sexual Exploitation and Abuse by United Nations Peacekeepers: Case Studies of the Democratic Republic of Congo and Central African Republic

Linda Mushoriwa, Esther Njieassam, and Pierre T. Bata

1 Introduction

The prevalence of sexual violence in conflict situations is not a novel phenomenon.[1] It has been, for a long time, considered as an inevitable

[1] Gloria Gaggioli, 'Sexual Violence in Armed Conflicts: A Violation of International Humanitarian Law and Human Rights Law' 96(894) *International Review of the Red Cross* (2014): 504.

L. Mushoriwa (✉) · E. Njieassam
South African Research Chair in International Law, University of Johannesburg, Johannesburg, South Africa

E. Njieassam
e-mail: esthere@uj.ac.za

P. T. Bata
Human Rights Department, Catholic University, Yaoundé, Cameroon

A. Budoo-Scholtz and E. C. Lubaale (eds.), *Violence Against Women and Criminal Justice in Africa: Volume II*, Sustainable Development Goals Series,
https://doi.org/10.1007/978-3-030-75953-7_6

by-product of war.[2] In a speech to mark the International Day for the Elimination of Sexual Violence in Conflict in 2017, the United Nations (UN) Secretary-General Antonio Guterres stated the following:

> Rape and sexual violence in conflict...should never be downplayed as war's inevitable by-product. Sexual violence is a threat to every individual's right to a life of dignity, and to humanity's collective peace and security.[3]

The UN Security Council Resolution on Women and Peace and Security recognises that sexual violence committed during armed conflict is a threat against international peace and security.[4] In 2003 the UN adopted a zero-tolerance policy against all forms of sexual violence with respect to all its personnel,[5] which includes the prohibition of sexual activity with minors, and exchange of money, employment, goods, or services for sex.[6] This zero-tolerance policy was reaffirmed by the Security Council in its Resolution on Sexual Exploitation and Abuse by UN Peacekeepers[7] and the Resolution Women, Peace and Security in which the Security Council demanded, '...the complete cessation with immediate effect by all parties to armed conflict of all acts of sexual violence'.[8]

Despite this zero-tolerance policy, the UN has continuously had to deal with allegations of sexual exploitation and abuse (SEA) against members of its peacekeeping missions including those deployed in

---

[2] United Nations, Women 2000: Sexual Violence and Armed Conflict: United Nations Response, April 10, 1998, http://www.un.org/womenwatch/daw/public/cover.pdf; Jelke Boesten, 'Of Exceptions and Continuities: Theory and Methodology in Research on Conflict-Related Sexual Violence' 19(4) *International Journal of Politics* (2017): 515.

[3] UN News, *Sexual Violence Is a Threat to Every Individual's Right to a Life of Dignity-UN Chief*, June 19, 2017, https://news.un.org/en/story/2017/06/559822-sexual-violence-threat-every-individuals-right-life-dignity-un-chief.

[4] UN Security Council, *Resolution on Women and Peace and Security* (2008), paragraph 1.

[5] UN Secretariat, Secretary General's Bulletin, *Special Measures for Protection from Sexual Exploitation and Sexual Abuse*, October 9, 2003 (hereinafter Secretary-General's 2003 Bulletin), https://www.un.org/en/ga/search/view_doc.asp?symbol=ST/SGB/2003/13.

[6] Ibid., section 3(2).

[7] United Nations Security Council, *Resolution on Sexual Exploitation and Abuse by United Nations Peacekeepers* (2016), Preamble.

[8] UN Security Council, *Resolution on Women and Peace and Security: Sexual Violence in Conflict* (2019), paragraph 1.

missions in African countries. There have been reports of SEA by UN peacekeeping forces since the 1990s in several countries including Somalia, Liberia, Haiti, Sierra Leone, Democratic Republic of Congo (DRC) and Central African Republic (CAR).[9] This chapter provides a detailed overview of the scale of SEA against women and children by peacekeepers in the DRC and CAR and asserts that the statistics point towards a culture of impunity. It is argued that this culture of impunity ought to be understood against the backdrop of the immunity enjoyed by the UN which extends to its civilian personnel[10]; and the Memoranda of Understanding (MOUs) and Status of Force Agreements (SOFAs) entered into between the UN and troop-contributing countries (TCCs) in terms of which TCCs retain exclusive prosecutorial jurisdiction over military peacekeepers.[11]

In the past decade there has been a proliferation of literature about SEA by UN peacekeepers, and recommendations on how to address the culture of impunity that seems to be prevalent.[12] Freedman and Lilly have given a detailed overview of the privileges and immunities enjoyed by the UN which extends to its peacekeeping personnel, and the MOUs and SOFAs between the UN and TCCs by which the TCCs retain exclusive prosecutorial jurisdiction over military personnel.[13] Freedman

---

[9] Human Rights Watch, 'UN: Stop Sexual Abuse by Peacekeepers', March 4, 2016, https://www.hrw.org/news/2016/03/04/un-stop-sexual-abuse-peacekeepers.

[10] Charter of the United Nations (1945), article 105; Convention on the Privileges and Immunities of the United Nations (1946), article V; Rosa Freedman, 'UN Accountable: A New Approach to Peacekeepers and Sexual Abuse' 29(3) *European Journal of International Law* (2018): 966–968; Francesca Lilly, 'Peacekeepers or Perpetrators? UN Accountability in the Face of International Immunities' 20–07 *University of South Wales Law Journal Student Series* (2020): 7, 3–5.

[11] Freedman, *supra* note 10, 968–969; Lilly *supra* note 10, 8–10.

[12] See for example Muna Ndulo, 'The United Nations Response to the Sexual Abuse and Exploitation of Women and Girls by Peacekeepers During Peacekeeping Missions' 27(1) *Berkeley Journal of International Law* (2009): 127; Zsuzsanna Deen-Racsmany, 'Exclusive Criminal Jurisdiction over UN Peacekeepers and the UN Project(s) on Criminal Accountability: A Self-Fulfilling Prophecy?' 53 *Military Law and Law of War Review* (2013): 247; Roisin Burke, 'Central African Republic Peacekeeper Sexual Crimes, Institutional Failings: Addressing the Accountability Gap' 14 *New Zealand Journal of Public and International Law* (2016): 97; Freedman, *supra* note 10, 963; Jayden van Leeuwen, 'Addressing the Gap: Accountability Mechanisms for Peacekeepers Accused of Exploitation and Abuse' 50 *Victoria University of Wellington Law Review* (2019):135–156; Lilly, *supra* note 10, 1.

[13] Freedman, *supra* note 10, 965–969; Lilly *supra* note 10, 3–5, 8–10.

and Lilly assert that although the privileges and immunities, and the MOUs and SOFAs are important to protect the peacekeepers against unwarranted interference by host states,[14] they significantly contribute to a culture of impunity.[15] Burke has proposed amending the SOFAs to provide civilian peacekeepers with only functional immunity as opposed to absolute immunity, and to provide for concurrent jurisdiction for military peacekeepers, as is the case with the North Atlantic Treaty Organisation (NATO) agreement.[16] Van Leeuwen has assessed the direct non-legal accountability measures taken by the UN to address the problem of SEA by peacekeepers, and suggested proposals for improvement. These measures include the appointment of a victims' rights advocate,[17] victim impact assessments and attendance at criminal trials,[18] and changes to the Victims' Trust Fund.[19]

This chapter seeks to contribute to the available literature by providing an up-to-date overview of the scale of SEA allegations against the UN Organisation Mission in the Democratic Republic of Congo (MONUC), the UN Organisation Stabilisation Mission in the Democratic Republic of Congo MONUSCO and the UN Multidimensional Integrated Stabilisation Mission in the Central African Republic (MINUSCA) peacekeepers. In this vein, the chapter analyses the available statistics on SEA by MONUC, MONUSCO and MINUSCA to highlight that despite efforts by the UN to curb SEA by peacekeepers and to support victims, the culture of impunity persists. It ought to be noted from the outset that the available statistics on SEA are inaccurate.[20] Nevertheless, an analysis of these statistics is considered essential to highlight the culture of impunity amongst UN peacekeepers. This analysis makes for a strong argument that in the absence of a review of the immunity provisions in MOUs and SOFAs, the measures adopted

[14] Freedman, *supra* note 10, 965; Lilly *supra* note 10, 3.

[15] Freedman, *supra* note 10, 969; Lilly *supra* note 10, 8–10.

[16] Burke, *supra* note 12, 116.

[17] Van Leeuwen, *supra* note 12, 149–150,153–154.

[18] Van Leeuwen, *supra* note 12, 150–153.

[19] Van Leeuwen, *supra* note 12, 154–155.

[20] UN Security Council Resolution Women and Peace and Security, paragraph 9 (calling for a more systematic and reliable approach to recording accurate SEA data).

by the UN to ensure legal accountability and to support victims and acknowledge their pain and suffering, cannot be said to be effective, comprehensive and commensurate with the scale of the problem at hand.

Part 2 of the chapter gives a detailed overview of the scale of SEA by peacekeepers in DRC and CAR, and part 3 examines the immunity and jurisdiction framework of the UN peacekeeping architecture. Part 4 evaluates the measures taken by the UN to address the problem of SEA by peacekeepers, and part 5 makes concluding remarks.

2 The Scale of Sexual Violence and Exploitation by United Nations Peacekeeping Forces

Before examining the scale of SEA by MONUC, MONUSCO and MINUSCA peacekeepers, it is pertinent to first define the terms conflict-related sexual violence and peacekeeping. Conflict-related sexual violence is defined as follows:

> …rape, sexual slavery, forced prostitution, forced pregnancy, forced abortion, enforced sterilisation, forced marriage, trafficking in persons when committed in situations of conflict for the purpose of sexual violence/exploitation and any other form of sexual violence of comparable gravity perpetrated against women, men, girls or boys that is directly or indirectly linked to a conflict.[21]

Peacekeeping is 'an intervention into an area of instability in order to facilitate the transition of that area back towards peace'.[22]

---

[21] UN Office of the Special Representative of the Secretary-General on Sexual Violence in Conflict, Our Mandate, June 27, 2020, https://un.org/sexualviolenceinconflict/-our-work/our-mandate.

[22] Mission Justice, *What Is Peacekeeping*, June 15, 2020, https://mission-justice.org/what-is-peacekeeping.html.

Both international humanitarian law[23] and international criminal law[24] prohibit sexual violence in conflict situations and recognise that it amounts to war crimes and crimes against humanity.[25] In the *Kunarac* Case,[26] the International Criminal Tribunal for the Former Yugoslavia (ICTY) held that sexual violence can be classified as an act of torture because it causes severe pain or suffering, and that the detention and repeated torture and rape of Bosnian Muslim women by the accused who were members of the Bosnian Serb army constituted war crimes and crimes against humanity.[27] In the *Akayesu* case, the International Criminal Tribunal for Rwanda (ICTR) held that sexual violence amounts to genocide when committed with the intent to destroy a particular group.[28] The criminalisation of sexual violence in armed conflict situations highlights the gravity of SEA by peacekeepers. In this vein it is argued that it is imperative for the UN and member states to strive to ensure the eradication of the culture of impunity amongst peacekeepers in this regard. UN peacekeepers ought to help communities broken by conflict, not to breach the trust bestowed upon them by perpetrating acts of SEA.[29]

One of the reasons why SEA against women and children by peacekeepers is rife in countries such as the DRC and CAR is because of

---

[23] Fourth Geneva Convention Relative to the Protection of Civilian Persons in times of War, August 12, 1949; Protocol Additional to the Geneva Conventions of August 12, 1949, and Relating to the Protection of Victims of International Armed Conflicts (Additional Protocol I) of June 8, 1977; Protocol Additional to the Geneva Conventions of August 12, 1949, and relating to the Protection of Victims of Non-International Armed Conflicts (Additional Protocol II).

[24] The Rome Statute of the International Criminal Court (1998) provides that 'Rape, sexual slavery, enforced prostitution, forced pregnancy, enforced sterilisation, or any other form of sexual violence of comparable gravity' constitute crimes against humanity when committed as part of a widespread or systemic attack against civilians' (article 7(1)(g)); and war crimes when committed as part of a plan or policy or part of a large scale commission of such crimes (article 8(e)(vi)).

[25] For a detailed overview see Gaggioli, *supra* note 1, 511–531.

[26] *Prosecutor v Dragolijub Kunarac and Others,* IT-96–238 23/1(Appeals Chamber), June 12, 2002.

[27] Ibid., paragraphs 125–133; See also Gaggioli, *supra* note 1, 526.

[28] *Prosecutor v Jean-Paul Akayesu,* ICTR-96-4, (Trial Chamber) Judgment, (September 2, 1998), paragraph 687.

[29] A comprehensive strategy to eliminate future sexual exploitation and abuse in United Nations peacekeeping operations (hereinafter Zeid Report) March 24, 2005, A/59/710, paragraph 8.

the vulnerable position which women and children in conflict situations find themselves in. As Ndulo explained, most local people in countries affected by conflict live in poverty.[30] High rates of unemployment mean that unemployed women turn to prostitution with peacekeepers who have higher income levels and access to resources which are not available to the locals. This is done as a means for survival in order to feed themselves and in some cases their children and families.[31] Unfortunately, some children in conflict-torn countries have also turned to prostitution as a means of survival.[32] Although the UN has had to deal with SEA allegations across its peacekeeping missions, available data shows that the problem is more widespread in DRC and CAR. Between 2007 and 2010, the UN received a total of 483 SEA allegations from across its peacekeeping missions, and of these 37,4% (181) were from MONUC.[33] Between 2010 and 2014, 339 SEA allegations were received across UN peacekeeping missions, with 30,9% (105) from MONUSCO.[34] From 2015 to date, a total of 396 SEA allegations have been received across UN missions, with 24,5% (97) from MONUSCO and 41,7 % (165) from MINUSCA.[35] SEA by UN peacekeepers is therefore taking place on a wider scale in MINUSCA and MONUSCO, and previously MONUC and it is for this reason that a detailed analysis of data from these missions is warranted.

---

30 Ndulo, *supra* note 12, 144.

31 Ibid.; See also Bonnie Kovatch, 'Sexual Exploitation and Abuse in UN Peacekeeping Missions: A Case Study of MONUC and MONUSCO' 7(2) *The Journal of the Middle East and Africa* (2016): 163–164.

32 Ndulo, *supra* note 12, 144; Kovatch, *supra* note 31.

33 United Nations, 'Conduct in UN Field Missions', May 17, 2020, https://conduct.unmissions.org/.

34 Ibid.

35 Ibid.

2.1 Democratic Republic of Congo

2.1.1 Monuc

The UN Security Council authorised the deployment of MONUC in November 1999, after the signing of a ceasefire between the DRC and five other African countries which had joined the conflict.[36] Following allegations of SEA by MONUC peacekeepers in the Ituri district in Bunia in north-east DRC, the UN Office of International Oversight Services (OIOS) investigated the allegations between May and September 2004.[37] Out of 72 allegations which were received, 68 were against military personnel and 4 against international civilian personnel.[38] The OIOS reported that many of the allegations could not be substantiated because of their nonspecific nature and, in some cases the witnesses and victims failed to clearly identify the alleged perpetrators.[39] As a result, the OIOS compiled 20 case reports, 19 involving military personnel and 1 involving international civilian personnel.[40] The case against the civilian staffer was substantiated, and 3 of the 19 cases against the military personnel were substantiated.[41]

Further to the OIOS investigation in Bunia, the Secretary-General appointed Prince Zeid, the then permanent representative of Jordan to the UN, to assist in determining the nature and extent of SEA in peacekeeping missions.[42] The Zeid report noted that SEA mainly involved the exchange of sex for money (averaging an amount of between USD 1

---

36 UN Security Council, *Resolution on* the Situation Concerning the Democratic Republic of the Congo (1999); UN, MONUC-United Nations Organisation Mission in the Democratic Republic of the Congo, June, 18 2020, https://peacekeeping.un.org/mission/past/monuc; For a detailed overview of the DRC conflict; see also Human Rights Watch, 'Democratic Republic of Congo: On the Brink', August 1, 2006, https://www.hrw.org/news/2006/08/01/democratic-republic-congo-brink.

37 Investigation by the OIOS into allegations of sexual exploitation and abuse in the UN Mission in the DR Congo (A/59/661), January 5, 2005.

38 OIOS, *supra* note 37, 7–8.

39 OIOS, *supra* note 37, paragraphs 8–11.

40 OIOS, *supra* note 37, paragraph 10.

41 Ibid.

42 Zeid Report, *supra* note 29, 8.

and USD 3 per encounter), food and jobs.[43] It also noted that in some instances the rape of young girls was disguised as consensual sex as they were given money or food after being raped.[44] A media report detailed how young girls known as 'basharati badogo' (Swahili for small prostitutes), most of whom had earlier allegedly been raped by peacekeepers, would loiter around the peacekeepers' camps in the hope of selling their bodies in exchange for food, and a dollar, which is what they charged per sexual encounter.[45] According to the report:

> ...often, the victims were vulnerable, poverty-stricken girls engaged in what Congolese call 'obligation' or 'survival sex.' In this war shattered society, a breakdown of cultural norms, combined with extreme poverty, has driven hundreds of 'basharati badogo' to the soldiers' doorsteps.[46]

As Ndulo has asserted, the prevailing economic conditions and the fact that in some cases the victims are willing participants is no excuse for the perpetration of SEA by peacekeepers.[47]

The UN took several steps in response to the allegations including: the banning of unofficial contact between peacekeeping forces and community members; the imposition of a night-time curfew on peacekeepers: the prohibition of civilian clothing for uniformed forces for easier identification and monitoring; and expanded training on UN codes of conduct and rules on SEA.[48] Despite this, the abuse continued.[49] In 2008, for instance, about 100 Indian troops were alleged to have participated in

---

43 Zeid Report, *supra* note 29, paragraph 6.

44 Zeid Report, *supra* note 29, paragraph 6.

45 Emily Wax, Congo's desperate 'One Dollar UN Girls,' *Washington Post*, March 21, 2005, https://washingtonpost.com/archive/politics/2005/03/21/congos-desperate-one-dollar-un-girls/26b5e610-d9ed-42e1-909a-03b2e061377d/; Susan Notar, 'Peacekeepers as Perpetrators: Sexual Exploitation and Abuse of Women and Children in the Democratic Republic of Congo' 14(2) *Journal of Gender, Social Policy and the Law* (2006): 417.

46 Wax, *supra* note 45.

47 Ndulo, *supra* note 12, 144.

48 Michael Fleshman, 'Tough UN Line on Peacekeeper Abuses: Action Initiated to End Sexual Misdeeds in Peacekeeping Missions', *Africa Renewal*, April 2005, www.un.org/africarenewal/magazine/april-2005/tough-un-line-peacekeeper-abuses.

49 UN News Service, Peacekeepers' Sexual Abuse of Local Girls Continuing in DRC, January 7, 2005, https://news.un.org/en/story/2005/01/125352-peacekeepers-sexual-abuse-local-girls-continuing-dr-congo-unfinds.

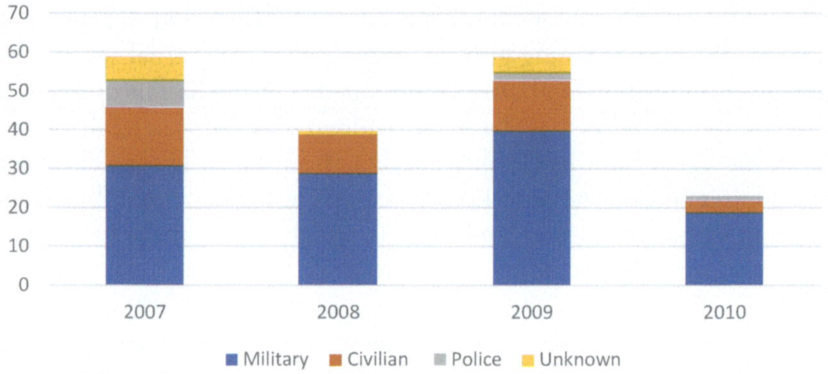

Fig. 1 MONUC total allegations per category of personnel (2007–2010) (*Source* United Nations, Conduct in UN Field Missions)

a child prostitution ring which paid for sexual encounters with young girls. However, the Indian army found all of them innocent.[50] The UN implemented an electronic tracking system for allegations of misconduct in 2008, and this incorporated some data from 2007. Before 2007 information was physically stored in files and is therefore not available for analysis.[51]

The graph below highlights the number of allegations made against MONUC personnel by category. The number of allegations against military peacekeepers is higher than other categories of personnel in all four years, and as shall be discussed below this has been attributed to the framework of jurisdictional bars applying to military personnel. The UN started recording data specifying the type of allegations in 2010, and the available data shows that in 2010 MONUC received a total of 23 SEA allegations.[52] Of these, 10 were abuse allegations, 12 exploitations and 1 was an allegation of both exploitation and abuse (Fig. 1).[53]

[50] James Akena, The Globe and Mail, 'Peacekeepers Gone Wild: How Much More Abuse Will the UN Ignore in Congo?', August 3, 2012, www.theglobeandmail.com/news/politics/second-reading/peacekeepers-gone-wild-how-much-more-abuse-will-the-un-ignore-in-congo/article4462151/.

[51] UN, *supra* note 33.

[52] Ibid.

[53] Ibid.

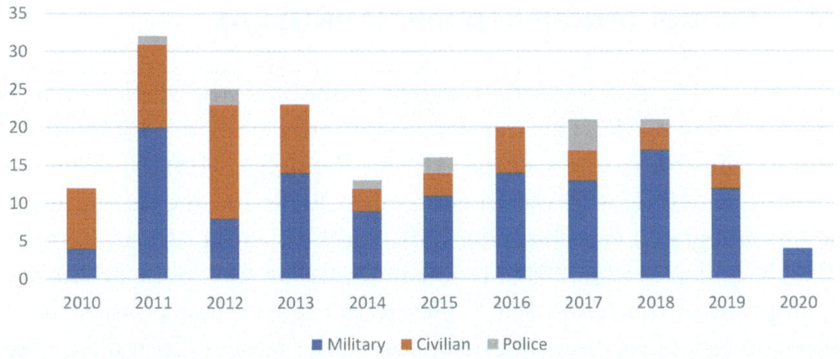

Fig. 2 MONUSCO total allegations per category of personnel (2010–2020) (*Source* United Nations, Conduct in UN field missions. The 2020 data is from January to June)

2.1.2 Monusco

In July 2010, the UN Security Council changed the name of MONUC to MONUSCO in line with developments regarding the implementation of the ceasefire,[54] with the primary mandate to protect civilians.[55] Kovatch has however asserted that the renaming was partly due to MONUC having lost credibility following the 2004 SEA scandal.[56] Despite the renaming of MONUC to MONUSCO, and the earlier interventions by the UN, allegations of SEA by peacekeepers in the DRC continued to surface. In April 2018 for instance, it was reported that a UN military observer had been suspended following allegations that he had fathered a child with an underage girl.[57] Available data on SEA allegations across UN peacekeeping missions highlights that MONUC and MONUSCO collectively have the highest number of SEA allegations compared to other peacekeeping missions (Fig. 2).[58]

---

[54] UN Security Council, *Resolution on Extension of the Mandate of the UN Organisation Mission in the Democratic Republic of the Congo* (MONUC), (2010).

[55] Ibid., paragraph 12(a).

[56] Kovatch, *supra* note 31, 158.

[57] BBC News, DR Congo: UN Peacekeepers Face Fresh Abuse Sex Claims, April 28, 2017, https://www.bbc.com/news/world-africa-39745357.

[58] UN, *supra* note 33.

2.2 Central African Republic (MINUSCA)

In April 2014, the Security Council authorised the deployment of MINUSCA to CAR. The transfer of authority from the International Support Mission to the Central African Republic (MISCA) (deployed in 2013) to MINUSCA was in September 2014; and the subsuming of the UN Integrated Peacebuilding Office in the Central African Republic (BINUCA, deployed in 2010) by the new mission took place on the date of adoption of the resolution.[59] Genovese explains that political instability and lack of socio-economic opportunities has left Central Africans, particularly women and children, vulnerable to SEA.[60] Consequently, women and children have had to trade their bodies for money, food, water and other basic needs.[61]

Between May and June 2014, a human rights officer and local UN staff uncovered allegations that foreign peacekeepers had allegedly abused young children in the M'Poko camp for the internally displaced in Bangui.[62] Most of the alleged perpetrators were from the French peacekeeping force, the Sangaris forces.[63] In one of six interviews conducted by the human rights officer with boys aged between eight or nine and 13, a nine-year old described what allegedly happened to him and his friend, also aged nine at the hands of two soldiers from the Sangaris forces as follows:

> They asked us what we wanted. We answered that we were hungry. The short man told me to suck his bangala (penis). I was afraid but because I was hungry, I accepted, and I entered first into the shack. My friend

---

[59] UN Security Council, *Resolution on Establishment of the UN Multidimensional Integrated Stabilisation Mission in the Central African Republic* (MINUSCA) until April 30, 2015 (2014).

[60] Sophia Genovese, 'Prosecuting UN Peacekeepers for Sexual and Gender-Based Violence in the Central African Republic' 43(2) *Brooklyn Journal of International Law* (2018): 617.

[61] Ibid.

[62] Marie Deschamps, Hassan Jallow and Yasmin Sooka, 'Taking Action on Sexual Exploitation and Abuse by Peacekeepers: Report of an Independent Review on Sexual Exploitation and Abuse by Peacekeeping Forces in the Central African Republic', December 17, 2015, https://rinj.org/documents/un/Justice-Marie-Deschamps-Independent-Review-Report.pdf, 17–20.

[63] Ibid., 19.

> followed me…At the end they gave us 3 packs of 'rasquette' (military food ration) and some cash.[64]

In 2015, four girls reported that in 2014 a French military commander had forced them into having sex with a dog, and that they had been given nine dollars in exchange for the act of bestiality.[65] Commenting on the vulnerability of women and children which leads them to perform sexual acts in exchange for money or services Genovese asserted that:

> …[t]he 'choice' to sell one's body, especially in conflict zones, is often a choice made in the absence of other viable options for survival. The coercive nature of these transactions, strictly within the context of war, conflict, and peacekeeping, cannot be seen as a meaningful one. Furthermore, transactional sex and/or survival sex can never be seen as consensual when a child is involved.[66]

In January 2016 the UN reported that MINUSCA had received allegations of sexual abuse against minors perpetrated by ten peacekeepers from Bangladesh, DRC, Morocco, Niger and Senegal.[67] In February 2016 the UN said it had identified seven new minor victims of sexual abuse in Bambari by peacekeepers from the DRC and the Republic of Congo.[68] Further, in October 2017 the UN reported that MINUSCA had received a report that UN peacekeepers had sexually abused a minor in Bambari.[69] The graph below gives an overview of SEA allegations

---

64 Ibid.

65 Samuel Oakford, 'French Peacekeepers Allegedly Tied Up Girls and Forced Them into Bestiality', *Vice News*, March 31, 2016, https://news.vice.com/article/french-peacekeepers-allegedly-tied-up-girls-and-forced-them-to-have-sex-with-dogs; Genovese, *supra* note 60, 618.

66 Genovese, *supra* note 60, 618.

67 UN News, 'UN Officials Name Countries Whose Troops Are Accused of Sexually Abusing Minors in Central African Republic', January 29, 2016, https://news.un.org/en/story/2016/01/521142-un-officials-name-countries-whose-troops-are-accused-sexually-abusing-minors.

68 UN News, 'New Allegations of Sexual Abuse Emerge Against UN Peacekeepers in Central African Republic', February 4, 2016, https://news.un.org/en/story/2016/02/521562-news-allegations-sexual-abuse-emerge-against-un-peacekeepers-central-african.

69 UN, 'New Allegation of Sexual Abuse Surfaces at UN Mission in CAR', October 11, 2017, https://peacekeeping.un.org/en/new-allegation-of-sexual-abuse-surfaces-un-mission.

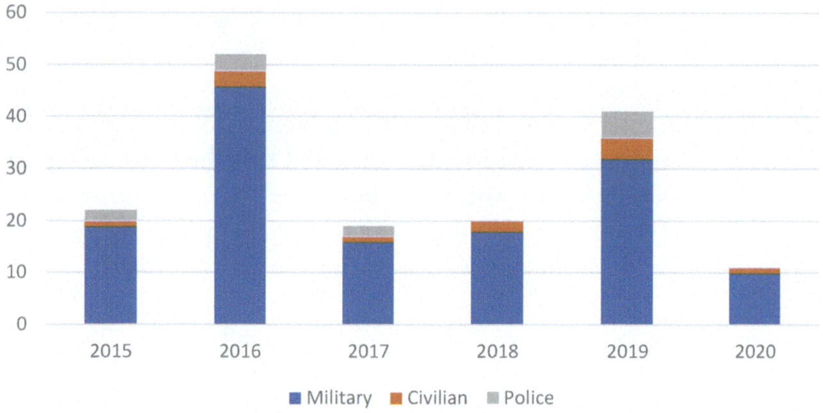

Fig. 3 MINUSCA total allegations per category of personnel (2015–2020) (*Source* United Nations, Conduct in UN Field Missions. The 2020 data is from January to June)

against MINUSCA peacekeepers.[70] The number of recorded SEA allegations against MINUSCA peacekeepers between 2015 and 2020 surpass those of MONUSCO peacekeepers between the same period (Fig. 3).

3 Accountability Mechanism for United Nations Peacekeepers

The above discussion on the scale of SEA by peacekeepers in the DRC and CAR has highlighted that there is a culture of impunity amongst peacekeepers, particularly military peacekeepers. This culture of impunity has largely been attributed to the framework of immunities and jurisdictional bars which regulates the accountability of UN peacekeepers for acts of misconduct.[71] Peacekeeping can be divided into two main categories: military, and civilian personnel.[72] As explained by Freedman, police peacekeepers can be classified as troops, civilians or

70 UN, *supra* note 33.

71 See for example Freedman, *supra* note 10, 966; Lilly, *supra* note 10, 8–9.

72 Freedman, *supra* note 10, 965.

experts,[73] and as such, the focus of this article is on accountability for military and civilian peacekeepers. This is notwithstanding that statistics for SEA allegations against police personnel were included in the above section to give a clearer picture of the situation in DRC and CAR.

3.1 Civilian Personnel

Civilian peacekeepers enjoy immunity from domestic laws and jurisdiction of the courts of host states,[74] as an extension of the immunity enjoyed by the UN by virtue of its status as a legal person.[75] High ranking staff including the Secretary-General and heads of agencies enjoy personal immunity which is absolute and applies regardless of whether the act in question was committed during the course of the official performing official duties.[76] All other civilian staff enjoy functional immunity which applies only in respect of acts committed as part of the official functions of the individual in question.[77] It has been asserted that this immunity, and the jurisdictional bars relating to peacekeeping troops, significantly contributes to the culture of impunity by peacekeepers.[78]

With respect to civilian peacekeepers, the UN is often reluctant to waive their immunity to pave way for investigations and possibly prosecution by the host state.[79] A prime example is when the UN barred a human rights officer from participating in a French investigation into allegations of SEA against minors by the Sangaris forces, on the basis of immunity.[80] This was notwithstanding that the human rights officer was

[73] Freedman, *supra* note 10, 965.

[74] Freedman, *supra* note 10, 966; Lilly, *supra* note 10, 8.

[75] Lilly, *supra* note 10, 2.

[76] Freedman, *supra* note 10, 966. For a detailed overview of the principle of immunities see Christopher Gevers and Patrick Vrancken, 'Jurisdiction of States', in *International Law*, edited by Hennie Strydom (2016): 234–265.

[77] Freedman, *supra* note 10, 966.

[78] See for example Freedman, *supra* note 10, 969, Lilly, *supra* note 10, 4, Van Leeuwen, *supra* note 12, 140–142. Zeid Report, *supra* note 29, paragraph 6 also noted that the jurisdictional bars make it difficult to ensure legal accountability.

[79] Freedman, *supra* note 10, 969.

[80] Genovese, *supra* note 60, 629; Deschamps and others, *supra* note 62.

privy to vital information which would be useful to the investigation. The UN only waived the immunity of the human rights officer after a year.[81] Although the immunity of the UN does not extend to military peacekeepers, the jurisdictional bars in bilateral agreements arguably lead to the peacekeepers enjoying absolute immunity. Accordingly, host states cannot investigate or prosecute peacekeepers regardless of whether or not the crimes they are accused of were committed as part of their official functions.[82]

3.2 Military Peacekeepers

The UN does not directly employ military peacekeepers,[83] but it enters into bilateral agreements in the form of MOUs and SOFAs with TCCs, which outline that the TCC retains jurisdiction over its troops for any acts of misconduct in the course of peacekeeping operations.[84] The 2011 Model MOU outlines issues of jurisdiction over peacekeeping forces,[85] and the 1990 Model SOFA provides that the TCCs retain exclusive jurisdiction over military peacekeepers.[86] As explained by Van Leeuwen, these bilateral agreements are standard and apply to all criminal offences.[87] The jurisdictional bars have their basis on the principle of state sovereignty, as states are reluctant to completely renounce jurisdiction over their troops.[88] The MOUs and SOFAs are therefore, according

[81] Genovese, *supra* note 60, 629; Deschamps and others, *supra* note 62, vi.

[82] Freedman, *supra* note 10, 969; Van Leeuwen, *supra* note 12, 141.

[83] Freedman, *supra* note 10, 968.

[84] Freedman, *supra* note 10, 972, Lilly, *supra* note 10, 8.

[85] Model Memorandum of Understanding in Manual on Policies and Procedures Concerning the Reimbursement and Control of Contingent-Owned Equipment of Troop/ Police Contributors Participating in Peacekeeping Missions (2011); Freedman, *supra* note 10, 968.

[86] See clause 47(b) of the Model Status of Forces Agreement for Peacekeeping Operations: Report of the Secretary-General UN Doc A/45/594 (9 /10/1990); Freedman, *supra* note 10, 968; Van Leeuwen, *supra* note 12, 140.

[87] Van Leeuwen, *supra* note 12, 141.

[88] Lilly, *supra* note 10, 9. For a detailed overview of the principle of state sovereignty see generally, Bardo Fassbender, 'Sovereignty and Constitutionalism in International Law' in Nel Walker (ed) *Sovereignty in Transition* (2003).

Table 1 Action taken against military peacekeepers by TCCs

Mission	Substantiated allegation(**s**)	Nationality	Victim	Date of incidence	Final action by TCC
MONUSCO	Sexual assault (1)	South Africa	Child	October 2015	Demotion in rank
MONUSCO	Sexual activity with a minor (2)	Benin	Child	May–October 2014	45 days imprisonment
MONUSCO	Sexual assault (1)	Morocco	Adult	October 2014	40 days imprisonment
MINUSCA	Rape (1)	Bangladesh	Child	November 2015	- Dismissal - 1-year imprisonment
MINUSCA	Rape (2)	Morocco	Child	Unspecified/2014–2015	1-year imprisonment

Source United Nations, UN Conduct in Field Missions

to Lilly, a necessary balancing act which serves as an incentive for TCCs to contribute their troops.[89]

Peacekeepers who are accused of SEA are rarely investigated and prosecuted by their home states. This has been attributed mainly to political considerations that prosecuting peacekeepers could lead to a wane in support for peacekeeping operations.[90] The absence of a legislative framework to prosecute sexual violence and exploitation crimes committed extraterritorially also contributes to such non-investigation and non-prosecution.[91] Where troops have been prosecuted by their home states, the sentences have often been lenient, as highlighted by the examples in the Table 1.

The UN acknowledges that there is a culture of impunity and refers to its efforts to end SEA as 'unyielding',[92] but it does not have the power to ensure legal accountability because of jurisdictional bars in bilateral agreements.[93] This is exacerbated by the fact that TCCs are reluctant

[89] Lilly, *supra* note 10, 9.

[90] Freedman, *supra* note 10, 973–974.

[91] Freedman, *supra* note 10, 973–974.

[92] Lilly, *supra* note 10, 10; United Nations Peacekeeping, quarterly update May 30, 2019.

[93] Lilly, *supra* note 10, 14.

to act upon assurances made in bilateral agreements to prosecute military peacekeepers for acts of misconduct.[94] The UN has two codes of conduct for its peacekeeping personnel. Rule 4 of the 'Ten Rules: Code of Personal Conduct for Blue Helmets',[95] states as follows: 'Do not indulge in immoral acts of sexual, physical or psychological abuse or exploitation of the local population or United Nations staff, especially women and children'.[96] The 'We are United Nations Peacekeepers' Code of Conduct contains a similar provision in article 3.[97] Field-based peacekeeping personnel has since 1998 been issued with pocket cards of the 'Ten Rules',[98] and from 2018 field personnel are issued with the 'no-excuses' card outlining the zero-tolerance policy.[99] These codes of conduct are however not legally binding on military peacekeepers and serve as mere guidelines as the UN has no jurisdiction over them.[100] The only action that the UN can take is to repatriate the accused peacekeeper(s) and to provide the TCC with evidence.[101] It is asserted that in view of the culture of impunity as highlighted above and the failure by TCCs to prosecute alleged offenders, it is time for the UN to review the accountability framework particularly the immunity provisions in the MOUs and SOFAs.

4 Measures Taken by the UN to Curb SEA: Towards a Victim-Centred Approach?

In response to the SEA allegations against MONUC peacekeepers in 2004, the then UN assistant Secretary-General for peacekeeping, Jane Holl Lute, said that '[t]he blue helmet has become black and blue

94 Ndulo, *supra* note 12, 154–155.

95 UN, *supra* note 33; Genovese, *supra* note 60, 626.

96 United Nations, 'Ten Rules', Rule 4.

97 http://www.un.org/en/peacekeeping/documents/un_in.pdf, May 28, 2020; Genovese, *supra* note 60, 627.

98 UN, *supra* note 33.

99 UN, *supra* note 33; Van Leeuwen, *supra* note 12, 139.

100 Genovese, *supra* note 60, 626.

101 Lilly, *supra* note 10, 19, Genovese, *supra* note 60, 627.

through self-inflicted wounds. We will not sit still until the lustre of that blue helmet is restored'.[102] True to Lute's words, the UN has taken a number of measures to curb SEA by its peacekeepers.

Since 2004, the successive Secretaries-General have published a yearly comprehensive report on SEA allegations throughout UN peacekeeping missions, and in 2007 the UN began to keep records of SEA allegations.[103] This made it easier in terms of assessing the scale of the problem, notwithstanding that the data cannot be said to be truly reflective of the scale of the problem. This is because of underreporting due to several factors including fear of stigmatisation.[104] The measures implemented by the UN can be divided into two broad categories, accountability, and remedial measures and these are discussed in turn below.

4.1 Legal Accountability Measures

As discussed above, the available data on SEA by UN peacekeepers points to a culture of impunity, and this has been attributed to gaps in the UN's accountability framework. Where allegations of SEA against civilian peacekeepers or experts on mission have been substantiated, the UN's policy is to refer the matter to the accused's country of nationality, through the Office of Legal Affairs.[105] The Secretary-General has called for member states to evaluate the applicability of their domestic legislative instruments to sex crimes committed by UN peacekeepers; and to update these laws to allow for active personality jurisdiction.[106] Whilst in theory this is a plausible policy for accountability, there is a worrying trend with respect to the referral of substantiated sexual abuse allegations against civilian personnel for criminal accountability.

Between 2015 and 2020 MINUSCA had no substantiated sexual abuse allegations, but it had one substantiated allegation of transactional

[102] Fleshman, *supra* note 48.

[103] UN, *supra* note 33.

[104] Van Leeuwen, *supra* note 12, 138–139.

[105] UN, *supra* note 33.

[106] Ibid.

sex and one of solicitation of transactional sex with adult victims.[107] MONUSCO had five substantiated allegations of sexual abuse, and one of solicitation of transactional sex where the victim was an adult.[108] According to available data, the UN does not refer allegations of transactional sex where the victim is an adult for criminal accountability.[109] This can be attributed to the distinction that ought to be drawn with respect to adults who willingly participate in transactional sex with peacekeepers.[110] It is however a cause for concern that referral for criminal accountability for a substantiated allegation of rape of a child reported in November 2017, and sexual activity with a minor reported in July 2015 is still pending,[111] whilst one allegation each of sexual activity with a minor and sexual assault on a child reported in September 2015 have been referred for criminal accountability.[112] Justice delayed is justice denied, and the delay by the UN in referring substantiated sexual abuse allegations for criminal accountability arguably amounts to undermining the gravity of the crimes. The Security Council acknowledged this in its Resolution on Women and Peace and Security: Sexual Violence in Conflict where it reiterated that, '… inaction and impunity for sexual violence crimes in conflict and post-conflict situation can send a message that the incidence of such crimes is tolerated'.[113] The UN should expeditiously refer substantiated sexual abuse allegations for criminal accountability for its response to SEA to be deemed to be commensurate with the scale of the problem. In the General Assembly Resolution on 'United Nations Actions on Sexual Exploitation and Abuse', the General Assembly requested the Secretary-General and all the relevant entities to immediately inform member states of allegations of SEA both by UN personnel system and non-UN personnel who serve under a mandate of

---

[107] Ibid.

[108] Ibid.

[109] Ibid.

[110] Ndulo, *supra* note 12, 143.

[111] UN, *supra* note 33.

[112] Ibid.

[113] UN Security Council, *Resolution Women and Peace and security: Sexual Violence in Conflict* (2019), Preamble, paragraph 15.

the Security Council.[114] If the UN could act upon this request by the General Assembly, this would go a long way in ensuring accountability for SEA.

With respect to military personnel, because of jurisdictional bars in MOUs and SOFAs with TCCs, the UN is extremely limited in terms of the measures it can take to ensure criminal accountability. As explained above, the TCCs retain exclusive prosecutorial jurisdiction over military personnel, and the UN can only repatriate the accused troops and bar them from future peacekeeping missions. Cognisant of this limitation, the UN has taken measures to try and force TCCs to prosecute troops accused of SEA. In the 2016 annual report on SEA, the then Secretary-General Ban Ki-Moon publicly revealed for the first time the nationalities of troops accused of SEA.[115] In March 2016, the Security Council authorised the Secretary-General, through Resolution 2272 (2016), to repatriate entire peacekeeping contingents where there is evidence of widespread and systemic SEA.[116] Where member states have shown reluctance to bring their peacekeepers to account, such countries can be barred from providing peacekeeping troops in future.[117] Lily[118] and Genovese[119] have suggested that in such circumstances the UN should cut its losses and refrain from dealing with such members states in future missions.

These measures, though they cannot guarantee that action will be taken by the TCCs, can be an effective way of ensuring accountability when one considers the economic and political dynamics involved in member states contributing troops for peacekeeping. As explained by Freedman, for many TCCs, contributing troops is associated with status and significant financial gain.[120] TCCs could therefore be forced into

114 General Assembly *Resolution United Nations Action on Sexual Exploitation and Abuse* (2017), paragraph 12.

115 Report of the Secretary-General 'Special Measures for Protection from Sexual Exploitation and Sexual Abuse' (February 16, 2016), paragraph 28.

116 *Resolution on Sexual Exploitation and Abuse by United Nations Peacekeepers* 2276 (2016), paragraph 1.

117 Ibid., paragraph 2 and 3.

118 Lilly, *supra* note 10, 21.

119 Genovese, *supra* note 60, 636.

120 Freedman, *supra* note 10, 973.

taking action for fear of being barred from future peacekeeping missions and therefore losing out on the financial gains and status. In view of the gravity of the SEA crimes, however, the UN ought to do more than just try to force TCCs to prosecute accused peacekeepers. Many scholars have made recommendations in this regard. Burke has proposed amending the SOFAs to provide civilian peacekeepers with only functional immunity as opposed to absolute immunity, and to provide for concurrent jurisdiction for military peacekeepers as is the case with the NATO agreement.[121] Lilly has recommended the establishment of an independent court mechanism in host countries to deal with SEA allegations.[122]

As observed by Van Leeuwen however, UN member states are unlikely to consent to the amendment of MOUs and SOFAs to provide for concurrent jurisdiction because of concerns over the human rights standards in some countries where peacekeepers operate.[123] Genovese has asserted that states are unlikely to sign agreements which have the effect of limiting their sovereignty.[124] Lily has argued in this vein that it would be more feasible to remodel the MOUs and SOFAs to ensure accountability whilst allowing the UN to maintain its immunity; and for TCCs to retain exclusive jurisdiction over their troops.[125] The Zeid Report suggested that obtaining formal assurances that TCCs will prosecute peacekeepers and the inclusion in MOUs of a clause requiring TCCs to report on action taken should be a precondition for the acceptance of an offer by member states to contribute troops to the UN.[126] The Secretary-General has called for the setting up of on-site court martial proceedings by TCCs to ensure the effectiveness of investigations, as called for by the Secretary-General.[127] This is arguably the most practical solution as it would not only ensure accountability but it will also

---

121 Burke, *supra* note 12, 116; See also Van Leeuwen, *supra* note 12, 144.

122 Lilly, *supra* note 10, 21.

123 Van Leeuwen, *supra* note 12, 144. For a similar view see Marco Odello and Roisin Burke, 'Between Immunity and Impunity: Peacekeeping and Sexual Abuses and Violence' 20 *The International Journal of Human Rights* (2016): 846–847.

124 Genovese, *supra* note 60, 636.

125 Lilly, *supra* note 10, 20.

126 Zeid Report, *supra* note 29, 6.

127 UN, *supra* note 33.

address the contentious issue of TCCs being reluctant to let host states exercise jurisdiction over their troops due to sovereignty concerns. It is recommended that the UN should take this a step further and make it mandatory for TCCs to set up the on-site court martial proceedings as a precondition to the deployment of peacekeepers.

From the above discussion it is clear that the root cause of impunity with respect to SEA by peacekeepers is the immunity granted to the peacekeepers. The effective eradication of the problem of SEA by peacekeepers is therefore dependent upon a review of the immunity provisions in the MOUs and SOFAs, to ensure that the peacekeepers are held accountable. Although all the above recommendations are commendable, they do fall short of addressing the root cause of SEA which is immunity of peacekeepers.

The UN acknowledges that accountability for SEA is of paramount importance. In his 2016 report on measures to prevent SEA, the Secretary-General stated the following:

> Transparency and accountability are the critical means through which the UN and its member states can demonstrate their collective commitment to the Secretary-General's zero-tolerance policy, retain trust of the international community and provide justice for victims.[128]

Lilly comments on the following on the importance of punishing perpetrators of SEA:

> If survivors are prohibited from seeking compensation from the organisation that has placed perpetrators in their communities, and failed to thoroughly investigate and pursue prosecution, the organisation must ensure adequate avenues of redress to punish perpetrators and ensure justice is served.[129]

It is hoped that the UN will continue to explore ways of ensuring accountability as this is arguably the key to eradicating impunity with respect to SEA by peacekeepers.

---

[128] Secretary-General's Report, *supra* note 114, paragraph 37.

[129] Lilly, *supra* note 10 21.

4.2 Remedial Measures

In addition to measures to ensure accountability, the UN has implemented remedial measures which seek to provide support and assistance to the victims, and to acknowledge their pain and suffering. In the yearly Secretary-General reports since 2004, the recurrent theme was exploring how to support victims of SEA.[130] Although in 2007 the General Assembly adopted the Resolution on Comprehensive Strategy on Assistance and Support to Victims of SEA by UN Staff and Associated Personnel (Comprehensive Strategy),[131] tangible frameworks to assist victims were not adopted until 2016.[132] In 2019, the Security Council recognised through the Resolution on Women, Peace and Security: Sexual Violence in Conflict, the need for a survivor centred approach and urged member States to adopt this approach in preventing and responding to SEA.[133] The question to be asked is whether the remedial measures implemented can be said to be comprehensive, effective and commensurate with the scale of the problem.

4.2.1 Trust Fund for Victims and Paternity Claims

Since July 2015 the UN has suspended payments of peacekeepers accused of SEA.[134] In March 2016, the Secretary-General established the Trust Fund in Support of Victims of SEA (Trust Fund).[135] The aims of the Trust Fund include engaging in community outreach and providing assistance and support to complainants, victims and children born as a result of SEA in line with the Comprehensive Strategy. However, it does not provide compensation to victims and complainants.[136] It is financed

---

[130] Van Leeuwen, *supra* note 12, 144–145.

[131] General Assembly Resolution *Comprehensive Strategy on Assistance and Support to Victims of Sexual Exploitation and Abuse by UN Staff and Associated Personnel* (2008).

[132] Van Leeuwen, *supra* note 12, 144.

[133] UN Security Council *Resolution on Women and Peace and Security: Sexual Violence in Conflict* (2019), paragraph 16.

[134] UN, *supra* note 33.

[135] Ibid.

[136] Ibid.

by voluntary contributions from member states, and from payments withheld from peacekeepers accused of SEA, where such allegations have been substantiated.[137]

To date, the Trust Fund has financed projects in the DRC, CAR and Liberia. In DRC, between February and December 2018, MONUSCO, in collaboration with a local organisation 'Sikuya Mazingira', (SYAM) launched three programmes for the benefit of Bujovu, Muningi, Kavumu and Sake communities.[138] There were 441 participants in total.[139] The programmes provided scholarships to 52 children, and 329 community members learned income-generating skills and became self-sustainable. SYAM supported SEA awareness programmes aimed at ensuring safe reporting of allegations. The Trust Fund provided USD 264,703 for these projects.[140] In CAR, MINUSCA identified the International Rescue Committee (IRC) to launch a country wide programme for victims of SEA.[141] IRC included SEA in its sexual and gender-based violence awareness initiative and by 2019 the programme had 2873 participants.[142] It had also approached the Protection from SEA network in the second quarter of 2019 to offer the organisation's services to victims of SEA by UN peacekeepers.[143] This programme was however completed in 2019. Another significant milestone in CAR was that during the last quarter of 2018 the Trust Fund of the Review Committee authorised a project to be established by the American Bar Association, Rule of Law Initiative, to provide legal assistance to victims of SEA where paternity is alleged and child care support required.[144]

In Liberia the Trust Fund Review Committee (Review Committee) approved an Adult Literacy Programme in 2018.[145] The aim of the

---

137 Ibid.

138 'Trust Fund in Support of Victims of Sexual Exploitation and Abuse' (UN Conduct in Field Missions) (2017–2018), 5.

139 Ibid.

140 2017–2018 Report, *supra* note 138, 6.

141 2017–2018 Report, *supra* note 138, 5.

142 Trust Fund in Support of Victims of Sexual Exploitation and Abuse (UN Conduct in Field Missions) (2019 update), 2.

143 Ibid.

144 Ibid.

145 2017–2018 Report, *supra* note 138, 5.

Literacy programme was to support education and vocational training for victims in order to promote awareness and prevention of SEA.[146] The project was implemented by the UN Educational, Scientific and Cultural Organisation (UNESCO) and the National Adult Education Association of Liberia to benefit eight communities of the Montserrado County; and it was projected to be completed in the first quarter of 2020.[147] In May 2019, the Review Committee approved proposals for six projects in the Beni, Bunia, Kalembe, Kisangani, Mwenga and Uvira in the DRC.[148] It is commendable that the Trust Fund has financed tangible projects aimed at assisting victims. However, the number of victims assisted still falls far short of the scale at which SEA is taking place. Although the problem is more widespread in DRC and CAR, these are not the only countries where communities already affected by conflict must live with the trauma and stigmatisation because of SEA by UN peacekeepers. It is noteworthy that a literacy programme has been launched in Libera, but there is need for a more holistic approach which would see the Trust Fund being used to implement projects in other countries such as Haiti. The 2019 Trust Fund update indicated that a proposal for an income-generating programme from South Sudan was under review,[149] and it is hoped that the Review Committee will approve of this project.

It is acknowledged that the Trust Fund relies on donations from member states and hence the availability of financial resources is a factor which constrains the UN in terms of what projects can be implemented with support from the Trust Fund. Hence, in order for the Trust Fund to benefit more victims and therefore become an effective and comprehensive strategy to deal with SEA, member states ought to show political will and donate more money. This would be in line with the member states' stated commitment to effectively deal with the problem of SEA as demonstrated by the Voluntary Compact on

[146] Ibid.

[147] 2019 Update, *supra* note 142, 2.

[148] Ibid.

[149] Ibid.

Preventing and Addressing SEA which was proposed by the Secretary-General in 2017.[150] As of September 2019, the Voluntary Compact had been signed by 103-member states.[151]

In particular, more needs to be done to address the problematic issue of children born as a result of SEA. As observed by Ndulo, the problem of peacekeepers fathering babies and abandoning them is widespread.[152] The situation is complicated by the fact that often the mothers of the children do not have enough details to trace the alleged fathers thereby making it difficult to establish paternity.[153] The Secretary-General has called upon TCCs to consent to the obtaining of DNA samples for troops accused of SEA to ensure accountability.[154] Although a DNA collection protocol was established in 2014, DNA can samples can only be collected where the domestic legislation of the TCC provides for recourse to DNA samples to determine paternity.[155] If the Trust fund could support more initiatives to deal with the issue of paternity claims, this could be an effective solution to the problematic issue.

4.2.2 Victims' Rights Advocate

The current Secretary-General indicated in his first annual report on SEA in 2017 that he was committed to 'a new approach' towards the problem of SEA.[156] Many recommendations were made in the report, key of which were the appointment of a Victims' Rights Advocate (VRA),[157] and the authorisation of withholding of payments by member states where TCCs do not expeditiously initiate or finalise SEA investigations.[158] The recommendation to withhold payments has not been

---

150 https://un.org/preventing-sexual-exploitation-and-abuse/content/voluntary-compact.

151 Ibid.

152 Ndulo, *supra* note 12, 157–158.

153 Ndulo, *supra* note 12, 158.

154 UN, *supra* note 33.

155 UN, *supra* note 33.

156 Report of the Secretary-General on Special Measures for protection from sexual exploitation and sexual abuse (2017).

157 Secretary-General (2017), *supra* note 156, paragraphs 27–33.

158 Secretary-General (2017), *supra* note 156, paragraph 34.

implemented, but in August 2017 the Secretary-General appointed the first VRA, Jane Connors.[159] The role of the VRA is to work alongside victims of SEA to serve their interests and to acknowledge their pain and suffering.[160] In the 2018 report on SEA, the Secretary-General indicated that the VRA had worked to ensure improved collaboration between the UN and national authorities to improve investigations into paternity claims emanating from SEA allegations.[161] In Haiti, the VRA worked towards fostering greater cooperation among UN entities dealing with SEA, and in South Sudan the VRA worked to ensure timely provision of legal, medical and psychological support.[162] The VRA is an effective mechanism which acknowledges that at the centre of the problem of SEA is the victim. Van Leeuwen convincingly said in this regard that:

> … the VRA is a mechanism that can be seen to provide a sense of moral vindication for the victim, providing for their interests and cathartically acknowledging that some wrong has been done for which support must now be given.[163]

5 Concluding Remarks

This chapter has provided a detailed overview of the scale of SEA by peacekeepers in DRC and CAR and asserted that the available data points to a culture of impunity on the part of UN peacekeepers, particularly the military peacekeepers. The chapter has highlighted how the immunities and privileges framework for the UN, and the MOUs and SOFAs by which TCCs retain prosecutorial jurisdiction over military peacekeepers, significantly contribute to the culture of impunity. The measures implemented by the UN to force TCCs to ensure legal

[159] Van Leeuwen, *supra* note 12, 145.

[160] Van Leeuwen, *supra* note 12, 146; Terms of Reference, Victims' Rights Advocate.

[161] Special measures for protection from exploitation and abuse (February 15, 2018), U.N Doc A/72/751, paragraph 29.

[162] Ibid.

[163] Van Leeuwen, *supra* note 12, 146.

accountability, and remedial measures implemented to assist victims and acknowledge their pain and suffering have also been assessed. The UN ought to be commended for adopting a paradigm of accountability which goes beyond state sovereignty and the bilateral agreements between the UN and TCCs. The UN further acknowledges that the victim is at the centre of the SEA problem.

Nevertheless, for the victim-centered approach to be effective and comprehensive, there is need for the UN to widen the scale of the programmes intended to empower the victims and vulnerable communities affected by conflict in general. This would go a long way towards ensuring that vulnerable women and girls do not look at prostituting themselves to peacekeepers and having babies with peacekeepers as a survival strategy. With respect to legal accountability, it is commendable that the UN has taken concrete steps in a bid to force TCCs into taking steps to ensure accountability. However, at the heart of the accountability problem lies the MOUs and SOFAs, and this is what must be addressed to ensure accountability. From the above discussion it is clear that the root cause of impunity with respect to SEA by peacekeepers is the immunity granted to the peacekeepers. The effective eradication of the problem of SEA by peacekeepers is therefore dependent upon a review of the immunity provisions in the MOUs and SOFAs. This is to ensure that the peacekeepers are held accountable. Due to the gravity of the crimes of SEA, the implementation of remedial measures which are victim centred can only be said to be effective, comprehensive and commensurate with the scale of the problem when accompanied by an effective framework of legal accountability.

References

BBC News, 2017, DR Congo: UN Peacekeepers Face Fresh Abuse Sex Claims, https://www.bbc.com/news/world-africa-39745357.

Boesten Jelke, 2017, 'Of Exceptions and Continuities: Theory and Methodology in Research on Conflict-Related Sexual Violence' 19(4) *International Journal of Politics*.

Burke Roisin, 2016, 'Central African Republic Peacekeeper Sexual Crimes, Institutional Failings: Addressing the Accountability Gap' 14 *New Zealand Journal of Public and International Law.*

Christopher Gevers and Patrick Vrancken, 2016, 'Jurisdiction of States', in *International Law,* edited by Hennie Strydom.

Deen-Racsmany Zsuzsanna, 2014, 'Exclusive Criminal Jurisdiction over UN Peacekeepers and the UN Project(s) on Criminal Accountability: A Self-Fulfilling Prophecy?' 53(2) *Military Law and Law of War Review.*

Emily Wax, 2005, Congo's Desperate 'One Dollar UN Girls,' *Washington Post,* https://washingtonpost.com/archive/politics/2005/03/21/congos-desperate-one-dollar-un-girls/26b5e610-d9ed-42e1-909a-03b2e061377d/.

Fassbender Bardo, 2003, 'Sovereignty and Constitutionalism in International Law', in *Sovereignty in Transition,* edited by Nel Walker.

Fleshman Michael, 2005, 'Tough UN Line on Peacekeeper Abuses: Action Initiated to End Sexual Misdeeds in Peacekeeping Missions', *Africa Renewal,* www.un.org/africarenewal/magazine/april-2005/tough-un-line-peacekeeper-abuse.

Francesca Lilly, 2020, 'Peacekeepers or Perpetrators? UN Accountability in the Face of International Immunities' 7 *UNSW Law Journal Student Series.*

Gloria Gaggioli, 2015, 'Sexual Violence in Armed Conflicts: A Violation of International Humanitarian Law and Human Rights Law' 96(894) *International Review of the Red Cross,* http://doi.org/10.1017/S1816383115000211.

Jayden van Leeuwen, 2019, 'Addressing the Gap: Accountability Mechanisms for Peacekeepers Accused of Exploitation and Abuse' 50 *Victoria University of Wellington Law Review.*

Kovatch Bonnie, 2016, 'Sexual Exploitation and Abuse in UN Peacekeeping Missions: A Case Study of MONUC and MONUSCO' 7(2) *The Journal of the Middle East and Africa.*

Marie Deschamps, Hassan Jallow and Yasmin Sooka, December 17, 2005 'Taking Action on Sexual Exploitation and Abuse by Peacekeepers: Report of an Independent Review on Sexual Exploitation and Abuse by Peacekeeping Forces in the Central African Republic', https://rinj.org/documents/un/Justice-Marie-Deschamps-Independent-Review-Report.pdf.

Ndulo Muna, 2009, 'The United Nations Response to the Sexual Abuse and Exploitation of Women and Girls by Peacekeepers During Peacekeeping Missions' 27(1) *Berkeley Journal of International Law.*

Odello Marco and Roisin Burke, 2016, 'Between Immunity and Impunity: Peacekeeping and Sexual Abuses and Violence' 20 *The International Journal of Human Rights*.

Prosecutor v Dragolijub Kunarac and Others, IT-96-238 23/1(Appeals Chamber), June 12, 2002.

Prosecutor v Jean-Paul Akayesu, ICTR-96-4 (Trial Chamber) Judgment, (September 2, 1998).

Rome Statute of the International Criminal Court (1998).

Rosa Freedman, 2018, 'Unaccountable: A New Approach to Peacekeepers and Sexual Abuse' 29(3) *European Journal of International Law*.

Samuel Oakford Samuel, 2016, 'French Peacekeepers Allegedly Tied Up Girls and Forced Them into Bestiality', https://news.vice.com/article/french-peacekeepers-allegedly-tied-up-girls-and-forced-them-to-have-sex-with-dogs.

Sophia Genovese, 2018, 'Prosecuting UN Peacekeepers for Sexual and Gender-Based Violence in the Central African Republic' 43(2) *Brooklyn Journal of International Law*.

Susan Notar, 2006, 'Peacekeepers as Perpetrators: Sexual Exploitation and Abuse of Women and Children in the Democratic Republic of Congo' 14(2) *Journal of Gender, Social Policy and the Law*.

UN News, 2016, 'New Allegations of Sexual Abuse Emerge Against UN Peacekeepers in Central African Republic', https://news.un.org/en/story/2016/02/521562-news-allegations-sexual-abuse-emerge-against-un-peacekeepers-central-african.

UN News, 2016, 'UN Officials Name Countries Whose Troops Are Accused of Sexually Abusing Minors in Central African Republic', https://news.un.org/en/story/2016/01/521142-un-officials-name-countries-whose-troops-are-accused-sexually-abusing-minors.

UN News, 2017, 'Sexual Violence Is a Threat to Every Individual's Right to a Life of Dignity-UN Chief', https://news.un.org/en/story/2017/06/559822-sexual-violence-threat-every-individuals-right-life-dignity-un-chief.

United Nations Charter (1945).

United Nations Convention on Privileges and Immunities of the United Nations (1946).

United Nations General Assembly Resolution, 2008, *UN Comprehensive Strategy on Assistance and Support to Victims of Sexual Exploitation and Abuse by UN Staff and Associated Personnel*.

United Nations General Assembly Resolution, 2017, *United Nations Action on Sexual Exploitation and Abuse*.

United Nations Security Council Resolution, 1999, *The Situation Concerning the Democratic Republic of the Congo.*

United Nations Security Council Resolution, 2008, *Women and Peace and Security.*

United Nations Security Council Resolution, 2010, *Extension of the Mandate of the UN Organisation Mission in the Democratic Republic of the Congo (MONUC).*

United Nations Security Council Resolution, 2015, *Establishment of the UN Multidimensional Integrated Stabilisation Mission in the Central African Republic (MINUSCA)* until April 30, 2015.

United Nations Security Council Resolution, 2016, *Sexual Exploitation and Abuse by United Nations Peacekeepers.*

United Nations Security Council Resolution, 2019, *Women and Peace and Security: Sexual Violence in Conflict.*

United Nations, 1998, 'Women 2000: Sexual Violence and Armed Conflict: United Nations Response', www.un.org/womenwatch/daw/public/cover.pdf.

United Nations, 2005, 'Peacekeepers' Sexual Abuse of Local Girls Continuing in DRC', https://news.un.org/en/story/2005/01/12532-peacekeepers-sexual-abuse-local-girls-continuing-congo-un-finds.

United Nations, 2017, 'New Allegation of Sexual Abuse Surfaces at UN Mission in CAR', https://peacekeeping.un.org/en/new-allegation-of-sexual-abuse-surfaces-un-mission.

7

Conflict-Related Sexual Violence in the North-East Nigeria: Strengthening Legal Responses

Iyabode Ogunniran

1 Introduction

Jama a Ahl al-sunnah li-da'wa wa al-jihad (otherwise known as Boko Haram) is an Islamic insurgency group globally characterised as a terrorist.[1] Since 2009, it has been ruthless and daring in its operations in the North-East Nigeria states of Borno, Adamawa and Yobe as

[1] The full meaning of Boko Haram is (*Jama a Ahl al-sunnah li-da'wa wa al-jihad*). Boko in Hausa means 'western education' and the Arabic word 'Haram' is sin. Yemi Oke, 'International Criminal Court, Crimes Against Humanity and the Nigerian Boko Haram Islamist Group: Can Two Wrongs Make a Right', *ISIL Year Book of International Humanitarian and Refugee Law* 12 (2012–2013): 157–173.

I. Ogunniran (✉)
Department of Public Law, Faculty of Law, University of Lagos, Lagos, Nigeria
e-mail: iogunniran@unilag.edu.ng

A. Budoo-Scholtz and E. C. Lubaale (eds.), *Violence Against Women and Criminal Justice in Africa: Volume II*, Sustainable Development Goals Series,
https://doi.org/10.1007/978-3-030-75953-7_7

well as neighbouring countries.[2] The intensity of force and its organisational structure has elevated the group to fighting an armed conflict of non-international character.[3] The group engages in conflict-related sexual violence as thousands of women and girls have been abducted and kidnapped from their communities.[4] The abduction of 276 Chibok school girls in 2014 drew international opprobrium and the Bring Back Our Girls Initiative. Though some have been released, as of 2019, 112 are still missing.[5] Several of such women and girls are being held captive in the dens of the group across the North East. The returnees, painfully recounted they were subjected to rape, gang rape and forced pregnancy. Sadly, members of the Nigerian Security Forces were also implicated in these serious violations.[6] Presently, they suffer psycho-social trauma due to their ordeal coupled with facing alienation and stigma of association with the insurgents.[7] In such a deeply cultural communities, their reintegration is a daunting task.

Various United Nations (UN) Security Council (UNSC) Resolutions and General Assembly Resolution mandate states to prosecute and punish perpetrators. UNSC 1325 (2000) obligates state parties 'to put an end to impunity and prosecute those responsible for' crime against humanity, including those relating to sexual violence against women and

[2] Shekau, the leader of the group, in a video openly dared the former US President Barak Obama, Former French President Francois Hollande and Israeli Prime Minister Benjamin Netanyahu to him, saying 'they are no match for me' (Sheaku). Precious Igbonwelundu and Adamu Sulaimon, 'Boko Haram Leader Shekau Dares Obama in Video,' *The Nation*, August 13, 2013; Ibid.

[3] 'Non International Armed Conflict in Nigeria, http://www.rulac.org/browse/conflicts/non-international-armed-conflict-in-nigeria#collapse4accord; Hilary Matfess, 'Boko Haram: History and Context,' *Oxford Research Encyclopaedia of African History* (2017): 1–24, https://oxfordre.com/africanhistory/view/10.1093/acrefore/9780190277734.001.0001/acrefore-9780190277734-e-119?print=pdf.

[4] International Crisis Group, Nigeria: Women and the Boko Haram Insurgency, https://www.crisisgroup.org/africa/west-africa/nigeria/nigeria-women-and-boko-haram-insurgency.

[5] Al Jazeera, Nigeria's Chibok School Girls: Five Years On, 112 Still Missing (2019), https://www.aljazeera.com/news/2019/04/nigeria-chibok-school-girls-years-112-missing-190413192517739.html.

[6] Human Rights Watch, 'Those Terrible Weeks in their Camp' (2014), https://www.hrw.org/report/2014/10/27/those-terrible-weeks-their-camp/boko-haram-violence-against-women-and-girls.

[7] International Crisis Group, *supra* note 4.

girls.[8] Resolution 2467 (2019) calls upon states 'to strengthen legislation and enhance investigation and prosecution of sexual violence in conflict and post conflict situations'; and 'prompt access to justice and reparation for victims'. It encourages survivor-centred approach in preventing and responding to such sexual violence.[9] The country has an obligation to implement these Resolutions.[10] Ultimately, in 2017, the insurgents were charged before a court and prosecuted. It is highly disturbing, as the writer discusses in the paper, that none of them was charged for rape, sexual slavery, forced pregnancy or sexual violence.

Boko Haram is a non-state armed group that commit violence against women and girls are committed during armed conflicts. The Rome Statute of the International Criminal Court (ICC) applies to such crimes. The 2019 Preliminary Activities of the ICC Report on Nigeria identified eight potential cases of crimes against humanity and war crimes, including six by Boko Haram.[11] Nigeria has signed but is yet to domesticate the Rome Statute. Presently, there appears to be no respite for the survivors, whether in terms of legal, economic or social support. It is also horrifying that these violations continue unabated. Human Rights Watch warned that there may not really be an accurate statistic of victims of Boko Haram violence.[12] This writer contends, against the backdrop of these international Resolutions and the country's obligation to domesticate the ICC that, it is urgent to institute a legal framework to prosecute perpetrators. The country took the right step by proposing the Crimes

[8] Paragraph 11, Adopted by the Security Council at its 4213th Meeting on October 31, 2000, https://undocs.org/S/RES/1325(2000); *UN General Assembly Resolution on Basic Principles and Guidelines on the Right to a Remedy and Reparation for Victims* mandates States in cases of serious violations of international humanitarian law constituting crimes under international law to investigate, prosecute and punish perpetrators. Resolution 60/147 of December 16, 2005, https://www.ohchr.org/en/professionalinterest/pages/remedyandreparation.aspx.

[9] Resolution 2467, *Women, Peace and Security: Sexual Violence in Conflict* (2019): Paragraphs 14–16, Adopted by the Security Council at its 8514th Meeting on April 23, 2019, https://undocs.org/S/RES/2467(2019).

[10] Arguably, the WPS Resolutions carry normative weight as certain aspect constitute already legal binding obligations. It reinforces normative standards to access to justice, law reform, protection of victims, witnesses, and remedies. Christine Chinkin and Madeleine Rees, *Commentary on Security Council Resolution 2467*, (2019), 11.

[11] International Criminal Court, *Report on Preliminary Examination Activities 2019*, https://www.icc-cpi.int/itemsDocuments/191205-rep-otp-PE.pdf.

[12] Human Rights Watch, *supra* note 6.

Against Humanity, War Crimes, Genocide and Related Offences Bill in 2012.[13] It is almost eight years and the Bill is yet to be passed by the National Assembly.

Hence, this chapter analyses the Bill to determine its adequacy to prosecute crimes against humanity and the non-international character of the conflict by Boko Haram, drawing comparative interpretation from the Rome Statute and notable judicial decisions. The first part is the introduction. It briefly traces the history of the insurgents and their acts of conflict-related sexual violence in the second part. In the third part, the paper interrogates the trial of the insurgents and contends that despite several documented reports, none was tried for sexual violence. The fourth part assesses Nigeria's status *vis-à-vis* the Rome Statute. The fifth part analyses the crucial provisions of the Bill, identifies gaps and suggests amendments for effective prosecution. It briefly considers other interventions and suggested it must be complemented with socio-economic measures targeted at the root causes of the insurgency and rebuilding the communities. The writer concludes that legal responses is urgently needed to put an end to the impunity.

2 Boko Haram and Conflict-Related Sexual Violence

Boko Haram started as a dissident religious sect that was founded in 2002 by Muhammed Yusuf in Borno State, Nigeria.[14] For about seven years, it launched occasional attacks. However, the first armed confrontations between Boko Haram and the Nigerian Government started in July 2009.[15] Over the years, Boko Haram established control of a significant amount of territory in North-Eastern Nigeria. This area was declared to be a Caliphate and it was used to launch military operations against

[13] https://www.pgaction.org/pdf/CRIMES-AGAINST-HUMANITY-WAR-CRIMES-GENOCIDE-AND-RELATED-OFFENCES-BILL-2012-Nigeria.pdf.

[14] Matfess, *supra* note 3.

[15] Ibid.

targets in Nigeria as well as in neighbouring countries.[16] Today, it has metamorphosed into a lethal and resilient force internationally recognised for its brutality.[17] Globally, Boko Haram is classified as a terrorist group.[18]

The Nigerian government responded to the group and established a Joint Task Force (JTF).[19] This was largely ineffective due to mischaracterisation of insurgency as urban phenomenon, high level of civilian casualties and limited flow of information from the civilian population to the JTF.[20] In 2015, to further whittle down the activities of the insurgent group, the government created the Multinational Joint Task Force (MNJTF) with neighbouring countries.[21] Since then, the attacks conducted by the armed group have changed in nature, relying predominantly 'on guerrilla warfare strategies and suicide bombings'.[22] The insurgency group due to the intensity of the force and organisational structure has attained the level of armed conflict of non-international character.[23]

Several reasons have been adduced for gender-based violence in times of armed conflict. Kamau asserts that the motivations range from actors

---

[16] Ibid.

[17] Yemi Oke, 'Insecurity Challenges in Nigeria-Boko Haram Insurgency, Bakassi Resettlement Crisis and the Niger Delta Militancy: A Thesis for Lasting Peace' 1 *International and Comparative Journal of Peace and Environment* (2014): 24–44.

[18] Oke 2014, *supra* note 1; Nanna Lord Mallam and Adejoh Sunday 'Terrorism and Conflict-Related Sexual Violence in Africa: North eastern Nigeria in Focus' 6(1) *Covenant University Journal of Politics & International Affairs* (2018): 76–88.

[19] Matfess, *supra* note 3.

[20] Ibid.

[21] A Multinational Joint Task Force was formed in the Lake Chad Basin in 2012 to deal with Boko Haram. In 2015, the African Union reconstituted it at a Summit level meeting; Isaac Olawale Albert, 'Rethinking the Functionality of the Multinational Joint Task Force in Managing the Boko Haram Crisis in the Lake Chad Basin' *Africa Development* 42(3) (2017): 120–123.

[22] International Humanitarian Rules to the War between Nigeria and the Boko Haram Sect, https://www.educationalresourceproviders; https://com/applying-international-humanitarian-law-rules-to-the-war-between-nigeria-and-the-boko-haram-sect/Applying.

[23] 'How Is the Term "Armed Conflict" Defined in International Humanitarian Law?' *International Committee of the Red Cross (ICRC) Opinion Paper*, March 2008, http://www.icrc.org/web/eng/siteegO.nsf/html/armed-conflictarticle-170308; Jide James-Eluyode, 'Enforcement of International Humanitarian Law in Nigeria' 3 *African Human Rights Law Journal* (2003): 264–274.

using it as weapon of war to random spoils of war.[24] According to Amnesty International:

> Evidence gathered…in recent years supports the view that conflict reinforces and exacerbates *existing pattern* of discrimination and violence against women. The violence women suffer in conflict is an *extreme manifestation* of the discrimination and abuse face in peacetime, and the unequal power relations between men and women in most societies. In peacetime, such attitudes contribute to the widespread acceptance of domestic violence, rape and other forms of sexual abuse against women. When political tensions and increasing militarisation spill over into outright conflict, these habitual attitudes and abuses take on new dimensions and distinct patterns, and all forms of violence increase, including rape and other forms of sexual violence against women.[25]

Conflict-related sexual violence include rape, sexual slavery, forced prostitution, forced pregnancy, forced abortion, enforced sterilisation, forced marriage and 'any other sexual violence of comparable gravity perpetrated against women or girls that are directly linked to a conflict'. The link may be evident in the profile of the perpetrator, who is often affiliated with a state or non-state armed group such as a terrorist group like Boko Haram. In a similar vein, the profile of the victim is that who is frequently an actual or perceived member of a political, ethnic, or religious minority group or targeted based on gender identity.[26] Relatedly,

---

24 Evelyn W Kamua, 'Domestic Adjudication of Sexual and Gender-Based Violence in Armed Conflict: Considerations for Prosecutors and Judges' 4(1) *African Journal of Legal Studies* (2011): 89.

25 Amnesty International, Lives Blown Apart Crime Against Women in Times of Conflict: Stop Violence Against Women (2004), https://www.amnesty.org/download/Documents/88000/act770752004en.pdf.

26 The abductees who escaped reported that the insurgents practiced forced conversion of abductees and strict enforcement of the sect's decrees. They were referred to as *mustadafin* an Arabic term that means the 'downtrodden' or 'oppressed.' According to the women, the *mustadafin* were instructed by the insurgents, through daily or near-daily Quranic education before entering the insurgency ranks as wives. Matfess notes that this underlines the insurgency ideological motivation; Matfess, *supra* note 3.

sexual violence can be used as a tactic of terrorism, as women and children were targeted for abduction and sexual abuse by extremist groups such as Boko Haram as part of financial calculus and self-perpetuation.[27]

As stated above, Boko Haram started as a dissident group. However, in 2014, in an unprecedented move that caught global attention, 276 Chibok secondary school girls were abducted.[28] Later that year, the group also attacked Damasak in Borno State and abducted an estimated 400 women and children, including 300 elementary school children.[29] From January 2014 and April 2015, over 2,000 women and girls were abducted.[30] As some of the abductees were released, many others are being taken. The MNJTF continues to tackle the insurgency. Clearly and sadly, the group persist in capturing women and girls, using sexual violence as a weapon.[31]

Several reports show that the abducted women and girls were repeatedly raped and gang raped.[32] The terrorist group made conscious effort to impregnate the abducted women.[33] Forced marriages and sexual slavery were perpetrated; some of those that were kidnapped were 'sold out'. Abducted girls who refuse marriage or sexual contact within marriage faced violence or death threats.[34] There were enforced disappearance as many of the abductees have been taken to different camps in the North East.[35] Back in their host communities or the Internally

---

27 *Report of the United Nations Secretary-General, Conflict Related Sexual Violence*, March 29, 2019: 5–6, https://www.un.org/sexualviolenceinconflict/report/s-2019-280/.

28 Human Rights Watch, *supra* note 6.

29 Human Rights Watch, 'Nigeria: A Year On: No Word on 300 Abducted Children' (2016), https://www.hrw.org/news/2016/03/29/nigeria-year-no-word-300-abducted-children.

30 The Guardian, 'The Chibok Girls Are Just One Part of the Ordeal of Women in North East Nigeria' (2016), https://www.theguardian.com/commentisfree/2016/aug/18/chibok-abducted-girls-women-north-east-nigeria-boko-haram-video.

31 Benjamin Maiangwa and Daniel Agbiboa, 'Why Boko Haram Kidnaps Women and Young Girls in North-Eastern Nigeria' 3 *Conflict Trends* (2014): 51–56.

32 Mia Bloom and Hilary Matfess, 'Women as Symbols & Swords in Boko Haram's Terror' 6(1) *Prism* (2016): 109–110.

33 Ibid.

34 *The Times of Israel*, 'UN Condemns Extremist se of Rape, Sexual Slavery', https://www.timesofisrael.com/un-2014-saw-extremists-use-rape-sexual-slavery/.

35 Sambisa Forest, Gullak Camp in Adamawa State; Amnesty International, 'Nigeria: Abducted Women and Girls Forced to Join Boko Haram Attacks', https://www.amnesty.org/en/latest/news/2015/04/nigeria-abducted-women-and-girls-forced-to-join-boko-haram-attacks/.

Displaced Camps, they are suffering from psycho-social trauma as well as the stigma of association. The stigma is heightened for those who have been raped or married (by force or choice) and have children for Boko Haram. Such children are said to have 'bad blood' from their fathers and potential future risks of harming the people.[36] In such a deeply cultural communities, their reintegration is a daunting task. It is only logical that perpetrators are made accountable for this dastardly act.

3 Trial of Boko Haram Insurgents

The congruence of opinion is that the insurgency group has committed reprehensible atrocities against their victims. Hence, they should be held accountable through prosecution, conviction and punishment.[37] Eventually, in 2017, the government began the trial of 1,669 suspects. The charges included murder, kidnapping, abduction of Chibok girls, 'providing material and non-violent support' to the group.[38] There were three rounds of trial. In the first round, 575 accused persons were tried, but the proceeding was shrouded in secrecy.[39] In the second round, 475 suspects were tried and discharged due to lack of sufficient evidence against them.[40] In the third round and importantly so, over 200 suspects were tried under the Terrorism (Prevention) Amendment Act 2013.[41] The courts convicted 113, acquitted 5 and discharged 97 due to no concrete evidence against them. Several procedural irregularities were

36 Ibid.

37 Human Rights Watch, *supra* note 29; Security Council Resolution 1325 (2000), *supra* notes 8 and 9; *UN General Assembly Resolution on Basic Principles and Guidelines on the Right to a Remedy and Reparation for Victims, supra* note 8.

38 Human Rights Watch, Nigeria: Flawed Trials of Boko Haram Suspects, https://www.hrw.org/news/2018/09/17/nigeria-flawed-trials-boko-haram-suspects#:~:text=In%20October%202017%2C%20authorities%20began,violent%20support%20to%20the%20group.

39 Ibid.

40 Ibid.

41 Ibid., See Terrorism (Prevention) Act 2011.

observed in the trial which is outside the purview of this paper.[42] Significantly, the Act does not criminalise sexual violence as an act of terrorism. Unsurprisingly, none of the suspects was convicted for sexual violence despite all the reported activities of sexual violence across the North East.[43] Brown warns that across the world, the feeling is that conflict-related sexual violence are acts of violence if there is a 'public dimension' to it. But where it is committed in private, it is seen as opportunistic and unrelated to the conflict. Hence, such crimes are rarely prosecuted, much less prosecuted as crimes against humanity.[44]

Just recently, the 2020 Report of the Secretary-General to the Security Council on Nigeria documented 826 allegations of conflict-related sexual violence, including rape, and forced marriage. 88% was attributed to Boko Haram and the JTF.[45] The 2015 Amnesty International report detailed Nigerian military's complicity in crimes against women and their children in Northern Nigeria.[46] Obviously, the country needs to urgently institute frameworks that will make perpetrators accountable for their unlawful actions. This writer quickly adds that UNSC Resolution 1820 (2008) is quite instructive. It mandates States to exclude sexual violence crimes from amnesty provisions in the context of conflict resolution processes.[47]

---

[42] Proceedings were very short; charges were vague; lack of official interpreters; charging previously discharged accused persons for the same offence; unclear orders for rehabilitation, etc. *supra* note 39.

[43] Report of the United Nations Secretary-General, *supra* note 28.

[44] Clare Brown, 'Sexual Exploitation and Abuse in Conflict: An International Crime,' *American University International Law Review* 34(3) (2019): 506.

[45] Office of the Special Representative of the Sec-General, Sexual Violence in Conflict, Nigeria, https://www.un.org/sexualviolenceinconflict/countries/nigeria/.

[46] Amnesty international, Boko Haram Survivors have been Starved and Raped by Nigerian Military, https://www.amnesty.org/en/latest/news/2018/05/boko-haram-survivors-have-been-starved-and-raped-by-nigerias-military/.

[47] Women, Peace and Security, UN Doc. S/RES/1820 (2008), June 19, 2008.

4 Nigeria and the International Criminal Court (ICC)

The Rome Statute was adopted in 1998 and came into force in 2002. Nigeria signed the Statute on the June 1, 2000 and ratified it on September 27, 2001. Article 11 of the Statute states that the court has jurisdiction with respect to crimes committed after its entry into force and the date of its entry into force in a country.[48] Relatedly, section 12 of the Nigerian Constitution provides that a treaty can only have the force of law in Nigeria if it has been re-enacted into law by the National Assembly.[49] Hence, the Rome Statute will only apply in Nigeria when it is domesticated into national laws. In addition, section 36(8) of the 1999 Constitution prohibits retroactive legislation.[50] In other words, the grave violations committed by the insurgency cannot be tried as international crimes in the Rome Statute until it is enacted as part of the Nigerian laws.

Meanwhile, the 2019 Preliminary Activities of the ICC Report on Nigeria identified eight potential cases of crimes against humanity, including six by Boko Haram.[51] The Preamble to the Rome Statute emphasises the duty of state parties to exercise criminal jurisdiction over those responsible for international crimes. Impliedly, once a State domesticate the Statute, national courts can adjudicate on the crimes. The ICC would be a court of last resort since it is complementary to national criminal jurisdictions.[52] In other words, the court can only intervene where Nigeria is unwilling or unable to investigate and prosecute. This may be an instance where proceedings are unduly delayed or intended to shield individuals from criminal responsibility.[53] Robinson

---

48 International Criminal Court, https://asp.icc-cpi.int/en_menus/asp/states%20parties/african%20states/Pages/nigeria.aspx.

49 1999 Laws of the Federal Republic of Nigeria, Abacha v Fawehinmi (2000) 6 NWLR (pt.660) 228 SC.

50 Ibid.

51 International Criminal Court Report, *supra* note 11.

52 Paragraphs 6 and 10.

53 Article 17(1)(a).

asserts that this inactivity is understood as signs of abdication of primary responsibility warranting ICC's intervention.[54]

There have been three failed attempts in Nigeria to domesticate the Rome Statute. Olugbuo explains that the ICC appears to target African countries as many of the cases before it are from Africa.[55] Hence, legal acceptance of international criminal justice is subject to political interest. Nigeria has to balance competing demands regarding its obligation to the international community *vis-à-vis* the leadership position on the continent.[56] The Nigerian Attorney General and Minister of Justice set up an inter-ministerial committee that produced a draft of the Crimes Against Humanity, War Crime, Genocide and Offences Bill in 2012. Olugbuo may be right, eight years after, the Bill is yet to be passed into law. Conversely, the country has obligations under the above international Statute and Resolutions to protect human rights, ensure international justice, enforce accountability, and grant reparation to survivors.

In the view of this writer, there is an urgent need to pass the Bill for an enforceable legal framework. The insurgency in the North East is ongoing and women's bodies continue to be used as swords and symbols of war. The survivors are entitled to justice as part of their healing process or there is a risk of having a section of the country consisting of traumatised and damaged people. The risk may be providing a fertile ground for future recruitments. The next section analyses the Bill against the backdrop of legal and institutional frameworks in Nigeria.

---

[54] Benson Chinedu Olugbuo, 'Acceptance of International Criminal Justice in Nigeria Legal Compliance, Myth or Reality?' *International Nuremberg Principles Academy* 7, https://www.nurembergacademy.org/fileadmin/media/pdf/acceptance/Nigeria.pdf.

[55] Ibid.

[56] African Union Passed a Resolution of non-cooperation with the ICC on the arrest and surrender of President Al-Bashir of Sudan. Ibid., 4–5.

5 The Crimes Against Humanity, War Crimes, Genocide and Related Offences Bill 2012

As indicated above, the Bill is on international crimes and provides the legal basis for the trial of the insurgency group. It is germane to review the sections and suggest ways of strengthening the implementation. The objectives of the Bill are: 'to provide for measures under Nigerian Law for the punishment and enforcement of international crimes'; 'to give effect to certain provisions of the Rome Statute'; and 'to enable Nigeria to cooperate with the' ICC.[57]

5.1 Jurisdiction

The national court has the primary jurisdiction to adjudicate on crimes. The Bill will apply to offences in Part II (international crimes and offences) committed after it comes into force.[58] It vests the court with extra territorial jurisdiction. Where an act constituting 'an offence is committed by a person outside the territory of Nigeria, proceedings may be instituted at the High Court if: 'the person is a citizen or permanent resident of Nigeria'; 'has committed the offence against a citizen of Nigeria or permanent resident of Nigeria'; or 'is present in Nigeria after the commission of the offence'.[59] In addition, where an act constituting an offence under Part II of the Bill is 'alleged to have been committed by a person outside Nigeria', proceedings 'may be instituted against the person for that offence' in a court in Nigeria 'having jurisdiction to try offences under this Bill' and that court 'shall have all the powers to try offences as if the offence had been committed within the territorial limits of the court's jurisdiction'.[60]

---

57 Part 1 s&ection 1.

58 Bill, s&ection 21.

59 Bill, s&ection 22.

60 Bill, s&ection 23; As part of the objectives of mutual cooperation, s&ection 51 of the Bill provides that Nigeria may request assistance from the ICC in relation to the investigation and prosecution of crimes under the Rome Statute for which the maximum penalty under the

Court in this regard is the Federal High Court, High Court of the Federal Capital Territory (FCT) and the State High Court.[61] According to the Nigerian Constitution, a High Court is duly constituted if it consists of a judge.[62] The International Criminal Court sits with three judges. It has three Divisions: Pre-trial, Trial and Appeal Chambers.[63] To resolve the constitutional conflict, Nigeria should create an International Crimes Division, similar to a High Court. This will be in a Central Division, preferably in the FCT.[64] Apart from the offences in the Bill, the court should adjudicate on all international crimes such as money laundering, drug trafficking, hostage taking, counterfeiting, hijacking, sabotage and terrorism. Kamau suggests raising a Unit consisting of 'prosecutors, investigators, doctors, nurses, counsellors, interpreters and witness assistants' who would have undergone training on how to handle the victims for the offences in the Rome Statute, that is, this Bill.[65] Kamau rationalises that the team would help to ensure that the necessary evidence is gathered while maintaining appropriate care and safety of the victims. Based on her experience in the Office of the Prosecutor of the ICC, Kamau said that successful prosecution and convictions are more likely to result from specially trained investigators 'conducting investigation under guidelines specially formulated particularly for handling of rape and other forms of sexual violence'.[66] In this writer's view, training

---

Nigerian law is a term of imprisonment of not less than 5 years; S&ection 69 of the Bill provides that Nigeria may act as a state of enforcement of sentences by the ICC, and for the Attorney General to notify relevant government ministries, departments, and agencies, including the National Security Adviser where the need arises; S&ection 70 states that if the person to enforce judgement upon is a foreigner, the Home State must consent; S&ection 87 provides that the prosecutor of the ICC may conduct investigation in Nigeria as provided for under the Rome Statute; By s&ection 88 Bill, the judges can sit in Nigeria to gather evidence, conduct or continue proceeding, or review a sentence imposed by the ICC.

61 Bill, s&ection 99.

62 1999 Constitution of the Federal Republic of Nigeria, s&ection 273.

63 Rome Statute, article 34.

64 Uganda International Crimes Division.

65 Kamau, *supra* note 24.

66 Factors such as number of victims and perpetrators, organised nature of the perpetrators, the manner in which the crimes are committed, the circumstances surrounding their commission, the sheer scale of the crimes and the unique elements of some of the crimes are drastically different from those concerned at the national level; Kamau, *supra* note 24.

should take the bottom-up approach and judges at the Court of Appeal and Supreme Court should be included.

5.2 International Crimes and Offences

The Bill defines Crimes against Humanity to include acts such as rape, sexual slavery, enforced prostitution, forced pregnancy, enforced sterilisation or any other forms of sexual violence of comparable gravity, enforced disappearance, 'when committed as part of a widespread or systematic attack directed against any civilian population with the knowledge of the attack'.[67] 'Directed against civilian population' means a 'course of conduct involving the multiple commission of the acts against the civilian population', 'pursuant to or in furtherance of a state or organisational policy to commit such attack'. Boko Haram has been targeting girls in schools probably because of their disdain for western education. They are deliberately pursuing girls and women as to entrench their ideological belief upon them.

The Bill provides that the section 5 will be interpreted in accordance with the element of crime adopted under article 9 of the Rome Statute.[68] The elements of the crime against humanity of rape[69] is as follows:

(1) The perpetrator invaded the body of a person by conduct resulting in penetration, however slight, of any of the body of the victim or the perpetrator touches the sexual organ, anal or genital opening of a victim with any object or any part of the body.

---

[67] Bill, s&ection 5: Forced pregnancy means the unlawful confinement of a woman forcibly made pregnant, with the intent of affecting the ethnic composition of any population or carrying out other grave violations of international law and this definition shall not in any way be interpreted as affecting Nigerian laws relating to pregnancy. Enforced disappearance of persons means the arrest, detention or abduction of persons by or with authorisation, support or acquiescence of any government official or political organisation, followed by a refusal to acknowledge that deprivation of freedom or to give information on the fate or whereabouts of those persons, with the intention of removing them from the protection of the law for a prolonged period of time.

[68] Elements of Crime, https://www.icc-cpi.int/NR/rdonlyres/336923D8-A6AD-40EC-AD7B45BF9DE73D56/0/ElementsOfCrimesEng.pdf.

[69] Article 7(1)g-1.

(2) Invasion was committed by force or threat of force or coercion caused by fear of duress, detention, psychological oppression or abuse of power, against such person or another person or by taking advantage of a coercive environment. (3) The conduct was committed as part of widespread or systematic attack and (4) the perpetrator knew the conduct was part or intended to be part of a widespread or systematic attack directed against a civilian population.[70]

The elements of crime state that crime against humanity entails individual responsibility. The last two elements (that is, 3 and 4) describe the context in which the conduct happened. It clarifies the requisite participation and knowledge of 'a widespread or systematic attack against a civilian population'. The perpetrator needs not 'have knowledge of all the characteristics of the attack' or the 'precise detail of the plan or policy of the state or organisation'.

The UN reported that hundreds of released female captives said they were repeatedly raped by Boko Haram and compelled to marry their captors. This revelation suggests that Boko Haram is not only destroying existing family and community structures but is bent on controlling the future composition of families.[71]

The elements of the crimes against humanity of forced pregnancy[72] are:

(1) The perpetrator confined one or more women, forcibly make them pregnant with the intent of affecting the ethnic composition of any population or carrying out other grave violations of international law.
(2) The conduct was committed as part of widespread or systematic attack and

[70] Article 7(1)(g)-1.

[71] Zainab Bangura, Special Representatives of the Sec-Gen of UN on Sexual Violence in Conflict United Nations News Condemning the use of Sexual Violence, UN Envoy warns Boko Haram aims to Destroy Family Structures, https://news.un.org/en/story/2015/05/499942-condemning-use-sexual-violence-un-envoy-warns-boko-haram-aims-destroy-family.

[72] Article 7(1)g-4.

(3) The perpetrator knew the conduct was part or intended to be part of a widespread or systematic attack directed against a civilian population.[73]

There is a general opinion that Boko Haram's sexual terrorism is a deliberate plan by them to ensure that women produce offspring that would continue the insurgency. The organised nature of the sexual violence point to a deliberate self-perpetuation plan.[74]

The elements of the crime against humanity of enforced disappearance[75] are:

(1) (a)The perpetrator arrested, detained or abducted one or more persons or (b) refused to acknowledge the arrest, detention or abduction and give information on the whereabouts.
(2) Such arrest or detention or abduction was followed or accompanied by a refusal to acknowledge that deprivation of freedom or give information on the whereabouts or (b) such refusal was preceded by deprivation of freedom.
(3) The perpetrator was aware that (a) such arrest or detention or abduction would be followed in the ordinary course by a refusal to acknowledge that deprivation of freedom or give information on the whereabouts or (b) such refusal was preceded by deprivation of freedom.
(4) Such arrest, detention or abduction was carried out by authorisation, support or acquiescence of a state or political organisation or such refusal to acknowledge the deprivation of freedom or give information as to whereabouts be carried out by authorisation or support of the state or political organisation.[76]

---

[73] Article 7(1)g-4.

[74] *The New York Times*, Boko Haram Militants Raped Hundreds of Female Captives in Nigeria, https://www.nytimes.com/2015/05/19/world/africa/boko-haram-militants-raped-hundreds-of-female-captives-in-nigeria.html.

[75] Article 7(1)i.

[76] Ibid.

Section 6(d) emphatically covers 'serious violations of the laws and customs applicable in armed conflict not of an international character, within the framework of international law' such as committing rape, sexual slavery, enforce prostitution, forced pregnancy as defined in article 7, paragraph 2 of the Rome Statute, also constituting a serious violation of Article 3 common to the Four Geneva Conventions 1949. Most of the elements of the crime for establishing section 6(d) are same as in section 5, except the last two (i.e. 3 and 4). First, the conduct 'must take place and be associated with an armed conflict of non-international character' and secondly, 'the perpetrator must have been aware of factual circumstances that established an armed conflict'.[77]

Based on the above, the insurgent group can be tried under sections 5 and 6(d) of the Bill. Reports and evidence abound on the perpetration of these crimes. The group attacks have been ongoing for over a decade, hence multiple and systematic attacks occurred against civilians.[78] It is time to put an end to this impunity through the speedy passage of the Bill to create the necessary prosecution framework for future trial.

As stated above, international crimes, because of the nature of the operation in relation to countries and armed conflict imposes individual responsibility on a commander. Section 19 of Bill highlights the responsibility of commander and superiors. A military commander is responsible for the crimes committed by forces under his or her effective control, as a result of his or her failure to exercise control properly over them where (a) 'he or she knew or ought to have known, that the forces were committing or about to commit the offence' or (b) 'failed to take reasonable measures within his or her power to suppress or prevent its commission or submit the matter to competent authority for investigation or prosecution'.[79]

Unlike the position in Nigeria, where the section is in the alternative, both the Rome Statute[80] and the International Criminal Tribunal

[77] For instance, article 8(2)(e)vi-1 (war crime of rape) article 8(2)(e)vi-4.

[78] David Sverdlov, 'Rape in War: Prosecuting the Islamic State of Iraq and the Levant and Boko Haram for Sexual Violence Against Women', *Cornell International Law Journal* 50(2) (2017): 333.

[79] Bill.

[80] Article 28.

Yugoslavia (ICTY) in *Prosecutor v Kunarac*[81] interpreted the section cumulatively. The Tribunal held that there must be existence of a superior-subordinate relationship. This is not formal, but that the superior had effective control over his suburbanites.[82] It was alleged that Kunarac was a commander of a group of soldiers as he requested for them on an ad hoc basis. The Trial Chamber noted that these soldiers went back to their respective brigades when the specific task he assigned to them had finished. During the periods that the operations continued, the soldiers were 'under the effective control' of the accused. However, the prosecutor has failed to show that the soldiers who committed the offences charged in the indictment were under the effective control of the accused at the time they committed the offence. Hence, he is not responsible as a superior under article 7(3) Statute (*Command Responsibility*).[83] This section is very important to prosecute the leader of the insurgency. He has both individual and command responsibility. The provision is cumulative, it is knowledge and inaction that produce liability.

5.3 Evidentiary Rules

The Bill is silent on the evidentiary procedure in the conduct of trial.[84] This is unlike when the elements of the crime was adopted from the Rome Statute. Hence, the germane issue here is whether the courts in prosecuting cases under the Bill would rely on the Nigerian Evidence Act or the Rules of Procedure and Evidence of the Rome Statute. Where the courts adopt the former approach, it is trite law that the evidence of a complainant of sexual offences must be corroborated.[85] The Nigerian

---

[81] IT-96-23-T & IT-96-23/1-T.

[82] Paragraphs 395–396.

[83] Paragraphs 626–629.

[84] See the Evidence Act 2011, Criminal Procedure Act (CPA) 1945 for Southern Nigeria, Criminal Procedure Code (CPC) 1965 for Northern Nigeria, Administration of Criminal Justice Act (ACJA) 2015 was enacted to repeal both the CPA and CPC. Presently only 11 out of the 36 states have adopted the ACJA.

[85] See the Criminal Code Act, Cap C38, Laws of the Federation, 2004, s&ection 218 on defilement of girls under 13 years, s&ection 221 defilements of girls under 16 years but above 13 years and idiots.

Supreme Court in *Edet Iko v State*[86] held that corroborative evidence goes to or strengthens the assertions of the complainant. There is no statutory provision in Nigeria that makes such corroboration mandatory. 'It has been considered expedient that, as a matter of practice, the court should be very slow to convict on the uncorroborated evidence of the complainant'. This has been the view held in quite a number of cases decided in the country.[87]

The second option is, following the element of crime, to apply the Rules of Procedure and Evidence of the Rome Statute.[88] It provides 'a Chamber shall not impose a legal requirement of corroboration to prove crimes of sexual violence'.[89] In *Prosecutor v Akayesu*,[90] the International Criminal Tribunal for Rwanda (ICTR) was confronted with only one testimony in support of a fact alleged in the indictment. The Tribunal noted that the proceedings before it was being conducted in accordance the Statute and Rules of the Tribunal, and not national rules of evidence. Rule 96(i) of the Rules deals with the issue of corroboration of testimony required by the Chamber and applies only to cases of testimony by 'victims of sexual assault', stipulate that 'no corroboration shall be required'. Hence, the Chamber can rule based on 'a single testimony provided such testimony is, in its opinion, relevant and credible'.[91] This option conflicts with the Nigerian position.

Both the Nigerian evidentiary rules and the Rules of Procedure of the ICC state the conditions for establishing consent in sexual offences. In the former, consent is vitiated if it is obtained by 'force', 'threats or intimidation', 'fear of harm' and 'false and fraudulent misrepresentation to the nature of the act'. Similarly, the latter provides that the consent cannot be inferred by words or conduct of the victim where: (1) 'force, threat of force, coercion or taking advantage of a coercive environment has

[86] (2001) 14 NWLR (pt. 732) 221; Jegede v State (2001) 1 NWLR (pt. 695) 623; Ibeakanna v Queen (1963) 2 SCNLR 191.

[87] *Na'an Upahar & Or v The State* (2003) 6 NWLR (pt. 816).

[88] Rules of Procedure and Evidence, https://www.icc-cpi.int/iccdocs/pids/legal-texts/rulesprocedureevidenceeng.pdf.

[89] Rule 63(4).

[90] ICTR-96-4-T.

[91] Notes 134 and 135.

undermined victim's ability to give voluntary and genuine consent'; (2) 'the victim is incapable of giving genuine consent' and (3) 'by reason of silence or lack of resistance of the victim'.[92] However, the Nigerian courts use the evidence of physical injuries on the complainant to determine lack of consent. According to the Court in *Posu v State*,[93] 'the bruises in the inner thighs showed lack of consent and that the appellants forced their way into the prosecutrix'. This writer contends that this approach will not work in establishing the crimes in sections 5 and 6(d) of the Bill.[94]

Significantly, the 'nature of evidence' is quite different from domestic cases. First, the act or series of act would have happened in times of armed conflict, even if it is of non-international character. There may not really be access to medical or the justice system to document bruises or the exact violation. Also, the victim may not even remember or know the name of the perpetrator.[95] Secondly, the sources of evidence for such crimes during the conflict 'is not limited to the victims themselves'. It 'can be collected or seen from the corpses of the victims', from the survivors 'and from other people who witnessed the rapes'.[96] This assertion is also true for Nigeria. Many of the offences are being committed in the insurgent's dens. In view of this, this writer submits that the present Nigerian case law on corroboration and consent will not allow effective prosecution of the insurgents under the Bill. This should be noted in the future amendment of the Evidence Act as regards international crimes of sexual type. Suffice to say, that in applying the evidentiary rules for now, judges must be trained on the 'nature' of this crime to develop jurisprudence in that regard.

[92] Rule 70.

[93] (2011) 2 NWLR (pt. 1234) 393–407.

[94] Iyabode Ogunniran, 'Male Offences, Female Trials: Rape and the Quest for Gender Justice in Africa' 18(1) *The Nigerian Journal of Contemporary Law* (2012): 9–38.

[95] Kamau, *supra* note 24, 106.

[96] Ibid.

5.4 Role of the Attorney General

The consent of the Attorney General is required for prosecution. Hence, proceedings for an offence under the Bill shall not be instituted without the consent of the Attorney General. However, a person charged with an offence under sections 4, 5 and 6 'may be arrested'; or 'warrant of arrest may be issued and executed', and 'may be remanded in custody or bail while waiting for the Attorney General's consent'.[97] Olugbuo rightly contends that the Attorney General 'is a political appointee and may be influenced by the Executive in the discharge of duties' under the Bill.[98] He rightly proposes consent to be obtained from the Director of Public Prosecution who is a career civil servant.[99]

5.5 Defences

The Bill states that 'a person charged with an offence may rely' on any defence under 'Nigerian or international laws'. But where the provision of the Nigerian law is inconsistent with the provision of international law, the latter prevails.[100] The Bill further provides that subject to constitutional provision, an offender cannot raise the defence that the act constituting the offence was 'in conformity with the law in force at the place at which the act was alleged to have been committed'.[101] The Constitution is the ground norm, and where there is any conflict between its provision and any international law, the Nigerian courts would always give preference to the constitutional provisions.[102]

[97] Bill, s&ection 16.

[98] Olugbuo, *supra* note 54.

[99] Ibid.; Uganda International Criminal Court Act, 2010, s&ection 17.

[100] Bill, s&ection 17.

[101] Ibid.

[102] *Fawehinmi v Abacha* (2000) 6 NWLR (pt.610) 289.

5.6 Punishment

The punishment for crimes against humanity and serious violations in armed conflict of non-international character are imprisonment for a term not exceeding 30 years or life imprisonment depending on the extreme gravity of the offence and the individual circumstances of the convicted person.[103] Other parties to the offence are liable on conviction, to the same penalty as the principal offender.[104] This is highly commendable as all the perpetrators of the heinous crime should serve the same punishment. There is a need for continuous training of judges on the underlying philosophy for this punishment. The courts should impose maximum sentences in contrast to the situation with domestic convictions of sexual violence.[105]

5.7 Victims Participation and Witness Protection

The Bill allows the court on a motion by or on behalf of the prosecuting authority or the application of the witness to protect a witness before it, if it is satisfied that the life of the witness is in danger. The court will take measures to keep the identity and address of the witness secret and ensure that the witness and his family is protected from intimidation, threats or reprisals from the offender, his associates or person in position of authority.[106] This protection is important in the Nigerian situation since the insurgency is ongoing. However, the Bill is silent on victim's participation. This is a big lacuna because it is a major innovation in

[103] Bill, s&ections 5(2)(b) and 6(2)(b).

[104] Bill, s&ection 9: any person who attempts; counsels or procures; orders, incites, solicits or induces; is an accessory; intentionally contributes in any way to the commission of the offence commits the offence.

[105] Iyabode Ogunniran, 'Criminal Law Through the Gender Lens: A Comparative of Rape Laws in England and Nigeria' 5 *University of Ibadan Law Journal* (2016): 31–49. The Nigerian Supreme Court awarded five years imprisonment to one of the few rape cases that went up to the apex court whereas the maximum sentence is life imprisonment.

[106] Bill, s&ection 94: In the Akayesu's case, all Prosecutor and Defence witnesses who requested for protection benefited from measures guaranteeing the confidentiality of their testimony. No information that could identify the witnesses were given. During the hearing, letters of the alphabet were used as pseudonym to refer to protected witnesses and screen isolated the said witnesses from the public but not the accused and his witness, paragraph 18.

prosecuting international crimes due of the nature of the atrocities. The Rome Statute emphatically states that the 'court shall take appropriate measures to protect the safety, physical and psychological wellbeing, dignity and privacy of victims and witnesses'. Also, '[w]here the personal interests of the victims are affected, the court shall permit their views and concerns to be presented and considered at stages of the proceedings'.[107] Though its use is a relatively new phenomenon, it is considered as an instrument to give victims of gross violation of human rights and intentional humanitarian law a voice and to promote reconciliation.[108] The Pre-Trial Chamber of ICC gave the first victim-related decision in 2006.[109] The Trial Chamber 1 rendered another landmark judgement on the issue of victim participation in 2008.[110] This writer submits that this is a crucial aspect of the trial that is personal to the victim. The judge has a discretion to allow it. Hence, victims' participation should be integrated into the Bill.

5.8 Special Victims Trust Fund[111]

This is for the benefit of the victims of crime and their families. A person convicted of an offence under the Act in the High Court may forfeit assets, properties or direct or indirect proceeds to the Fund. The 'court may order money and other property collected through fines or forfeiture to be transferred to the Fund'. The Attorney General shall ensure that forfeited assets or properties are 'effectively transferred and vested' in the Fund as well as issue guidelines for its management. A victim of

[107] Article 68.

[108] Elisabeth Baumgartner, 'Aspects of Victim Participation in the Proceedings of the International Criminal Court' 90(870) *International Review of the Red Cross* (2008): 409–411.

[109] January 17, 2006, *Decision on the Application for Participation in the Proceedings of Victim Participation and Reparation Section* (VPRS) 1–6. Pre-Trial Chamber 1 admitted a group of applicants to participate as victims in the investigation proceedings when examining the situation in the Democratic Republic of Congo (DCR). The Prosecutor referred to this group of victims as 'Situation victims' as opposed to 'case Victims'. Ibid.

[110] January 18, 2008, Trial Chamber 1 Decision on Victims' Participation. This decision formed part of the preparation of the trial proceedings in the case of *The Prosecutor v Thomas Lubanga Dyilo* in DCR. Ibid.

[111] Bill, s&ection 93; Rome Statute, s&ection 75.

crime under the Bill, has the 'right to institute civil action against appropriate parties, and is entitled to compensation, restitution and recovery for economic, physical and psychological damage' which shall be met from the Fund. The writer submits that this initiative is laudable as the survivors and their families can restart their lives with such assistance. In addition, civil action can be instituted in a designated court for that purpose at the High Court. Such court is aware that a criminal case has been concluded to fast-track trial. The Administration of Criminal Justice Act (ACJA) 2015 is instructive in this regard. The Criminal Court can award compensation and restitution or during the pendency of the criminal trial, a civil action can also be instituted.[112] Most importantly, the process should be speedily conducted so that the survivors can access the Fund for necessary exigencies.

5.9 Other Interventions

In 2013, Nigeria developed a National Plan of Action (NAP) for the Implementation of UNSCR 1325. The first NAP is based on five pillars of prevention, participation, protection, prosecution and promotion. One of the strategies is the Ministry of Women Affairs forming a coalition with the civil society organisation (CSO) called Legislative Advocacy Coalition on Violence Against Women (LACVAW) to campaign for legislation and policies that are fundamental to the implementation of the Resolutions and the NAP. To take care of current realities, the second NAP (2017–2020) includes reintegration of victims of insurgency, gender-based violence survivors.[113]

Several national and international organisations are also at the forefront of ending the Boko Haram impunity and granting succours to the victims. The Bring Back our Girls Initiative; Human Rights Watch who conduct annual report on the insurgency activities and monitor prosecution of the Insurgent Group; Put Nigeria First that has worked diligently to support Nigerian soldiers; Nigeria Regional Transitional

---

[112] S&ections 319–321.

[113] Federal Ministry of Women Affairs and Social Development, Abuja, Nigeria, http://www.lse.ac.uk/women-peace-security/assets/documents/2019/NAP/Nigeria-NAP-2-2017-2020.pdf.

Initiative working to counter terrorism and the United States Agency for International Development providing humanitarian assistance in the North-East Nigeria.[114] Amnesty International continues to urge the Nigerian government to investigate and prosecute culpable military officers.[115] Nigeria Coalition for ICC has been active in pursuit of justice for international crimes.[116]

However, there is a need to take a holistic approach to the issue of conflict in the North East. This writer asserts that economic, political and social complexities that created and nurtured the insurgency have resulted into crises in the communities. The Federal Government as well as the Governors in those states should complement international humanitarian assistance by strategically providing and rebuilding the communities as conducive environment will enable justice to thrive.

6 Conclusion

The UNSC Resolutions 1325 (2000) and 2467 (2019) obligate States to strengthen legislation to prosecute and punish perpetrators of crimes against humanity. The Boko Haram insurgents have committed a series of acts of sexual violence against the women and girls in the North-East which amount to Crimes against Humanity. These are hapless and helpless citizens of Nigeria whose bodies are being used as frontline.

It is crucial to urgently domesticate the Crimes Against Humanity, War Crimes, Genocide and Related Offences Bill against the backdrop of the suggested amendments. This is the time for the Coalition for ICC and related CSOs to lobby the National Assembly to pass the Bill. The Covid-19 pandemic has exacerbated sexual gender-based violence across the country and the National Assembly is presently revisiting passing

[114] Harry K Tiwari, 'Taking Off the Blindfold: An End to Impunity in Nigeria', 42(2) *Brooklyn Journal of International Law* (2017): 887–924.

[115] Amnesty international, Boko Haram Survivors have been Starved and Raped by Nigerian Military, https://www.amnesty.org/en/latest/news/2018/05/boko-haram-survivors-have-been-starved-and-raped-by-nigerias-military/.

[116] Coalition for the International Criminal Court, http://www.coalitionfortheicc.org/country/nigeria.

bills on such issues. For instance, the Sexual Harassment Bill 2020 has just been passed to law.

The Bill provides for the Victims Trust Fund. It is gladdening that it goes further by stating that fines levied and forfeited assets of the perpetrators will go into the Fund. This writer submits that funding is imperative in providing reparation to survivors. It is equally essential for the Federal Government to source for financing of the Fund from private sectors to foreclose a situation where there is no money in it. In addition, they need psycho-social support such as counselling, medical and mental health treatments, economic empowerment and financial support to facilitate their reintegration into their communities.

Generally, the Federal Government and Ministry of Justice should accommodate the special Division of the FCT in the yearly budget. This is a perquisite to sustain the operations of this court based on the nature of trial it will be conducting. The court requires a physical structure, furnishing it, trained interpreters, investigators and judges, amongst others. Strengthening the court will enable it to perform optimally to repose public confidence in its activities.

Nigeria cannot continue to sit on the fence in prosecuting international crimes. The passage of the Bill into law will clearly activate prosecution. The insurgency is ongoing, prosecuting and punishing the perpetrators is one of the ways of putting an end to this impunity.

References

Abacha v Fawehinmi (2000) 6 NWLR (pt.660) 228 SC.

Administration of Criminal Justice Act (ACJA) 2015.

Amnesty International, 2018, Boko Haram Survivors Have Been Starved and Raped by Nigerian Military, https://www.amnesty.org/en/latest/news/2018/05/boko-haram-survivors-have-been-starved-and-raped-by-nigerian-military/.

Benjamin Maiangwa and Daniel Agbiboa, 2014, 'Why Boko Haram Kidnaps Women and Young Girls in North-Eastern Nigeria' 3 *Conflict Trends*.

Benson Chinedu Olugbuo, 2016, 'Acceptance of International Criminal Justice in Nigeria Legal Compliance, Myth or Reality?' 7 *International Nuremberg Principles Academy*, https://www.nurembergacademy.org/fileadmin/media/pdf/acceptance/Nigeria.pdf.

Christine Chinkin and Madeleine Rees, 2019, *Commentary on Security Council Resolution 2467*, The London School of Economics and Political Science.

Clare Brown, 2019, 'Sexual Exploitation and Abuse in Conflict: An International Crime' 34(3) *American University International Law Review.*

Coalition for the International Criminal Court, http://www.coalitionfortheicc.org/country/nigeria.

Criminal Code Act, Cap C38, Laws of the Federation, 2004.

Criminal Procedure Act (CPA) 1945 Southern Nigeria.

Criminal Procedure Code (CPC) 1965 Northern Nigeria.

David Sverdlov, 2017, 'Rape in War: Prosecuting the Islamic State of Iraq and the Levant and Boko Haram for Sexual Violence Against Women' 50(2) *Cornell International Law Journal*.

Elisabeth Baumgartner, 2008, 'Aspects of Victim Participation in the Proceedings of the International Criminal Court' 90(870) *International Review of the Red Cross.*

Evelyn W Kamua, 2011, 'Domestic Adjudication of Sexual and Gender-Based Violence in Armed Conflict: Considerations for Prosecutors and Judges', 4(1) *African Journal of Legal Studies.*

Evidence Act 2011.

Federal Ministry of Women Affairs and Social Development, Abuja, Nigeria, http://www.lse.ac.uk/women-peace-security/assets/documents/2019/NAP/Nigeria-NAP-2-2017-2020.pdf.

Harry K Tiwari, 2017, 'Taking Off the Blindfold: An End to Impunity in Nigeria' 42(2) *Brooklyn Journal of International Law.*

Hilary Matfess, 2017, 'Boko Haram: History and Context'.

Human Rights Watch, 2014, Those Terrible Weeks in Their Camp, https://www.hrw.org/report/2014/10/27/those-terrible-weeks-their-camp/boko-haram-violence-against-women-and-girls.

Human Rights Watch, 2016, Nigeria: A Year On: No Word on 300 Abducted Children, https://www.hrw.org/news/2016/03/29/nigeria-year-no-word-300-abducted-children.

Ibeakanna v Queen (1963) 2 SCNLR 191.

International Committee of the Red Cross, 2008, *Opinion Paper*, 'How Is the Term "Armed Conflict" Defined in International Humanitarian

Law?', http://www.icrc.org/web/eng/siteegO.nsf/html/armed-conflictarticle-170308.
International Criminal Court, 2019, 'Report on Preliminary Examination Activities', https://www.icc-cpi.int/itemsDocuments/191205-rep-otp-PE.pdf.
International Crisis Group, 2016, Nigeria: Women and the Boko Haram Insurgency, https://www.crisisgroup.org/africa/west-africa/nigeria/nigeria-women-and-boko-haram-insurgency.
Isaac Olawale Albert, 2017, 'Rethinking the Functionality of the Multinational Joint Task Force in Managing the Boko Haram Crisis in the Lake Chad Basin' 42(3) *Africa Development*.
Iyabode Ogunniran, 2012, 'Male Offences, Female Trials: Rape and the Quest for Gender Justice in Africa' 18(1) *The Nigerian Journal of Contemporary Law*.
Iyabode Ogunniran, 2016, 'Criminal Law Through the Gender Lens: A Comparative of Rape Laws in England and Nigeria' 5 *University of Ibadan Law Journal*.
Jegede v State (2001) 1 NWLR (pt. 695) 623.
Jide James-Eluyode, 2003, 'Enforcement of International Humanitarian Law in Nigeria' 3 *African Human Rights Law Journal*.
Mia Bloom and Hilary Matfess, 2016, 'Women as Symbols & Swords in Boko Haram's Terror' 6(1) *Prism*.
Na'an Upahar & Or v The State (2003) 6 NWLR (pt. 816).
Nanna Lord Mallam and Adejoh Sunday, 2018, 'Terrorism and Conflict-Related Sexual Violence in Africa: Northeastern Nigeria in Focus' 6(1) *Covenant University Journal of Politics & International Affairs*.
Office of the Special Representative of the Sec-General, Sexual Violence in Conflict, Nigeria, https://www.un.org/sexualviolenceinconflict/countries/nigeria/.
Report of the United Nations Secretary-General, Conflict Related Sexual Violence March 29, 2019, https://www.un.org/sexualviolenceinconflict/report/s-2019-280/.
Terrorism (Prevention) Act 2011.
The Guardian, 2016, The Chibok Girls are just one part of the Ordeal of Women in North—East Nigeria, https://www.theguardian.com/commentisfree/2016/aug/18/chibok-abducted-girls-women-north-east-nigeria-boko-haram-video.

The New York Times, 2015, Boko Haram Militants Raped Hundreds of Female Captives in Nigeria, https://www.nytimes.com/2015/05/19/world/africa/boko-haram-militants-raped-hundreds-of-female-captives-in-nigeria.html.

The Times of Israel, 2015, UN Condemns Extremist se of Rape, Sexual Slavery, https://www.timesofisrael.com/un-2014-saw-extremists-use-rape-sexual-slavery/.

UN General Assembly Resolution on Basic Principles and Guidelines on the Right to a Remedy and Reparation for Resolution 60/147 of December 16, 2005, https://www.ohchr.org/en/professionalinterest/pages/remedyandreparation.aspx.

Yemi Oke, 2012–2013, 'International Criminal Court, Crimes Against Humanity and the Nigerian Boko Haram Islamist Group: Can Two Wrongs Make a Right' 12 *ISIL Year Book of International Humanitarian and Refugee Law*.

Yemi Oke, 2014, 'Insecurity Challenges in Nigeria-Boko Haram Insurgency, Bakassi Resettlement Crisis and the Niger Delta Militancy: A Thesis for Lasting Peace' 1 *International and Comparative Journal of Peace and Environment*.

Zainab Bangura, 2015, Special Representatives of the Sec-Gen of UN on Sexual Violence in Conflict United Nations News Condemning the Use of Sexual Violence, UN Envoy Warns Boko Haram Aims to Destroy Family Structures, https://news.un.org/en/story/2015/05/499942-condemning-use-sexual-violence-un-envoy-warns-boko-haram-aims-destroy-family.

8

Prospects for Reparations for Victims of Conflict-Related Sexual Violence in Uganda

Josephine Ndagire

1 Introduction

The concept of reparation dates back to the 1648 Treaty of Westphalia and the law of remedies.[1] Remedies are a form of legal redress for harms and wrongful acts.[2] Therefore, broadly, reparations are a form of legal remedy. Reparations may be procedural or substantive. The procedural component refers to the process of seeking redress, while the substantive

[1] Rashida Manjoo, Promotion and Protection of All Human Rights, Civil, Political, Economic, Social and Cultural Rights including the Right to Development: Report of the Special Rapporteur on the Violence Against Women, Its Causes and Consequences, A/HRC/14/22, April 19, 2010.

[2] Ibid., at 8.

J. Ndagire (✉)
Makerere University, Kampala, Uganda
e-mail: jndagire@law.mak.ac.ug

A. Budoo-Scholtz and E. C. Lubaale (eds.), *Violence Against Women and Criminal Justice in Africa: Volume II*, Sustainable Development Goals Series,
https://doi.org/10.1007/978-3-030-75953-7_8

aspect emanates from a pronouncement of harm by a judicial or quasi-judicial entity.[3] Collectively, the procedural and substantive aspects of reparations symbolically atone aggrieved parties for harms such as violations of human rights.[4] In recent years, reparations have been established as a right, deriving from customary international law and other legal sources.[5] To that end, fulfilment of the right to reparations plays a critical role in post-conflict reconstruction. The South African Committee on Reparation and Reconciliation, for instance, construed reparations as a counterbalance to amnesty.[6]

Recent years have shown that reparations may result from administrative processes or negotiations, and not necessarily some form of judicial process.[7] For instance in 2013, the British government settled a claim of rights violations during colonial times by veteran Mau Mau fighters.[8] This trend has primarily been driven by prolonged conflicts, which created mass victims for widespread violations.[9] The process leading to reparations is therefore largely determined by the context (nature of conflict) and the number of victims.[10]

For years, the conflict in Northern Uganda was regarded as one of Africa's most tragic catastrophes.[11] After President Museveni overthrew a

---

[3] Ibid.

[4] Naomi Roht-Arriaza, 'Reparations Decisions and Dilemmas' 27(2) *Hastings International and Comparative Law Review* (2004): 157–291, https://repository.uchastings.edu/hastings_international_comparative_law_review/vol27/iss2/1.

[5] Jean- Marie Kamatali, 'Accountability for Genocide and Other Gross Human Rights Violations: The Need for an Intergrated and Victim Based Transitional Justice' 9(2) *Journal of Genocide Research* (2007): 275–295, https://doi.org/10.1080/14623520701368685.

[6] Pablo De Greiff, *HandBook of Reparations* (2006): 193.

[7] Jamie E Malamud et al., 'Reparations and Civil Litigation' in *Compensation for Human Rights Violations in Transitional Democracies: The Hand Book of Reparations* edited by Pablo de Greiff (2006): 539–559.

[8] BBC, *Mau Mau Torture Victims to Receive Compensation*, June 6, 2013, https://www.bbc.com/news/uk-22790037.

[9] For instance, the holocaust created mass victims and led to decades long reparation programmes by the German government. Similar experiences include victims of the apartheid regime in South Africa.

[10] Dinah Shelton and Ingadottir Thordis, The International Criminal Court Reparations to Victims of Crimes (article 75 of the Rome Statute) and the Trust Fund (article 79): Recommendations for the Court Rules of Procedure and Evidence, Centre on International Cooperation (1999 http://www.pictpcti.org/publications/PICT_articles/REPARATIONS.PDF

[11] Ibid.

Northern-led government in the 1980s,[12] several rebel groups sprouted in the Northern part of the country, including, the Lord's Resistance Army (LRA)—an offshoot of the Holy Spirit Movement (HSM). The LRA, under Joseph Kony, waged a brutal war in the Northern part of the country for over two decades years. Although the rebel outfit was pushed out of Uganda around 2006, it is still active to this day, and believed to operate in Obo, Central African Republic.[13] The LRA is believed by many to be a cult.[14] The group is notorious for perpetrating the most heinous crimes including, indiscriminate (civilian) attacks, forced recruitment, abductions, mutilations and all forms of conflict-related sexual violence (CRSV). Over the years, the LRA received support from sympathisers, mostly Ugandans in the diaspora and reportedly, the government of Sudan.[15]

This article specifically assesses the harm caused by CRSV and how survivors, in thousands, can obtain meaningful redress. The LRA abducted several girls and young women over the years and subjected them to sexual slavery.[16] Indeed, in the 1990s, about 800 children were born to LRA fighters, in a single camp.[17] While girls and women were conscripted into the rebel group as fighters, spies and potters, sexual violence was a calculated tactic of the conflict.[18] In addition to sexual

[12] Khristopher Carlson and Dyan Mazurana, *Forced Marriage Within the Lord 's Resistance Army* (2008): 12.

[13] Catherine Byaruhanga, 'Has Ugandan Rebel Leader Joseph Kony Been Defeated?' *BBC*, May 23, 2017, https://www.bbc.com/news/world-africa-39999324.

[14] Payam Arkhavan, 'Developments at the International Criminal Court: The Lord 's Resistance Army Case: Uganda 's Submission of the First State Referral to the International Criminal Court' 99 *American Journal of International Law* (2005): 403.

[15] BBC, *Uganda Mystic Rebel Leader Dies*, January 18, 2007, http://news.bbc.co.uk/2/hi/africa/6274313.stm. According to the Sudan Tribune, this support continued until 2012, See Sudan Tribune, *Sudan Is Backing Joseph Kony 's LRA, Says Uganda*, May 1, 2012, http://www.sudantribune.com/spip.php?article42451.

[16] Amnesty International, 'Uganda: Justice System Fails Victims of Sexual Violence' November 30, 2007.

[17] Arkhavan, *supra* note 14.

[18] The Daily Monitor, *Last of Abducted Aboke Girls Back Home*, http://www.monitor.co.ug/artman/publish/news/Last_of_abducted_Aboke_girls_back_home_81437.sht.

slavery, the girls and women were also forced into marriage and repeatedly raped. In many ways, each suffered multiple forms of CRSV.[19] Over the years, the LRA conducted several massacres and abductions.

The most memorable of these, and perhaps, one that drew global attention to the conflict, is the 1996 night abduction of 152 secondary school girls from St Marys College, Aboke.[20] The girls were aged between 13 and 16 years.[21] While 122 girls were released the following day, 5 died and each of the remaining 25 bore at least one child as a result of repeated rapes and sexual enslavement.[22] The men had multiple 'wives', as many as 40, in some instances.[23] The Aboke girls represent just a tiny fraction of the number of female abductees. CRSV served several purposes including, rewarding fighters, bolstering morale, inflicting pain and asserting the subjugation of girls and women in the cult. The collective experiences of women culminated into heinous crimes—war crimes and crimes against humanity.

In the aftermath of the conflict in Northern Uganda, prosecution of CRSV crimes proved challenging due to the number of victims, unwillingness of victims to participate, a lack of suitable legislative framework for several years and a general preference for traditional justice mechanisms. Administrative remedies, in this particular context, seem better suited, due to predictability, relatively limited time involved and certainty pertaining to the outcome of the process.

The concept of reparations is novel to Uganda's legal system and remains largely unexplored in jurisprudence and scholarly literature. In recent years, civil society organisations (CSOs) have taken a keen interest in the concept and have framed it as central to meaningful peace and reconstruction efforts in post-conflict Northern Uganda. The United

---

[19] Sarah Tumwebaze, *The 20-Year Old War That Tore Their Families Apart*, The Daily Monitor Newspaper, April 30, 2011, http://www.monitor.co.ug/Magazines/Full+Woman/-/689842/1153386//8ydw7sz/-/index.html.

[20] Els De Temmerman, Aboke Girls: Children Abducted in Northern Uganda (2001).

[21] Thernstrom, *Melanie, Charlotte, Grace, Janet and Caroline Come Home*, The New York Times, May 22, 2005.

[22] Ibid.

[23] The New Vision, *Former LRA Commander Kwoyelo Free*, http://www.newvision.co.ug/D/8/12/765742.

Nations[24] and CSOs[25] have documented the atrocities of the conflict at length, while others, have called for reparations. Several engagements with victims of the conflict have repeatedly prioritised truth and reparations.

The precise meaning of the concept of reparations for victims of the Northern Uganda remains abstract. The government has implemented reconstruction and development programs in the region[26] and perceives the same as some form of reparation (National Transitional Justice Policy 2019). However, as a marginalised region, the government was bound to undertake development projects, regardless of the conflict and ensuing ravages (article 36 Constitution, 1995). This notwithstanding, there could be intersections between reparations and development programs.[27] Reparations must follow an acknowledgement of harm and should at the very minimum, encompass an appropriate compensatory sum that reflects the socio-economic circumstances. The Nairobi Declaration on Women's and Girls' Right to a Remedy and Reparation (Nairobi Declaration), builds on to the UN Basic Principles and Guidelines on the Right to a Remedy and Reparation for Victims of Gross Violations of International Human Rights Law and Serious Violations of International Humanitarian Law (Basic Principles) by drawing attention to the specific experiences of women in conflict.[28] The conventional understanding

[24] Office of the United Nations High Commissioner for Human Rights, Making Peace Our Own: Victims ' Perceptions of Accountability, Reconciliation and Transitional Justice in Northern Uganda (2007), https://uganda.ohchr.org/Content/publications/Making%20Peace%20Our%20Own.

[25] International Crisis Group, Northern Uganda: Seizing the Opportunity for Peace, Africa Report No 124–26 (2007); Amnesty International, 'Uganda: Justice System Fails Victims of Sexual Violence' November 30, 2007*;* Human Rights Watch, 'Abducted and Abused: Renewed Conflict in Northern Uganda' (2003), https://www.hrw.org/reports/2003/uganda0703/uganda0703.pdf; Human Rights Watch, 'Uprooted and Forgotten Impunity and Human Rights Abuses in Northern Uganda', https://www.hrw.org/reports/2005/uganda0905/.

[26] The development programs include Northern Uganda Social Action Fund (NUSAF) I and II; *The Peace Recovery and Development Plan (PRDP) I, II and III. Together, these programs aimed to improve service delivery and access to services by the citizens in the region.*

[27] International Center for Transitional Justice, *Building Blocks for Reparations: Providing Interim Relief to Victims Through Targeted Development Assistance*, September 2020, https://www.ictj.org/sites/default/files/ICTJ_Report_Uganda_InterimRelief_Web.pdf.

[28] The Nairobi Declaration on Women's and Girls' Right to a Remedy and Reparation (Nairobi Declaration), 2007.

of restitution in the Basic Principles, would for instance, perpetuate gender inequality and discrimination which led to CRSV, in the first place.[29] The Nairobi Declaration underscores the importance of women's participation in reparation programs,[30] and warns against undertaking development programs instead of a reparation program.[31]

The important work cited above does not go into the specifics of a reparation program for girls and women subjected to CRSV. This article offers a glimpse into what an actual reparation program for survivors of CRSV might look like. Since reparations are determined by harm, this article discusses specific harms caused by CRSV and how they may be redressed.

2 Conflict-Related Sexual Violence Harms

The effects of CRSV were articulated by the UN Security Council in Resolution 1325.[32] Resolution 1325, essentially, drew links between gender, conflict and conflict resolution, for the first time.[33] Resolution 1325 states as follows:

> ...understanding of the impact of armed conflict on women and girls, effective institutional arrangements to guarantee their protection and full participation in the peace process can significantly contribute to the maintenance and promotion of international peace and security...[34]

---

[29] Valérie Couillard, 'The Nairobi Declaration: Redefining Reparation for Women Victims of Sexual Violence' 1 *The International Journal of Transitional Justice* (2007): 9. https://doi.org/10.1093/ijtj/ijm030.

[30] Nairobi Declaration *supra* note 28, Principle 2.

[31] Ibid., Principle 3(b).

[32] UN Security Council, *Security Council Resolution 1325 (2000) [on women and peace and security]*, October 31, 2000, S/RES/1325 (2000), https://www.refworld.org/docid/3b00f4672e.html.

[33] Andrew Sheriff and Karen Barnes, Enhancing the EU Response to Women and Armed Conflict with Particular Reference to Development Policy, Study for the Slovenian EU Presidency, European Centre for Development Policy Management, Discussion Paper No. 8, (2008): 9, https://www.europarl.europa.eu/document/activities/cont/200805/20080507ATT28495/20080507ATT28495EN.pdf; See also, Nairobi Declaration, supra note 28, paragraph 3.

[34] Resolution 1325, preamble 10.

The lived experiences of women and girls should inform all interventions relating to their redress in post-conflict situations. This requires an in-depth analysis of the forms and effects of CRSV on the victims and survivors. Put differently, it is important to examine specific harms and how they impact the lives upon which they are inflicted. Such examination is crucial in guiding reparation programs and how they may be applied on an individual basis because reparations should redress specific and not abstract harms. The discussion that follows assesses various forms of harms and how they impact women and girls.

2.1 Fistula

CRSV is far more brutal than other forms of sexual violence. During the 1994 genocide in Rwanda, women were invaded with gun barrels, wood and other objects.[35] Similar experiences were reported in the Democratic Republic of Congo, while gang rapes characterised the conflicts in Sierra Leone, Liberia and Northern Uganda.[36] CRSV has dire and dramatic consequences including fistula and chronic pain in the pelvic area.[37] This situation is exacerbated by the practice of female genital mutilation (FGM), in some cases. FGM increases the risk of tears of tissue in the reproductive system.[38] In extreme cases, traumatic fistulae resulting from brutal rapes could develop into permanent injury to the uterus

35 CW Mullins, 'He Would Kill Me with His Penis: Genocidal Rape in Rwanda as a State Crime' 17 *CritCrim* (2009): 15–33, https://doi.org/10.1007/s10612-008-9067-3; See also, Janet Fleischman and Nowrojee Binaifer, In Rwanda, Too, Rape, Was a War Crime and Must Be Punished, *The New York Times*, July 25, 1996; Eleni Coundouriotis, 'You Only Have Your Word: Rape and Testimony' 35(2) *Human Rights Quarterly* (2013): 365–385, http://www.jstor.org/stable/24518020; *The Prosecutor v Akayesu (Judgment)* (September 2, 1998) ICTR¬96¬4¬T, paragraph 507 (Chamber I, ICTR).

36 Kim Thuy Seelinger, *Domestic Accountability for Sexual Violence: The Potential of Specialised Units in Kenya, Liberia, Sierra Leone and Uganda*, https://international-review.org/sites/default/files/irrc-894-seelinger.icrc.pdf.

37 Ines Nissou Dossa et al., 'Fistula and other Adverse Reproductive Health Outcomes Among Women Victims of Conflict-related Sexual Violence: A Population-based Cross-sectional Study' 41(1) *Birth Berkeley, Calif* (2014): 5–13. https://doi.org/10.1111/birt.12085.

38 Katie Thomas, *Sexual Violence: Weapon of War*, file:///C:/Users/HP500B ~ 1/AppData/Local/Temp/Sexual_Violence_Weapon_of_War.pdf.

and deformity of the reproductive tract.[39] These kinds of fistula are commonly reported in post-conflict communities, including, Northern Uganda.[40] The trauma suffered by girls and women in the reproductive tract are largely responsible for the predominance of fistulae in post-conflict communities.

2.2 Psychological Trauma

CRSV may result in lasting psychological trauma and depression.[41] This particular harm may not show physical symptoms, and is often, overlooked or even disregarded. One observer notes that 'concessions—made for the person suffering such obvious war-related incapacity as loss of a limb are unlikely to be made for those with equally severe wounding inflicted by sexual violence'. They further note that 'trauma is recurring, and continues long after the end of the conflict'.[42] In the event of pregnancy arising out of rape, depression poses serious risks to a child's development.[43] The invisible scars of sexual violence last a lifetime. It would require appropriate reparations to alleviate the traumatic effects of CRSV. A wholesome approach to reparations is necessary if victims bearing invisible scars are to obtain a remedy that would be regarded effective in law.

---

39 ACQUIRE Report, *Traumatic Gynaecologic Fistula: A Consequence of Sexual Violence in Conflict Settings, Acquire Project* (2006): 3, https://www.engenderhealth.org/files/pubs/maternal-health/tf-report-english.pdf.

40 Ibid.

41 International Committee of the Red Cross, 'Women and War: Women and Armed Conflict and the Issue of Sexual Violence' ICRC (2014) 29, file:///C:/Users/HP500B ~ 1/AppData/Local/Temp/icrc_report_women_and_war-1.pdf.

42 Thomas, *supra* note 38.

43 Children's Defense Fund, Minnesotta, *Zero to Three Research to Policy Project: Maternal Depression and Early Childhood* (2011), http://www.cdf-mn.org/research-library/maternal-depressionreport.pdf.

2.3 Forced Pregnancy

The weaponisation of sexual violence in conflict situations is a serious human rights violation and undermines human dignity. Forced impregnation is one of several consequences of the weaponisation of sexual violence. It is an international crime when committed in the context of an armed conflict or war.[44] Force impregnation is recognised by the Rome Statute of the International Criminal Court (Rome Statute) as a war crime and crime against humanity.[45] The Rome Statute defines forced pregnancy as:

> [T]he unlawful confinement of a woman forcibly made pregnant, with the intent of affecting the ethnic composition of any population or carrying out other grave violations of international law. This definition shall not in any way be interpreted as affecting national laws relating to pregnancy.[46]

In Northern Uganda, the LRA took several girls and women as wives, and sired several children with them.[47] Many women gave birth at a very young age and suffered gynaecological complications, with no access to professional health care services.[48] Beyond physical harm, the girls/women lost opportunities such as education, and were faced with a bleak future, marked by poverty.[49] Moreover, children born out of rape face considerable challenges, including rejection, ill-treatment, abuse and

---

[44] Boon Kristen, 'Rape and Forced Pregnancy under the ICC Statute: Human Dignity, Autonomy, and Consent' 32 *Columbia Human Rights Law Review* (2001): 655.

[45] UN General Assembly, Rome Statute of the International Criminal Court (Rome Statute) (last amended 2010), July 17, 1998, ISBN No. 92–9227-227–6, article 7 (1) (g). See also, Rome Statute, article 6 (a) – (d).

[46] Rome Statute, article 7 (2) (f).

[47] Amnesty International, *supra* note 16.

[48] Ibid.

[49] Women's Advocacy Network, *Petition Before the Parliament of the Republic of Uganda* (2014), http://justiceandreconciliation.com/wp-content/uploads/2014/03/Womens-Advocacy-Network-Petition-24-February-2014.pdf.

denial of a social status within a community such as a surname or inheritance rights.[50]

3 The International Framework on Reparations

For years, the right to reparations was implicit in the right to a remedy.[51] The UN Basic Principles for the Protection and Promotion of Human Rights through Action to Combat Impunity, establish the right to reparations for victims of all human rights violations.[52] Under these principles, states bear the responsibility to ensure respect and enforce norms of international human rights and international humanitarian law that are incorporated in treaties to which they are party, and those that have been incorporated in their domestic legal systems.[53] This obligation, *inter alia,* includes provision of reparations to the victims. The International Law Commission Articles on State Responsibility for Internationally Wrongful Acts (ILC Articles) 2001 provide for the full reparation of victims for injury caused by internationally wrongful acts and guarantees of non-repetition (Article 31(1)).[54] Where the responsible party is unable or unwilling to provide reparations to victims; the state should endeavour to provide reparations, especially where there has been serious bodily injury, physical or mental impairment.[55]

---

[50] Joanne Neenan, 'Closing the Protection Gap for Children Born of War: Addressing Stigmatisation and the Intergenerational Impact of Sexual Violence in Conflict' *Centre for Women Peace and Security, LSE* (2018): 34.

[51] Instruments include: Article 8 of the UDHR; article 2(3) International Convenenant on Civil and Political Rights; Declaration of the Basic Principles of Justice for Victims of Crime and Abuse of Power, UN Doc. A/RES/40/34, adopted by the General Assembly Resolution 40/34, 29 November 1985 and Articles 75 & 79 of the Rome Statute.

[52] Updated Set of principles for the protection and promotion of human rights through action to combat impunity, E/CN.4/2005/102/Add.1, February 8, 2005.

[53] Basic Principles, Principle 10.

[54] Annex, General Assembly resolution 56/83 of 12 December 2001.

[55] The United Nations Basic Principles and Guidelines on the Right to a Remedy and Reparation for Victims of Gross Violations of International Human Rights Law and Serious Violations of International Humanitarian Law, Principle 18. It should be noted that these are non-binding norms but persuasive and authoritative interpretation.

The Basic Principles detail several forms of reparations. They establish a standard for an effective remedy which includes: 'equal and effective access to justice'; 'reparation for harm suffered' and 'access to information'.[56] Further, victims of 'gross violations of international human rights law and serious violations of international humanitarian law' have the right to be 'provided with full and effective reparations in its five forms'—restitution, compensation, satisfaction, guarantees of non-repetition and rehabilitation, which is discussed in detail below.[57] There should be proportionality between the reparations and the gravity of harm suffered.[58] The higher the degree of gravity of the harm suffered by the victim, the more severe the distress.[59]

General Comment 31 of the Human Rights Committee (HRC) provides that the duty to protect covenant rights includes the vindication of those rights by making available accessible and effective remedies.[60] In addition, states have a duty to align the available remedies with the peculiar needs of special interest or vulnerable groups.[61] From this perspective, a right is as good as available redress. Where states fail to provide meaningful avenues for rights enforcement, the duty to protect is breached. While the HRC singles out children, victims and survivors of CRSV would without a doubt, fall in the same category.

It follows that states should 'establish appropriate judicial and administrative mechanisms for addressing claims of rights violations under domestic law'. The HR notes that 'the enjoyment of the rights recognised under the Covenant' can be effectively assured by the judiciary in many different ways such as 'including direct applicability of the Covenant, application of comparable constitutional or other provisions of law, or the interpretive effect of the Covenant in the application of national

---

[56] Basic Principles, Principle 11.

[57] Amnesty International, *Truth, Justice and Reparation: Establishing an Effective Truth Commission,* Pol 30/009 (2007); *See also*, International Law Commission Articles *on State Responsibility*, G.A Res 56/83 of December 12, 2001.

[58] Basic Principles, Principle 15.

[59] *Loayza Tamayo v Peru* Judgment of November 27,1998,43 Inter-Am.Ct.H.R (Ser.C) (1998).

[60] General Comment No. 31 [80] *Nature of the General Legal Obligation Imposed on States Parties to the Covenant*: 05/26/2004. CCPR/C/21/Rev.1/Add.13.

[61] Ibid.

law'.[62] The HRC also stresses on administrative mechanisms 'to give effect to the general obligation to investigate allegations of violations promptly, thoroughly and effectively through independent and impartial bodies'.[63] If a state fails to investigate allegations of violations, it is in contravention of its obligations under the Covenant. The states needs to ensure '[c]essation of an ongoing violation' which 'is an essential element of the right to an effective remedy'.[64] Paragraph 16 emphasises that violations are not remedied unless reparations rendered are effective. This emphasis is necessary for sexual offenses because the remedies and reparation programs seldom address the peculiar needs of CRSV victims.

4 Domestic Framework for Reparations

Article 32 of the 1995 Constitution of the Republic of Uganda (Constitution) recognises affirmative action in favour of marginalised groups. Reparations provide a means through which the marginalised and isolated are reintegrated into society. Objective III(iii) of the Constitution calls for tolerance, appreciation and respect for various 'customs, traditions and beliefs'. Objective III(iv) further provides for the establishment of 'institutions and procedures for resolution of conflicts fairly and peacefully'. It also calls for the integration of Ugandans 'while at the same time recognising the existence of their ethnic, religious ideological and cultural diversity'.[65] When read in light of the spirit in the preamble, there is support to the assumption that the legislators wanted to promote

[62] *Supra* note 60, paragraph 15.

[63] Ibid.

[64] Ibid., paragraph 16: 'Articles 2 & 3, require that States Parties make reparation to individuals whose Covenant rights have been violated. Without reparation to individuals whose Covenant rights have been violated, the obligation to provide an effective remedy, which is central to the efficacy of article 2 & 3, is not discharged. In addition to the explicit reparation required by articles 9& 5, and 14 & 6, the Committee considers that the Covenant generally entails appropriate compensation. The Committee notes that, where appropriate, reparation can involve restitution, rehabilitation and measures of satisfaction, such as public apologies, public memorials, guarantees of non-repetition and changes in relevant laws and practices, as well as bringing to justice the perpetrators of human rights violations'.

[65] Constitution of Uganda, Objective (III)(ii).

reconciliation and redress for past and ongoing wrongs. The Constitution was promulgated in 1995, at the peak of LRA atrocities in Northern Uganda. In addition to the spirit of the Constitution and national objectives articulated in the preamble, article 50(1) of the Constitution affirms the right of individuals to seek redress for rights violations. Article 50(2) further allows the enforcement of rights on behalf of victims. Such third-party enforcement may be undertaken by an individual or organisation. In this regard, the Constitution takes a critical step in ensuring the protection of human rights. More critically, article 126(2) establishes the foundation for the reparations. It enjoins courts to provide adequate compensation to victims of wrongs (article 126(2)(c)) and to promote reconciliation (article 126(2)(d)). In these two provisions, the Constitution looks beyond justice—which is no doubt, a form or reparation, and underpins the importance of monetary compensation and reconciliation between adversaries.

In addition to establishing formal courts as rights enforcement mechanisms (article 50), the Constitution establishes a quasi-judicial mechanism to expedite redress for rights violations. Article 51 establishes the Uganda Human Rights Commission (UHRC). The mandate of UHRC is to, among others investigate human rights violations and make recommendations related to rights promotion to the legislative body. The powers of the UHRC are enunciated in article 53 of the Constitution and include, performance of functions and powers of a court, such as, calling witnesses, issuing summons, committing persons for contempt and more importantly, ordering the release of restricted or detained persons and ordering the 'payment of compensation' or other 'legal remedy or redress'. The details of its operations are elaborated in the Uganda Human Rights Commission Act 1997.

Uganda domesticated the Rome Statute on the heels of the Review Conference of the Rome Statute, which was held in Uganda, from May 31 to June 11, 2010. The International Criminal Court Act (ICC Act) was promulgated on May 25, 2010 and commenced on June 25, 2010. Section 20(1)(a)(xiii) of the ICC Act provides for the enforcement of orders of the ICC in respect to 'fines, penalties and reparations'. The ICC Act is silent on orders for reparations and fines emanating from trials in Uganda courts.

Despite the aforementioned legal framework, for decades, there was no procedure for enforcing rights in the manner envisaged by article 50(4) of the Constitution. In 2019, the legislative body passed the Human Rights (Enforcement) Act (HREA) of 2019. This Act is significant in several ways. In the first instance, HREA broadens the concept of victimhood by recognising that the effects rights violations transcend the individual victim. Section 1 of the HREA defines a victim as:

> ...a person who suffers a human right violation and includes the person's immediate family or dependents or any other person whose rights have been violated as a result of the violation of the victim's rights and freedoms.

A critical analysis of this definition suggests that the law now recognises that single rights violation could, advertently or inadvertently cause other human rights violations. Put differently, a human rights violation should result into rights violations of persons other than the initial victim before they can be regarded as victims. While an important first step, this law seems oblivious to family and community disruptions and vulnerabilities that may arise out of single human rights violation. And while such disruptions and vulnerabilities may not amount to a specific human rights violation immediately, they may and generally tend to, several years later.

The HREA embodies the concept of reparations in several ways. It affirms the importance of redress for rights violations by establishing a procedure for such a process. Section 3(1) of the HREA goes further by recognising threats to fundamental rights and freedom as a basis for seeking redress. More importantly, however, it bestows upon the courts power to order several forms of reparation in human rights matters including, compensation (Section 9(1)), restitution (Section 9(2)(a)), rehabilitation (Section 9(2)(b)), satisfaction including establishing the truth through the full and public disclosure of facts (Section 9(2)(c)(ii)), 'public apology including, acknowledgement of the facts and acceptance of responsibility' (Section 9(2)(c)(iv)) and 'guarantees of non-repetition (Section 9(2)(c)(vi)).

There is broad mention of compensation in legislation preceding the HREA. For instance, Section 199 of the Magistrates Courts Act (MCA) confer upon magistrates the power to make an order for compensation if they are satisfied that a party to the criminal proceedings—including the prosecution, suffered some form of harm due to the acts of the other party). In a similar fashion, courts of record—High Court, Court of Appeal, which also sit as the Constitutional Court and the Supreme Court, may by virtue of Section 126(1) of the Trial on Indictment Act (TIA), make orders for compensation.

There is limited precedent of compensation orders in sexual violence cases. Section 199 of the MCA and 126 of the TIA have mostly been invoked in cases involving property. This notwithstanding, Section 129B of the Penal Code Act, explicitly provides for compensation in cases of defilement (sexual intercourse with persons below 18 years of age). It is to the effect that where the victim suffered harm of a physical, sexual, or psychological nature, the court may order the perpetrator to pay compensation to the victim. To be clear, sexual offences/violations *always* cause the kind of harm stipulated in the aforementioned provision, including emotional distress. Unfortunately, the law presupposes such harm to be the exception and not the rule. This notwithstanding, the courts have made compensation orders in a handful of sexual offences. In *Mubiru Kisingiri v Uganda*, the accused was convicted of aggravated defilement, sentenced to 10 years in prison and ordered to compensate the victim 50,000,000 Uganda Shillings (USD 13,500).[66] On appeal, the conviction was quashed and the sentence set aside due to inconsistencies in the evidence submitted to the trial court. In *David Otema v Uganda*, the trial judge noted the medical expenses incurred by the victim as a result of rape and ordered the perpetrator to pay 300,000 Uganda Shillings (USD 81).[67] Clearly, the courts are taking steps to ensure appropriate redress for victims of sexual violence, although the practice varies widely and is inconsistently applied.

---

[66] *Mubiru Kisingiri v Uganda* (HCT-0OCR-CN-O108 - 2015) [2016] UGHCCRD 6 (April 19, 2016).

[67] *David Otema vs Uganda*, Criminal Appeal No. 155 of 2008) [2015] UGCA 42 (June 15, 2015).

The concept of reparations for conflict-related crimes, made its way into Uganda's policy for the first time in Juba Peace Agreement on Accountability and Reconciliation (Juba Agreement). This agreement followed protracted peace talks between the government of Uganda and the LRA. Clause 11 and 12 of the Juba Agreement specifically calls for reparations for women and children.[68] In many ways, the Juba Agreement acknowledges the importance of reparations to peacebuilding and incorporates concepts such truth and reconciliation.

The Ugandan government adopted the National Transitional Justice Policy (NTJP) on June 17, 2019 to address post-conflict situations.[69] The policy is a combination of judicial and non-judicial processes and mechanisms including, prosecution, truth telling, reparations programs and institutional reforms.[70] The NTJP is a significant milestone, in as far as it acknowledges the absence of a comprehensive legal framework for reparations, victims' frustrations as a result of the failure to provide reparations, and challenges pertaining to establishing a reparation program.[71] The absence of a policy of children born in captivity is highlighted, although there is no mention of the women who bore them and the circumstances under which they were born. More importantly, the NTJP adopts a broad interpretation of reparations to include, compensation and symbolic reparations.[72] In a major setback, the NTJP appears to confuse development initiatives and reparations. The former is a duty that states owe to citizens while the latter is a recognised and enforceable right.

The liability of the government to provide reparations to the affected districts, stems from its acts and omissions, including, the failure to exercise due diligence in protecting civilians. Uganda has a duty to perform treaty obligations in good faith.[73] Failure to act in good faith

[68] The Justice Law and Order Sector: Republic of Uganda, *Special Report: The National Transitional Justice Policy (NTJP)*, 3 July 2019, https://www.jlos.go.ug/index.php/com-rsform-manage-directory-submissions/services-and-information/press-and-media/latest-news/item/698-special-report-the-national-transitional-justice-policy, 11.

[69] Ibid., 12.

[70] Ibid.

[71] Ibid.

[72] Ibid.

[73] Article 26 of the Vienna Convention on the Law of Treaties (1969).

by exercising due diligence may be deduced from: the deployment arrow wielding auxillary forces (Amuka Boys), who were few in number and unable to engage the LRA,[74] initial absence of the UHRC in Northern Uganda and perpetual underfunding of the entity,[75] and objection to the United Kingdom (UK) proposals in a joint resolution in 2006 that sought to investigate the external sources of LRA support.[76] While this resolution primarily aimed at enabling the arrest of LRA leaders indicted by the International Criminal Court (ICC), the UK also proposed an investigation of the external sources of support of the rebel group. The Uganda government rejected this proposal and ultimately, efforts towards establishing culpability for the heinous crimes, and by extension, potential sources of compensation were frustrated. The National objectives in the preamble to the Constitution clearly state that foreign policy shall be based on respect for international law and treaty obligations.[77] Article 45 of the Constitution also recognises rights, duties, declarations and guarantees relating to the fundamental human rights and freedoms that are provided by other human rights instruments.

5 Reparations for CRSV Victims in Northern Uganda

Given the number of offences committed in Northern Uganda and the multitude of victims/survivors, any reparations for CRSV victims would have to be part of a broader reparation program. The UN broadly defines a reparations program to include both administrative and out of court

[74] Office of the United Nations High Commissioner for Human Rights, Making Peace Our Own: Victims' Perceptions of Accountability, Reconciliation and Transitional Justice in Northern Uganda, United Nations (2007), https://uganda.ohchr.org/Content/publications/Making%20Peace%20Our%20Own.pdf..

[75] Human Rights Watch, *Abducted and Abused: Renewed Conflict in Northern Uganda* (2003), https://www.hrw.org/reports/2003/uganda0703/uganda0703.pdf.

[76] International Crisis Group, *Northern Uganda: Seizing the Opportunity for Peace, Africa* Report No 124–26, (2007): 16.

[77] Objective XXVIII (i) (b), Constitution of the Republic of Uganda (1995).

settlements.[78] It should be noted that these programs do not necessarily follow judicial/quasi-judicial processes, but are nonetheless premised on the acknowledgement of wrong doing, and the concomitant harm that creates victims.

Reparation programs generally have a tendency to focus on the persons who directly suffer harm, and in doing so, exclude victims or inadvertently, rank rights violations. Such an approach does little to redress collective harm. In the case of CRSV, the harm goes far beyond the individual woman and affects the resulting children, families and the communities. According to the UN, victims of CRSV include persons who individually or collectively suffered such violence, family members (partners and children) and children born as a result of pregnancy from rape.[79] Principle 8 of the Basic Principles construes victims as persons who collectively or individually suffer harm. The Basic Principles construe harm in a much broader sense than HREA to include:

> ...physical or mental injury, emotional suffering, economic loss or substantial impairment of their fundamental rights, through acts or omissions that constitute gross violations of international human rights law, or serious violations of international humanitarian law.[80]

This broad categorisation of harm extends to a victim's family members or community, who may suffer emotional harm or economic loss. For emphasis, sexual violence is harm against the individual but the reality is that in complex cultural, social and religious contexts, communities also suffer harm. Until those factors are neutralised, communities fall victim.

[78] United Nations, *Guidance Note of the Secretary General on Reparations for Conflict-related Sexual Violence*, June (2014): 6, https://www.ohchr.org/Documents/Press/GuidanceNoteReparationsJune-2014.pdf.

[79] Ibid.

[80] Basic Principles, Principle 8.

5.1 Restitution

Restitution is the body of law where liability is based on a defendant's unjust enrichment.[81] The law of remedies primarily aims at undoing the effects of wrongs suffered and restoring what was taken from the victim. Restitution may 'include performance of an obligation', 'revocation of the offending act' or 'abstention of the unlawful conduct'.[82] The ILC Articles provide that a state 'is under an obligation to make restitution and to re-establish the situation which existed before the wrongful act'. The ILC Articles further provide that restitution is not the appropriate form of reparations in circumstances where it is—materially impossible or would—involve a burden out of all proportion from the benefit deriving from restitution instead of compensation.[83] Principle 19 of the Basic Principles further provides that restitution 'should whenever possible, restore the victim to the original situation before gross violations of international human rightslaw or serious violations of international humanitarian law occurred'. It includes: 'restoration to liberty, enjoyment of human rights, identity, family life and citizenship, return to one's place of residence, restoration of employment and return of property where it was deprived'.[84]

The war in Northern Uganda adversely affected the entire region leaving the inhabitants with a perception that they were unfairly marginalised through economic deprivation. Deprivation was allegedly a strategic way of rendering communities incapable of fighting the government.[85] The government should therefore endeavour to economically uplift these communities so that they can regard themselves as being treated with a sense of equality with other regions. There is constitutional authorisation for the proposal under article 193(4) of the Constitution. It states as follows:

---

[81] Bryan Garner, *Black's Law Dictionary*, 8th Edition (2004).

[82] Linda Malone, *International Law* (2008): 50.

[83] International Law Commission Articles, Article 35 (a) & (b).

[84] Basic Principles, Principle 19.

[85] Paul Omach, 'Understanding Obstacles to Peace in Northern Uganda: Actors Their Interests and Strategies, in Africa's Great Lakes Region' in *Understanding Obstacles to Peace: Actors, Interests and Strategies in Africa's Great Lakes Region* edited by Mwesiga Baregu (2011): 273.

> [E]qualisation grant is the money to be paid to local governments for giving subsidies or making special provisions for the least developed districts and shall be based on the degree to which a local government unit is lagging behind the national average standard for a particular service.[86]

Prior to the war, the affected districts enjoyed relatively good security which allowed the people to live a normal life and to engage in activities such as agriculture, pastoralism and education. Girls and women enjoyed security although not necessarily gender equality, the right to marry and found a family due to patriarchal societal structures. The conflict exacerbated this situation by forcing women and girls into marriages. The children born as a result of these unions have largely been rejected. In accordance with the Nairobi Declaration, restitution for victims of CRSV does not mean a return to the gender discriminatory practices of the past. Rather, restitution should put in place measures that would ensure that the equal enjoyment of rights by both sexes, personal security and means of survival or a source of livelihood, for the women and their families.

5.2 Compensation

Compensation is monetary payment as recognition for harm done and as means of making good the losses suffered.[87] The calculation and assessment of damages is complex because an injury can be psychological. Moreover, even physical injury as a result of criminal activity may be hard to atone for in terms of damages because there is no scale to measure the degree of severity. Monetary compensation includes pecuniary losses, non-pecuniary damage and costs and expenses. Assessment

---

[86] Indeed, the principle of affirmative action in favour of marginalised groups is well entrenched by article 32 of the Constitution, which provides that: —…the State shall take affirmative action in favor of groups marginalised on the basis of... or any other reason created by history... for the purpose of redressing imbalances which exist against them.|| Uganda's history certainly has a lot to do with the marginalisation and even if the North was not deliberately targeted for marginalisation, the insecurity has exacerbated the situation. To achieve institutional development, the government should work within the existing northern Uganda Reconstruction Program.

[87] Black's Law Dictionary, *supra* note 81.

for each monetary award should be accurate because excessive or inadequate awards are likely to frustrate the compensatory, retributive and deterrent aims of reparations.

Article 36 of the ILC Articles affirms the obligation to compensate for the damage caused in so far as damage is not made good by restitution. The Basic Principles state that 'compensation should be provided for any economically assessable damage as appropriate and proportional to the gravity of the violation and circumstances of each case'. Examples include, 'physical or mental harm', 'lost opportunities including employment, education and social benefits', 'material damages and loss of earnings, loss of earning potential', 'moral damage', 'costs required for legal or expert assistance, medicine and medical services', psychological and social services.[88]

In light of the large number of victims, an administrative approach to compensation would be feasible in Uganda. The ICC Trust Fund for Victims (TFV), has over the years, rendered assistance to victims of the conflict in Northern Uganda.[89] It should be noted that the assistance rendered under the TFV is independent of reparations of the ICC.[90] As of 2016, 43,000 victims had benefitted from the fund.[91] While the ICC has played a pivotal role in providing reparative assistance to victims of the conflict, such assistance should not substitute the role that states must play in redressing harm. To that end, the government should establish a Reparation Fund. The Reparation Fund should be funded by the government through annual allocation of money by the Ministry of Finance in the national budget. The defence ministry has over the years consumed the largest part of the country's resources due to the war. For example, in 1999, defence expenditure more than doubled from USD 150 to USD 350 million[92] and has seen a steady increase over

---

[88] Basic Principles, Principle 20.

[89] International Criminal Court, *The Trust Fund for Victims Launches New Assistance Projects in Northern Uganda*, July 2015, https://www.icc-cpi.int/Pages/item.aspx?name=pr1126.

[90] Ibid.

[91] Lino Owor Ogora, *Why Reparations Will Be Central in Determining the Sucess of Ongwen's Trial, International Justice Monitor: A Project of the Open Society Initaitive*, November 9, 2016, https://www.ijmonitor.org/2016/11/why-reparations-will-be-central-in-determining-the-success-of-ongwens-trial/.

[92] Monthly News about Africa, *The New People African Feature Service*, Issue 87, June 1999.

the years.[93] The national budget should make room for the Fund, by reducing expenses elsewhere, for instance, in the defence ministry. Other sources would be donations from non-governmental or private sources. In addition, as was the case with South Africa,[94] the donor community should be requested to directly contribute to the Fund, and to allow unspent monies from other projects, to be diverted to the fund. The government should compile the official list of CRSV victims and survivors.

Victims should be categorised by harm and the amount awarded should correspond to the degree of harm. One of the tragic effects of war was the disruption of education for over two decades. Women were abducted as young girls, forced to join the rebellion for several years, returning as adults with children.[95] Lost time and deprivation of education cannot be remedied by restitution, hence making compensation indispensable. The factors to be considered could include: the number of dependents the victim has, the opportunities lost such as education, whether or not the victim was incapacitated and incapable of earning income, among others. CRSV victims would unfortunately fall in all the enumerated categories because the majority were recruited young and spent years in captivity, thereby, losing education opportunities. CRSV victims and survivors, suffered multiple injuries. For instance, having more than one child with one or more perpetrators further complicates the situation. Guided by the foregoing factors, the government should determine the amount of compensation to be paid to each category. Payments should be made on a monthly basis and depending on the resources, perhaps, spread out, over a number of years.

In South Africa, the Truth and Reconciliation Committee recommended about USD 3,500 for all victims because it would be difficult

93 The East African Newspaper, March 31, 2003.

94 Ginger Thompson, South Africa to Pay $3,900 to Each Family of Apartheid Victims, *The New York Times*, April 16, 2003. See also, Penelope E Andrews, 'Reparations for Apartheid's Victims: The Path to Reconciliation?' 53 *DePaul Law Review* (2004): 1155, https://via.library.depaul.edu/law-review/vol53/iss3/9.

95 K Amone-P'Olak et al., 'Sexual Violence and General Functioning Among Formerly Abducted Girls in Northern Uganda: The Mediating roles of Stigma and Community Relations–the WAYS Study' 16 BMC Public Health (2016): 64, https://doi.org/10.1186/s12889-016-2735-4.

to rank harm/suffering.[96] For CRSV victims, this approach would be untenable because some victims/survivors clearly need more compensation than others. For instance, some victims may need lifelong treatment for conditions such as fistula, while others may have multiple children. Compensation relating to CRSV victims must be critically thought through and appropriate. The challenge is that not all harm can be economically assessed. However, the average wages that the women could have earned, had they attained an education, are ascertainable. Compensation for time and lost opportunity could also take the form of vocational training that could provide skills, adult education and grants to set up businesses, among other initiatives.

5.3 Rehabilitation

Rehabilitation has been defined as a service that restores a traumatised person to the 'fullest physical, psychological, social, vocational and educational level of functioning of which he or she is capable, consistent with physiological or anatomical impairments and environmental limitation'.[97] The Basic Principles provide that rehabilitation should include medical and psychological care, as well as legal and social services.

Prior to the conflict, women may not have enjoyed perfect physical health, but they did to a great extent enjoy mental and psychological health. Rehabilitation programs should work towards enabling victims to experience a normal life. Community-based organisations and non-governmental organisations in northern Uganda, are at the forefront of providing mental and psychosocial support for CRSV survivors. However, there is a need for targeted and continuous counselling for women who bore children as a result of the conflict, in order to cope with motherhood, through complimentary services provided by the government, such as, provision of free psychological assistance, as part of trauma recovery, provided by skilled psychiatrists and psychologists.

---

96 Truth and Reconciliation Committee of South Africa, Final Report, volumes 1-5 (1998), hereafter 1-5 Final Report, 175–184.

97 Trauma System Agenda for the Future, http://www.nhtsa.dot.gov/people/injury/ems/emstraumasystem03/glossary.htm.

The fistula conditions which further victimise the victims because of strong bodily odours, must be treated.[98] Neither the government nor private actors can solely meet all the rehabilitation needs of the affected communities, including the treatment of fistula. Interventions should be concerted and complementary. Additionally, medical workers must have the capability to support the legal process should victims decide to pursue justice. This can be done through proper documentation and collection of forensic evidence,[99] where possible. Coordination between various administration and state departments is to that end crucial.[100] Medical personnel must work hand in hand with police and the prosecution office in order to allow for a comprehensive assessment of damage.[101] Liberia's National Task Force devised a Gender-Based Violence Plan of Action which coordinates multi-sectoral efforts within the government and other organisations has proved very effective.[102] The difficulties of coordination among various players particularly local ones must be addressed through the establishment of a coordination body, ideally, a body responsible for the entire reparation program.

For efficiency and in order to avoid duplication of roles, cooperation is inevitable. The integration effort could, for instance, see organisations working on CRSV, taking up different themes and special focus such as reproductive health, mental health, successful community reintegration of victims and ex-women combatants, elderly women, girls, male victims, among others. Special focus on each of the specific groups of survivors is imperative, because they each have special needs, which cannot be met by a single organisation. The thematic focus on different victims by organisations will meet the Security Council's call for:

[98] Population Reference Bureau, Uganda's Fistula Patients Lack Knowledge of Prevention and Treatment, https://www.prb.org/ugandasfistulapatientslackknowledgeofpreventionandtreatment/.

[99] Ibid.

[100] Ibid.

[101] Ibid.

[102] Ibid.

> ... all those involved in the planning for disarmament, demobilisation and reintegration to consider the different needs of female and male ex-combatants and to take into account the needs of their dependents.[103]

This resolution clearly calls for an acknowledgement of the peculiar situation in which survivors of CRSV find themselves today, and efforts to provide appropriate redress.

5.4 Satisfaction

Satisfaction includes every other form of reparation and is meant to address any non-material damage.[104] The obligation to give satisfaction arises where the injury caused cannot be made good by restitution or compensation.[105] Satisfaction should include where applicable: 'effective measures aimed at cessation of continuing violations'; 'verification of facts and full and public disclosure of the truth'; 'to the extent that such disclosure does not cause further harm or threaten the safety and interests of victims, victim's relatives, witnesses or persons who have intervened to assist to assist the victim or to prevent occurrence of further violations'; 'the search for the whereabouts of the of the disappeared, identities of children abducted, and for bodies of those killed, assistance in recovery'; 'identification and reburial of bodies in accordance with the expressed or presumed wish of the victims, or cultural practices of families and communities'; 'and an official declaration or a judicial decision restoring the dignity'.[106] Other measures, include, 'the rights of the victim and of persons closely related to the victim'; 'public apology including acknowledgement of facts and acceptance of responsibility'; 'judicial and administrative sanctions against people liable for

---

[103] Bouta Tsjeard, *Gender and Disarmament, Democratisation and Reintegration: Building Blocs for Dutch Policy*, Conflict Research Unit, Netherlands Institute for International Relations (2005), https://www.oecd.org/derec/netherlands/35112187.pdf.

[104] Barbara R Johnston, 'Waging War, Making Peace: The Anthropology of Reparations' in *Waging War, Making Peace: Reparations and Human Rights* edited by Barbara R Johnston and Susan Slyomovics (2009): 14.

[105] International Law Commission, Articles on State Responsibility for Internationally Wrongful Acts, Article 37.

[106] Basic Principles, Principle 22.

violations'; 'commemorations and tributes to the victims'; and 'inclusion of an accurate account of the violations that occurred'.[107]

An accurate record is critical in Northern Uganda where the facts surrounding the atrocities are heavily contested.[108] Most important, the government should take responsibility for atrocities committed by the army and should acknowledge that its failure to protect the regions exacerbated the situation. Former rebels who have been granted amnesty need to take responsibility for these crimes. They should issue a public apology to the victims. It is impossible to achieve satisfaction unless victims feel a sense of recognition for the harms suffered by those responsible. Sexual crimes should feature among the top list of heinous crimes of the war.

Symbolic reparations have a very positive effect on victims or survivors at a psychological level.[109] Symbolic reparations permanently recognise the harm done and portray a very deep sense of atonement. To this end, major streets, schools, hospitals, *inter alia* should be renamed after the victims. Every effort should be made to exhume and rebury the massacre victims in a decent and respectable national ceremony. In the event of mass graves, monuments should be set up and the names of the victims were ascertained, engraved. Investigations should be undertaken in order to establish the whereabouts of missing persons and these should include abductees that never returned.

5.5 Guarantees of Non-Repetition

According to the Basic Principles, guarantees of non-repetition should include, 'ensuring effective civilian control of military and security forces', 'ensuring that all civilian and military proceedings abide by international standards of due process, fairness and impartiality'; 'strengthening the independence of the judiciary'; and 'protecting persons in the legal, medical and health care professions'.[110] Other guarantees include,

[107] Ibid.

[108] Human Rights Watch, *Uprooted and Forgotten Impunity and Human Rights Abuses in Northern Uganda*, https://www.hrw.org/reports/2005/uganda0905/.

[109] Christie Daniel, The Encyclopedia of Peace Psychology (2012): 1153.

[110] Basic Principles, Principle 23.

'providing on a priority basis, humanitarian law education to all sectors of society and training of law enforcement officials and military and security forces'; 'promoting observance of rules of conduct and ethnic norms, in particular, international standards by public servants, law enforcement officials, media, medical, psychological, social service and military personnel as well as by economic enterprises'; 'promoting mechanisms for preventing and monitoring social effects and their resolution'; and 'reviewing and reforming laws contributing to or allowing violations to take to place'.[111]

According to the Guidelines for Gender-based Violence Interventions in Humanitarian Settings,[112] humanitarian agencies and personnel must assume the existence of sexual violence whether or not evidence exists. Interventions should encompass three phases: emergency preparedness; minimum prevention and response and comprehensive prevention and response.[113] While there has been a cessation of hostilities for over ten years, occasionally, communities are anxious about rebel attacks.[114] During emergency situations, the government should immediately ascertain and acknowledge the peculiar vulnerabilities of civilians and act in response to such vulnerability.

Police, security personnel and national armed forces should be trained and educated about sexual violence on recruitment. This strategy has been adopted by the UN Peacekeeping mission in order to combat the incidence of sexual harassment by peacekeeping personnel in the field. The UN strategy is built around three principles, namely: deterrence, punishment and accountability.[115] The army must be professionalised

---

[111] Ibid., Principle 23.

[112] Inter- Agency Standing Committee Task Force on Gender and Humanitarian Assistance, Guidelines for Gender-based Violence Interventions in Humanitarian Settings: Focusing on Prevention of and Response to Sexual Violence in Emergencies (2005): 2, https://www.unhcr.org/453492294.pdf.

[113] Ibid.

[114] Refugee Law Project, *Compendium of Conflicts in Uganda: Findings of the National Reconciliation and Transitional Justice Audit* (2014): 153.

[115] Muna Ndulo, 'The United Nation's Response to the Sexual Abuse and Exploitation of Women by Peacekeepers During Conflict' *Cornell Law Faculty Publication* (2009): 127–161, https://scholarship.law.cornell.edu/cgi/viewcontent.cgi?article=1058&context=facpub; see also Estelle Zisstag, *Criminal Justice, Social Policy and Society* (2005): 137–148.

and new policies and measures that ensure safety and sensitivity in the investigation of CRSV within the army should be adopted.

The Brussels Call for Action emphasises the need for full and active participation of women and other vulnerable populations in the development of national plans that address sexual violence. Gender-based violence adversely affects post-conflict peace and reconciliation efforts.[116] It is imperative that women are involved in peace processes in order to achieve and maintain durable peace and reconciliation.[117] Resolution 1325 in essence reaffirms the contribution of women to conflict prevention and resolution in peace building.[118] In sum it calls for: women's equal involvement 'at all decision making levels' in peace processes; protection of women and girls; gender mainstreaming in UN reporting and implementation systems; inclusion of gender training in peacekeeping operations; and the need to end impunity for violence against women.

In accordance with Resolution 1325, women should be regarded as active participants in post-conflict reconstruction programs including peacekeeping, conflict prevention and reconciliation processes. The importance of participation of women was reiterated in Resolution 1820 in 2008. The Security Council noted that women play an important role in the prevention and resolution of conflicts and called for their equal participation and increase in their role regarding the maintenance of peace and security as well as decision making. Full involvement of Northern Ugandan women in these decision making positions will signal—at the very least, a symbolic resolve, not to repeat the violations suffered.

116 Resolution 1325, preamble, 4.

117 Ibid.

118 Resolution 1325, 5.

6 Conclusion

CRSV is an affront to human dignity and imparts several and varied harms—some of which are lifelong, on the victims and survivors. Unfortunately, over a decade later, there is neither a concrete legislative framework on reparations for these grave crimes nor efforts by the government to alleviate or redress the harm suffered by victims. The NTJP which was passed in 2019 is commendable and lays the foundation for a reparation program. Unfortunately, the NTJP is largely silent about the victims of CRSV, and generally, appears to regard development and reconstruction programs as reparations. Many CRSV victims suffer from stigma and as a result, have generally been unable to integrate, marry and start families. In addition, several are bearing the burden of raising the children born in conflict by themselves or with minimal support from their families. The NTJP fails to acknowledge these realities and, like preceding legislation, narrowly construes reparations.

This chapter documents the specific harms caused by CRSV, in order to demonstrate why, and how reparations for CRSV, must be broadly construed, specific and appropriate. The chapter heavily relies on international instruments, such as, the Basic Principles and the Nairobi Declaration to provide a comprehensive set of normative and structural proposals, for reparations for CRSV survivors in Northern Uganda.

In accordance with the Basic Principles, 'victims' must be construed in the broadest sense, possible. This chapter, therefore argues for various reforms, ranging from legal reform to practical solutions, that would go beyond the limits of the law. Whereas it may not always be feasible to specifically cater to all special categories of victims of the conflict, the harm caused by sexual violence warrants special treatment. Reparations should therefore have a gender component, that ensures that the needs of CRSV victims/survivors are taken into consideration. The effectiveness of a remedy in law is crucial; ineffective remedies are not remedies. Although the government is not in a position to meet every single need of each victim, effort to do so must be demonstrated. The Basic Principles list various forms of reparations. The diversity of the forms of reparations provide an opportunity for the government to build special needs into the reparation program.

References

ACQUIRE Report, 2006, *Traumatic Gynaecologic Fistula: A Consequence of Sexual Violence in* Conflict Settings, Acquire Project, https://www.engenderhealth.org/files/pubs/maternal-health/tf-report-english.pdf.

Amnesty International, 2007, *Truth, Justice and Reparation: Establishing an Effective Truth Commission*, Pol 30/009.

Amnesty International, November 30, 2007, *Uganda: Justice System Fails Victims of Sexual Violence.*

Andrew Sheriff and Karen Barnes, 2008, *Enhancing the EU Response to Women and Armed Conflict with Particular Reference to Development Policy, Study for the Slovenian EU Presidency*, European Centre for Development Policy Management, Discussion Paper No. 8, https://www.europarl.europa.eu/document/activities/cont/200805/20080507ATT28495/20080507ATT28495EN.pdf.

Barbara R Johnston, 2009, 'Waging War, Making Peace: The Anthropology of Reparations' in *Waging War, Making Peace: Reparations and Human Rights*, edited by Barbara Rose Johnston and Susan Slyomovics.

BBC, 2007, *Uganda Mystic Rebel Leader Dies*, http://news.bbc.co.uk/2/hi/africa/6274313.

Bouta Tsjeard, 2005, *Gender and Disarmament, Democratisation and Reintegration: Building Blocs for Dutch Policy*, Conflict Research Unit, Netherlands Institute for International Relations, https://www.oecd.org/derec/netherlands/35112187.pdf.

Bryan A Garner, 2004, *Black's Law Dictionary*, 8th Edition.

Catherine Byaruhanga, 2017, *Has Ugandan rebel leader Joseph Kony Been defeated?*, https://www.bbc.com/news/world-africa-39999324.

Children's Defense Fund, Minnesotta, 2011, *Zero to Three Research to Policy Project: Maternal Depression and Early Childhood*, http://www.cdf-mn.org/research-library/maternal-depressionreport.pdf.

CW Mullins, 2009, *He Would Kill Me with His Penis: Genocidal Rape in Rwanda as a State Crime'* 17 *Crit Crim*, https://doi.org/10.1007/s10612-008-9067-3.

Daniel J Christie, 2012, *The Encyclopedia of Peace Psychology.*

David Otema v Uganda, Criminal Appeal No. 155 of 2008) [2015] UGCA 42 (June 15, 2015).

Declaration of the Basic Principles of Justice for Victims of Crime and Abuse of Power, UN Doc. A/RES/40/34, adopted by the General Assembly Resolution 40/34, November 29, 1985.

Dinah L Shelton and Thordis Ingadottir, 1999, *The International Criminal Court Reparations to Victims of Crimes (Article 75 of the Rome Statute) and the Trust Fund (Article 79): Recommendations for the Court Rules of Procedure and Evidence,* Centre on International Cooperation, http://www.pictpcti.org/publications/PICT_articles/REPARATIONS.PDF.

Dossa Nissou, Maria Victoria Zunzunegui, Marie Hatem and William Fraser, 2014, 'Fistula and other Adverse Reproductive Health Outcomes Among Women Victims of Conflict-related Sexual Violence: A Population-based Cross-sectional Study' 41(1) *PubMed*.

E De Temmerman, 2001, *Aboke Girls: Children Abducted in Northern Uganda.* Fountain.

Eleni Coundouriotis, 2013, 'You Only Have Your Word: Rape and Testimony' 35(2) *Human Rights Quarterly*, http://www.jstor.org/stable/24518020.

Estelle Zisstag, 2005, *Criminal Justice, Social Policy and Society.*

General Assembly resolution 56/83 of December 12, 2001.

General Comment No. 31 *Nature of the General Legal Obligation Imposed on States Parties to the Covenant:* 05/26/2004. CCPR/C/21/Rev.1/Add.13,

Human Rights Watch, 2003, *Abducted and Abused: Renewed Conflict in Northern Uganda*, https://www.hrw.org/reports/2003/uganda0703/uganda0703.pdf.

Human Rights Watch, 2005, *Uprooted and Forgotten Impunity and Human Rights Abuses in Northern Uganda*, https://www.hrw.org/reports/2005/uganda0905/.

Inter- Agency Standing Committee Task Force on Gender and Humanitarian Assistance, 2005, *Guidelines for Gender-based Violence Interventions in Humanitarian Settings: Focusing on Prevention of and Response to Sexual Violence in Emergencies*, https://www.unhcr.org/453492294.pdf.

International Center for Transitional Justice, 2020, *Building Blocks for Reparations: Providing Interim Relief to Victims Through Targeted Development Assistance*, https://www.ictj.org/sites/default/files/ICTJ_Report_Uganda_InterimRelief_Web.pdf.

International Committee of the Red Cross, 2014, *Women and War: Women and Armed Conflict and the Issue of Sexual Violence*, file:///C:/Users/HP500B~1/AppData/Local/Temp/icrc_report_women_and_war-1.pdf.

International Criminal Court, 2015, *The Trust Fund for Victims Launches New Assistance Projects in Northern Uganda*, https://www.icc-cpi.int/Pages/item.aspx?name=pr1126.

International Crisis Group, 2007, *Northern Uganda: Seizing the Opportunity for Peace, Africa* Report No 124–26.

International Law Commission Articles on State Responsibility, G.A Res 56/83 of December 12, 2001.

Jamie E Malamud et al., 2006, 'Reparations and Civil Litigation: Compensation for Human Rights Violations in Transitional Democracies' in *The Handbook of Reparations*, edited by Pablo De Greiff.

Janet Fleischman, July 25, 1996, In Rwanda, Too, Rape, Was a War Crime and Must Be Punished, *The New York Times.*

Jean-Marie Kamatali, 2007, 'Accountability for Genocide and Other Gross Human Rights Violations: The Need for an Intergrated and Victim Based Transitional Justice' 9(2) *Journal of Genocide Research* (2007).

Joanne Neenan, 2018, 'Closing the Protection Gap for Children Born of War: Addressing Stigmatisation and the Intergenerational Impact of Sexual Violence in Conflict' *Centre for Women Peace and Security, LSE.*

K Amone-P'Olak et al., 2016, 'Sexual Violence and General Functioning Among Formerly Abducted Girls in Northern Uganda: The Mediating Roles of Stigma and Community Relations--the WAYS Study' *BMC public health*, https://doi.org/https://doi.org/10.1186/s12889-016-2735-4.

Kristen Boon, 2001, 'Rape and Forced Pregnancy under the ICC Statute: Human Dignity, Autonomy, and Consent' 32 *Columbia Human Rights Law Review.*

Kristopher Carlson and Dyan Mazurana, 2008, *Forced Marriage Within the Lord's Resistance Army.*

Linda Malone, *International Law* (2008).

Loayza Tamayo v Peru Judgment of November 27,1998,43 Inter-Am.Ct.H.R (Ser.C) (1998).

Mubiru Kisingiri v Uganda (HCT-0OCR-CN-O108 - 2015) [2016] UGHCCRD 6 (April 19, 2016).

Myers v Bethlehem Ship Building Corp, 303 U.S.41, (1938): 5–51.

Naomi Roht-Arriaza, 2004, 'Reparations Decisions and Dilemmas' 27(2) *Hastings International and Comparative Law Review*, https://repository.uchastings.edu/hastings_international_comparative_law_review/vol27/iss2/1.

Ndulo Muna, 2009, 'The United Nation's Response to the Sexual Abuse and Exploitation of Women by Peacekeepers During Conflict' *Cornell Law*

Faculty Publication, https://scholarship.law.cornell.edu/cgi/viewcontent.cgi?article=1058&context=facpub.

Office of the United Nations High Commissioner for Human Rights, 2007, *Making Peace Our Own: Victims Perceptions of Accountability, Reconciliation and Transitional Justice in Northern Uganda*, https://uganda.ohchr.org/Content/publications/Making%20Peace%20Our%20Own.pdf.

Ogora Lino Owor, 2016, *Why Reparations Will Be Central in Determining the Success of Ongwen's Trial, International Justice Monitor: A Project of the Open Society Initiative*, https://www.ijmonitor.org/2016/11/why-reparations-will-be-central-in-determining-the-success-of-ongwens-trial/.

Pablo De Greiff, 2006, *HandBook of Reparations.*

Paul Omach, 2011, 'Understanding Obstacles to Peace in Northern Uganda: Actors their Interests and Strategies, in Africa's Great Lakes Region' in *Understanding Obstacles to Peace: Actors, Interests and Strategies in Africa's Great Lakes Region*, edited by Mwesiga Baregu.

Payam Arkhavan, 2005, 'Developments at the International Criminal Court: The Lord's Resistance Army Case: Uganda's Submission of the First State Referral to the International Criminal Court' 99(2) *American Journal of International Law.*

Penelope E Andrews, 2004, 'Reparations for Apartheid's Victims: The Path to Reconciliation' 53 *DePaul Law Review*, https://via.library.depaul.edu/law-review/vol53/iss3/9.

Population Reference Bureau, *Uganda's Fistula Patients Lack Knowledge of Prevention and Treatment*, https://www.prb.org/ugandasfistulapatientslackknowledgeofpreventionandtreatment/.

Prosecutor v Akayesu (Judgment), September 2, 1998, ICTR¬96¬4¬T, para 507 (Chamber I, ICTR).

Prosecutor v Dragan Nikolic, IT-9–2, 203.

Rashida Manjoo, 2010, *Promotion and Protection of all Human Rights, Civil, Political, Economic, Social and Cultural Rights including the Right to Development: Report of the Special Rapporteur on the Violence against Women, its Causes and Consequences*, A/HRC/14/22.

Refugee Law Project, 2014, *Compendium of Conflicts in Uganda: Findings of the National Reconciliation and Transitional Justice Audit.*

Sarah Tumwebaze, April 30, 2011, *The 20-Year Old War That Tore Their Families Apart*, The Daily Monitor Newspaper, http://www.monitor.co.ug/Magazines/Full+Woman/-/689842/1153386//8ydw7sz/-/index.html.

Seelinger Kim Thuy, *Domestic Accountability for Sexual Violence: The Potential of Specialised Units in Kenya, Liberia, Sierra Leone and Uganda*, https://international-review.icrc.org/sites/default/files/irrc-894-seelinger.pdf, 545–558.

The Constitution of the Republic of Uganda (1995).

The Justice Law and Order Sector, 2019, *Republic of Uganda, Special Report: The National Transitional Justice Policy (NTJP)*, https://www.jlos.go.ug/index.php/com-rsform-manage-directory-submissions/services-and-information/press-and-media/latest-news/item/698-special-report-the-national-transitional-justice-policy.

The Nairobi Declaration on Women's and Girls' Right to a Remedy and Reparation (2007).

The New People African Feature Service, 1999, *Monthly News about Africa*, Issue 87.

Thernstrom, May 22, 2015, Melanie, Charlotte, Grace, Janet and Caroline Come Home, *The New York Times*.

Thomas Katie, 2007, *Sexual Violence: Weapon of War*, file:///C:/Users/HP500B~1/AppData/Local/Temp/Sexual_Violence_Weapon_of_War.pdf.

Thompson Ginger, April 16, 2003, South Africa to Pay $3,900 to Each Family of Apartheid Victims, *The New York Times*.

Trauma System Agenda for the Future, http://www.nhtsa.dot.gov/people/injury/ems/emstraumasystem03/glossary.htm.

Truth and Reconciliation Committee of South Africa, 1998, *Final Report*, volumes 1–5 (1998).

United Nations Security Council *Resolution 1325*, S/RES/1325 (2000).

United Nations, 2014, *Guidance Note of the Secretary General on Reparations for Conflict-related Sexual Violence*, https://www.ohchr.org/Documents/Press/GuidanceNoteReparationsJune-2014.pdf.

Valérie Couillard, 2007, 'The Nairobi Declaration: Redefining Reparation for Women Victims of Sexual Violence' 1 *The International Journal of Transitional Justice*.

Women's Advocacy Network, 2014, *Petition Before the Parliament of the Republic of Uganda*, http://justiceandreconciliation.com/wp-content/uploads/2014/03/Womens-Advocacy-Network-Petition-24-February-2014.pdf.

9

Incorporating Human Rights in the Fight Against Police Sexual Violence in Malawi

Pachalo Mwenelupembe

1 Introduction

The Malawi Demographic Health Survey of 2015–2016 revealed that of the surveyed women between the ages 15 to 49 years, 20% reported to 'have experienced some form of sexual violence in their life'. Of these women, 4% had experienced sexual violence before the age of 18.[1] The survey focussed on sexual spousal violence which is defined as follows:

> ...[to] physically force you to have sexual intercourse with him even when you did not want to; physically force you to perform any other sexual acts you did not want to; force you with threats or in any other way to perform sexual acts you did not want to.[2]

[1] Malawi Demographic and Health Survey (MDHS) (2015–2016): 282 https://dhsprogram.com/publications/publication-FR319-DHS-Final-Reports.cfm.

[2] Ibid., 280.

P. Mwenelupembe (✉)
BookerSimon Law Practice, Lilongwe, Malawi

A. Budoo-Scholtz and E. C. Lubaale (eds.), *Violence Against Women and Criminal Justice in Africa: Volume II*, Sustainable Development Goals Series,
https://doi.org/10.1007/978-3-030-75953-7_9

Based on the foregoing definition, the common perpetrator of sexual spousal violence is the husband. This definition could, however, be misleading as the perpetrator could also be a wife in a relationship.

The available data in Malawi does not go far in indicating the number of women who have reported to have experienced sexual violence generally, and more specifically, at the hands of police. This, however, does not mean that women and girls have not been victims of sexual violence at the hands of police. The police in Malawi have been accused of demanding sex from women, especially sex workers to avoid arrests or for bail. A study by the Southern Africa Litigation Centre, revealed that 9% of sex workers reported to have been raped by the police and 2.6% reported to have been forced to pay bribes just so they are not arrested.[3] In recent times, following the post-election violence in Nsundwe, the High Court of Malawi in the case of *The State and The Inspector General of Police and others Ex parte M.M and 18 others*[4] found that due to the failure by the police to investigate allegations of sexual violence, the police was in violation of the rights of the women involved, including their right to an effective remedy. The court subsequently ordered that the women be compensated for violation of their rights and further ordered the police to investigate and arrest the perpetrators of the sexual violence against the women.

The above case exposed the lack of commitment by the police to investigate allegations against its members. A recent report by the Malawi Human Rights Commission[5] established that policemen raped 13 women, defiled one girl and sexually assaulted three girls during their

[3] Southern Africa Litigation Centre (SALC), *No Justice for the Poor: A Preliminary Study of Enforcement of Nuisance Related Offences in Blantyre, Malawi* (2013): 90, http://www.southernafricalitigationcentre.org.

[4] *The State and The Inspector General of Police, the Clerk of the National Assembly, The Minister of Finance Ex-parte M.M, Women Lawyers Association and 17 Others*, Judicial Review Cause No. 7 of 2020.

[5] Malawi Human Rights Commission (MHRC), *Investigation Report into the Alleged Rape, Defilement and Indecent Assault by Police Officers on some Women and Girls in Lilongwe West (M'bwatalika, Kadziyo and Mpingu Areas)*, HRC/05/51/300, 2019 (Unpublished).

peace- keeping operations in the area Despite the fact that the report recommended to the Inspector General of Police an investigation of the allegations, no investigation or report was released by the police until they were compelled by the court.

The lack of available data on police sexual violence can be attributed to the reluctance of the police to investigate fellow officers and the secrecy that comes with this nature of the offence. It has been explained that:

> ...victims of sexual violence in general have few incentives to pursue a formal complaint and well as many disincentives including the fear of being blamed for the incident or the fear of not being believed...[6]

This fear may be elevated when the offender is a police officer. As recognised by the Malawi Human Rights Commission report, the usual perpetrators of these crimes are those in the position of trust to the victims and this increases the chance of the victim's failure to report the violations.[7]

Clearly, the fear to report police sexual violence has contributed to the lack of information on the subject. This means that specific ways of preventing and combating the violence have not been developed and as such, women and girls continue to be sexually violated by the police. However, the information and cases referred to in this chapter based on selected criminal proceedings before courts, some published reports on sexual violence, and cases that have been reported in the newspapers give a picture of the situation.

From the onset, it must be recognised that a state is the custodian of human rights and is assigned the role of protecting and enforcing human rights. This has been envisaged under Section 12(1)(d) of the Constitutional Principles which states that the 'inherent dignity and worth of each human being requires that the State and all persons' to 'recognise and protect human rights and afford the fullest protection to the rights and views of all individuals, groups and minorities whether or not they are entitled to vote'. The state protects human rights through its various

[6] Peter B Kraska and Victor E Kappeler, 'To Serve and Pursue: Explaining Police Sexual Violence Against Women' 12 *Justice Quarterly* (1995): 85–111.

[7] MHRC, *supra* note 5, 10.

agents and one of them is the police. In this article, state actors mean parties under the control of the state and carrying out various functions of the state. For purposes of this chapter, the focus is placed on the police as one of the organs of the state in Malawi.

General Recommendation No. 35 of the Committee on the Elimination of Discrimination Against Women (CEDAW Committee), provides that under the Convention on the Elimination of All forms of Discrimination Against Women (CEDAW) and general international law a state party is responsible for 'acts and omissions by its organs and agents that constitute gender-based violence against women and these include acts or omissions of officials in its executive, legislative and judicial branches'.[8] This position has further been entrenched in several holdings by the African Commission on Human and Peoples' Rights including in the *Ogoni* case where the Commission found that Nigeria had violated the *ogoni* peoples' right to food through actions of the military that had destroyed and contaminated food.[9] A state therefore breaches its obligation to protect women from violence where such violence is inflicted by itself, or, where it is unable to prevent third parties from doing so.

The World Health Organisation (WHO) has defined sexual violence as follows:

> ...any sexual act, attempt to obtain a sexual act, unwanted sexual comments or advances, or acts to traffic or otherwise directed against a person's sexuality using coercion, threats of harm or physical force, by any person regardless of relationship to the survivor, in any setting.[10]

At the African Union level, a broader definition of sexual violence has been provided by the African Commission on Human and Peoples' Rights' Guidelines on Combating Sexual Violence and Its Consequences in Africa (ACHPR Guidelines) which provide that, 'sexual violence

[8] CEDAW, Committee *General Recommendation No. 35 on Gender-Based Violence Against Women, Updating General Recommendation No. 19*, July 26, 2017 CEDAW/C/GC/35 page 7.

[9] *Social and Economic Rights Action Centre (SERAC) and another v Nigeria*, 155/96 http://www.achpr.org.

[10] World Health Organisation, *Sexual Violence* (2020) http://www.who.int/reproductivehealth/topics/violence/sexual_violence/en.

means any non-consensual sexual act, a threat or attempt to perform such an act or compelling someone else to perform such an act on a third person'.[11] As per the ACHPR Guidelines, these acts are 'non-consensual when they involve violence, the threat of violence, or coercion'.[12] It has further been elaborated that coercion can be the result of 'psychological pressure, undue influence, detention, abuse of power or someone taking advantage of a coercive environment, or the inability of an individual to freely consent'.

The ACHPR Guidelines also clarify that not all forms of sexual violence require physical contact and this is particularly important because sexual violence manifests itself in many forms. The ACHPR Guidelines provides a wide range of acts of sexual violence including 'sexual harassment', rape (including marital rape), 'attempted rape', 'sexual assault', 'anal and vaginal virginity tests', 'violent acts to the genitalia (such as burning, electrical shocks or blows)', 'forced marriage', 'forced pregnancy', 'forced sterilisation', 'forced abortion', 'forced prostitution', 'forced pornography', 'forced nudity', 'forced masturbation and any other forced touching that the victim is compelled to perform on himself/herself or a third person', and 'threats of sexual violence used to terrorise a group or a community'.

The chapter proceeds by discussing and critically analysing the laws that address sexual violence in Malawi and the obligations such laws impose on the state in protecting women from sexual violence. The discussion focuses on sexual violence by police in Malawi and how such cases have been handled in the criminal justice system, including the courts. Lastly, recommendations that advance combatting sexual violence through human rights are made. While the focus is on literature such as laws and court cases that are specific to Malawi, other jurisdictions are also referred to for inspirations.

---

11 ACHPR Guidelines, paragraph 3.1.

12 Ibid.

2 Applicable Laws on Sexual Violence in Malawi

The Constitution of Malawi provides that women have the 'right to full and equal protection by the law'.[13] The state therefore bears the primary obligation to protect women from all forms of violence, including sexual violence. Under Section 24(2)(a) of the Constitution, the state has the obligation to pass legislation aimed at eliminating 'customs and practices that discriminate against women, particularly practices such as' 'sexual abuse', 'harassment' and 'violence'. Sexual violence against women and girls has been recognised as gender-based violence, with such kind of acts being gender-specific and discriminatory against women.[14] Through Sections 139 to 140, the Penal Code Act of Malawi criminalises several sexual offences including rape, defilement, sexual harassment and sexual assaults.

Of specific application is the Gender Equality Act enacted on April 9, 2013. The Act has defined sexual harassment as:

> ...any form of unwanted verbal or non-verbal or physical conduct of a sexual nature in circumstances in which a reasonable person, having regard to all the circumstances, would have anticipated that the other person would be offended, humiliated and intimidated.

The Gender Equality Act has also provided specific duties to health officers in addition to those under the Public Health Act. Among others, health officers are required to 'respect the dignity and integrity of every person accessing sexual and reproductive health services'[15] and 'obtain a written consent from the person being offered sexual and reproductive health services or family planning services before performing any procedure and offering services'.[16] A person commits an offence and is liable

[13] The Constitution of the Republic of Malawi (1994), Section 24(1).

[14] *Egyptian Initiative for Personal Rights and Interights v Arab Republic of Egypt African Commission*, December 16, 2011 Communication No. 323/2006.

[15] Gender Equality Act (2012), Section 20 (1) (b).

[16] Gender Equality, Section (2013) 20(1)(f).

to a prison sentence of three years if they contravene the duties provided above.

The Gender Equality Act has not prescribed any powers and duties to the police in dealing with women as it has done with health workers. Police are required to act as per Section 152 of the Constitution which mandates them to protect the 'rights of persons in Malawi according to the prescriptions of the Constitution and any other law'. Other than the Constitution, the Police Act supplements and elaborates on the various powers and functions of the police. However, it would have been of great impact if specific obligations were prescribed in the Gender Equality Act outlining the role of police officers in their dealings with women considering that the range of powers given to the police.

The police have as much interaction with women and girls as health workers. In Malawi, the police and health workers are the first access point for victims of rapes, defilement and other sexual-related crimes. The police conduct night-time patrols on the streets and have powers to enter, search and detain any person, including women. Also, police officers are engaged in the investigation and prosecution of sexual offences. The constant interface between the police and women would have required the Gender Equality Act to specifically contain provisions outlining the obligations on the part of the police. Despite the silence of the Gender Equality Act on the role of the police, the police have developed guidelines and regulations to be used when dealing with women and girls. For example, a male police officer cannot search women and male police officers cannot be left alone with females.[17] The enforceability of these regulations depends on whether female police officers are available. In the absence of female officers, male police officers carry out the task. Most unfortunately, these regulations or codes of conduct do not have legal force as law would have. Hence, failure to follow such regulations by the police would usually lead to disciplinary action against the police and not necessarily criminal action.

[17] At the time of submitting this chapter, I could not be provided with the actual document containing such regulations due to police protocol not to release such documents. This information was however confirmed by a senior police commissioner who did not want to be quoted.

Furthermore, despite the Gender Equality Act being a recent legislation that was aimed at domesticating some parts of the Protocol to the African Charter on Human and Peoples' Rights on the Rights of Women in Africa (Maputo Protocol), there are still many areas that were not covered and included. For example, the Act does not recognise the various ways through which sexual violence manifests itself. As a result, sexual violence has only been regarded and treated as a mere criminal act limited to rape or defilement, thus, forgetting the many forms sexual violence manifests in such as sexual harassment and other forms of non-contact sexual violence.

It is, however, interesting to note that Malawi ratified both the Maputo Protocol and the CEDAW on May 2005 and September 1987 respectively. While the provisions of the Maputo Protocol need domestication for them to be legally binding, the ratification itself signifies Malawi's intention to be bound by the provisions of the Maputo Protocol. Sexual violence is explicitly prohibited by article 4(2) of the Maputo Protocol and an obligation is imposed on states to 'enact and enforce laws to prohibit all forms of violence against women including unwanted or forced sex whether the violence takes place in private or public'. The state is further required under article 4(2)(b) to adopt 'legislative, administrative, social and economic measures as may be necessary to ensure the prevention, punishment and eradication of all forms of violence against women'.

In General Recommendation No. 35 by the CEDAW Committee, 'gender-based violence against women constitutes discrimination against women' and states have an immediate obligation to pursue 'by all appropriate means and without delay a policy of eliminating discrimination against women, including gender based violence against women'.[18] States have to also '[e]nsure that all forms of gender-based violence against women in all spheres, which amount to a violation of their physical, sexual, or psychological integrity, are criminalised'. Further, states have to introduce and strengthen legal sanctions for crimes against women.[19] A critical issue that the CEDAW Committee has also placed emphasis on is

[18] CEDAW, *supra* note 8, 8.

[19] Ibid., 10.

the need to make provision for civil remedies and to repeal all legal provisions that discriminate against women, in particular, the discriminatory evidentiary rules.[20]

3 State Obligations in Combating Sexual Violence

States have general obligations to respect, protect and fulfil human rights. Sexual violence is a violation of several women's rights including the right to life, dignity, health, security of the person and privacy. A state has the obligation to protect women from sexual violence and this entails ensuring that third parties are prevented from committing any acts of sexual violence on women.

The ACHPR Guidelines have, in detail, explained the states obligations regarding sexual violence. The Guidelines provide that states have several obligations including prevention of sexual violence, protection and support to victims of sexual violence, ensuring their access to justice through effective investigation and prosecution of perpetrators of sexual violence and provision of effective remedies to victims of sexual violence.[21] Furthermore, states are required to act with due diligence when dealing with sexual violence. This means that states must ensure that allegations of sexual violence are thoroughly investigated and prosecuted and that survivors have an effective remedy under the criminal justice system as well as damages and reparations in civil court. States must have 'an effective and accessible legal and services framework in place to address all forms of gender-based violence against women committed by state agents, on their territory or extraterritorially'.[22] In

[20] Ibid.; See also Lubaale's discussions on reforms to criminal laws in Africa with a view to advancing the rights of women and children. Emma Charlene Lubaale, 'Human Rights Reforms of Criminal Law in Africa' in *Governance, Human Rights, and Political Transformation in Africa* edited by M Addaney, M Nyarko and E Boshoff (2020): 149–171; Lubaale Emma Charlene, *Bridging the Justice Gap in the Prosecution of Acquaintance Child Sexual Abuse: A Case of South Africa and Uganda* (PhD Thesis, University of Pretoria 2015).

[21] ACHPR Guidelines, *supra* note 11, 18.

[22] CEDAW, *supra* note 8, 7.

protecting women from sexual violence, 'agents acting on a state's behalf or under their effective control must refrain from committing any acts of sexual violence'. The state must also 'adopt necessary legislative and regulatory measures to act with due diligence to prevent and investigate acts of sexual violence committed by state and non-state actors', 'prosecute and punish perpetrators' and 'provide a remedy to victims'.

In the context of Malawi, there are a number of laws criminalising the various forms of sexual violence. However, the enforcement of such laws is lacking and this is attributable to multiple reasons including poor accountability by the police. Lack of accountability for crimes by police is particularly a challenge because the police carry the mandate of investigating and prosecuting crimes against women. The selectiveness in investigations and prosecutions by the police translates to a failure by the state to protect women from sexual violence and violates their right to access to justice and an effective remedy.

4 Sexual Violence by the Police and the Criminal Justice System in Malawi

In Malawi, police sexual violence manifests itself in several forms including harassment, assaults, rape and defilement.[23] Other forms include demanding sexual acts from women including sex workers. Often, sex becomes the mode of payment women have to offer to avoid arrests or to be released from custody. This is very unfortunate considering that Section 153(2) of the Constitution clearly states that 'police shall enjoy only such powers as are necessary for the protection of rights under the Constitution' and 'the maintenance of public safety and public order'. Powers exercised out of the bounds of the law are illegal and constitute a breach of guaranteed rights. Section 4 of the Police Act

[23] *The Case of the State and the Inspector General of Police, the Clerk of the National Assembly, the Minister of Finance Ex-parte M.M, Women Lawyers Association and 17 Others*, Judicial Review Cause No. 7 of 2020. The complainants made allegations of sexual violence by the police including rape, groping of private parts, stripping women naked and other physical assaults.

of 2010 gives the police powers and functions to: 'prevent, investigate and detect crime', 'apprehend and prosecute offenders', 'preserve law and order', 'protect life, property, fundamental freedoms and rights of individuals'. These powers have the effect of elevating their status and influence to the public.[24]

In total disregard of the obligation under the Constitution and the Police Act, some police officers have used their power to perpetrate various crimes, including sexual violence against women. It is worth noting that of all the reported incidences of sexual violence, there has been none reported of police sexually assaulting men. This confirms the reality that sexual violence has been a targeted form of violence against women and as such, a form of gender-based violence.

The courts in Malawi have recognised the being a police officer aggravates crimes committed against citizens and can therefore constitute an aggravating factor in sentencing a convicted police officers.[25] The courts are of the view that the position held by the police is one of trust and breach of such trust constitutes a breach of the inherent trust that citizens have in the state. The courts have also considered it an abuse of power and an abdication of the state's obligation to protect women. Sexual violence by the police represents a breach of trust because states are trusted to protect the rights and fundamental freedoms of all persons in Malawi. This trust bestowed upon the police is further recognised under Section 12(1)(b) of the Constitution which states that:

> ...all persons responsible for the exercise of powers of State do so on trust and shall only exercise such power to the extent of their lawful authority and in accordance with their responsibilities to the people of Malawi.

The police are trusted representatives of the state and it is for this reason that women and girls approach the police to access various services. Women and girls have the inherent trust that if they approach

---

[24] Independent Police Complaints Commission, *The Abuse of Police Powers to Perpetrate Sexual Violence* (2012) 1, https://www.policeconduct.gov.uk/sites/default/files/Documents/research-learning/abuse_of_police_powers_to_perpetrate_sexual_violence.

[25] *Republic v Gregory Chikuni* Criminal Case No. 569 of 2018, in the Senior Resident Magistrate Court of Malawi, (unreported).

these men in uniforms, they can and will be assisted. Therefore, when such agents perpetrate acts of violence, there is a total breach of trust by the state and its ability to protect and operate in the interest of the people.

Sexual violence by the police is also a gross abuse of power and a violation of the constitutional mandate to protect the rights of women. The abuse of police powers for purposes of sexual exploitation, or, even violence, is something that fundamentally betrays the trust that communities and individuals place in the police. It therefore has a serious impact on the public's confidence in individual officers and the service in general. It is essential to ensure that systems are in place to prevent, monitor and deal swiftly with any individual who exploits that trust.[26]

Sexual violence by state agents can also be viewed as an abdication of the state's obligation to protect women. The state bears the primary responsibility of protecting women from sexual violence and indeed any forms of violence. Where a state, through its agents participates in perpetrating violence, the acts of violence may be seen as being sanctioned by the state.

As explained above, there are hardly any reported cases on sexual violence committed by the police. However, women and girls are susceptible to sexual violence while in police custody, while being searched and interrogated. Unfortunately, the criminal laws in Malawi have maintained the use of the corroboration rule in sexual offences which has the potential of hindering victims of sexual violence from reporting, especially where the incidences occurred in private.[27]

However, as already noted, in passing sentences, the court considers the fact that the convicted person is a police officer as an aggravating factor. In essence, the court recognises that offences committed by persons who have been entrusted with constitutional powers and duties to protect human rights should be condemned in the highest sense. In *R v Chikuni*,[28] for example, the court in handing down its sentence stated that:

---

[26] Independent Police Complaints Commission, *supra* note 24, foreword ii.

[27] Lubaale Emma Charlene, 'Admissibility of Evidence Presented by Children in Sex Abuse Prosecutions in Uganda: The Case for Reforms' 5 *African Journal of Law and Criminology* (2015): 1–15.

[28] *Chikuni* Case, *supra* note 25.

> ...further aggravating the present case is the fact that the accused person pre-planned the commission of the present offence. He took advantage of the victim's age and vulnerability and then carnally knew her. Him being a serving police officer, he was supposed to be in the forefront protecting her and not sexually abusing her. He has breached the position of trust bestowed upon him.

Despite such ground-breaking decisions, what can be observed from the available case law is that courts have generally treated cases of sexual violence as a matter of criminal law. The courts have not highlighted the human rights impact that such cases have on women and girls. A further examination of court cases also reveals a huge gap in the law regarding the protection of women from sexual violence by the police. Courts have not been proactive in calling on the state to ensure that measures are put in place to protect and prevent women from abuse. While this can be attributed to the fact that the legal framework is already limiting,[29] courts should be able to make pronouncements that reflect the human rights guarantees that are enshrined in the Constitution and in other applicable human rights treaties that Malawi has ratified, such as the Maputo Protocol.

By merely treating sexual violence as criminal offences, the courts fail to highlight the human rights implications of the offence, thereby silencing the human rights obligations that the state has towards ending sexual violence. The court also excluded the state from the violations that are committed against women as the perpetrator bears the sole responsibility for the crimes committed. The state bears no consequences whatsoever unless the victim elects to pursue the matter further in a civil court with a view to seeking civil remedies. While a responsive criminal justice system is important in ensuring the punishment of the offender and retributive justice for the victims, effective justice must include the development of measures and practices that prevent further occurrence of the violence and the state being held accountable for its failure to protect victims of sexual violence. The obligation to protect under human rights is very clear and specific.

---

[29] See discussion by Lubaale, *supra* note 20 on the continent-wide nature of this challenge.

5 Recommendations

5.1 Specific and Targeted Laws

The state must acknowledge that sexual violence is a complex and multifaceted problem and that it requires targeted efforts directed towards the specific violation.[30] This is specifically essential in combating sexual violence by police, whose acts of sexual misconduct are not adequately covered by the existing laws. States must therefore engage in deliberate and direct efforts towards reforming laws and repealing rules and practices that perpetuate discrimination against women. The CEDAW Committee has recommended that states repeal all legal provisions that 'discriminate against women, and enshrine, encourage, facilitate, justify or tolerate any form of gender-based violence against them'.[31] Such legal provisions include 'discriminatory evidentiary rules and procedures and all laws that prevent or deter women from reporting gender-based violence'.

For a long time, one such practice has been the use of the 'corroboration rule', adopted by Malawian courts from the English Legal System. This rule required that in sexual offences, there must be independent testimony from a source other than the complainant who implicated the accused person. This rule deters women from reporting cases of rape and defilement due to lack of corroborative evidence, consequently, violating their right to access to justice.[32]

In a recent[33] decision by the High Court of Malawi in *Steven Kaliyati v Republic,*[34] the court held that the practice requiring corroboration in sexual offences is blatantly discriminatory against women and contrary to Section 20 of the Constitution. The court stated that:

---

30 Commissioner Asuagbor, 'Special Rapporteur on the Rights of Women in Africa on Combatting Sexual Violence and Its Consequences' 2016, https://www.reliefweb.int/report/world/report-commissioner-asuagbor-special-rapporteur-rights-women-africa-combatting-sexual-violence.

31 CEDAW, *supra* note 8, 10.

32 Bernadette W Malunga, 'The Rule on Corroboration In sexual offences and Women's Access to Justice in Malawi' 46 *Zam. L.J* (2015): 121, http://www.heinonline.org; See similar discussion by Lubaale in the context of Uganda, *supra* note 27.

33 This judgement was issued on July 7, 2020.

34 Criminal Appeal No. 109 of 2018.

> ...in view of our current constitutional dispensation, the practice requiring corroboration in sexual offences based on the fact that women are unreliable witnesses, must be called out for what it is. It is discrimination against women based on their sex and or gender and cannot be sustained.' Despite such pronouncements, the rule remains alive and well and there has not been an explicit repealing of the law regarding it.

The legislative reform and policy measures should be focussed on building a legal and policy framework that broadly criminalises all forms of sexual harassment, abuse and violence and should expressly prohibit non-consensual and inappropriate sexual contact between police with women and girls.[35] The ACHPR Guidelines have recommended that states ensure that their national legal framework criminalises all forms of sexual violence. The legal framework in Malawi is lacking in this aspect. The Penal Code which is essentially old common law only defines and criminalises rape and defilement. The Gender Equality Act only provides a lukewarm definition of sexual harassment which is not broad enough to include the many other forms of sexual violence. This essentially means that other forms of sexual violence are treated as mere sexual assaults.

It is important to introduce legislation that is specific and covers as many forms of sexual violence as possible. For example, Zambia through the Anti-Gender Based Violence Act of 2011, has broadened the definition of physical, mental, social and economic abuse to include sexual abuse and abuse 'delivered from cultural or customary rites or practices' such as forced virginity testing, FGM, child marriage and sexual cleansing.[36] Namibia also passed the Combating of Rape Act of 2000 which introduced comprehensive definitions of rape and provides for 'aggravated sentences for offences involving minors when perpetrated by a person in a position of trust or authority' such as police and health officers.

---

[35] Christina Beninger, 'Combating Sexual Violence in Schools in Sub-Saharan Africa: Legal Strategies Under Regional and International Human Rights Law' 13 *African Human Rights Law Journal* (2013): 281–301.

[36] Anti-Gender Based Violence Act 2011, Section 3.

5.2 Judicial Officers Trained on Application of Available Laws

A proactive judiciary which recognises and understands the nature of sexual offences and applies the relevant laws in the quest for justice is a necessary weapon against sexual violence against women and girls. It is of no use for a state to promulgate national laws or ratify international laws that target sexual violence when practitioners of such laws are not trained to apply them. This is especially relevant in the judiciary which is a crucial institution in the criminal justice system. It is important for presiding judges and magistrates to recognise not only the criminal element of sexual violence, but also its human rights violations. Courts must always consider human rights guarantees even in criminal trials to ensure that victims of sexual violence are treated with dignity and in accordance with all relevant laws. The approach by Justice Mwale in *Steven Kaliyati v Republic* is not only bold but commendable. It shows a judicial officer who understands the impact of human rights principles even in criminal proceedings. General Comment No. 2 of the ACHPR[37] stresses the importance of law practitioners, judges and magistrates acquiring training and sensitisation on states obligations in the Maputo Protocol as this contributes to the implementation of the human rights guarantees.

Not only must the judiciary recognise that sexual violence is an abuse of human rights, it must also call for specific actions to be taken by the other branches of government in order to combat the violence. In *The State v Inspector General of Police & others ex Parte MM and 18 others*,[38] the court ordered the police to report to the court on the steps taken to investigate and arrest perpetrators of sexual violence within a specified number of days. In some cases, the court condemns the violence but does no more than that. In the case of *R v Kalipinde* for example, the court in sentencing a health officer found guilty of attempted rape stated that '.....cases of this nature are rampant nowadays, and this only shows how

[37] ACHPR General Comment No. 2 on Article 14.1 (a), (b), (c) and (f) and Article 14. 2(a) and (c) of the Protocol to the African Charter on Human and Peoples' Rights on the Rights of Women in Africa, paragraph 49.

[38] *Women Lawyers Association* case, *supra* note 4, 44.

unsafe our women and girls are in the society'. That is why Malawi as a country has joined the global village in protecting our women and girls against sexual related offences.'[39] The court must go further to state the protective measures which Malawi has taken against sexual offences and how the offence has violated such measures.

5.3 Use of Specialised and Independent Expertise

The United Nations adopted a Model Strategies and Practical Measures on the Elimination of Violence against women in the field of Crime Prevention and Criminal Justice[40] in order to 'assist criminal justice systems and professionals in meeting their due diligence obligations'. One such strategy was the use of specialised expertise in investigating and prosecuting sexual violence against women and girls. The model provides that specialised approaches to violence against women may include establishing special police and prosecutorial units and even special courts.

As recognised by the Special Rapporteur on the Rights of Women in Africa:

> ...across Africa, a major challenge to combat sexual violence is the lack of a comprehensive and effective system through which victims of sexual violence can report the matter, access services and demand accountability.[41]

Most victims of sexual violence by the police refrain from reporting the incidences to the same police because of fear and lack of trust in a system that has violated them. In *Ex Parte MM and 18 others*, all women indicated that they were afraid to report to the police because they had been violated by the same police.[42]

[39] *Republic v Stain Kalipinde*, criminal case No. 167 of 2019, in the senior resident magistrate court.

[40] United Nations Resolution 65/228 http://www.unodcs.org.

[41] Commissioner Asuagbor, *supra* note 30, page 3.

[42] *Women Lawyers Association* case, *supra* note 4, page 44.

In some countries, this has led to the establishment of independent police oversight bodies which have powers to investigate complaints from the public. Despite the Independent Complaints Commission (ICC) being established under Section 128 of the Police Act in 2010, an official call setting up the ICC was only made in March 2020, and it is yet to start operating. The ICC is established to 'receive and investigate complaints by the public against police officers and the police service', to 'investigate death and injury as a result of police action' and to 'investigate all deaths and injuries which occur in police custody'.[43] The functions of the ICC appear to only be restricted to the ones provided under Section 129 of the Police Act unless a broader interpretation is adopted to include even an investigation of sexual violence. Since this law had specified death and injuries, it would have made logical sense for it to also specify sexual offences committed by the police, or, which occur at the hands of the police. This is because as discussed above, sexual violence against women is a form of gender-based violence requiring specific attention due to the nature of the violence as well as the perpetrator.

Notwithstanding the above, the ICC has also only been given powers to 'receive and investigate complaints by the public against police officers and the police service'. Upon carrying out the investigations, the ICC is required to make recommendations to the Police Service Commission and the Minister on its findings. It is up to those authorities to decide what action to take regarding the recommendations. The fact that the ICC is established under the Police Act also raises issues of independence. In as much as Section 131 of the Police Act provides that the ICC shall operate independently from the Malawi Police Services, there may still be an appearance of impartiality because it is established by the laws that govern the police. In other jurisdictions such as South Africa, the Independent Police Investigation Directorate is established under a separate legislation as mandated by Section 206(6) of the South African Constitution. The Act which establishes the directorate in South Africa comprehensively provides for the functions and administration of the directorate and these are independent of the police. A similar approach should have been taken in the establishment of the ICC in Malawi since

[43] Police Act, 2010, Sections 129(a)(b) and (c).

Malawi has followed a similar approach regarding institutions such as the Ombudsman and the Human Rights Commission under Chapters 10 and 11 of the Malawian Constitution respectively.

6 Conclusion

The scarcity of information on sexual violence by the police indicates that this is an area that requires specific attention. The laxity shown by the police in investigating the allegations in *Ex parte MM and others*, for example, indicates a state institution that is not transparent and not willing to be accountable. There is no doubt that the legal framework satisfies the minimum requirements to combat sexual violence against women. However, in addition to the laws, we must go further to ensure that all other supporting institutions such as the judiciary and the Independent Complaints Commission are functional to ensure that all allegations of sexual violence are adequately investigated and prosecuted. In the context of Malawi, an active judiciary conversant with the constitutional human rights guarantees is also required in order to make relevant and necessary orders to the police.

The protection of women from sexual violence will also require a collective effort involving civil society organisations which are able to stand up for vulnerable women in ensuring access to justice and an effective remedy. The role of the Women Lawyers Association in Malawi in *Ex Parte MM and others* demonstrates how a vibrant civil society led by practitioners knowledgeable in human rights law can positively have an impact on the rights of women in Africa. Equipped with the existing national and international laws and a strengthened monitoring and protective reporting system, it is possible to fight the sexual violence pandemic and to ensure that every woman and girl is protected from sexual violence including at the hands of the police.

References

African Commission on Human and Peoples' Rights, 2005, 'General Comment No. 2 on Article of the Protocol to the African Charter on Human and Peoples' Rights on the Rights of Women in Africa (2005).

Bernadette W Malunga, 2015, The Rule on Corroboration in sexual Offences and Women's Access to Justice in Malawi 46 *Zam. L.J*, http://www.heinonline.org.

CEDAW Committee, 2017, *General Recommendation No. 35 on Gender-based Violence Against Women, Updating General Recommendation No. 19* CEDAW/C/GC/35.

Christina Beninger, 2013, 'Combating Sexual Violence in Schools in Sub-Saharan Africa: Legal Strategies Under Regional and International Human Rights Law' 13 *African Human Rights Law Journal*.

Commissioner Asuagbor, Special Rapporteur on the Rights of Women in Africa on Combatting Sexual Violence and Its Consequences, http://www.peaceau.org/uploads/commissioner-asuagbor-on-combatting-sexual-violence-and-its-consequences.pdf.

Constitution of the Republic of Malawi, 1994.

Egyptian Initiative for Personal Rights and Interights v Arab Republic of Egypt African Commission, December 16, 2011 Communication No. 323/2006.

Emma C Lubaale, 2015, 'Admissibility of Evidence Presented by Children in Sex Abuse Prosecutions in Uganda: The Case for Reforms' 5 *African Journal of Law and Criminology*.

Emma C Lubaale, 2020, 'Human Rights Reforms of Criminal Law in Africa' in *Governance, Human Rights, and Political Transformation in Africa* edited by M Addaney, M Nyarko and E Boshoff.

Emma C Lubaale, *Bridging the Justice Gap in the Prosecution of Acquaintance Child Sexual Abuse: A Case of South Africa and Uganda* (PhD Thesis, University of Pretoria 2015).

Independent Police Complaints Commission, 2012, *The Abuse of Police Powers to Perpetrate Sexual Violence*, https://www.policeconduct.gov.uk/sites/default/files/Documents/research-learning/abuse_of_police_powers_to_perpetrate_sexual_violence.pdf.

Malawi Demographic and Health Survey (MDHS) (2015–16), https://dhsprogram.com/publications/publication-FR319-DHS-Final-Reports.cfm.

Malawi Human Rights Commission, 2019, *Investigation Report into the Alleged Rape, Defilement and Indecent Assault by Police Officers on some Women*

and Girls in Lilongwe West (M'bwatalika, Kadziyo and Mpingu Areas), HRC/05/51/300.
Malawi, Gender Equality Act (2013).
Namibia, Combating of Rape Act of 2000.
Peter B Kraska and Victor E Kappeler, 1995, 'To Serve and Pursue: Explaining Police Sexual Violence Against Women' 12 *Justice Quarterly*.
Police Act of Malawi (2010).
Republic v Gregory Chikuni, Criminal Case No. 569 of 2018, in the Senior Resident Magistrate Court of Malawi, (unreported).
Republic v Stain Kalipinde, criminal case No. 167 of 2019.
Social and Economic Rights Action Centre (SERAC) and another v Nigeria, 155/96 http://www.achpr.org.
Southern Africa Litigation Centre, 2013, *No Justice for the Poor: A Preliminary Study of Enforcement of Nuisance Related Offences in Blantyre, Malawi*, http://www.southernafricalitigationcentre.org.
The State and The Inspector General of Police, the Clerk of the National Assembly, The Minister of Finance Ex-parte M.M, Women Lawyers Association and 17 others, Judicial Review Cause No. 7 of 2020.
United Nations Resolution 65/228, http://www.unodcs.org.
Zambian Anti-Gender Based Violence Act 2011.

Part III

Criminal Justice and Women in Situations of Vulnerability in Africa

10

The Invisible Woman: Limits to Achieving Criminal Accountability for Violence Against Women with Disabilities in Africa

Adetokunbo Johnson and Satang Nabaneh

1 Introduction

Women encounter gender-based violence daily in countries throughout Africa. For instance, it has become the norm for African women to be beaten, raped and in extreme circumstances murdered simply on the

[1] Ingrid van der Heijden, Naeemah Abrahams and Jane Harries, 'Additional Layers of Violence: The Intersections of Gender and Disability in the Violence Experiences of Women with Physical Disabilities in South Africa' *Journal of Interpersonal Violence* (2016): 2. For example, in South Africa, a woman is murdered by her intimate partner every 8 hours.

[2] Cheluchi Onyemelukwe, 'Intersections of Violence Against Women and Health: Implications for Health Law and Policy in Nigeria' 22 *William and Mary Journal of Women and the Law* (2015): 611.

A. Johnson (✉)
University of the Free State, Bloemfontein, South Africa

S. Nabaneh
University of Pretoria, Pretoria, South Africa

A. Budoo-Scholtz and E. C. Lubaale (eds.), *Violence Against Women and Criminal Justice in Africa: Volume II*, Sustainable Development Goals Series,
https://doi.org/10.1007/978-3-030-75953-7_10

grounds of their gender.[1] Chilling research confirms how one in three African women have encountered one form of gender-based violence at some point in their lives.[2] This insight exposes this violence as one of the most severe and widespread human rights infringements committed against women in Africa and globally.[3] The severity and global prevalence of violence against women have earned significant attention amidst urgent call for actions at the international stage.[4] In a 2011 report the Special Rapporteur on Violence Against Women, its Causes and Consequences (Special Rapporteur on Violence Against Women) issued a stark warning on how violence intensifies women's tendency to develop injuries that could subsequently become disabilities.[5] She described how, once disabled, violence is amplified dramatically for women with disabilities in a way that validates the correlation between violence and disability.[6]

With 82% of the global estimated 300 million women with disabilities[7] living in developing countries in Africa,[8] there are well-documented accounts of the prevalence of violence against women with disabilities in African countries.[9] However, the truth is that indigenous research on this

---

3 van der Heijden et al., *supra* note 1, 2; See generally, Kathleen Cornelsen, 'Doubly Protected and Doubly Discriminated: The Paradox of Women with Disabilities after Conflict' 19 *William and Mary Journal of Women and the Law* (2013):109.

4 Christine Chinkin, 'Addressing Violence Against Women in the Commonwealth Within States' Obligations under the International Law' 40(3) *Commonwealth Law Bulletin* (2014): 474.

5 Human Rights Council, *Report of the Special Rapporteur on Violence Against Women, Its Causes and Consequences, Rashida Manjoo*, May 2, 2011 (A/HRC/17/26), paragraph 28. See generally Human Rights Council, *Thematic Study on the Issue of Violence Against Women and Girls and Disability Report of the Office of the United Nations High Commissioner for Human Rights*, March 30, 2012 (A/HRC/20/5), paragraph 27.

6 Ibid., paragraph 28. See generally *Amplifying the Voice of Women with Disabilities Affected by Gender-based Violence and Sexual Violence*, http://www.hlanganisa.org.za/wp-content/uploads/2019/03/JGF_AMPLIFYING-VOICES-OF-WWD.pdf.

7 Disabled women and women with disabilities are used interchangeably in the chapter. Disability is a contentious term but its use in this chapter draws inspiration from the social and human rights understandings. For information on the human rights understanding of disability, see generally: Theresia Degener, 'Disability in a Human Rights Context' 5 *Laws* (2016): 1.

8 Rangita De Silva De Alwist, 'Mining the Intersections: Advancing the Rights of Women and Children with Disabilities Within an Interrelated Web of Human Rights' 18(1) *Pacific Rim Law & Policy Journal* (2009): 295.

9 See generally, Ilze Grobbelaar-du-Plessis, 'African Women with Disabilities: The Victims of Multi-layered Discrimination' 22 *South African Public Law* (2007): 406. See generally Talia

topic is still limited and scattered.[10] Insights from Meer and Combrinck about the difficulties involved in gathering accurate and empirical information on violence against women with intellectual disabilities validate this point.[11] This limited and scattered indigenous research on violence against women with disabilities is evident, mainly when the violence is sexual.[12] Referring specifically to South Africa, Meer and Combrinck mention how the nature and extent of sexual violence against women with intellectual disabilities are almost impossible to capture.[13]

Against this backdrop, this chapter questions whether African countries can achieve criminal accountability for violence against women with disabilities. For this analysis, the definition of criminal accountability for violence against women with disabilities rests on the question; is violence against women with disabilities recognised as a criminal offence in Africa? This question is crucial for two reasons. One, without the criminalisation or criminal liability for violence against women with disabilities, criminal prosecution would be difficult, if not impossible, to achieve. Two, without the criminalisation of violence against women with disabilities, redress and reparations for women with disabilities who are victims of violence in Africa would be non-existent. In advancing this discussion, this chapter proceeds in six sections as follows. Section one provides an introduction. This introduction is followed in section two by a contextual exploration of violence encountered by women with disabilities daily in Africa. Section three takes the conclusions in the preceding section forward by discussing intersecting forms of marginalisation for

---

Meer and Helene Combrinck, 'Invisible Intersections: Understanding the Complex Stigmatisation of Women with Intellectual Disabilities in Their Vulnerability to Gender-based Violence' *Agenda: Empowering Women for Gender Equity* (2015): 1, http://dx.doi.org/10.1080/10130950.2015.1039307; Serges Alain Djoyou Kamga, 'A Call for a Protocol to the African Charter on Human and Peoples' Rights on the Rights of Persons with Disabilities in Africa' 21(2) *African Journal of International and Comparative Law* (2013): 222.

[10] Louis O. Oyaro, 'Africa at Crossroads: The United Nations Convention on the Rights of Persons with Disabilities' 30(2) *American University International Law Review* (2015): 351; Meer and Combrinck, *supra* note 9, 2.

[11] Meer and Combrinck, *supra* note 9, 2.

[12] Marit Hoem Kvam and Stine Hellum Braathen, 'I Thought... Maybe This Is My Chance' Sexual Abuse Against Girls and Women with Disabilities in Malawi' 20(1) *Sexual Abuse: A Journal of Research and Treatment* (2008): 8, https://doi.org/10.1177/1079063208.

[13] Meer and Combrinck, *supra* note 9, 2.

women and girls with disabilities. Insights drawn from this exploration lays a good background for section four which provides an outline of the normative legal development for addressing violence against women with disabilities in Africa. Specifically, we explore how global and regional criminal frameworks have ensured criminal accountability for violence against women with disabilities. After that, in the fifth section, with evidence from African jurisdictions, we identify challenges and remedies to achieving criminal accountability for violence against women with disabilities. Finally, the last section offers conclusions. The conclusions that emerge from this analysis demonstrate the need for the development of an intersectional lens in criminal justice systems to ensure greater criminal accountability for violence that women with disabilities face daily in African countries.

2 The Situation of Violence Against Women with Disabilities in Africa

Established in scholarship is the reality that women with disabilities make up at the very least, half of the estimated 80 million persons with disabilities that inhabit Africa.[14] For example, there is evidence that the majority of the 7.5% of the South African populace with a disability are women.[15] Similarly, the more significant chunk of the over 22 million persons with disabilities in Nigeria are women.[16] These figures are an endorsement of literature that describes disability[17] and violence as deeply gendered in Africa.[18] The reality is that African women with disabilities face similar acts of violence experienced by their sisters without disabilities inflicted

[14] Kamga, *supra* note 9, 222.

[15] van der Heijden et al., *supra* note 1, 2.

[16] C Jonah Eleweke and Janine Ebenso, 'Barriers to Accessing Services by People with Disabilities in Nigeria: Insights from a Qualitative Study' 6 *Journal of Educational and Social Research* (2016): 118.

[17] Gabi Mkhize, 'Problematising Rhetorical Representations of Individuals with Disability—Disabled or Living with Disability?' 29(2) *Agenda* (2015): 138, https://doi.org/10.1080/10130950.2015.1040692.

[18] van der Heijden et al., *supra* note 1, 2.

by mainly intimate partners, relatives and neighbours in and outside the home or community and state.[19] However, with empirical data mostly derived from the Global North, scholarship has reported that women with disabilities are two and sometimes three times more likely to experience physical assault than their sisters without disabilities.[20] In the situation of sexual violence, the picture is even more alarming with accounts of how compared to the female population without disabilities, women with disabilities are up to three or four times more likely to be raped and sexually violated by a family member, acquaintance or stranger.[21]

African women with disabilities face violence significantly due to negative beliefs.[22] This situation links to the fact that Africans are very religious and traditional, usually relying on their beliefs to explain disability.[23] Disability is often perceived as a consequence of punishment from the gods for sin, misdemeanour, misfortune and a curse.[24] Besides, disability, commonly portrayed as demonic and evil,[25] or an affliction that Ndlovu defines as an abnormality that represents a 'diminishment or destruction of the force of life in dire need of restoration fuels violence'.[26] These beliefs are perhaps why, women with disabilities, are so often suspected of witchcraft in Africa and why they are violently attacked and lynched vigilante style.[27]

---

[19] Human Rights Council 2012; *supra* note 5, paragraph 21.

[20] Arlene S Kanter and Carla Villarreal Lopez, 'A Call for an End to Violence Against Women and Girls with Disabilities under International and Regional Human Rights Law' 10(2) *Northeastern University Law Review* (Summer 2018): 589–590.

[21] Ibid., 590.

[22] Human Rights Council 2012, *supra* note 19, paragraph 22.

[23] Hebron L Ndlovu, 'African Beliefs Concerning People with Disabilities: Implications for Theological Education' 20(1–2) *Journal of Disability & Religion* (2016): 31, http://dx.doi.org/10.1080/23312521.2016.1152942.

[24] Edwin Etieyibo and Odirin Omiegbe, 'Religion, Culture, and Discrimination Against Persons with Disabilities in Nigeria' 5(1) *African Journal of Disability* (2016): 5, http://dx.doi.org/10.4102/ajod.v5i1.192.

[25] Ibid., 3.

[26] Ndlovu, *supra* note 23, 31.

[27] For accounts on witchcraft and ritual killings in Uganda, Malawi, South Africa and Nigeria, see generally John Alan Cohan, 'The Problem of Witchcraft Violence in Africa' 44(4) *Suffolk University Law Review* (2011): 865. See generally Human Rights Council 2011, *Report of the*

Evidence suggests that witchcraft violence particularly on women with disabilities, for instance, is rife in at least 25 African countries.[28] A recent study by Etieyibo and Omiegbe documents how a woman with intellectual disabilities was labelled a witch and subsequently burnt to death in Nigeria is worthy of mention.[29] This story coupled with the accounts of the frightful attacks and ritual murder of women with disabilities, particularly women living with albinism for the sole intent of using their body parts for wealth in several African countries is problematic.[30] All of these violent acts are pervasive in Africa today, perhaps because of the cultural and religious acceptance of the reasoning that women with disabilities are social outcasts who live for the benefit of the population without disabilities.[31] Armed with such cultural and religious explanations, sometimes reinforced by law, these acts of violence on women with disabilities in most African countries become culturally and legally acceptable and, in some cases, praiseworthy,[32] in the name of cleansing the society.[33]

Also, because of negative stereotypes and myths, the violence of women with disabilities manifests in distinct forms.[34] The stereotypes and portrayal of women with disabilities according to Grobbelaar-du-Plessis as sick, ill, childlike, dependent, passive, needy, in need of care, incompetent, helpless, asexual, genderless and 'role-less inflicts on them an 'invisible social status'.[35] For example, harmful myths about the sexuality of women with disabilities render it subject to continued violence.[36] This violence happens because of the invisible status imposed on the woman with disabilities, reinforced by, for example, the myth that she is

---

Independent Expert on the Enjoyment of Human Rights by Persons with Albinism, January 18, 2016 A/HRC/31/63 paragraph 16, 21.

28 Human Rights Council 2016, *supra* note 27, paragraphs 16, 21.

29 Etieyibo and Omiegbe, *supra* note 24, 3.

30 Human Rights Council 2016, *supra* note 27, paragraphs 20, 21.

31 Etieyibo and Omiegbe, *supra* note 24, 3.

32 Cohan, *supra* note 27, 865.

33 Etieyibo and Omiegbe, *supra* note 24, 3.

34 Human Rights Council 2012, *supra* note 5, paragraph 22.

35 Grobbelaar-du-Plessis, *supra* note 9, 406.

36 Kamga, *supra* note 9, 222.

sexually inactive, overactive, unattractive and incapable of childbearing and motherhood.[37]

Eleweke and Ebenso share the story of a woman with disabilities:

> There was a case where a woman in a wheelchair was raped. The case was not taken seriously. Even the family members did not want us to pursue it. They felt that if a woman with disabilities got raped, she should have been grateful that someone wanted to have sex with her![38]

This scenario confirms arguments in research that violence against women with disabilities is trivialised.[39] It is possible to speculate that this triviality happens because the expectation is that women with disabilities should be grateful that men are willing to have sex with them.[40]

This case confirms insight from literature that links the prevalence of sexual violence in African countries to unequal power relations as opposed to the sexual act itself.[41] This insight could explain why, on the one hand, women with disabilities are perceived as sexually undesirable, thereby failing the feminine qualities of what it is to be a woman.[42] On the other hand, they tend to meet the patriarchal criteria that view women as inferior, passive and dependent, making them susceptible to sexual assault and violence.[43] This patriarchal criterion could be why, as research demonstrates, men are willing to have sex with women with disabilities in private but are unwilling to be associated with them in

---

37 Meer and Combrinck, *supra* note 9, 4.

38 Eleweke and Ebenso, *supra* note 16, 118.

39 Meer and Combrinck, *supra* note 9, 4.

40 Eleweke and Ebenso, *supra* note 16, 118.

41 Advantage Africa, 'An Assessment of the Social, Cultural and Institutional Factors That Contribute to the Sexual Abuse of Persons with Disabilities in East Africa' (2016), https://www.advantageafrica.org/file/advantage-africa-full-research-report-sexual-abuse-of-persons-with-disabilities-pdf, 34.

42 Margaret Lloyd, 'The Politics of Disability and Feminism, Discord or Synthesis' 35(3) *Sociology* (2001): 716, 718, https://doi.org/10.1177%2FS0038038501000360.

43 Virginia Kallianes and Phyllis Rubenfeld, 'Disabled Women and Reproductive Rights' 12(2) *Disability & Society* (1997): 206, http://dx.doi.org/10.1080/09687599727335.

public.[44] The truth is that this susceptibility of the woman with disabilities to rape in this case as Meer and Combrinck have accurately shown stems from the misguided perception of women with disabilities as 'perfect victims'—compliant, silent and invisible'.[45]

Research widely captures the implications of this 'invisible status' on violence against women with disabilities.[46] Insight from Meer and Combrinck reveals that the perception of women with disabilities as easy targets render them vulnerable to abuse in South Africa.[47] For them, because invisibility is tantamount to isolation, women with disabilities are rendered defenceless and powerless without the means to protect and fend for themselves properly.[48] This situation is particularly the case for women that have speech difficulties who might be unable to call or shout for help.[49] Besides, the woman with disabilities' plight in recognising and identifying violence as a crime[50] as well as its endorsement increases its severity and potency in Africa.[51] A typical scenario captured in literature is the intentional deprivation of the use of important mobility and communication equipment as well as assistive devices by personal attendants, caregivers and guardians entrusted with caring for women with disabilities.[52] Unfortunately, the implications of this deprivation could end up potentially life-threatening for the woman with disabilities.[53]

---

44 NSRP and Inclusive Friends, 'What Violence Means to us: Women with Disabilities Speak' (2015), http://www.nsrp-nigeria.org/wp-content/uploads/2015/09/What-Violence-Means-to-us-Women-with-Disabilities-Speak.pdf, 5.

45 Meer and Combrinck, *supra* note 9, 4.

46 Ibid., 6,7. See generally, Robyn White, Juan Bornman and Ensa Johnson, 'From Silence to Justice: Implications for Persons with Little or No Functional Speech Accessing the Criminal Justice System' 31(1) *Acta Criminologica: Southern African Journal of Criminology* (2018): 20. Grobbelaar-du-Plessis, *supra* note 9, 406.

47 Meer and Combrinck, *supra* note 9, 6.

48 Ibid., 6.

49 White, Bornman and Johnson, *supra* note 46, 20.

50 Carolyn Frohmader and Stephanie Ortoleva, 'The Sexual and Reproductive Rights of Women and Girls with Disabilities' (2013): Issue paper https://womenenabled.org/pdfs/issues_paper_srr_women_and_girls_with_disabilities_final.pdf.

51 Ereshnee Naidu, Sadiyya Haffejee, Lisa Vetten and Samantha Hargreaves, *On the Margins: Violence Against Women with Disabilities*, Centre for the Study of Violence and Reconciliation 13 (2005), http://www.csvr.org.za/docs/gender/onthemargins.pdf, 25.

52 Kanter and Villarreal Lopez, *supra* note 20, 590.

53 Ibid., 590.

With these scenarios, it is evident that perpetrators can exploit the woman with disabilities' perceived invisibility to continue committing the violence with impunity without showing any fears or remorse.[54] This exploitation worsens when the perpetrators of these violent actions are caregivers and relatives that women with disabilities depend on and trust.[55] The kind of intimate relationship shared with perpetrators aggravated by physical, economic and financial dependence, coupled with the fear of retribution makes it difficult, if not impossible, for most women with disabilities in violent relationships to find a way of escape.[56] As such, the fear of loneliness, isolation, abandonment might inform the preference of women with disabilities to suffer violence in silence and stay trapped in abusive relationships.[57]

Most times, because of mobility and communication challenges aggravated by the increased stigma associated with both violence and disability, women with disabilities discover that they are stuck in violent situations.[58] Sometimes, the severity of the disability makes it difficult for most victims with disabilities to identify what appropriate and inappropriate sexual behaviour is. Besides, the severity of the disability makes it difficult for most female victims with disabilities to speak about the violent situation, and decreases the likelihood of escape or reporting.[59] Women with communication disabilities might not be able to report or be believed if, and when, they do report the abuse.[60] This is true for different reasons for women living with albinism[61] as well as women with intellectual and communication difficulties who largely depend on the gravity of disability, and who might be unlikely to report if they

---

54 Ibid.

55 Stephanie Ortoleva, 'Women with Disabilities: The Forgotten Peace Builders' 33(83) *Loyola of Los Angeles International and Comparative Law Review* (2010–2011): 96.

56 Ibid., 97.

57 De Silva De Alwist, *supra* note 8, 296.

58 Ortoleva, *supra* note 55, 97.

59 Ibid., 97; See also, Meer and Combrinck, *supra* note 9, 8.

60 White, Bornman and Johnson, *supra* note 46, 20.

61 See generally Human Rights Council 2011, *supra* note 27, paragraph 22.

are considered unable to express or communicate what has happened to them.[62]

More so, the absence of required language skills to understand the victim with disabilities might be potentially appealing to abusers and exacerbates violence.[63] Moreover, although the culture of silence is a common feature of violence against women without disabilities, women with disabilities experience this silence culture in more problematic ways for multiple reasons.[64] For instance, similar to women without disabilities, women with disabilities also experience feelings of shame or self-blame, worsened for the woman with disabilities who might not have the right knowledge about the workings of the criminal justice system.[65] Ortoleva echoes this point, by describing the possibilities that women with disabilities might be unaware of vital information that might be readily available to their sisters without disabilities.[66] Given the situation, it is most unlikely that perpetrators get caught and held accountable for violent acts committed. This failure to apprehend perpetrators is true if police officers share a common perception that women with disabilities should be grateful for the rape.[67] The truth is that where such demeaning mindsets permeate in society, it leads to a situation in Nigeria, for instance, where a woman with a disability is treated like dogs and not as human beings.[68] According to Eleweke and Ebenso, '[a]ny person with a physical disability or any deformity in Nigeria is treated like a dog depending on where (s)he comes from. Some may not regard a physically challenged person as a human being'.[69]

Conclusively, the above sketch is a striking confirmation of available scholarly and anecdotal evidence that shows how the violence of African

62 White, Bornman and Johnson, *supra* note 46, 20.

63 Ibid., 20.

64 Ortoleva, *supra* note 55, 97.

65 White, Bornman and Johnson, *supra* note 46, 20.

66 Ortoleva, *supra* note 55, 97.

67 Eleweke and Ebenso, *supra* note 16, 118.

68 Ibid., 118.

69 Ibid., 118.

women with disabilities can be of a physical,[70] emotional,[71] sexual[72] and economic nature.[73] Importantly, it gives credence to speculations that indicate the enormity and gravity of violence encountered by women with disabilities in Africa.

3 Intersecting Forms of Marginalisation for Women and Girls with Disabilities

The term 'intersectionality' introduces the thought that discrimination, including violence against women, can be based on several grounds simultaneously rather than one or two.[74] For example, Crenshaw credited to be the originator of the term 'intersectionality' used the lives of African American women to demonstrate how discrimination and violence can occur based on both race and sex at the same time.[75]

As documented by the United Nations (UN) Independent Expert on the Enjoyment of Human Rights by Persons with Albinism, African women with disabilities experience multiple and reinforcing layers of discrimination and unique forms of violence that women without disabilities do not.[76] Similarly, in the preamble to the UN Convention on the Rights of Persons with Disabilities (CRPD), attention is drawn to the particular susceptibility of women and girls with disabilities to violence.[77] Specifically, article 6 recognises that women with disabilities face multiple and intersecting forms of both gender-based and disability-based violence.[78] Also, echoed in the well-documented

---

70 Human Rights Council 2016, *supra* note 5, paragraph 22.

71 Ibid., paragraph 22. See generally van der Heijden et al., *supra* note 1, 2.

72 Ibid., paragraph 21. See generally Kvam and Braathen 'I thought' 6.

73 van der Heijden et al., *supra* note 1, 11.

74 Kimberlé Crenshaw, 'Demarginalizing the Intersection of Race and Sex: A Black Feminist Critique of Antidiscrimination Doctrine, Feminist Theory and Antiracist Politics' *University of Chicago Legal Forum* (1989): 151.

75 Ibid., 149.

76 Human Rights Council 2016, *supra* note 5, paragraph 41; Naidu et al., *supra* note 51, 12.

77 Preamble to the Convention on the Rights of Persons with Disabilities (CRPD).

78 CRPD, article 6, 14, 23.

research by the 2011 Report of the UN Special Rapporteur on Violence Against Women, is the multiple and intersecting forms of discrimination that contribute to and exacerbate violence against women.[79] Specifically, the report discussed the plight that African women with disabilities encounter, amplified by multiple factors such as ethnicity/race, ability, age, poverty and access to resources, minority status, and social status, language, religion, sexual orientation and gender identity, and class.[80] For example, based on geographical location and poverty,[81] scholarship has accurately hinted to the reality that incidences of violence against women with disabilities may be more severe and substantially higher in African countries than in European countries.[82]

At this juncture, it is clear that African women with disabilities are in a plight. This plight occurs because the woman with disabilities embodies multidimensional identities[83] which makes it difficult, if not impossible, to identify on what grounds, violence has occurred. Compared with their sisters without disabilities, when gender intersects with disability, women with disabilities experience violence at a greater severity, manifesting in different and distinct forms with additional abusers.[84] Women with disabilities, because of their intersecting identities, hold a heightened tendency to encounter extreme violence frequently that would probably persist over a protracted and extended period, developing into more extreme and severe injuries.[85]

The question to be asked is whether violence against women with disabilities is recognised as a criminal offence in Africa? At first glance, this question may appear simplistic. However, proof from some African

[79] Human Rights Council 2011, *supra* note 5, paragraph 28.

[80] Ibid., paragraph 67.

[81] Kamga, *supra* note 9, 222.

[82] Ingrid Van der Heijden, Jane Harries and Naeemah Abrahams, 'Barriers to Gender-based Violence Services and Support for Women with Disabilities in Cape Town, South Africa' *Disability & Society* (2019): 3, https://doi.org/10.1080/09687599.2019.1690429.

[83] See Human Rights Council 2012, *supra* note 5, paragraphs 18, 19.

[84] Ortoleva, *supra* note 55, 96. See also; Kanter and Lopez, *supra* note 20, 591.

[85] See generally, Ortoleva, *supra* note 55, 96. Stephanie Ortoleva and Hope Lewis, '*Forgotten Sisters—A Report on Violence Against Women with Disabilities an Overview of Its Nature, Scope, Causes and Consequences*' (2012): 16.

jurisdictions on how certain intersecting forms of sexual and gender-based violence against women with disabilities is unrecognisable as a crime[86] gives this argument validity. For example, asides from the Northern Nigerian Penal Code[87] that encourages domestic violence on women, forced sterilisation is a specific example of intersectional violence on women with intellectual disabilities not explicitly criminalised in Nigeria yet.[88] This practice is sometimes state sanctioned under the guise of acting in her best interest.[89] Her best interest is in the form of hindering menstruation, pregnancy, or childbirth without seeking explicit consent of the girl or woman usually with an intellectual disability.[90] Although Section 42 of the Nigerian Constitution implicitly forbids forced sterilisation, Ofuani finds that this harmful gendered practise continues with impunity in the country.[91] Such practices confirm how criminal accountability, defined as the criminalisation of violence against women with disabilities, is almost impossible to achieve without specific legislation that recognises the multiple and intersectional discrimination that women with disabilities face daily.

4 Global and Regional Normative Frameworks

Various global and regional instruments address violence against women. The objective of this section is to undertake a comprehensive analysis of the normative and institutional framework for the protection of women with disabilities against violence. These global and regional standards

[86] CRPD Committee *Concluding Observations in relation to the initial report of Gabon* adopted at its fourteenth session (August 17 to September 4, 2015).

[87] Northern Nigerian Penal Code, Section 55 (1)(d).

[88] Anwuli Irene Ofuani, 'Protecting Adolescent Girls with Intellectual Disabilities from Involuntary Sterilisation in Nigeria: Lessons from the Convention on the Rights of Persons with Disabilities' 17 *African Human Rights Law Journal* (2017): 554, http://doi.org/10.17159/1996-2096/2017/v17n2a9.

[89] Ibid., 554. A number of scholars also corroborates this assertion. See generally, Kanter and Lopez, *supra* note 20, 593–595.

[90] Kanter and Villarreal Lopez, *supra* note 20, 594.

[91] Ofuani, *supra* note 88, 554.

play a role in transforming national law reform and influencing domestic court decisions.

4.1 United Nations Human Rights Treaties

At the UN level, various human rights treaties and standards address the issue of violence against women, including violence against women with disabilities.[92]

4.1.1 Convention on the Elimination of All Forms of Discrimination Against Women

The Convention on the Elimination of All Forms of Discrimination against Women (CEDAW)[93] was adopted in 1979 and entered into force in 1981. The CEDAW does not comprehensively address violence against women, given that it has only article 6, which prohibits trafficking and prostitution. Through its General Recommendations, the Committee on the Elimination of Discrimination against Women (CEDAW Committee) had tried to remedy the gap in standards relating to violence against women in CEDAW. For instance, in 1992, the CEDAW Committee adopted General Recommendation No. 19, stating that violence is a form of discrimination against women and making the link with existing human rights norms.[94] In particular, it states that:

> The Convention in article 1 defines discrimination against women. The definition of discrimination includes gender-based violence, that is, violence that is directed against a woman because she is a woman or that affects women disproportionately. It includes acts that inflict physical, mental or sexual harm or suffering, threats of such acts, coercion and

[92] For a comprehensive analysis of normative standards at the UN level, see Rashida Manjoo, 'Normative Developments on Violence Against Women in the United Nations System' in *The Legal Protection of Women from Violence: Normative Gaps in International Law* edited by Rashida Manjoo and Jackie Jones (2018): 79–108.

[93] Convention on the Elimination of All Forms of Discrimination Against Women (CEDAW) GA Res 54/180 UN GAOR 34th session Supp 46 UN Doc A/34/46 1980.

[94] CEDAW Committee General Recommendation 19 *Violence against women* (1992).

other deprivations of liberty. Gender-based violence may breach specific provisions of the Convention, regardless of whether those provisions expressly mention violence.[95]

In 1993, the Declaration on the Elimination of Violence against Women (DEVAW),[96] a soft law was adopted by the General Assembly. While not minding, the DEVAW mirrors General Recommendation No. 19. It provides a framework that defines violence against women, and the obligations of states to act in due diligence in combatting it.

The mechanism of Special Rapporteur on Violence against Women was subsequently created in 1994.[97] In discharging her mandate, she is required to prepare annual thematic reports as well as to conduct country visits. Such rallied attention in the global recognition of violence against women was reflected in the Beijing Declaration and Platform for Action (BPfA), which was adopted by member states of the UN during the Fourth World Conference on Women.[98] Violence against women was identified as one of the 12 critical areas of concern.[99]

Furthermore, General Recommendation No. 28 adopted in 2010, provides guidance on article 2 and recognises that violence against women is a 'form of discrimination that seriously inhibits women's ability to enjoy and exercise their human rights and fundamental freedoms based on equality with men'.[100] Other standards include General Recommendation No. 30 of 2013 that deals with women in conflict

---

[95] General Recommendation No 19 paragraph 6.

[96] Declaration on the Elimination of Violence against Women GA Res 48/104 of December 20, 1993.

[97] United Nations Commission on Human Rights Resolution 1994/45 on the question of integrating the rights of women into human rights mechanisms of the UN and the elimination of violence against women, adopted on March 4, 1994.

[98] Report of the Fourth World Conference on Women, A/CONF.177/20, chap. I, resolution 1, annex II, (1995).

[99] Ibid., paragraph 44.

[100] UN Committee on the Elimination of Discrimination against Women. 2010. CEDAW General Recommendation 28: Core obligations of States UN Doc. CEDAW/C/GC/28.

prevention, conflict and post-conflict situations[101] and General Recommendation No. 35 of 2017, updating general recommendation No. 19, which provides detailed and expansive identification of manifestations, causes and consequences.[102] In particular, as it relates to women with disabilities, CEDAW Committee General Recommendation No. 18 recognises that women with disabilities face double discrimination on account of gender and disability.[103] In line with this, the former Special Rapporteur on Violence against Women has also noted that '[v]iolence against women is deeply rooted in multiple layers of discrimination and inequality. As these layers of discrimination intersect, violence against women intensifies'.[104]

4.1.2 Convention on the Rights of Persons with Disabilities

The CRPD adopted in 2006 is the first legal treaty applicable to persons with disabilities.[105] The rights-based approach adopted in the CRPD focuses on ensuring the human rights of persons with disabilities.[106] According to Viljoen, the CRPD ensures 'accountability and legal obligations on states'.[107]

---

[101] UN Committee on the Elimination of Discrimination against Women. 2013. CEDAW General Recommendation No. 30: Women in conflict prevention, conflict and post conflict situations. UN Doc. CEDAW/C/GC/30.

[102] UN Committee on the Elimination of Discrimination against Women. 2017. CEDAW General Recommendation No. 35 on gender-based violence against women, updating General Recommendation No. 19.

[103] General Recommendation No 18: Disabled women (1991).

[104] *See* HRC 'Report of the Special Rapporteur on Violence Against Women, Its Causes and Consequences' A/HRC/17/26, (2 May 2011).

[105] Adopted by the UN General Assembly on December 13, 2006 and came into force on May 3, 2008.

[106] For an in-depth analysis of the CRPD with a special focus on Africa, see TP Van Reenen & H Combrinck 'The UN Convention on the Rights of Persons with Disabilities in Africa: Progress after 5 Years' 18 *SUR International Journal of Human Rights* (2011): 133;

[107] Frans Viljoen, *International human rights law in Africa* (2012) 140.

Article 6 of the CRPD recognises that women with disabilities are subject to multiple discrimination.[108] Article 16 of the CRPD guarantees protection from violence against every person with a disability, including the protection of women with disabilities. The provision further mandates states parties to eliminate acts of exploitation, abuse and violence that are committed by third parties. Besides, article 15 of the CRPD requires member states to ensure that persons, including women with disabilities, are not subjected to' torture or cruel inhuman or degrading treatment or punishment'. Articles 12, 17 and 25 forbid coerced or involuntary treatment and confinement, all of which constitute acts of violence.

As of October 2020, there are 164 signatories and 182 ratifications of the CRPD.[109] Two African countries made reservations, which are Egypt, Libya. Libya's declaration states that the State:

> ... interprets article 25 (a) thereof, concerning the provision of health-care services without discrimination based on disability, in a manner that does not contravene the Islamic sharia and national legislation...[110]

Several states including Denmark objected to Libya's declaration noting that subjecting the application of one of the Convention's provisions to Islamic sharia and national legislation is incompatible with the object and purpose of the Convention and as such one not permitted according to article 46(1).[111] Furthermore, in its concluding observations on women with disabilities, the Committee on the Rights of Persons with Disabilities (CRPD Committee) has expressed concern about: 'the persistence of violence against women and girls with disabilities, including sexual violence and abuse; female genital mutilation; and

---

108 See also Committee on the Rights of People with Disabilities General Comment 3: *Women and Girls with Disabilities* (2016).

109 See https://treaties.un.org/Pages/ViewDetails.aspx?src=TREATY&mtdsg_no=IV-15&chapter=4&clang=_en.

110 Ibid.

111 Ibid.

sexual and economic exploitation'.[112] In 2019, the CRPD Committee expressed concern with the 'lack of specific legislation, policies and programmes' to protect women with disabilities from all forms of violence, abuse and economic exploitation.[113]

There is continued effort on the part of the various UN mechanisms in contributing to a more holistic understanding of violence against women as well as amplifying calls for more action to combat it. The few above examples show the means through which international norms on violence against women have been developed. However, as noted by Manjoo, their effectiveness has been limited 'because of the reliance on the lack of specific provisions on violence against women and thus a reliance on non-binding interpretations of the treaty'.[114] The CRPD Committee in its General Comment No. 3 on women and girls with disabilities[115] adopted in 2016 has noted that 'international and national laws and policies on disability have historically neglected aspects related to women and girls with disabilities'.[116]

4.2 African Human Rights Treaties

The African Union (AU) formerly the Organisation of African Unity (OAU) is a union of African countries that promotes integration and development of the countries and people across the continent. The AU Constitutive Act was adopted in 2000.[117] Article 4(l) of the Constitutive Act of the AU (Constitutive Act) establishes the 'promotion of gender equality' as one of the principles according to which the African Union should function. The Assembly of Heads of States and Governments adopts human rights treaties and protocols. The past few decades

---

112 General Comment No. 3, paragraph 10.

113 Concluding observations on the initial report of Senegal, CRPD/C/SEN/CO/1 (2019), paragraph 29(a).

114 Manjoo, *supra* note 92.

115 General Comment No. 3 (2016) on women and girls with disabilities CRPD/C/GC/3.

116 Ibid., paragraph 3.

117 Adopted by African Heads of State in 2000, entry into force in 2001.

have shown an increasing appreciation for women's rights in the African region.

At the regional level, various human rights instruments have several provisions that seek to promote and protect the rights of persons with disabilities, including the protection of women with disabilities from violence. The instruments include the African Charter on Human and Peoples' Rights (African Charter),[118] the Protocolto the African Charter on Human and Peoples' Rights on the Rights of Women (Maputo Protocol),[119] the African Charter on the Rights and Welfare of the Child (African Child Charter),[120] and the African Youth Charter.[121] This section will focus on the instruments mainly related to the protection of women with disabilities.

4.2.1 The African Charter on Human and Peoples' Rights

The African Charter[122] entered into force in 1986 and has since been ratified by 54 of the 55 AU member states except for its newest returning member Morocco.[123] The African Charter includes civil and political rights, economic, social and cultural rights, and group rights, for the first time in one international treaty. Article 2 provides that individuals are entitled to 'rights and freedoms on an equal basis and without discrimination', including based on sex or 'other status,' which has been interpreted to include disability. Article 18(3) relates more explicitly to

---

[118] The African Charter on Human and Peoples' Right adopted in 1981 and came into force in 1986, Article 2.

[119] Protocol to the African Charter on Human and Peoples' Rights and on the Rights of Women in Africa, adopted July 11, 2003, 2nd Ordinary Session of the Assembly of the African Union, AHG/Res. 240 (XXX) (entered into force November 25, 2005), Article 23.

[120] African Charter on the Rights and Welfare of the Child, OAU Doc CAB LEG/24.9/49, adopted on July 11, 1990, entered into force on November 29, 1999, Article 13. The African Youth Charter, adopted in 2006 and came into force in 2009, article 2.

[121] The African Youth Charter, adopted in 2006 and came into force in 2009, Article 2.

[122] The African Charter on Human and Peoples' Right adopted in 1981 and came into force in 1986.

[123] List of countries which have signed, ratified/acceded to the African Charter, https://au.int/sites/default/files/treaties/36390-sl-african_charter_on_human_and_peoples_rights_2.pdf.

women by requiring states to 'ensure the elimination of every discrimination against women and also ensure the protection of the rights of the woman and the child as stipulated in international declarations and conventions'. Article 18(4) also provides special protection for persons with disabilities, including women with disabilities.

The African Charter established the African Commission on Human and Peoples' Rights (African Commission), a quasi-judicial body within the African human rights system.[124] The African Commission is established to promote human and peoples' rights and to ensure their protection within Africa.

4.2.2 Protocol to the African Charter on Human and Peoples' Rights on the Rights of Women in Africa

The Maputo Protocol[125] was adopted by the AU on 11 July 2003 and came into force on 25 November 2005. As of June 2020, 42 Member states of the AU has made commitments to the obligation specifically by ratifying the Maputo Protocol.[126] The Maputo Protocol was adopted to address the shortcomings evident in the African Charter on women's rights issues.[127]

The Maputo Protocol provides a comprehensive framework to guide all rights-based action for gender equality and ensure the empowerment of women and girls in Africa. It is celebrated universally for its various innovations in women's rights. For example, the legal prohibition of female genital mutilation is prescribed as well as the authorisation of

---

124 Article 30 of the African Charter. See also R Murray, The African Commission on Human and Peoples' Rights and International Law (2000).

125 Protocol to the African Charter on Human and Peoples' Rights and on the Rights of Women in Africa, adopted July 11, 2003, 2nd Ordinary Session of the Assembly of the African Union, AHG/Res. 240 (XXX) (entered into force November 25, 2005), Article 23.

126 List of countries which have signed, ratified/acceded to the Maputo Protocol, https://au.int/sites/default/files/treaties/37077-sl-PROTOCOL%20TO%20THE%20AFRICAN%20CHARTER%20ON%20HUMAN%20AND%20PEOPLE%27S%20RIGHTS%20ON%20THE%20RIGHTS%20OF%20WOMEN%20IN%20AFRICA.pdf.

127 Frans Viljoen, 'An Introduction to the Protocol to the African Charter on Human and Peoples' Rights on the Rights of Women in Africa,' 16(19) *Washington and Lee Journal of Civil Rights and Social Justice* (2009). See also Fareda Banda, 'Blazing a Trail: The African Protocol on Women's Rights Comes into Force' 50(1) *Journal of African Law* (2006): 84.

abortion in cases of sexual assault, rape, incest, and where the continued pregnancy endangers the mental and physical health of the mother or the life of the mother or the foetus.

The Maputo Protocol generally provides a robust normative framework for the protection of women from violence. It defines violence against women as follows:

> ...all acts perpetrated against women which cause or could cause them physical, sexual, psychological, and economic harm, including the threat to take such acts; or to undertake the imposition of arbitrary restrictions on or deprivation of fundamental freedoms in private or public life in peacetime and during situations of armed conflicts or war.[128]

This definition guides in terms of interpretation of the Maputo Protocol. The Maputo Protocol also contains several substantive provisions on the protection of women against violence. Article 2 of the Maputo Protocol focuses on the elimination of discrimination against women. States parties should adopt 'appropriate legislative, institutional and other measures' to fight discrimination against women. Under this obligation, states need to ensure that the principle of equality is integrated into its laws and that there is an effective application of the concept.[129]

The Maputo Protocol further commits state parties to the adoption of specific measures to combat violence against women, especially sexual violence (article 3(4), article 4, article 5, article 6, article 11 (3)); and authorises medical abortions in situations involving sexual assault, rape and incest (article 14(2)(c)).

In ensuring that women enjoy their right to dignity, article 3(4) provides that states have a duty to:

> ...adopt and implement appropriate measures to ensure the protection of every woman's right to respect for her dignity and protection of women from all forms of violence, particularly sexual and verbal violence.[130]

[128] Maputo Protocol, Article 1(j).

[129] Maputo Protocol, Article 2(1)(a).

[130] Emphasis added.

Article 4 further elaborates on the measures that state parties need to take to ensure respect for her life and the integrity and security of her person. Significantly, a list of state obligation is provided, which include enacting and enforcing laws and other administrative measures; understanding the root causes and consequences in order to prevent violence; and implementing programmes for rehabilitation of victims.[131] These multi-pronged requirements, among others, obligate states to ensure that they provide adequate administrative, social and economic measures to 'prevent, punish and eradicate all forms of violence against women'. Importantly, states need to not only punish perpetrators but also to provide rehabilitation to victims and reparations where necessary.

In addition to general provisions that apply to all women and girls, article 23 of the Maputo Protocol addresses the special protection of women with disabilities. It requires state parties to ensure that women with disabilities are free from violence, sexual abuse and discrimination.

The African Commission, for its part, has also put in place various mechanisms and developed several standards to elevate attention paid to women's rights concerns pursuant to article 45(1)(b) of the African Charter which mandates the African Commission to 'formulate and lay down principles and rules aimed at solving legal problems relating to human and peoples' rights and fundamental freedoms upon which African Governments may base their legislation'.

Consequently, the African Commission established the mandate of the Special Rapporteur on the Rights of Women in Africa. Through this mandate, the African Commission has been able to achieve various things, including the development of several General Comments to provide clarification and promote understanding of the Maputo Protocol's substantive content.[132]

---

131 Maputo Protocol, Article 4(2).

132 See African Commission on Human and Peoples' Rights, 'General Comments No. 1 on Article 14 (1) (d) and (e) of the Protocol to the African Charter on Human and Peoples' Rights on the Rights of Women in Africa', https://www.achpr.org/legalinstruments/detail?id=14; and African Commission on Human and Peoples' Rights, 'General Comment No. 2 on Article 14.1 (a), (b), (c) and (f) and Article 14. 2 (a) and (c) of the Protocol to the African Charter on Human and Peoples' Rights on the Rights of Women in Africa', https://www.achpr.org/legalinstruments/detail?id=13.

The African Commission also adopted Resolution 111 on the Right to a Remedy and Reparation for Women and Girls Victims of Sexual Violence (2007).[133] The Resolution condemned all forms of sexual violence against women and urged African states to criminalise all forms of sexual violence. In 2014, the African Commission adopted Resolution 283 on the situation of women and children in armed conflict.[134] The African Commission called on African states to adopt all necessary measures to prevent and eradicate all forms of violence against women and prosecute and punish perpetrators. It noted the importance of the provision of rehabilitation of survivors of sexual and gender-based violence.

The African Commission adopted the Guidelines on Combating Sexual Violence and its Consequences in Africa (Niamey Guidelines)[135] during its 60th Ordinary Session held in Niamey, Niger from May 8 to May 22, 2017. The premise of the drafting of the guidelines was based on Resolution 365 of 2017, which empowered the Special Rapporteur on the Rights of Women to develop such a guideline.[136] Thus, the goal of the Niamey Guidelines is to guide and support the member states of the AU in effectively implementing their commitments and obligations to combat sexual violence and its consequences. The Niamey Guidelines are designed as a tool to offer a methodology to African states and to serve as 'the foundation for an adequate legal and institutional framework'. They offer a set of practical, specific and concrete measures, and were developed pursuant to article 45(1)(b) of the African Charter, which gives the African Commission a mandate to create and draught the principles and regulations relating to human rights, which African governments may

---

[133] African Commission on Human and Peoples' Rights, 'Resolution 111 of 2007 on the Right to a Remedy and Reparation for Women and Girls Victims of Sexual Violence', https://www.achpr.org/sessions/resolutions?id=163.

[134] African Commission on Human and Peoples' Rights, 'Resolution 283 of 2014 on the Situation of Women and Children in Armed Conflict', https://www.achpr.org/sessions/resolutions?id=330.

[135] African Commission on Human and Peoples' Rights, 'The Guidelines on Combating Sexual Violence and its Consequences in Africa' (2017), https://www.achpr.org/legalinstruments/detail?id=4.

[136] African Commission on Human and Peoples' Rights, 'Resolution 365 of 2017 on Developing Guidelines on Combatting Sexual Violence and its Consequences,' https://www.achpr.org/sessions/resolutions?id=305.

use as the basis for their domestic legislation. The Guidelines are now at the popularisation stage.

Also, the continental political body, the AU in 2018, adopted its new Strategy on Gender Equality and Women's Empowerment, which seeks to 'maximize opportunities for women and girls, ensuring their security, dignity and resilience, making laws and institutions more effective and strengthening their leadership, voice and visibility'.[137] This Strategy also promotes full implementation of women's rights instruments. It proposes the development of a Programme titled 'All for Maputo Protocol', which supports the universal ratification, domestication and implementation of Maputo Protocol. The significance of gender equality and women's empowerment have been further encompassed in Agenda 2063, Africa's framework for sustainable development, whose aspiration 6 is '[a]n Africa where development is people-driven, unleashing the potential of women and youth'.

a. Monitoring and Implementation

An essential component in monitoring the implementation of the Maputo Protocol is state reporting as provided in article 62 of the African Charter and article 26 of the Maputo Protocol. State parties must submit reports on the measures they have taken including but not limited to legislative, administrative institutional and programmatic, to give effect to the provisions of these instruments.

While many of the African Commission's concluding observations issued to state parties mention violence against women,[138] it largely does not address the issues of women with disabilities. Even where there are recommendations pertaining to women with disabilities, they are usually too broad and do not address the specific concerns of the population who are victims of violence. African states, in their reports to the African Commission, usually neglect to address the experience of women with

[137] African Union, 'Strategy for Gender Equality & Women's Empowerment 2018–2028,' https://au.int/sites/default/files/documents/36817-doc-52569_au_report_eng_print.pdf.

[138] See for example, Concluding Observations on Kenya (2007); Ethiopia (2010); Togo (2012); Burundi (2013); Malawi (2015); and Côte d'Ivoire (2018), https://www.achpr.org/statereportsandconcludingobservations.

disabilities.[139] In terms of enforcement, interpretation of the Maputo Protocol falls to both the African Commission and the African Court on Human and Peoples' Rights (African Court). The Maputo Protocol in article 27 provides that the African Court 'shall be seized with matters of interpretation arising from the application or implementation of this Protocol'. This, therefore, makes the African Court a potentially strong platform to remedy women's rights violations and advance the protection agenda for women in Africa. Access to the African Court is either direct or indirect through specified organs such as the African Commission.

Given the role of domestic courts as the watchdog of other organs of government, litigation plays a vital role in the realisation of women's rights. While the African Commission has dealt with cases relating to gender-based violence,[140] it has not recorded a communication generally on women with disabilities, in particular as it relates to violence.

It is noteworthy that on May 11, 2018, the African Court issued a landmark judgement in the case of *Association pour le progres et la defense des droits des femmes Maliennes (APDF) and Institute for Human Rights and Development in Africa (IHRDA) v Republic of Mali.*[141] For the first time in its history, the African Court found a violation of the Maputo Protocol. The African Court held that the Malian Family Code violates women's rights as recognised under international law and ordered the state of Mali to modify its legislation accordingly. However, it is important to note that neither the African Commission nor African Court has not dealt with cases on issues pertaining to women with disabilities, in particular on the violence that they face.

---

[139] See for example Nigeria's 6th periodic report (2015-2016) to the African Commission on Human and Peoples' Rights.

[140] See for example, *Equality Now and Ethiopian Women Lawyers Association (EWLA) v Federal Republic of Ethiopia*, Communication 341/2007 (2007); *Sudan Human Rights Organisation & Centre on Housing Rights and Evictions (COHRE) v. Sudan*, Communication No. 79/03–296/05; *Egyptian Initiative for Personal Rights and Interights v. Egypt* Communication No. 323/06 (2011).

[141] Application No. 046/2016, African Court on Human and Peoples' Rights (2018).

4.2.3 Protocol to the African Charter on Human and Peoples' Rights on the Rights of Persons with Disabilities

The Protocol to the African Charter on Human and Peoples' Rights on the Rights of Persons with Disabilities in Africa (African Disability Rights Protocol) was adopted on January 30, 2018.[142] The African Disability Rights Protocol has not come into force as it has yet to be ratified by at least 15-member states.[143] According to Durojaye and Nabaneh:

> The African Disability Rights Protocol is a binding legal document protecting the human rights of persons with disabilities taking into account their lived realities in the continent while maintaining the core values and principles as set out in the CRPD.[144]

Article 1 of the African Disability Rights Protocol notes that its purpose is 'to promote, protect and ensure the full and equal enjoyment of all human and peoples' rights by all persons with disabilities, and to ensure respect for their inherent dignity'. The African Disability Rights Protocol contains several provisions that address violence against women. The African Disability Rights Protocol, in its preamble, acknowledges that women with disabilities are at a greater risk of violence. Article 9 requires state parties to take effective and appropriate measures to ensure that persons with disabilities are protected from all forms of exploitation, violence and abuse on an equal basis with others.[145] Article 9(3) further obligates states parties to investigate and prosecute the perpetrators of violence. Article 11 of the African Disability Rights Protocol

---

[142] Protocol to the African Charter on Human and Peoples' Rights on the Rights of Persons with Disabilities https://au.int/sites/default/files/treaties/35475-treaty-protocol_to_the_achpr_on_the_rights_of_persons_with_disabilities_in_africa_e.pdf.

[143] The Protocol has registered so far only one signature from the Central African Republic. The Protocol can only come into force when it is ratified by 15 of the 54 AU member states that have accepted to be bound by the African Charter.

[144] Ebenezer Durojaye and Satang Nabaneh, 'Human Rights and Access to Healthcare for Persons with Albinism in Africa' 7(40) *African Disability Rights Yearbook* (December 2019).

[145] African Disability Rights Protocol Article 9(2)(c).

addresses harmful practices such as witchcraft, abandonment, concealment and ritual killings. Article 27, on the rights of women and girls with disabilities, explicitly obligates state parties to ensure that women with disabilities are protected from gender-based violence and are provided with rehabilitation and psychosocial support. In some instances, it goes beyond the CRPD on which it is modelled on. For example, article 13 provides for the right to legal aid of persons with disabilities. This article is vital in ensuring access to justice for persons with disabilities, including women with disabilities.

As illustrated above, the understanding of violence against women has evolved through the global and regional human rights frameworks. There is growing recognition of the impact of violence against women in serving as a barrier to the full realisation of their rights. Yet, the risks factors for gender-based violence that are unique to women with disabilities as compared to other women have not been comprehensively addressed. It is posited that significant attention has not been paid to the situation of women and girls with disabilities in Africa, particularly, as it relates to gender-based violence.

5 Influence of Human Rights Norms on National-Level Law Reform and Jurisprudence on Violence Against Women with Disabilities

At the national level, many gains have been made since the adoption of the Maputo Protocol, not only evidenced by the number of countries that have signed and ratified the Maputo Protocol, but also evident through increased adoption of legislation addressing discrimination against women. For example, between 2007 and 2018, countries such as Zimbabwe, Uganda, South Sudan, Kenya, Guinea Bissau, Mozambique, The Gambia, and Cameroon all adopted laws that punish the practice of female genital mutilation (FGM). Either new laws have been introduced, or existing laws have been amended.[146] Addressingdiscrimination through the law presents a crucial starting point that eventually translates to substantive equality on the ground.

However, it is evident how in most African countries, women with disabilities remain at the bottom of what Abu-Habib has described as a metaphorical ladder of legal and human rights protection.[147] Nowhere is this assertion clearer than the absence of legislation that recognises the multiple and intersectional discrimination of the woman with disabilities. For example, disability is missing as a prohibited ground of discrimination in several African constitutions.[148] In Ghana and Liberia's state report to the CRPD Committee, for instance, the government acknowledged that it had no specific laws dealing with the particular concerns and violent acts targeted on women with disabilities.[149] Besides, disability is not explicitly recognised as a prohibited ground of discrimination in Section 42 of the 1999 Nigerian Constitution.[150] This is notwithstanding arguments that claim that this oversight in the Nigerian Constitution should not be read as exhaustive but as purposive.[151]

---

[146] Satang Nabaneh and Adamson Muula, 'Female Genital Mutilation/Cutting: A Complex Legal and Ethical Landscape' 2 *International Journal of Gynecology & Obstetrics* (2019): 145, https://doi.org/10.1002/ijgo.12792: 253–257.

[147] Lina Abu-Habib, 'Women and Disability Don't Mix! 'Double Discrimination and Disabled Women's Rights' 3(2) *Gender and Development* (1995): 52.

[148] CRPD Committee, *Concluding Observation on the initial report of the Niger* adopted during its 21st session in 1 May 2019; CRPD Committee, *Concluding Observation on the initial report of Algeria* adopted during its 20th session in 27 June 2019.

[149] Republic of Liberia, *Initial report on the implementation of the Convention on the Rights of Persons with Disabilities* submitted to the Convention on the Rights of Persons with Disabilities on April 24, 2020 paragraph 16. Republic of Ghana, *Initial report on the implementation of the Convention on the Rights of Persons with Disabilities* submitted to the Convention on the Rights of Persons with Disabilities on March 8, 2019 paragraphs 59–61.

[150] Section 42 Nigerian Constitution. See generally; Ibrahim Imam and M Abdulraheem-Mustapha, 'Rights of People with Disability in Nigeria: Attitudes and Commitment' 24(3) *African Journal of International and Comparative Law* (2016): 440.

[151] See generally Ofuani, *supra* note 88, 552–553. Umeh 'Ngozi Chuma Umeh, 'Reading Disability into the Non-discrimination Clause of the Nigerian Constitution' 4 *African Disability Rights Yearbook* (2016): 72. Ebenezer Durojaye and Yinka Owoeye, 'Equally Unequal or Unequally Equal: Adopting a Substantive Equality Approach to Gender Discrimination in Nigeria' 17(2) *International Journal of Discrimination and the Law* (2017): 71.

Unfortunately, what these examples prove is that the majority of African states do not even have an adequate legal framework for persons with disabilities much less on violence against women with disabilities. Even African countries that have legislations that ostensibly forbid discrimination on the grounds of disability derive inspiration mainly from the medical understanding of disability.[152] Forexample, in several concluding observations, the CRPD Committee has expressed concerns about legislation that still rely on the medical understanding of disability.[153] Ironically, South Africa, widely hailed for its progressive regulatory framework, also applies the medical understanding of disability in certain aspects of its legislation, particularly with persons with severe and profound intellectual disabilities.[154]

However, South Africa is one of the few African countries that explicitly recognises and forbids discrimination on more than one ground.[155] The problem is that even in South Africa, similar to other African countries, as confirmed by Meer and Combrinck, sexual and gender-based violence, particularly on women with intellectual disabilities, continues and remains widespread.[156] In the case of *Velasquez Rodrigues v Honduras*, the InterAmerican Court of Human Rights has proven that adequate legal architecture is crucial in cases of violence against women.[157] Even having adequate legal architecture, according to the Court is not enough: it must function in an effective system.[158] Elaborating, in an effective system, laws must be accompanied by efficient realisation with the political will and adequate resources to achieve criminal accountability.[159]

---

152 See generally, CRPD Committee, *Concluding Observations in Relation to the initial report of Rwanda* adopted at its 21st session on 3 May 2019 paragraph 5. CRPD Committee, *Concluding Observations in relation to the initial report of Morocco* adopted at 18th session on 25 September 2017 paragraphs 6.

153 See generally, CRPD Committee, *Concluding Observations in relation to the initial report of Rwanda* paragraph 5. CRPD Committee *Concluding Observations in relation to the initial report of Morocco* paragraphs 6.

154 CRPD Committee, *Concluding Observations in relation to the initial report of South Africa* adopted at its 20th session on 23 October 2018 paragraph 4.

155 Section 9(3) 1996 South African Constitution.

156 Meer and Combrinck, *supra* note 9, 2.

157 *Velasquez Rodrigues v Honduras* (1986); Chinkin, *supra* note 4, 478.

158 Ibid., 478.

159 Chinkin, *supra* note 4, 478.

In Malawi's state report to the CRPD Committee, the government acknowledged that despite its laws, there is a scarcity of resources to ensure effective implementation.[160] As such, even in African jurisdictions that explicitly forbid discrimination based on disability, they still fall short without adequate resources to ensure effective realisation.

To recap, backed by *Velasquez Rodrigues v Honduras*, it is established that the inadequate and lack of specific laws in African jurisdictions that recognise the intersectional positioning of women with disabilities is perhaps one main reason gender and sexual violence continues unabated. A one size fits all legislation is inadequate because of the flawed view that persons with disabilities are internally similar or homogeneous and share the same encounters with dominant group members. In other words, such laws fall into the trap of erroneously treating vulnerable groups as homogeneous, failing to recognise their internal differences. Forced sterilisation is an example of sexual violence used above, that is unique to women with disabilities, constituting a combination of gender-based violence and disability-based violence simultaneously.[161] The Namibian High Court in *LM and Others v Namibia*[162] found that forced sterilisation of women without informed consent due to their HIV- positive status was unlawful.

This kind of intersectional violence is not necessarily targeted at women or the disabled as similar groups but is targeted particularly at women with disabilities. In the absence of intersectional laws, it is difficult to identify forced sterilisation as a crime. By refusing to recognise women's intersectional positioning, the woman with disabilities is not just denied legal protection, but she ends up invisible within the criminal justice system.

---

[160] Republic of Malawi, *Initial report on the implementation of the Convention on the Rights of Persons with Disabilities* submitted to the Convention on the Rights of Persons with Disabilities on March 8, 2019 paragraph 59, 232.

[161] Ofuani, *supra* note 88, 552;

[162] Case no: SA 49/2012. See also Chantal J Badul and Ann Strode, '*LM and Others v Government of the Republic of Namibia:* The First Sub Saharan African Case Dealing with Coerced Sterilizations of HIV-Positive Women—Quo Vadis?' 13 *African Human Rights Law Journal* 2013: 214–228.

6 Challenges and Remedies in Addressing Violence Against Women with Disabilities

Despite the significant milestones achieved in advancing women's rights and gender equality and addressing violence against women, at the national, regional and global levels, there remains both continuing and new sets of challenges that hamper efforts to promote and protect the human rights of women. Some of these critical challenges include failure of states to act with due diligence, barriers to accessing justice, limitations to addressing root causes and scarcity of data.

6.1 Failure of States to Act with Due Diligence

Despite the general guiding principles of due diligence in which states have an obligation to protect, prevent, punish and prosecute violence against women cases, they fail in this area.[163] The Niamey Guidelines further provides that:

> States must ensure that state agents do not commit any act of sexual violence. States are required to enact appropriate laws and regulatory steps to act with due diligence to prevent and investigate acts of sexual violence committed by State and non-State actors, prosecute and punish perpetrators, and provide remedies to victims.[164]

In *Equality Now and Ethiopian Women Lawyers Association v the Federal Republic of Ethiopia*,[165] a 13-year-old girl who experienced abduction and rape brought a complaint to the African Commission alleging that Ethiopia had violated various articles of the African Charter such as the general non-discrimination clause, (article 2); the right to equal protection of the law (article 3); integrity, liberty and security of the person,

[163] African Charter, Article 60; and Maputo Protocol, Article 4.

[164] Niamey Guidelines, 18.

[165] *Equality Now and Ethiopian Women Lawyers Association (EWLA) v Federal Republic of Ethiopia*, Communication 341/2007 (2007).

including freedom from cruel, inhuman and degrading treatment (article 4, 5 and 6) as well as protection from discrimination against women (article 18(3).

The African Commission held that Ethiopia violated articles 1 and 2 of the African Charter as it has failed in its duty to protect. Moreover, it was unable to prevent rape due to its failure to enact and implement laws as well as take steps to prevent private actors from infringing the rights of women and girls.

The CRPD in its concluding observations to Senegal noted the lack of mechanisms for identifying, investigating and prosecuting cases of exploitation, violence and abuse,[166] which is contrary to the state's due diligence obligation. Subsequently, the Committee recommended that Senegal:

> conduct investigations into cases of exploitation, violence and abuse against persons with disabilities, prosecute suspects, duly sanction perpetrators, ensure that victims are provided with effective redress, including compensation and rehabilitation.[167]

Women with disabilities must therefore be protected from gender-based violence.

6.2 Barriers to Accessing Justice

The CRPD Committee has also underscored that women with disabilities face unique barriers to accessing justice, particularly following violence, exploitation, and abuse.[168] Accessto justice including legal aid remains a challenge for women with disabilities that hinder their ability to seek and obtain redress,[169] due in part to the number of lawyers

[166] Concluding observations on the initial report of Senegal, CRPD/C/SEN/CO/1 (2019), paragraph 29(c).

[167] Ibid., paragraph 30(b).

[168] CRPD Committee, General Comment No. 3 (2016) on women and girls with disabilities, U.N. Doc. CRPD/C/GC/3 (2016), paragraph 52.

[169] See CRPD Committee, General Comment No. 3: Article 6: Women and girls with disabilities, U.N. Doc. CRPD/C/GC/3 (2016).

who take up pro bono cases, as well as the location of the legal aid services mainly in the urban areas.[170] This challenge, in part, contributes to the inadequate number of reporting and consequent investigation of cases.[171] Other barriers that women with disabilities face in accessing justice in Africa include limited access to information and services.[172] Moreover, owing to prejudices, barriers to the justice system are largely predicated on the intersection between gender and disability stereotypes.[173] As the former UN Special Rapporteur on Violence against Women, Rashida Manjoo noted, this stereotype results to 'systematic failure of the court system to acknowledge them as competent witnesses'.[174]

The foregoing is worsened by the gross indifference shown by police and law enforcement officers towards reports of violence against women with disabilities.[175] Most times, women with intellectual disabilities are mainly doubted with the credibility of their testimony and their evidence often questioned and dismissed by the courts.[176] This doubt, according to White, Bornman and Johnson stems from the misconception that women with communication disabilities are unable to testify in court as competent and reliable witnesses.[177] These authors explain how police officers may have an unfounded fear that they will not be able to gather complete, accurate and dependable information from the woman with disabilities, particularly if she has communication difficulties.[178] Unfortunately, without a legal personality, it will be almost impossible to apprehend and prosecute abusers successfully. It is perhaps this lack of legal personality and invisibility that could explain the scarcity of court cases involving women with disabilities in most African states.[179]

---

170 UN Special Rapporteur on Violence against Women, Report of the Special Rapporteur on violence against women, its causes and consequences, U.N. Doc. A/67/227 (2012), 43.

171 Ibid., 43.

172 Naidu et al., *supra* note 51, Section 3.5.

173 Special Rapporteur, *supra* note 5, 41–42.

174 Ibid., 41.

175 Ortoleva, *supra* note 55, 97.

176 Ibid., 141.

177 White, Bornman and Johnson, *supra* note 46, 20.

178 Ibid., 20.

179 Ngozi Chuma Umeh, *supra* note 151, 71.

Additionally, long and tedious legal procedures, as well as law enforcement officers driven by negative stereotypes have led to the impunity of violence committed against the woman with a disability in Africa.[180]

Effective access to justice is essential for challenging human rights violations.[181] The necessary legal aid must be provided to women with disabilities and survivors of violence at all levels of the criminal justice system. The CRPD Committee has emphasised that states' obligations in ensuring access to justice for persons with disabilities should include 'recognition of diverse communication methods, allowing video testimony in certain situations, procedural accommodation, the provision of professional sign language interpretation and other assistive methods'.[182] For example, in the Democratic Republic of Congo, measures to ensure access to justice include mobile courts for victims of gender-based violence based in Eastern Congo who are unable to access a courthouse.[183] These mobile courts ensure that women with disabilities, for instance, can access the justice system even when they live in remote areas.[184] This measure largely addresses issues around accessibility due to transportation and financial barriers.[185]

6.3 Lack of Transformative Remedies that Address Root Causes

There are several factors, as highlighted above, that expose women with disabilities to a greater risk of experiencing violence. These include

180 Ortoleva, *supra* note 55, 97.

181 See generally, Committee on the Elimination of Discrimination against Women (CEDAW Committee), General Recommendation No. 33: Women's Access to Justice, U.N. Doc. CEDAW/C/GC/33 (2015).

182 CRPD Committee, General Comment No. 1: Article 12: Equality before the law, U.N. Doc. CRPD/C/GC/1 (2014): 39.

183 Open Society Justice Initiative, 'Justice in DRC: Mobile Courts Combat Rape and Impunity in Eastern Congo' (2013), https://www.justiceinitiative.org/uploads/972ab1f9-fae9-49d0-b098-b5238433a859/justice-drc-20130114.pdf; Katyla Cengel, 'DRC: Mobile Courts Deliver Justice to Remote Areas' *ALJAZEERA* (September 2016), https://www.aljazeera.com/features/2016/09/26/drc-mobile-courts-deliver-justice-to-remote-areas/.

184 Ibid.

185 Ibid.

prejudices against their disability status, isolation from society, and dependence on others. These factors can lead to impunity. Thus, a holistic approach that addresses individual, institutional and structural factors that are cause and a consequence of violence against women with disabilities are required.

6.4 Data and Analysis Shortcomings

There is a general lack of systematic collection and analysis of data related to women with disabilities and violence that they face. States must ensure that they collect data to understand the issues that women with disabilities face to be able to develop effective solutions to address those challenges. There is a need for systematised and disaggregated data on violence against women and girls with disabilities. Further research on manifestations and prevalence rates, law, policy and institutional responses is needed.

7 Conclusion

The global and African human rights system have a plethora of human rights instruments that not only protect women, including women with disabilities, from violence but can have an impact on national laws and jurisprudence on addressing violence against women with disabilities. States have clear and specific obligations under international human rights law to enact legislation prohibiting all acts of violence. Women with disabilities must be recognised as equal rights holders to access the justice system and ensure that they seek redress when their rights are violated. Increased accountability is needed to hold states accountable to protect, prevent, punish, prosecute perpetrators of violence and to provide reparations to female survivors with disabilities.

Finally, the above analysis demonstrates how efforts to tackle and eliminate all forms of violence committed against African women with disabilities. States' legislation criminalising violent acts must develop an intersectional lens that recognises the intersections that exist between gender and disability.

References

1996 South African Constitution.
1999 Constitution of the Federal Republic of Nigeria.
Advantage Africa, 2016, 'An Assessment of the Social, Cultural and Institutional Factors That Contribute to the Sexual Abuse of Persons with Disabilities in East Africa', https://www.advantageafrica.org/file/advantage-africa-full-research-report-sexual-abuse-of-persons-with-disabilities-pdf.
African Charter on Human and Peoples' Rights (African Charter).
African Charter on the Rights and Welfare of the Child.
African Commission on Human and Peoples' Rights, 2017, *Guidelines on Combating Sexual Violence and Its Consequences in Africa.*
African Commission on Human and Peoples' Rights, *General Comment No. 2 on Article 14.1 (a), (b), (c) and (f) and Article 14. 2 (a) and (c) of the Protocol to the African Charter on Human and Peoples' Rights on the Rights of Women in Africa.*
African Commission on Human and Peoples' Rights, *General Comments No. 1 on Article 14(1)(d) and (e) of the Protocol to the African Charter on Human and Peoples' Rights on the Rights of Women in Africa.*
African Commission on Human and Peoples' Rights, Resolution 111 of 2007 on *the Right to a Remedy and Reparation for Women and Girls Victims of Sexual Violence.*
African Commission on Human and Peoples' Rights, *Resolution 283 of 2014 on the Situation of Women and Children in Armed Conflict*'.
African Commission on Human and Peoples' Rights, *Resolution 365 of 2017 on Developing Guidelines on Combatting Sexual Violence and its Consequences.*
African Union, 'Strategy for Gender Equality & Women's Empowerment 2018–2028 *Amplifying the Voice of Women with Disabilities Affected by Gender-based Violence and Sexual Violence*, http://www.hlanganisa.org.za/wp-content/uploads/2019/03/JGF_AMPLIFYING-VOICES-OF-WWD.pdf.
Anwuli Irene Ofuani, 2017, 'Protecting Adolescent Girls with Intellectual Disabilities from Involuntary Sterilization in Nigeria: Lessons from the Convention on the Rights of Persons with Disabilities' 17 *African*

Human Rights Law Journal, http://dx.doi.org/l 0.17159/1996–2096/2017/v17n2a9.

Arlene S Kanter and Carla Villarreal Lopez, 2018, 'A Call for an End to Violence Against Women and Girls with Disabilities under International and Regional Human Rights Law' 10(2) *Northeastern University Law Review*.

Brief on violence against women and girls with disabilities, 2019, https://www.vawgresourceguide.org/sites/vawg/files/briefs/vawg_resource_disability_formatted_v6.pdf.

C Jonah Eleweke and Jannine Ebenso, 2016, 'Barriers to Accessing Services by People with Disabilities in Nigeria: Insights from a Qualitative Study' 6(2) *Journal of Educational and Social Research*, Doi:https://doi.org/10.5901/jesr.2016.v6n2p113.

Carolyn Frohmader and Stephanie Ortoleva, 2013, 'The Sexual and Reproductive Rights of Women and Girls with Disabilities' Issue paper https://womenenabled.org/pdfs/issues_paper_srr_women_and_girls_with_disabilities_final.pdf.

CEDAW Committee, 1991, *General Recommendation No 18: Disabled Women*.

CEDAW Committee, 1992, General Recommendation 19 *Violence Against Women*.

CEDAW Committee, 2013, CEDAW *General Recommendation No. 30: Women in Conflict Prevention, Conflict and Post Conflict Situations*, UN Doc. CEDAW/C/GC/30.

CEDAW Committee, 2015, General Recommendation No. 33: *Women's Access to Justice*, U.N. Doc. CEDAW/C/GC/33.

CEDAW Committee, 2017, *General Recommendation No. 35 on Gender-based Violence Against Women, Updating General Recommendation No. 19*.

CEDAW Committee, *General Recommendation 28: Core Obligations of States* UN Doc. CEDAW/C/GC/28.

Chantal J Badul and Ann Strode, 2013, '*LM and Others v Government of the Republic of Namibia:* The First Sub Saharan African Case Dealing with Coerced Sterilizations of HIV-Positive Women—Quo Vadis?' 13 *African Human Rights Law Journal.*

Cheluchi Onyemelukwe, 2015, 'Intersections of Violence Against Women and Health: Implications for Health Law and Policy in Nigeria' 22 *William and Mary Journal of Women and the* Law.

Christine Chinkin, 2014, 'Addressing Violence Against Women in the Commonwealth Within States' Obligations under the International Law' 40(3) *Commonwealth Law Bulletin.*

Committee on the Rights of People with Disabilities, 2016, General Comment 3: *Women and Girls with Disabilities* CRPD/C/GC/3.
Convention on the Rights of Persons with Disabilities.
CRPD Committee, *Concluding Observations in relation to the initial report of Gabon* adopted at its 14th session (August 17, to September 4, 2015).
CRPD Committee, *Concluding Observation on the initial report of Algeria* adopted during its 20th session in June 27, 2019.
CRPD Committee, *Concluding Observation on the initial report of the Niger* adopted during its 21st session in May 1, 2019.
CRPD Committee, *Concluding Observations in relation to the initial report of Morocco* adopted at 18th session in September 25, 2017.
CRPD Committee, *Concluding Observations in relation to the initial report of Rwanda* adopted at its 21st session on May 3, 2019.
CRPD Committee, *Concluding Observations in relation to the initial report of South Africa* adopted at its 20th session on October 23, 2018.
CRPD Committee, *Concluding observations on the initial report of Senegal*, CRPD/C/SEN/CO/1 (2019).
CRPD Committee, General Comment No. 1: Article 12: Equality before the law, U.N. Doc.CRPD/C/GC/1 (2014) 39.
Declaration on the Elimination of Violence against Women GA Res 48/104 of December 20, 1993.
Ebenezer Durojaye and Satang Nabaneh, 2019, 'Human Rights and Access to Healthcare for Persons with Albinism in Africa' 7(40) *African Disability Rights Yearbook,* http://doi.org/https://doi.org/10.29053/2413-7138/2019/v7a2.
Ebenezer Durojaye and Yinka Owoeye, 2017, 'Equally Unequal or Unequally EQUAL: Adopting a Substantive Equality Approach to Gender Discrimination in Nigeria' 17(2) *International Journal of Discrimination and the Law.*
Edwin Etieyibo and Odirin Omiegbe, 2016, 'Religion, Culture, and Discrimination Against Persons with Disabilities in Nigeria' 5(1) *African Journal of Disability,* http://dx.doi.org/https://doi.org/10.4102/ajod.v5i1.192.
Egyptian Initiative for Personal Rights and Interights v. Egypt Communication No. 323/06 (2011).
Equality Now and Ethiopian Women Lawyers Association (EWLA) v Federal Republic of Ethiopia, Communication 341/2007 (2007).
Ereshnee Naidu et al., 2005, 'On the Margins: Violence Against Women with Disabilities' Centre for the Study of Violence and Reconciliation 13 http://www.csvr.org.za/docs/gender/onthemargins.pdf.

Fareda Banda, 2006, 'Blazing a trail: The African Protocol on Women's Rights comes into Force' 50(1) *Journal of African Law*, doi:https://doi.org/10.1017/S0021855306000076.

Frans Viljoen, 2009, 'An Introduction to the Protocol to the African Charter on Human and Peoples' Rights on the Rights of Women in Africa' 16(19) *Washington and Lee Journal of Civil Rights and Social Justice*.

Frans Viljoen, 2012, *International Human Rights Law in Africa*.

Gbenga Emmanuel Afolayan, 2015, 'Contemporary Representations of Disability and Interpersonal Relationships of Disabled Women in South-Western Nigeria' 29(2) *Agenda*, http://dx.doi.org/https://doi.org/10.1080/10130950.2015.1061780.

General Assembly Resolution, Convention on the Elimination of All Forms of Discrimination Against Women, 54/180 UN GAOR 34th session Supp 46 UN Doc A/34/46 1980.

Human Rights Council, January 18, 2016, *Report of the Independent Expert on the Enjoyment of Human Rights by Persons with Albinism* A/HRC/31/63.

Human Rights Council, March 30, 2012, *Thematic Study on the Issue of Violence Against Women and Girls and Disability Report of the Office of the United Nations High Commissioner for Human Rights* (A/HRC/20/5).

Human Rights Council, May 2, 2011, *Report of the Special Rapporteur on Violence Against Women, Its Causes and Consequences, Rashida Manjoo* (A/HRC/17/26).

Human Rights Watch, 2010, 'As If We Weren't Human': Discrimination and Violence Against Women with Disabilities in Northern Uganda, https://www.hrw.org/report/2010/08/26/if-we-werent-human/discrimination-and-violence-against-women-disabilities-northern.

Ibrahim Imam and M Abdulraheem-Mustapha, 2016, 'Rights of People with Disability in Nigeria: Attitudes and Commitment' 24(3) *African Journal of International and Comparative Law*.

Ilze Grobbelaar-du-Plessis, 2007, 'African Women with Disabilities: The Victims of Multi-layered Discrimination' 22 *South African Public Law*.

Ingrid Van Der Heijden, 2014, 'What Works to Prevent Violence Against Women with Disabilities', https://assets.publishing.service.gov.uk/media/57a089ade5274a27b20001e9/What_Works_Inception_Report_June_2014_AnnexW_Interventions_for_abuse_against_WWD.pdf.

Ingrid Van der Heijden, Jane Harries and Naeemah Abraham, 2016, 'Additional Layers of Violence: The Intersections of Gender and Disability in the Violence Experiences of Women with Physical Disabilities in South Africa' *Journal of Interpersonal Violence*.

Ingrid Van der Heijden, Jane Harries and Naeemah Abraham, 2019, 'Barriers to Gender-based Violence Services and Support for Women with Disabilities in Cape Town, South Africa' *Disability & Society*, https://doi.org/https://doi.org/10.1080/09687599.2019.1690429.

International Network of Women with Disabilities, 2011, 'Violence Against Women with Disabilities' Barbara Faye Waxman Fiduccia Papers on Women and Girls with Disabilities, Center for Women Policy Studies.

Jill Hanass-Hancock et al., 2018, '*Preventing Violence Against Women and Girls with Disabilities in Botswana: Situation Analysis*' https://www.samrc.ac.za/sites/default/files/attachments/2018-11-09/ALIGHTSItuationAnalsys.pdf.

John Alan Cohan, 2011, 'The Problem of Witchcraft Violence in Africa' 44(4) *Suffolk University Law Review*.

Kathleen Cornelsen, 2013, 'Doubly Protected and Doubly Discriminated: The Paradox of Women with Disabilities after Conflict' 19 *William and Mary Journal of Women and the Law*.

Katyla Cengel, 2016, 'DRC: Mobile Courts Deliver Justice to Remote Areas' *Aljazeera* https://www.aljazeera.com/features/2016/09/26/drc-mobile-courts-deliver-justice-to-remote-areas/.

Kimberley Crenshaw, 1989, 'Demarginalizing the Intersection of Race and Sex: A Black Feminist Critique of Antidiscrimination Doctrine, Feminist Theory and Antiracist Politics' *University of Chicago Legal Forum*.

Lina Abu-Habib, 1995, 'Women and Disability Don't Mix! Double Discrimination and Disabled Women's Rights' 3(2) *Gender and Development*.

LM and Others v Namibia Case no: SA 49/2012.

Louis O Oyaro, 2015, 'Africa at Crossroads: The United Nations Convention on the Rights of Persons with Disabilities' 30(2) *American University International Law Review*.

M Pavan Kumar and SE Anuradha, 2009, 'Nonconformity Incarnate': Women with Disabilities, 'Gendered' Law and the Problem of Recognition' 44(44) *Economic and Political Weekly*.

Margaret Llyod, 2001, 'The Politics of Disability and Feminism, Discord or Synthesis' 35(3) *Sociology*, doi:10.1177/2FS003803850.1000360.

Marit Hoem Kvam and Stine Hellum Braathen, 2008, 'I Thought . . . Maybe This Is My Chance' Sexual Abuse Against Girls and Women with Disabilities in Malawi' 20(1) *Sexual Abuse: A Journal of Research and Treatment*.

Michelle Fine and Adrienne Asch, 1981, 'Disabled Women: Sexism Without the Pedestal' 8(2) *The Journal of Sociology & Social Welfare*.

Mkhize Gabi, 2015, 'Problematising Rhetorical Representations of Individuals with Disability Disabled or Living with Disability?' 29(2) *Agenda*, https://doi.org/10.1080/10130950.2015.1040692.

Ngozi Chuma Umeh, 2016, 'Reading 'Disability' into the Non-discrimination Clause of the Nigerian Constitution' 4 *African Disability Rights Yearbook*.

Nigeria's 6th periodic report (2015–2016) to the African Commission on Human and Peoples' Rights.

NSRP and Inclusive Friends, 'What Violence Means to Us: Women with Disabilities Speak' (2015) http://www.nsrp-nigeria.org/wp-content/uploads/2015/09/What-Violence-Means-to-us-Women-with-Disabilities-Speak.pdf.

Open Society Justice Initiative, 2013, 'Justice in DRC: Mobile Courts Combat Rape and Impunity in Eastern Congo', https://www.justiceinitiative.org/uploads/972ab1f9-fae9-49d0-b098-b5238433a859/justice-drc-20130114.pdf.

Peter Blanck, Meera Adya and Maria Veronica Reina, 2007, 'Defying Double Discrimination' 8(1) *Georgetown Journal of International Affairs*.

Protocol to the African Charter on Human and Peoples' Rights on the Rights of Women in Africa.

Protocol to the African Charter on Human and Peoples' Rights on the Rights of Persons with Disabilities.

Rachel Murray, 2000, *The African Commission on Human and Peoples' Rights and International Law*.

Rangita De Silva De Alwist, 2009, 'Mining the Intersections: Advancing the Rights of Women and Children with Disabilities Within an Interrelated Web of Human Rights' 18(1) *Pacific Rim Law & Policy Journal*.

Rashida Manjoo, 2018, 'Normative Developments on Violence Against Women in the United Nations System' in *The Legal Protection of Women from Violence: Normative Gaps in International Law* edited by Rashida Manjoo and Jackie Jones.

Report of the Fourth World Conference on Women, A/CONF.177/20, chap. I, resolution 1, annex II, (1995).

Republic of Ghana, *Initial report on the implementation of the Convention on the Rights of Persons with Disabilities* submitted to the Convention on the Rights of Persons with Disabilities on March 8, 2019.

Republic of Liberia, *Initial report on the implementation of the Convention on the Rights of Persons with Disabilities* submitted to the Convention on the Rights of Persons with Disabilities on April 24, 2020.

Republic of Malawi, *Initial report on the implementation of the Convention on the Rights of Persons with Disabilities* submitted to the Convention on the Rights of Persons with Disabilities on March 8, 2019.

Robyn White, Juan Bornman, and Ensa Johnson, 2018, 'From Silence to Justice: Implications for Persons with Little or No Functional Speech Accessing the Criminal Justice System' 31(1) *Acta Criminologica: Southern African Journal of Criminology.*

Rosemary Kayess and Philip French, 2008, 'Out of Darkness into Light? Introducing the Convention on the Rights of Persons with Disabilities' 8(1) *Human Rights Law Review.*

Satang Nabaneh and Adamson Muula, 2019, 'Female Genital Mutilation/Cutting: A Complex Legal and Ethical Landscape' 145(2) International *Journal of Gynecology & Obstetrics*, https://doi.org/10.1002/ijgo.12792.

Serges Alain Djoyou Kamga, 2013, 'A Call for a Protocol to the African Charter on Human and Peoples' Rights on the Rights of Persons with Disabilities in Africa' 21(2) *African Journal of International and Comparative Law.*

Stephanie Ortoleva, 2010–2011, 'Women with Disabilities: The Forgotten Peace Builders' 33(83) *Loyola of Los Angeles International and Comparative Law Review.*

Stephanie Ortoleva and Hope Lewis, 2012, 'Forgotten Sisters—A Report on Violence Against Women with Disabilities an Overview of Its Nature, Scope, Causes and Consequences'.

Sudan Human Rights Organisation & Centre on Housing Rights and Evictions (COHRE) v. Sudan, Communication No. 79/03–296/05.

Talia Meer and Helene Combrinck, 2015, 'Invisible Intersections: Understanding the Complex Stigmatisation of Women with Intellectual Disabilities in Their Vulnerability to Gender-based Violence' *Agenda: Empowering Women for Gender Equity*, http://dx.doi.org/https://doi.org/10.1080/10130950.2015.1039307.

The African Youth Charter.

Theresia Theresia, 2016, 'Disability in a Human Rights Context' 5 *Laws.*

Thomas J Gerschick, 2000, 'Toward a Theory of Disability and Gender' 25(4) *Signs: Journal of Women in Culture and Society.*

Tobias P Van Reenen and Helene Combrinck, 2011, 'The UN Convention on the Rights of Persons with Disabilities in Africa: Progress after 5 Years' 8(14) *SUR International Journal of Human Rights.*

Tony Emmett and Erna Alant, 2006, 'Women and Disability: Exploring the Interface of Multiple Disadvantage' 23(4) *Development Southern Africa*, http://dx.doi.org/https://doi.org/10.1080/03768350600927144.

United Nations Commission on Human Rights Resolution 1994/45 on the question of integrating the rights of women into human rights mechanisms of the UN and the elimination of violence against women, adopted on March 4, 1994.

Virginia Kallianes and Phyllis Rubenfeld, 1997, 'Disabled Women and Reproductive RIGHTS' 12(2) *Disability & Society*, http://dx.doi.org/https://doi.org/10.1080/09687599727335.

11

The Right to Maternal Healthcare of Migrant and Refugee Women in South Africa and Uganda: Criminal Accountability as a Tool to Addressing Violation

Jackline N. Hakim, Annette Lansink, and Emma Charlene Lubaale

1 Introduction

An estimated 79.5 million people were forcibly displaced around the world at the end of 2019, 26.0 million of these being refugees and

[1] The United Nations High Commissioner for Refugees (UNHCR), *Global Trends Forced Displacement in 2019*, June 4, 2020, https://www.unhcr.org/globaltrends2019/; UNHCR, *Women*, September 4, 2020, http://www.unhcr.org/women.html.

J. N. Hakim (✉)
Centre for Human Rights, University of Pretoria, Pretoria, South Africa

A. Lansink
School of Law, University of Venda South Africa, Thohoyandou, South Africa
e-mail: annette.lansink@univen.ac.za

E. C. Lubaale
Faculty of Law, Centre for Human Rights, University of Pretoria, Hatfield, Pretoria, South Africa

A. Budoo-Scholtz and E. C. Lubaale (eds.), *Violence Against Women and Criminal Justice in Africa: Volume II*, Sustainable Development Goals Series,
https://doi.org/10.1007/978-3-030-75953-7_11

women making up 49–50% of the total refugee population.[1] Similarly, migrant populations around the globe had risen to 272 million in 2019 with Africa experiencing a significantly high rise in migrant population growth; South Africa and Uganda are among the African countries most affected by the influx of migrants and refugees within the continent.[2]

Migrants and refugees are generally categorised as 'vulnerable groups' because they are not only victims of their circumstances but the risk of having their rights violated is relatively higher in comparison to that of citizens of their host countries. These rights include the right to dignity, freedom from torture and discrimination, equality before the law, access to justice, access to socio-economic rights (SER) among which are the right to housing and healthcare.[3] Due to their status, migrant/refugee women are more susceptible to discrimination, racism, sexual and gender-based violence[4] with many experiencing substantial sexual and reproductive health rights (SRHR) challenges including access to maternal healthcare goods and services.[5] It is also a common practice for most countries hosting migrants and refugees to consider them as 'non-nationals' as they are often termed as 'aliens' or 'foreigners'.[6] This often sets the pace for ill and differential treatment of migrants and refugees. Some States have gone as far as enacting laws and policies which hardly accord due regard to the rights of migrants and refugees or discriminate against them directly or indirectly.[7] Although host countries are responsible for protecting migrants and refugees, the integration of these groups into the society is still a challenge. Migrants' limited access

---

[2] International Organisation for Migration, *World Migration Report* (2020).

[3] Amnesty International Report 2017/2018, *The State of the World's Human Rights* (2018).

[4] The Forced Migration Research Network, *The World's Biggest Minority? Refugee Women and Girls in the Global Compact on Refugees* (2017).

[5] World Health Organisation, *Refugee and Migrant Health: Draft Global Action Plan: Promoting the Health of Refugees and Migrants* (2019–2023), June 15, 2020, https://www.who.int/migrants/en/.

[6] Section 2(a) (xvii) of the Immigration Amendment Act 2004 of South Africa consider non-nationals as 'foreigners' and Section 3(1) of the Control of Aliens Refugees Act 1960 consider non-nationals as 'aliens.'.

[7] T Achiume 'Beyond prejudice: Structural xenophobic discrimination against refugees' 45 *Georgetown Journal of International Law* (2014): 331–332.

to maternal healthcare is escalated by xenophobia,[8] as this contributes to the unequal treatment of migrant and refugee women. This is despite the well-established international, regional and sub-regional frameworks on the rights of migrants and refugees.

In an era where human rights remain indispensable in the advancement of democratisation, a national framework which does not recognise the rights of all, including migrants and refugees becomes questionable. A HRBA, among others, underscores the need to respect, protect, promote and fulfil the rights of not only citizens but also non-nationals within the territory of a State.[9] Moreover, in the current era of globalisation, there is a legitimate concern by the international community for the protection of the rights of migrants and refugees in host States, who are at an increased risk of being abused and discriminated against. This state of affairs underscores the need for a critical analysis of the right to maternal healthcare at the national level with a view to identifying some good practices and issues warranting redress.

South Africa and Uganda were selected for comparison for various reasons, some of which are highlighted below. South Africa is considered a thriving democratic society with a globally lauded Constitution and progressive national health policies. It also has a self-resettlement and urban integration policy which focuses on reducing xenophobia and improving social inclusion.[10] Its 1996 Constitution has a specific right to health which encompasses the right to maternal healthcare as a justiciable socio-economic right. Its Refugee Act of 1998 is also considered to have adopted a HRBA as it guarantees refugees rights accorded in the Bill of Rights (BOR) including the right to health which is provided for under Section 27(g) of the Act. South African courts are also obliged by the Constitution to consider international law when interpreting the BOR.

[8] Paragraph 39 of the New York Declaration for Migrant and Refugees 2016; Y. Munyaneza, & E. Mhlongo, 'Challenges of women refugees in utilising reproductive health services in public health institutions in Durban, KwaZu-Natal, South Africa' *Journal of Interdisciplinary Health Sciences* (2019): 1–8.

[9] A. D'Amato, 'Human Rights as part of Customary International Law: A plea for change of paradigm' *Georgia Journal of International & Comparative Law* (2010): 20–21.

[10] Department of Cooperative Government and Traditional Affairs, *Integrated Urban Development Framework* 2016, June 5, 2020, https://www.africancentreforcities.net/wp-content/uploads/2017/05/IUDF-2016_WEB-min.pdf.

In contrast, the Ugandan 1995 Constitution has no justiciable right to health and adopts the dualist approach, and courts have no obligation to consider international law in their interpretation of human rights, which raises the question of how the international human right to maternal healthcare may be enforced. It is within this ambit that this chapter explores the implementation of the right to access maternal healthcare in both countries. Significantly, lessons may be drawn from both countries on the realisation of the right to maternal healthcare of migrant and refugee women. Before delving into the assessment of the law and practice relating to access to maternal healthcare in both countries, an appraisal of the international human rights obligation in both countries with regards to the right to maternal healthcare is conducted.

The discussion in this chapter will contribute to this subject in light of the current gaps in the literature. Much has been written about the challenges faced by migrants and refugees in South Africa and Uganda, all of which cannot be exhausted. Therefore, the work of some authors is discussed to demonstrate the scope of research thus far with a view to assessing the contribution this chapter makes to existing literature.

Carciotto and D'Orsi, are of the view that refugees, especially refugee women and girls who make up half of the refugee population,[11] are disproportionately affected as they encounter challenges in accessing healthcare and SRHR services[12] in South Africa despite the properly crafted legislative and constitutional provisions.[13] Vearey et al. take the view that there is a mismatch between the law and practice when it comes to the accessibility of healthcare by migrants in South Africa.[14] Crush and Tawodzera refer to the unequal treatment of migrants and refugees in accessing healthcare as 'medical xenophobia', a term the authors use to argue that migrants and refugees often encounter hostility when seeking medical care which is greatly influenced by healthcare

---

[11] United Nations High Commissioner for Refugees, *Women*, June 5, 2020, https://www.unhcr.org/women.html.

[12] https://iawg.net/search?q=refugee+women, September 7, 2020.

[13] S. Carciotto, & C. D'Orsi 'Access to socio-economic rights for refugees: A comparison across six African countries' *The Scalabrini Institute for Human Mobility in Africa* (2017): 38–39.

[14] J. Veary et al. 'Towards a migration-aware health system in South Africa: A strategic opportunity to address health inequity' *South African Health Review* (2017): 89.

providers.[15] According to Vearey and Richter, migrants have been deliberately excluded from the South African society even though the South African urban policy encourages migrants and refugees to integrate and re-settle.[16] They add that migrants do not receive prompt access to healthcare because of the existing challenges deliberately driven by medical personnel including receptionists undermining their right to health.[17]

In the context of Uganda, Addaney has argued that access to healthcare is one of the basic rights yet it continues to be violated, particularly among refugees in Uganda.[18] The Refugee Law Project in Uganda also conducted research on refugees living in Uganda and found that language is the main impediment to accessing healthcare.[19] Medical xenophobia is also practised within the health facilities often by the healthcare providers who mistreat refugees and overcharge them for medication.[20] Twinomugisha who has written extensively on the right to health including maternal healthcare in Uganda, submits that the barrier to accessing healthcare is attributed mainly to unethical practices of healthcare providers, inadequate allocation of resources by the government, medical fees and non-affordability of drugs.[21]

It is conceded that much has been written on maternal healthcare. However, not many writers have approached the subject from a comparative perspective that places South Africa and Uganda at the centre of the study. What also makes the present research unique is that it anchors the discussion within the broader international, regional and sub-regional

---

[15] J. Crush, & G. Tawodzera, 'Medical xenophobia and Zimbabwean migrant access to public health services in South Africa' 40 *Journal of Ethnic and Migration Studies* (2013): 656.

[16] J. Veary, & M. Richter 'Challenges to the successful implementation of policy to protect the right of access to health for all in South Africa' 4 *Migrant Health Forum* (2008): 15.

[17] J. Veary 'Healthy migration: A Public health and development imperative for south(ern) Africa' 10 *South African Medical Journal* (2014): 663–664.

[18] M. Addaney 'A step forward in the protection of urban refugees: The legal protection of the rights of refugees in Uganda' 17 *African Human Rights Law Journal* (2017): 243.

[19] Refugee Law Project 'A drop in the ocean: Assistance and protection for forced migrants in Kampala' 34 *Refugee Working Paper* (2005): 16.

[20] Urban Refugees.Org, *Concerned Population*, June 15, 2020, http://urban-refugees.org/Kampala/.

[21] B. K. Twinomugisha, 'Maternal health rights, politics and the law' *Professional Inaugural Lecture* (2017): 20.

normative framework on the maternal healthcare rights of migrant and refugee women. This framework then becomes a benchmark against which to measure the extent to which this right is realised with the hope that if South Africa and Uganda align their national framework with the international, regional and sub-regional normative framework, other benefits including realisation of Sustainable Development Goals (SDGs) will accrue. A major contribution of the chapter also lies in its emphasis on criminal accountability as one of the means to ensuring that those responsible for violation of the rights of migrant and refugee women are held to account.

2 Maternal Healthcare and the Global Development Agenda

The promotion of maternal healthcare was first reflected under the objectives of the World Health Organisation (WHO) under article 2(l) of its 1948 Constitution which, *inter alia,* underscored the need to 'promote maternal and child health and welfare and to foster the ability to live harmoniously in a changing total environment'. This was followed by other international platforms geared towards advancing the right to maternal healthcare including the 1994 International Conference on Population and Development, Programme of Action (ICPD, PoA) which expressly declared under paragraph 7.2 that women have the right to access appropriate healthcare services that will enable them to go through safe pregnancy and childbirth to ensure the possibility of bearing a healthy child.

Maternal healthcare has time and again been buttressed so much so that states are now deemed to have an obligation to ensure that women receive medical services before, during and after pregnancy and should be granted free maternal healthcare services where necessary under article 12(1, 2) of the Convention on the Elimination of all Forms of Discrimination Against Women (CEDAW). The Committee on CEDAW first noted under its General Recommendation No 24: Article 12 of the Convention (Women and Heath) adopted in 1999 that it is the duty of States to ensure women's right to safe motherhood and emergency obstetric care (EmOC).[22] States are required to include in their reports how they ensure safe pregnancies through free maternal healthcare services,[23] and ensure the removal of all barriers to women's access to health services including in the area of sexual reproductive health services.[24] The Committee also reiterated the obligation of States under article 12 of CEDAW in *Alyne da Silva Pimentel Teixera v Brazil*,[25] following the death of an Afro-Brazilian woman after childbirth. It found the State Party in violation of article 12 of CEDAW for failing to provide adequate maternal healthcare services which also constituted discrimination against women under articles 1 and 2 of CEDAW.[26] In its recommendation to the State, the Committee noted that Brazil must ensure the right to safe motherhood and affordable access to EmOC in accordance with paragraph 27 of General Comment No. 24.[27]

Maternal healthcare encompasses other services like antenatal care (ANC), delivery care, postnatal care (PNC), newborn care, basic essential obstetric care (BEOC) and EmOC.[28] Twinomugisha submits that the right to access EmOC is universally recognised as a human rights issue because it is an integral part of a woman's right to life and thus may be judicially enforced when violated.[29] Consequently, access to and improvement of maternal healthcare services by States is related to the target to reduce maternal mortality rate (MMR) and child mortality rate (CMR) which target was endorsed by the United Nations (UN) under the SDGs with the objective to 'leave no one behind'[30] which is infused in the 2030 Agenda. Notably, the health target for SDG 3.1 is to 'By

---

[22] CEDAW, A/54/38/Rev. 1, Chap. I (1999), June 15, 2020, https://www.refworld.org/docid/453882a73.html.

[23] Ibid., Paragraphs 26 and 27.

[24] Ibid., Paragraph 31(b).

[25] Alyne da Silva Pimentel Teixera v Brazil; CEDAW/C/49/D/17/2008, Paragraph 7.3.

[26] Ibid., Paragraph 7.6.

[27] Ibid., Paragraph 8(2)(2).

[28] The Demographic and Health Surveys programme, *Maternal Health Services* (2004): 109–110.

[29] B. K. Twinomugisha 'Exploring judicial strategies to protect the right of access to emergency obstetric care in Uganda' 7 *African Human Rights Law Journal* (2007): 289.

[30] United Nations general assembly resolution on transforming our world: The 2030 agenda for sustainable development A/RES/70/1 (2015).

2030, reduce the global MMR to less than 70 per 100,000 live births.'[31] SDG 3 encompasses measurable goals which include the improvement of maternal healthcare; prevention and reduction of maternal mortality and achievement of universal access of SRHR.[32] The goals to reduce MMR and CMR by half,[33] were also adopted under the '[g]oals for children and development in the 1990s' during the World Summit for Children in 1990.[34] Additionally, one of the objectives of the ICPD, PoA include the reduction of child and maternal mortality by providing universal access to SRHR services including family planning.[35]

According to the WHO, about 810 women die daily from preventable causes of pregnancy and childbirth.[36] Sub-Saharan Africa suffers the highest MMR accounting for 68% of maternal deaths per worldwide,[37] despite a worldwide focus on the need to improve maternal healthcare.[38] MMR and CMR are very high and it is documented that the health status of women and children in Africa is one of the lowest in the world, with the MMR in Africa at 546 per 100,000 live births.[39] It is thus discernible that the survival of a child and reduction in child mortality is largely dependent on the improvement of maternal healthcare services and reduction in MMR.[40]

The SDGs infused in the 2030 Agenda, provide a renewed commitment for States to further reduce MMR. The international community has since called on States to implement their international obligation

---

[31] WHO, September 4, 2020, https://www.who.int/sdg/targets/en/.

[32] Ibid.

[33] United Nations Children's Fund, *United Nations World Summit for Children* (1990), June 15, 2020, https://www.unicef.org/wsc/plan.htm.

[34] United Nations Children's Emergency Fund, June 15, 2020, https://www.unicef.org/wsc/.

[35] Ibid., Paragraph 1.12.

[36] WHO, *Maternal* Mortality (2019), June 15, 2020, https://www.who.int/news-room/fact-sheets/detail/maternal-mortality.

[37] United Nations Children's Emergency Fund, June 15, 2020, https://www.who.int/news-room/fact-sheets/detail/maternal-mortality.

[38] Umar H. et al. *Improving Access and Utilization of Maternal Healthcare Services Through Focused Antenatal Care in Rural Ghana: A Qualitative Study* (2019).

[39] United Nations Children's Emergency Fund, June 15, 2020, https://data.unicef.org/topic/maternal-health/maternal-mortality/#v.

[40] United Nations Department of Economic and Social Affairs, June 15, 2020, https://www.un.org/esa/devagenda/UNDA_BW5_Final.pdf.

to provide accessible and quality healthcare services to migrant/refugee women that it is often overlooked.[41] The Human Rights Council (HRC) resolution on preventable maternal mortality and morbidity and human rights also called on State Parties to fulfil their obligations under international treaties including CEDAW, Beijing Declaration and Platform for Action (BDPA), ICPD, PoA and SDG 3.[42]

This emphasis is based on the recognition of the fact that there is an unacceptably high global rate of preventable maternal mortality and morbidity which is a health and human rights challenge and which according to the HRC constitute violation of human rights.[43] The HRC has also expressed that States could reduce MMR and CMR through the integration of a human rights perspective in international and national responses to maternal mortality and morbidity. Furthermore, the WHO considers health to be a 'shared responsibility',[44] with States being under the obligation to provide universal access to sexual and reproductive health (SRH) services and integrate reproductive healthcare into national strategies and programmes which extends to all women including migrant and refugee women.[45] This is with due regard to the increasing number of migrant and refugee women of child-bearing age whose specific needs relate to maternal healthcare services. Furthermore, the New York Declaration for migrants and refugees which embodies the commitments made by UN Member States also adopts the SDGs that commit States to protecting the rights of all migrants and refugees regardless of status and provide essential healthcare services for them[46] including access to SRH services and tackle different forms of discrimination against migrant/refugee women and girls.[47]

---

[41] United Nations Fund for Population Activities, *Refugees' and Migrants' Reproductive Health Needs Overlooked*, June 15, 2020, https://www.unfpa.org/news/refugees'-and-migrants'-reproductive-health-needs-overlooked.

[42] A/HRC/RES/11/8 (2008).

[43] Ibid.

[44] WHO, June 16, 2020, http://www.who.int/about/en.

[45] SDG 3.7.

[46] A/RES/71/1 (2016), Paragraph 83.

[47] Ibid., Paragraph 31.

3 The Right to Maternal Healthcare Under International and Regional Instruments

SRHR is a key aspect in a woman's right to health,[48] and 'play[s] a crucial role in improving women's health and rights around the world'.[49] Sexual Reproductive Health Rights empowers women to live a dignified life which includes enjoying SER including access to quality healthcare services.[50] Therefore, States are under international obligation to make quality healthcare facilities and services available, accessible, acceptable and adaptable.[51] That said, the right to maternal healthcare is guaranteed under international instruments like article 25(2) of the Universal Declaration of Human Rights (UDHR) and article 12(2) of CEDAW which provides that State Parties shall ensure women appropriate services in connection with pregnancy, confinement and the postnatal period, granting free services where necessary, as well as adequate nutrition during pregnancy and lactation. Article 12(1) of the International Covenant on Economic Social and Cultural Rights (ICESR) 1966 also impliedly provides for the right to maternal healthcare under the obligation of States to recognise the right of everyone to the enjoyment of the highest attainable standard of physical and mental health, including 'the reduction of the stillbirth-rate and of infant mortality and for the healthy development of the child'.[52] It also implores State Parties to take necessary measures to provide medical care for persons within their jurisdictions in the event of sickness.[53]

Article 24(2)(d) of the United Nations Convention on the Rights of the Child (UNCRC) also provides that States should ensure appropriate prenatal and postnatal healthcare for mothers. Under General

[48] Report on the 55th Session of the Economic and Social Council, Commission on the Status of Women, Paragraph 3 (2011).

[49] R. J. Cook et al. *Reproductive Health and Human Rights: Integrating Medicine, Ethics and Law: Overview* (2003).

[50] ESCR General Comment No. 14: The Right to the Highest Attainable Standard of Health (Article 12), Paragraph 12.

[51] Ibid.

[52] ESCR, Article 12(2)(a).

[53] ESCR, Article 12(2)(d).

Comment No. 15 on the right of the child to the enjoyment of the highest attainable standard of health (article 24 of the UNCRC), the UNCRC Committee elaborates that States must realise the mother's right to health and ensure that care is received by women before, during and after their pregnancy. It further stated that by fulfilling this obligation States shall ensure universal access to a comprehensive package of SRHR interventions based on the concept of a continuum of care from pre-pregnancy, through pregnancy, childbirth and throughout the postpartum period. Article 41 of the Vienna Declaration and Programme of Action 1993 also recognises the human rights of women to include the right to safe maternity and healthcare services.

The right to maternal healthcare is also protected by other human rights instruments including articles 11(1)(f), 12(2) and 14(2)(b) of CEDAW; article 5(e)(iv) of the International Convention Against all forms of Racial Discrimination (CERD); and articles 25(1)(a), 28, 43(1)(e) and 70 of the International Convention on the Protection of the Rights of all Migrant Workers and Members of their Families (ICRMW). Under General Recommendation XXX (30) on Discrimination against Non-Citizens (2005), the CERD Committee stated that State Parties must respect the right of non-citizens to an adequate standard of physical and mental health by, *inter alia*, refraining from denying or limiting their access to preventive, curative and palliative health services.[54] This is also supported by paragraph 7(n) of General Recommendation XXIX (24) on article 1, paragraph 1 of CERD, which provides that States shall provide equal access to healthcare and social security services for members of descent-based communities.

The right to maternal healthcare also finds backing in regional instruments. Article 16 of the African Charter on Human and Peoples' Rights 1981 (Banjul Charter) and article 14(2) (b) of the Protocol to the African Charter on Human and Peoples' Rights on the Rights of Women in Africa 2003 (Maputo Protocol) both buttress this right in very clear and strong terms. The right to maternal healthcare is also enshrined under article 1 and 3(n) of the African Union (AU) Constitutive Act 2000, Annex 2 of the Continental Policy Framework on SRHR and

[54] *Supra*, Note 50, 36.

the Glossary of the Maputo Plan of Action. The Pretoria Declaration on Economic Social and Cultural Rights (ESCR) in Africa (2004) also adds weight to this protection, providing in its article 7(d) that the right to health under article 16 of the Banjul Charter entails, among other things, access to reproductive, maternal and child healthcare based on the life cycle approach to health. The AU Declaration on 'Actions on maternal, newborn, and child health and development in Africa by 2015' which was adopted during the AU Assembly in 2010 also *inter alia* launched the Campaign on Accelerated Reduction of Maternal Mortality in Africa (CARMMA) in their respective countries to promote maternal and neonatal health.[55]

Under the 2010 African Commission on Human and Peoples' Rights (The Commission) Principles and Guidelines on the Implementation of ESCR in the African Charter, States must ensure the right of access to appropriate healthcare services that enable women to go safely through pregnancy and childbirth.[56] The Commission also provided that States should develop systems that respond to and make available integrated SRH services.[57] Additionally, several Resolutions have been adopted to guarantee the right to maternal healthcare. For instance, the Resolution on the programme of essential medicines for children and their mothers,[58] recognises that women and children are the wealth of the African continent hence States must ensure their welfare as they are the most vulnerable of categories.[59] Also, the Resolution on Access to Health and needed Medicines in Africa which recognises the right to the 'highest attainable standard of health' under article 16 of the Banjul Charter also recognises that States should make medicine accessible for treatment and for a healthy and dignified life.[60]

---

[55] Assembly/AU/Decl.1(XI), Article 2(i).

[56] *Supra*, Note 50.

[57] Banjul Declaration of the 59th Ordinary Session of the Commission Under the Theme 'Women's Rights: Our Collective Responsibility' (2016), Paragraph 46.

[58] Resolution on the Integration of Women in Development CM/Res. 1215 (L) (1989).

[59] Ibid.

[60] African Charter, Resolution141 (XXXXIIII) 08 (2008).

Mention may also be made of the Resolution on MMR in Africa by The Commission which recognises women's right to maternal healthcare and recommended that States should accord due regard to the right to health in their periodic reports.[61] In terms of the content of their periodic reports, States are implored to report on the general state of maternal healthcare, including all levels of mortality and morbidity and challenges faced in implementing the related programmes; the policy and institutional measures taken to give effect to the provisions of article 16 of the Banjul Charter on the best attainable state of physical and mental health for women; the budgetary and institutional measures dedicated to securing maternal health; and other programmes and activities undertaken to secure mental health with results.[62] In addition to Resolutions, The Commission General Comments also recognises that women in Africa have the right to the highest attainable standard of health which includes SRHR.[63]

At the sub-regional level, article 16(d) of the Southern African Development Community (SADC) Protocol on health in the SADC provides that State Parties shall formulate standardised policies, strategies, programmes and procedures for reproductive health particularly in the area of fertility. Article 26 of the SADC Protocol on Gender and Development which is in line with the SADC Protocol on Health and other international and regional commitments by States also requires States to adopt legislative frameworks among others and provide for affordable quality healthcare in particular to reduce MMR and address SRH needs of others. The East African Community (EAC) Treaty (1999) adopts provisions along similar lines. The EAC Legislative Assembly recently passed the EAC SRHR Bill 2017 which seeks to provide for universal access to SRH and promote safe motherhood across the region in a bid to lower maternal and newborn mortality rates.[64] All these norms provide guidelines for States, including South Africa and Uganda to draw on to promote maternal healthcare.

---

61 Ibid.

62 Ibid.

63 General Comments on article 14 (1) (d) and (e) of the Maputo Protocol, Paragraph 5 (2012).

64 The East African Community, SRHR Bill 2017, June 15, 2020, http://www.eala.org/documents/view/theeac-sexual-and-reproductive-health-rights-bill2017.

4 The Rights of Migrants and Refugees to Maternal Healthcare in South Africa and Uganda

4.1 Legal Frameworks

Constitutions often encompass rights and freedoms guaranteed under international law. While some may be clustered under the BOR,[65] others are clustered as 'fundamental rights and freedoms of human right'.[66] The Constitution being the supreme law of the land sets the pace for States to implement their international, regional and sub-regional frameworks to respect, protect, promote and fulfil rights and freedoms of individuals in their respective jurisdictions. The right to health which includes SRHR is explicitly provided for under Section 27(1)(a) of South Africa's Constitution. It could be inferred from this provision that the Constitution makes provision for healthcare including maternal healthcare for all women in South Africa including migrant/refugee women.[67] Section 27(3) also provides that no one shall be denied emergency healthcare which includes EmOC. This, again, is a commendable provision since a generous interpretation of the section suggests that migrants/refugees are entitled to the same emergency healthcare as it pertains to maternal healthcare.

In addition to the express guarantee of the right to health in the Constitution, South Africa's Constitution has laudable provisions that set the pace for the invocation of international law standards. Notably, Section 39(1)(b) mandates courts to consider international law in the interpretation of the BOR.[68] Hence, where national laws on migration and refugees do not measure up to international human rights standards,

[65] South African Constitution, Chapter 2.

[66] Constitution of Uganda, Chapter 4.

[67] Maternal Factsheet on South Africa, June 12, 2020, https://countryoffice.unfpa.org/filemanager/files/southafrica/Maternal_health.pdf.

[68] *Nonkululeko Letta Bhe & Others v Magistrate, Khayelitsha & Others (*CCT 49/03) (2004) ZACC 17; 2005 (1) SA 580 (CC), Paragraph 218.

courts are to prefer an interpretation that advances international human rights.[69]

The Ugandan Constitution, on the other hand does not 'explicitly recognise' the right to health and thus there is no specific provision for the right to healthcare in Uganda.[70] However, the right to maternal healthcare is entrenched under article 33(3) which recognises all women's right to maternal healthcare and EmOC. The deliberate omission of a specific provision on the right to access healthcare under the Ugandan Constitution, could arguably lead to failure to effectively hold the government accountable for violation of the right to health. This also directly impedes migrant/refugee women from accessing the right to maternal healthcare. This position could, of course, be contrasted with South Africa's position where the right to health is very explicit.

Another important issue to take note of is the fact that the Constitution of Uganda does not explicitly make detailed provision for the place of international law in Ugandan courts. With Uganda adopting a dualist approach to the implementation of international law, arguably explicit provisions similar to Sections 39 and 233 of the South African Constitution would be helpful. While it cannot be argued that these provisions are a magic bullet in light of the fact that many factors are usually at play in judicial decision-making, the case law in South Africa suggests that the said provisions have played an important role in making international standards a reality.[71] Uganda continues to have a challenge of judicial enforcement of international law, with courts sometimes not being keen on invoking international human rights standards.[72] Perhaps provisions similar to those of South Africa would add persuasive momentum to the need for courts to take international law including that pertaining to maternal healthcare of migrants/refugees seriously.

---

[69] South African Constitution, Section 233.

[70] J. C. Mubangizi, & B. K. Twinomugisha 'The right to healthcare in the specific context of access to HIV/AIDS medicines: What can South Africa and Uganda learn from each other' 10 *African Human Rights Journal* (2010): 120.

[71] *S v Makwanyane* (3) SA (391) (CC) (1995), Paragraphs 35, 304,305 and 362.

[72] *Uganda Association of Women Lawyers & Others v Attorney General Constitutional* Petition 2 of 2003 UGCC 1 (2004), Paragraph 9(5).

Additionally, although the Ugandan Constitution 1995 does not make explicit provision for migrants/refugees, it provides under its article 21 in Chapter Four that all persons shall be equal before the law and shall enjoy freedom from discrimination; and all other rights guaranteed thereunder. A generous interpretation of this provision leads to a reasonable conclusion that migrants and refugees are included in the category of individuals who are to be protected from discrimination.

The Refugee Act 130 of 1998 is the seminal piece of legislation on the rights of refugees in South Africa. This Act is considered to take a HRBA[73] with Chapter Five of the Act guaranteeing extensive rights including SER.[74] The Act is considered to be one of the most progressive domestic instruments on promotion and protection of refugees in the world.[75] This is based on the fact that refugees are treated almost as citizens and enjoy to a large extent, similar rights and freedoms as citizens.[76] This Act has, however, been criticised for a number of reasons including its poor implementation and its failure to accord due regard to the rights of asylum seekers.[77] Moreover, although refugees have the liberty not to live in camps, a challenge arises with regard to blending into the society which exposes them to vulnerabilities including xenophobic attacks.[78]

In substantive terms, Section 27(g) of South Africa's Refugees Act provides for the right to health of refugees, which would reasonably encompass maternal healthcare. Its counterpart, Uganda's Refugee Act and its Regulations 9 of 2010, do not have a specific provision on the right to health.[79] With regard to refugee women, Section 33(2) of Uganda's Refugee Act provides that refugee women shall be entitled to

---

[73] Southern African Catholic Bishop's Conference 'Overview of the implementation of the Refugee Act of 1998' Briefing Paper 167, Paragraphs 3.1 and 9 (2006).

[74] Refugee Act, Sections 27, 29, 30 and 32.

[75] M. Makhema *Social Protection for Refuges and Asylum Seekers in the Southern Africa Development Community* (2009) 23.

[76] Ibid.

[77] C. Johnson 'Failed asylum seekers in South Africa' 1 *African Human Mobility Review* (2015): 2.

[78] S. M. Madue 'South Africa's foreign and migration policies missteps: Fuels of xenophobic eruptions?' 11 *The Journal for Transdisciplinary Research in Southern Africa* (2015): 63.

[79] Refugee Act, Section 28 and its regulation, Article 9.

all the rights and freedoms including SER guaranteed under the Constitution and any other relevant instruments Uganda is a party to especially CEDAW and the Banjul Charter. It is thus, submitted that refugee women in Uganda are entitled to maternal healthcare by virtue of the right guaranteed under article 33(3) of the Ugandan Constitution and other international instruments.

Despite the decrease of asylum seekers since 2017,[80] South Africa still has a high number of pending asylum cases which has a negative impact on migrant/refugee women who are denied their right to access maternal healthcare facilities for failing to provide 'valid permits'. Not surprisingly, research has proven that some refugee women in South Africa opt to give birth outside medical facilities by avoiding antenatal visits due to the hostile behaviour towards them by some of the healthcare providers. Other challenges these women face on a day-to-day basis include language barrier, financial challenge, ill treatment, failure to seek consent as well as medical xenophobia.

In Uganda, Section 28 of the Refugees Act provides that refugees are entitled to the rights and freedoms as guaranteed under the 1951 Convention relating to the Status of Refugees and the 1969 Organisation of African Unity (OAU) Convention Governing the Specific Aspects of Refugee Problems in Africa. Under the Uganda's Refugees Regulations, a person from any country within the EAC, upon application is granted refugee status, is to enjoy all the rights and privileges conferred on 'Community nationals' as guaranteed under the EAC Treaty and its Protocols which extends to refugee's dependant(s).[81] However, this raises a number of questions, particularly, whether such preferential treatment conforms to the principle of non-discrimination on account of one's nationality. On the basis of this preferential treatment, it is obvious that refugees from countries other than those from EAC do not receive the same treatment as those from the EAC which may in fact be considered problematic.[82]

---

80 Department of Home Affairs, *Annual Report 2017–2018* (2018), September 5, 2020, http://www.dha.gov.za/files/Annual%20Reports/AnnualReport2017-18.pdf.

81 Refugees Act, Section 55(2).

82 H. Kezie-Nwoha et al. 'Forced to flee: Voices of Congolese women refugees in Uganda' *Women's International Cross-Cultural Exchange* (2014): 56.

The reception of refugees in Uganda is twofold; some refugees reside in refugee resettlements[83] while other urban refugees who are the central focus of this study live in Kampala and other cities in Uganda and as studies have shown face a myriad of challenges including accessing basic healthcare services.[84]

In terms of legislative framework on migrants, South Africa's Immigration Amendment Act 19 of 2004 considers migrants as 'foreigners' who are neither South African citizens nor permanent resident holders but not illegal residents.[85] Based on its preamble, the Act is considered to be alive to human rights standards. Furthermore, it states under Section 1(p) that the members of the civil society organisation (CSO) will be educated on the rights of foreigners and refugees and also condemns xenophobic attacks against foreigners under Section 1 (m) of the Act, all of which are praiseworthy provisions on protection of migrants. However, it has been argued that the Act is more interested in state security than prioritising the human rights of migrants/refugees[86] as migrants face deportation where they are unable to produce valid permits of entry into South Africa.[87]

In Uganda, the Citizenship and Immigration Control Act 2006 and the Refugee Act including the Refugee Regulations have been commended for adopting a HRBA by guaranteeing rights and freedoms under international treaties.[88] Additionally, the Act requires migrants to produce valid passports from their country of origin or nationality[89] and to produce entry permit at all times[90] but failing to do so will result

[83] United Nations Development Programme, *Uganda's Contribution to Refugee Protection and Management*, September 5, 2020, https://data2.unhcr.org/en/documents/details/64687.

[84] K. Jacobsen 'Refugees and asylum seekers in urban areas: A livelihoods perspective' 19 *Journal of Refugee Studies.*

[85] Refugee Act, Section 2(a) (xvii).

[86] V. Ramoroka *The Determination of Refugee Status in South Africa: A Human Rights Perspective* (Master's Degree dissertation, University of South Africa 2014) 10.

[87] *Lawyers for Human Rights v Minister of Home Affairs and Others* CCT 38/16 (2017).

[88] V. Vemuru *Engendering Hope: Uganda's Progressive Policies on Refugee Management*, June 16, 2020, http://blogs.worldbank.org/nasikiliza/engendering-hope-ugandas-progressivepolicies-on-refugee-management.

[89] Refugee Act, Section 52.

[90] Refugee Act, Section 58.

to deportation.[91] With such stringent procedures, it is hard to envisage a situation where migrants battling to secure permits can effectively approach healthcare facilities for maternal healthcare.[92]

4.2 Courts and the Realisation of the Right to Maternal Healthcare

Courts can play a role in the enforcement of international human rights standards.[93] Therefore, the practice of domestic courts can also provide information on the extent to which the right to maternal healthcare is accorded due regard at the national level. Three cases are briefly discussed with a view to assessing how the courts in South Africa and Uganda have interpreted the right to health in relation to the rights of migrant/refugee women. These are: *Minister of Health and Others v Treatment Action Campaign and Others* (*TAC* case) for South Africa,[94] *Center for Health, Human Rights and Development (CEHURD) and Others v Attorney General* (*CEHURD* case) for Uganda[95] and the recently decided case of *CEHURD & 3 Ors v Attorney General Constitutional.*[96]

4.2.1 The TAC Case in South Africa

The *TAC* case is significant because it directly interprets women's SRHR under Section 27 of the Constitution. The case pertained to the restriction of nevirapine to two sites in a province which was meant to prevent mother to child transmission of HIV/AIDS during pregnancy, even

---

[91] Refugee Act, Section 60.

[92] M. Sharpe, & S. Namusobya 'Refugee status determination and the rights of recognized refugees under Uganda's Refugee Act 2006' 24 *International Journal of Refugee Law* (2012): 561–578.

[93] M. Killander, & H. Adjolohoun (eds.) *International and Domestic Human Rights Litigation in Africa: An Introduction* (2010): 15–16.

[94] *Minister of Health and Others v Treatment Action Campaign and Others* (2) 2002 (5) SA 721 (CC).

[95] *Center for Health, Human Rights and Development (CEHURD) and Others v Attorney General* 2012 4 UGCC, Constitutional Court Petition No. 16 of 2011.

[96] Petition No. 16 of 2011 [2020] UGCC 12 (August 19, 2020).

though it had been offered to the government for free.[97] The Constitutional Court *inter alia* also held that Sections 27(1) and 27(2) of the Constitution must be read together as defining the scope of the positive rights that everyone has and the corresponding obligations on the State to respect, protect, promote and fulfil these rights.[98] The Court made a series of declarations requiring the government under Sections 27(1) and (2) to devise and implement within its available resources a comprehensive programme that progressively realises the rights of pregnant women and their newborn children to have access to health services to combat mother-to-child-transmission of HIV/AIDs.[99]

4.2.2 The CEHURD Case in Uganda

The first CEHURD case concerned the alleged failure of the government of Uganda to provide maternal healthcare to expectant mothers in Uganda, which was argued, often results to their death.[100] This, as argued by the petitioners, constituted a violation of, among others, article 33(3) of Uganda's Constitution which provides for maternal healthcare services as well as EmOC. Even though the case which was litigated on behalf of Ugandan women[101] was struck out by the Constitutional Court without hearing its merits, it also extends to migrant/refugee women and their realisation to the right to maternal healthcare in Uganda by virtue of article 33(3) of the Constitution and Section 33(2) of the Ugandan Refugee Act.

The second *CEHURD* Case brought before the Constitutional Court declared the State's omission to prevent MMR and CMR, and improve performance on key maternal indicators, and adequately provide EmOC despite its obligation under national and international law a violation of the right to health under its Constitution.[102] This was also attributed

[97] *Supra,* Note 95, Paragraph 19.

[98] *Supra,* Note 95, Paragraphs 39 & 100.

[99] *Supra,* Note 95, Paragraph 135(2)(a).

[100] *Supra,* Note 95, Paragraph 1.

[101] S. Tamale, 'Controlling women's fertility in Uganda' 13 *International Journal on Human Rights* (2013): 124.

[102] *Supra,* Note 95, 57.

to staff negligence and lack of basic health facilities in health centres to support women. This landmark case decided in 2020 sets the pace for the realisation of maternal healthcare of women including migrant/refugee women as the Court emphasised the obligation of the State to prioritise and provide sufficient funds for maternal healthcare in the next financial year as well as train maternal healthcare providers and equip medical facilities within the next two financial years.[103]

These cases highlight the related challenges of how the vulnerabilities of migrant/refugee women are heightened when governments fail to fulfil their immediate obligation on non-discrimination[104] and fulfil their rights to ESCR including access to maternal healthcare services. Furthermore, they also depict that weak implementation of laws and policies can produced increased systemic discrimination and structural violation of these vulnerable groups of women by healthcare providers who directly/indirectly distinguish, deny, exclude, restrict and deprive migrant/refugee women from enjoying quality healthcare services resulting in preventable death in pregnancy and childbirth. Their risks are exacerbated when they are unable to seek recourse in courts for fear of reprisal/retaliation due to their status as migrant/refugee women.

5 The Right to Maternal Healthcare in Practice: Lessons from Treaty Monitoring Bodies

This section utilises the state reporting system before treaty bodies to gauge the practical implementation of the right to maternal healthcare of migrants and refugees in South Africa and Uganda beyond the international and national frameworks discussed in earlier sections. South Africa only ratified the ICESCR in 2015 thus there are no records of reports to the Committee on ICESCR. It also ratified several human rights treaties discussed in the preceding chapters including CEDAW in 1995, CERD in 1998, International Covenant on Civil and Political Rights (ICCPR)

---

103 *Supra,* Note 95, 58.

104 Committee on ESCR, non-discrimination in ESCR, Article 2, Paragraph 2.

in 1998, Banjul Charter in 1996 and the Maputo Protocol in 2002. Hence, reference is made to other treaty monitoring bodies including CEDAW Committee, CERD Committee and the Commission. In its first report to the CEDAW Committee[105] South Africa submitted that a HRBA has been adopted under its Constitution to guarantee access to healthcare services including free maternal and child healthcare.[106] It also submitted that it had developed the Gender Policy Guidelines for the Public Health Sector to ensure that an effective framework is in place to develop, implement and monitor laws, policies, programmes, procedures and practices for women's health. It was also submitted on refugees specifically, that it had reviewed its regulatory framework to ensure that all refugees including refugee women are treated with dignity and that they have equal access to healthcare. To the Commission, South Africa submitted that its policy on Universal Access to Primary Healthcare (1994) provides for free maternal care to pregnant women.[107] Before the CERD Committee, it submitted that a policy on the integration of refugees into South African society is also being developed and that it has continuously taken measures to ensure primary healthcare for all.[108]

However, a report by Non-Governmental Organisations (NGOs) to the CEDAW Committee noted that there are correspondingly low levels of maternal health, which has increased MMR in South Africa. This is attributed to the significant disparities in coverage of maternal and neonatal health interventions and thus the goal to deliver district-level healthcare in all district remains elusive.[109] To the CERD Committee, the South African Human Rights Commission (SAHRC) noted that there is a discrepancy between law and practice with regard to treatment of migrants and refugees in South Africa. It also noted that migrants are required to pay an extra medical service fee of R1,800 (over $150)

105 South African CEDAW Report, 'Progress made on the implementation of the Convention for the period 1998 to 2008' (2008).

106 *Supra*, Note 95, Paragraph 12.2.

107 Combined Second Periodic Report under the Banjul Charter and the Initial Report under the Maputo Protocol of the Republic of South Africa (2015), Paragraph 133.

108 South Africa's combined fourth and eighth periodic report to the Committee on CERD (2016), Paragraph 4.

109 Joint NGO South African shadow report on the implementation of CEDAW (2011), Paragraph 5.3.3.

and that both migrants and refugees are often at the receiving end of medical xenophobia as hospital staff are unable and unwilling to distinguish between different classes of migrants and refugees.[110] It reported an incident where a Somali refugee was denied maternal healthcare services on the basis that her condition did not qualify as an 'emergency' under Section 27(3) of the Constitution and also because she was unable to pay the medical service fee levied on foreigners.[111] Before the Commission, the NGOs noted that refugees and asylum seekers face rejection when trying to access healthcare including maternal healthcare services from primary and secondary healthcare facilities by frontline staff and also experience medical xenophobia by the healthcare providers.[112] They also noted that South Africa is still lacking in its HRBA to health and access to health services for women.[113]

In response, the CEDAW Committee noted that South Africa has an uneven distribution of healthcare services and recommended that the South African government continues to ensure equitable access to healthcare.[114] It also recommended that South Africa must ensure the implementation of the Maternal Child and Women's Health Strategy (2009–2014) and improve access to healthcare.[115] Similarly, the CERD Committee noted with concern the treatment of migrants and refugees in South Africa as regards discrimination, xenophobia and racism and how it has created difficulty in accessing basic services such as healthcare.[116] Hence, it recommended that it takes measures to ensure non-citizens have access to basic services such as healthcare without discrimination and provide language interpretation services to eliminate barriers in accessing basic services and conduct trainings of health and social service providers on the rights of non-citizens.[117]

---

110 SAHRC on South Africa's compliance with the provisions of CERD (2006).

111 Ibid.

112 South African NGO shadow report on the South Africa state report on the Banjul Charter and the Maputo Protocol (2016): 103.

113 Ibid., Paragraph 383.

114 CEDAW Concluding Observations CEDAW/C/SR. 387, 388 and 393 (1998), Paragraphs 133–134.

115 CEDAW Concluding Observations CEDAW/C/ZAF/CO/4 (2011), Paragraph 38.

116 CERD's observation on South Africa CERD/C/ZAF/CO/4 (2016), Paragraph 26(b).

117 Ibid., Paragraph 27(b).

The Commission in its Concluding Observations and Recommendations on the Combined South African Second Periodic Report under the Banjul Charter and the Initial Report under the Maputo Protocol 2016, highlighted the challenges faced by the public health sector in terms of service delivery,[118] acts of xenophobia and other intolerances directed at foreign nationals.[119] Hence, it recommended that South Africa enhances the conditions and access to healthcare and strengthen various initiatives taken in the fight against acts of xenophobia directed at foreign nationals to bring about a more coordinated response to the increased protection needs of foreign nationals.[120]

Uganda acceded to the ICESCR in 1987, to CERD in 1980, to the ICCPR in 1995, to CEDAW in 1985, to the Banjul Charter in 1986 and the Maputo Protocol in 2001. In its initial periodic report to the Committee on ICESCR in 2012, Uganda submitted that it had developed the Uganda Minimum Healthcare Package consisting of the most cost-effective priority care interventions and services addressing the high disease burden that is acceptable and affordable within the total resource envelope of the sector. One of the clusters under this package includes maternal and child health services.[121] However, Uganda admitted that MMR is still unacceptably high.[122] To the CEDAW Committee, Uganda admitted that maternal healthcare issues are yet to be realised at the 'policy and implementation level'.[123]

A Report to the Committee on ICESCR by the National Coalition on ESCR confirmed that MMR is still very high in Uganda as a result of poor reproductive healthcare services. It also reported that universal access to SRH is far from being realised in Uganda.[124] To CEDAW Committee, CEHRUD stated that women lack access to

---

[118] Ibid., Paragraph 31(iv).

[119] Ibid., Paragraph 41(iii).

[120] Ibid., Paragraph 57(ii).

[121] Ibid., 143.

[122] Ibid., Paragraphs 170–171.

[123] Combined fourth, fifth, sixth and seventh periodic report of Uganda CEDAW/C/UGA/7 (2009), Paragraph 139.

[124] National Coalition on ESCR to the CESCR on the occasion of its consideration of Uganda's first periodic report, (2015), Paragraph 11.24.

quality maternal healthcare and noted the failure to prioritise maternal health issues as reflected in the government's budgetary allocations.[125] It was also reported that the challenges in accessing health centres and the lack of medicine and medical personnel have therefore not adequately addressed MMR and CMR.[126]

The Commission observed that Uganda had failed to make reference to migrants and refugees in its report.[127] It recommended that Uganda expedites the process for the enactment of the draught bill on the National Health Insurance Scheme which aims at addressing high out-of-pocket spending and to improve equity in healthcare service.[128] In 2009, the CEDAW Committee noted that the near universal first attendance at antenatal clinic had only marginally improved and did not match with availability of EmOC;[129] that women had limited access to quality SRHR services;[130] and that MMR remains high.[131] Hence, it recommended that the government takes all necessary measures to improve women's access to healthcare and health-related services within the framework of the Committee's General Recommendation No. 24 and urged the government to strengthen its efforts to reduce the incidence of maternal and infant mortality and to raise awareness of and increase women's access to healthcare facilities and medical assistance by trained personnel.[132]

The Committee on ICESCR, in its first Concluding Observation to Uganda, noted that there is a decrease in the healthcare services accessible to everyone.[133] It also noted that the implementation and related

125 CEHURD Supplementary information on Uganda to CEDAW (2010) 2.

126 CSOs Alternative report on Uganda's implementation of CEDAW (2010), Paragraph 145.

127 The Commission's concluding observations and recommendations on the state report of the Republic of Uganda (2010–2012), Paragraph 73.

128 Ibid., Paragraph 115.

129 Consideration of reports submitted by Uganda under article 18 of CEDAW CEDAW/C/UGA/7, (2009), Paragraph 136.

130 Concluding Observation of CEDAW on Uganda CEDAW/C/UGA/CO/7, (2010), Paragraph 35.

131 Ibid.

132 Ibid., Paragraph 36.

133 E/C.12/UGA/CO/1, (2015), Paragraph 32.

laws on maternal healthcare are inadequate.[134] It recommended that the Ugandan government includes the right to health in the Constitution and ensures that everyone enjoys access to quality healthcare and that the government adopt a HRBA and implements policies and programmes to reduce preventable maternal mortality.[135]

6 A Case for Criminal Accountability for Violation of the Right to Maternal Healthcare in South Africa and Uganda

It can be gleaned from the preceding discussions that violations of the right to maternal healthcare for refugee/migrant women in both South Africa and Uganda is indisputable. Documented forms of abuse include medical xenophobia, ill treatment, unprofessionalism, financial challenge, language barrier, medical negligence, poor communication and other forms of impact abuse.[136] There is a consensus internationally that accountability will go a long way in improving the healthcare system, in particular, the mortality of mothers. At the AU level, accountability has been documented as a key component of advancing the SRHR of African people.[137] Conversely, this viewpoint was echoed by the special rapporteur on the right to health in his report to the HRC.[138] The UN does not prescribe a formula for advancing accountability for violations

[134] Ibid., Paragraph 33.

[135] Ibid.

[136] Liz Miller, 'The irony of refuge: Gender-based violence against female refugees in Africa' *Human Life and Human Welfare* (2012): 77–90; Ulrike Krause 'Violence against women in camps? Exploring links between refugee camp conditions and the prevalence of violence' *Health in Diversity—Diversity in Health* (2020): 187–208.

[137] The Maputo plan of action review report, the reproductive health and rights of the African people: Looking ahead (ST/EXP/HP/IV(I) (2015).

[138] Special Rapporteur on the right of everyone to the enjoyment of the highest attainable standard of physical and mental health, Paul Hunt, Promotion and Protection of all Human Rights, Civil, Political, Economic, Social and Cultural Rights (2008).

to the right to health.[139] However, it does make it clear that accountability can be ensured through various mechanisms at the national level. At a minimum, these mechanisms have to be 'accessible, transparent and effective.[140] It is submitted that this discretion creates an avenue for reliance on criminal law to ensure that those responsible for undermining the right to maternal healthcare are held accountable.

To ensure criminal accountability, The Penal Code Act of Uganda Chapter 120 and the various Common law offences under South African criminal law can be a basis for criminal charges and prosecution against those responsible for these abuses which is a good starting point. Notably, the various forms of violations including physical and verbal abuse are criminalised as assault and *crimen injuria* under the criminal laws of both South Africa and Uganda. In as far as asking for bribes in exchange for healthcare services, charges can be preferred through recourse to offences such as bribery. More severe offences such as culpable homicide can also be considered where negligent treatment results into death. The principles of criminal law, in this regard, the notion of *dolus eventualis*, can be a basis for establishing intention on the part of healthcare practitioners even though there was no direct intention on their part to cause death.

It is submitted that advancing criminal prosecution through creatively resorting to the existing criminal law framework will go a long way in ensuring accountability for the right to maternal health care in both countries. Such accountability has the effect of sending a clear message on the severity of violation of this right and the fact that those who undermine the health rights of mothers will be held accountable. Also critical in ensuring that victims of violation of the right to maternal health access justice is addressing the evidentiary barriers that exist in the criminal justice systems, especially Uganda.[141] There are laws that

139 United Nations High Commissioner for Human Rights and WHO, *The Right to Health: Fact Sheet No. 31*, Page 31, June 3, 2020, https://www.ohchr.org/Documents/Publications/Factsheet31.pdf.

140 Ibid.

141 On evidentiary barriers in Uganda's criminal justice system, see generally Lubaale Emma Charlene, *Bridging the Justice Gap in the Prosecution of Acquaintance Child Sexual Abuse: A Case of South Africa and Uganda* (PhD Thesis, University of Pretoria 2015); See also Lubaale Emma Charlene, 'Admissibility of evidence presented by children in sex abuse prosecutions in Uganda: The case for reforms' *African Journal of Law and Criminology*, 5 (2015): 1–15.

found their way to Africa's criminal justice system through colonialism. Notable is the rule of corroboration. The dogmatic application of these rules continues to be a hindrance to criminal accountability for offences involving women, thus, bringing the need for law reform to the fore.[142]

Pickles also submits that the reason for the lack of criminal accountability lies in the fact that these abuses are either invisible or not considered serious enough to warrant criminal investigation and prosecution.[143] For migrant/refugee women, this gap is heightened by challenges such as xenophobia and their illegal status in these respective countries. Under these circumstances, commencing criminal proceedings against abuses by healthcare workers would mean either exposing these women to further abuse, or, subjecting these women to further abuse and prejudice. It follows therefore that calls for criminal accountability for violation of maternal healthcare rights need to seriously consider the underlying factors that make it close to impossible for migrant/refugee women to bring these abuses to the attention of the criminal justice system.

7 Conclusion and Recommendations

The aim of this chapter is to provide a critical reflection on the plight of migrant/refugee women's access to maternal healthcare in South Africa and Uganda which issue to this date 'remains a major unresolved challenge in the human rights agenda' thus contributing to violations against women's rights in Africa and the increase of MMR and CMR. This chapter equally exposes the different manifestations of intersectional, systemic and structural discrimination in healthcare facilities by healthcare providers in service delivery which includes laws, policies, norms and practices against migrant/refugee women in South Africa and Uganda. In addition, the lack of implementation of international,

[142] Ibid.

[143] C. Pickles 'Eliminating abusive care: A criminal law response to obstetric violence in South Africa' *South African Crime Quarterly* (2015): 1–16.

regional and sub-regional human rights treaties and policies despite ratification and domestication by both countries that guarantee the right to quality maternal healthcare have been translated into privileges for migrant/refugee women in both countries. Furthermore, this chapter addresses the different aspects of migrant/refugee women's status as vulnerable groups which causes them to be excluded and marginalised from accessing quality, affordable and accessible maternal healthcare services.

Hence, it is established that there is a clear dichotomy between law and practice in both countries. The implementation framework is extremely weak as formal equality has not resulted in substantive equality for migrant/refugee women. These States have continuously failed to fulfil their core minimum obligation under international law to ensure the right of access to health facilities including goods and services on a non-discriminatory basis, especially for vulnerable or marginalised people including migrant/refugee women. The lack of accountability measures has resulted in the persistent discriminatory practices of health workers which consequence is reflected in the total number of maternal mortality and morbidity rate in these countries. Thus, despite their commitments to reduce MMR, this aspiration is far from being achieved.

This chapter therefore contributes towards existing literature on migrant/refugee women and barriers to access healthcare facilities of migrant/refugee women in South Africa and Uganda and it is devoted to analysing South Africa and Uganda's obligations under national, regional and international law with a view to addressing policy inadequacy and health-related discrimination against migrant/refugee women in South Africa. However, this chapter offers a comparative approach to analysing the jurisprudence and practice in both countries and how it has adversely affected migrant/refugee women. This chapter plays a significant role in presenting productive strategies to prevent further violations by holding the perpetrators accountable thus prevent violations against women with impunity.

This chapter also recommends that discriminatory laws, policies must be strengthened and harmonised with international principles of equality and non-discrimination. Consequently, the governments of South Africa and Uganda need to adopt an intersectional approach as a method to end racial discrimination and introduce gender justice as a means to ending violence against women in Africa. These should include developing roadmaps and continuously collecting relevant data on the accessibility of maternal healthcare services to migrant/refugee women. The Ugandan government can emulate some of the steps taken by South Africa, including, initiating an accountability mechanism like the National Committee for Confidential Enquiry into Maternal Deaths (NCCEMD) that would report on causes of maternal deaths through the vital statistics of all registered births; and make recommendations based on the analysis conducted on maternal deaths with the aim of reducing MMR. At the macro policy level, both countries should adopt a universal access to quality healthcare, for all in an acceptable and affordable way and medical facilities should be transformed into socially responsive institutions that do not discriminate on the basis of race or nationality. This would require the training and recruitment of more healthcare professionals and raising awareness through the media about the need to ensure equal access for all women including migrant/refugee women.

The right to maternal healthcare as part of the right to health should be expressly guaranteed as an enforceable constitutional right in the Ugandan constitution. It should also clarify the status of international law in its municipal legal system. Specifically, it is recommended that it adopt South Africa's example of requiring courts to take international law into consideration when enforcing human rights. This will enable courts to offer broader protection to maternal healthcare rights of migrants/refugees where national legal and policy frameworks are inadequate.

On another note, financial barriers such as the requirement of refugees/migrants to pay exorbitant fees for particular healthcare services should be removed to ensure these women are able to access maternal healthcare services on equal basis with nationals.

In addition, National Human Rights Institutions (NHRIs) and CSOs also have an important role to play in ensuring equitable access to maternal healthcare services for migrant/refugee women. They hold the government accountable by monitoring and reporting on the challenges that migrant/refugee women face in accessing maternal healthcare and lobbying government to implement relevant reforms. NHRIs and CSOs can also contribute to reform by providing training and raising awareness with healthcare providers and among migrant/refugee committees on the rights of migrant and refugee women to access maternal healthcare services on equal basis with nationals. This will ensure that negative attitudes and xenophobia that is faced by migrant and refugee women in accessing maternal healthcare services is reduced, if not completely eradicated.

The use of litigation as a strategy could improve access to maternal healthcare and prevent violence against women with impunity should be made a priority as it draws the attention of states to enforce guaranteed rights and force them to fulfil their minimum core obligations to the ICESCR and other international treaties. Closely related to litigation is criminal accountability. Accountability remains crucial in bringing an end to violation of the right to maternal healthcare. It is critical for the criminal justice systems of both Uganda and South Africa to start taking these abuses seriously by ensuring that those responsible for these abuses are criminally prosecuted. The existing legal frameworks of both countries provide avenues for criminal prosecution of those responsible for abuse. For migrant/refugee women, however, effective criminal accountability will require that underlying challenges such as xenophobia and other forms of discrimination against foreign nationals are addressed.

Suffice it to conclude that, human rights are a collective responsibility, and can only be effectively realised if all relevant stakeholders play their part. The right to maternal healthcare of migrant and refugee women will only be effectively realised in South Africa and Uganda if, governments, healthcare providers, NHRIs, CSOs and stakeholders play their respective roles in making it a reality.

References

African Commission, 2012, *General Comments on Article 14 (1) (d) and (e) of the Maputo Protocol*.

Amnesty International Report 2017/18, *The State of the World's Human Rights*, 2018.

Ben Twinomugisha, 2007, 'Exploring Judicial Strategies to Protect the Right of Access to Emergency Obstetric Care in Uganda' 7 *African Human Rights Law Journal*.

C. Pickles, 'Eliminating Abusive Care: A Criminal Law Response to Obstetric Violence in South Africa' *South African Crime Quarterly* (2015): 1–16.

CEDAW, 2010, *Concluding Observations on Uganda* CEDAW/C/UGA/CO/7.

CEDAW, 2011, *Concluding Observations* CEDAW/C/ZAF/CO/4.

CEHURD, 2010, Supplementary Information on Uganda to CEDAW.

CESCR, *General Comment No. 14: The Right to the Highest Attainable Standard of Health*, Article 12.

Combined Fourth, Fifth, Sixth and Seventh Periodic Report of Uganda CEDAW/C/UGA/7 (2009).

Combined Second Periodic Report Under the Banjul Charter and the Initial Report Under the Maputo Protocol of the Republic of South Africa (2015).

Committee on CEDAW, 1999, 'A/54/38/Rev.1, chap. I', https://www.refworld.org/docid/453882a73.html.

Consideration of Reports Submitted by Uganda Under Article 18 of CEDAW CEDAW/C/UGA/7 (2009).

Constitution of South Africa.

Constitution of Uganda.

Corey Johnson, 2015, 'Failed Asylum Seekers in South Africa' 1 *African Human Mobility Review*.

CSOs Alternative Report on Uganda's Implementation of CEDAW (2010).

Department of Cooperative Government and Traditional Affairs, 2016, *Integrated Urban Development Framework*, https://www.africancentreforcities.net/wp-content/uploads/2017/05/IUDF-2016_WEB-min.pdf.

Department of Home Affairs, 2018, *Annual Report 2017–2018*.

Emma Charlene Lubaale, 2015, 'Admissibility of Evidence Presented by Children in Sex Abuse Prosecutions in Uganda: The Case for Reforms' 5 *African Journal of Law and Criminology*.

Emma Charlene Lubaale, 2015, *Bridging the Justice Gap in the Prosecution of Acquaintance Child Sexual Abuse: A Case of South Africa and Uganda* (Ph.D. Thesis, University of Pretoria).

Haruna Umar et al., 2019, *Improving Access and Utilization of Maternal Healthcare Services Through focused Antenatal Care in Rural Ghana: A Qualitative Study*, https://www.hindawi.com/journals/aph/2019/9181758/.

Helen Kezie-Nwoha et al., 2015, Forced to Flee: Voices of Congolese Women Refugees in Uganda' *Women's International Cross-Cultural Exchange*.

Ines Keygnaert et al., 2016, *What Is the Evidence on the Reduction of Inequalities in Accessibility and Quality of Maternal Healthcare Delivery for Migrants? A Review of the Existing Evidence in the WHO European Region*, Health Evidence Synthesis Report, No. 45.

International Organisation for Migration, 2020, *World Migration Report.*

John Mubangizi and Ben Twinomugisha, 2010, 'The Right to Healthcare in the Specific Context of Access to HIV/AIDS Medicines: What Can South Africa and Uganda Learn from Each Other?' 10 *African Human Rights Law.*

Joint NGO South African Shadow Report on the Implementation of CEDAW (2011).

Jonathan Crush and Godfrey Tawodzera, 2013, 'Medical Xenophobia and Zimbabwean Migrant Access to Public Health Services in South Africa' 40 *Journal of Ethnic and Migration Studies.*

Karen Jacobsen, 2006, 'Refugees and Asylum Seekers in Urban Areas: A Livelihoods Perspective' 19 *Journal of Refugee Studies.*

Lawyers for Human Rights v Minister of Home Affairs and Others CCT 38/16, 2017.

Liz Miller, 2012, 'The Irony of Refuge: Gender-Based Violence Against Female Refugees in Africa' *Human Life and Human Welfare.*

M. Killander and H. Adjolohoun, 2010, *International and Domestic Human Rights Litigation in Africa: An Introduction.*

Malcolm Langford, Bruce Porter, Rebecca Brown and Julieta Rossi, 2016, *The Optional Protocol to the International Covenant on Economic, Social and Cultural Rights: A Commentary.*

Marina Sharpe and Salima Namusobya, 2012, 'Refugee Status Determination and the Rights of Recognized Refugees Under Uganda's Refugee Act 2006' 24 *International Journal of Refugee Law.*

Maternal Health Factsheet on South Africa, https://countryoffice.unfpa.org/filemanager/files/southafrica/Maternal_health.pdf.

Mpho Makhema, 2009, *Social Protection for Refuges and Asylum Seekers in the Southern Africa Development Community* (The World Bank).

National Coalition on ESCR to the CESCR on the Occasion of Its Consideration of Uganda's First Periodic Report (2015).

New York Declaration for Migrant and Refugees (2016).

Nonkululeko Letta Bhe & Others v Magistrate, Khayelitsha & Others (CCT 49/03) (2004) ZACC 17; 2005 (1) SA 580 (CC), paragraph 218.

R. Brown, L. Chenwi and A. M. Stein, 2016, 'Equality and Non-discrimination' in *The Optional Protocol to the International Covenant on*

Economic, Social and Cultural Rights: A Commentary edited by Malcolm Langford, Bruce Porter, Rebecca Brown & Julieta Rossi.

Rebecca Cook et al., 2003, *Reproductive Health and Human Rights: Integrating Medicine, Ethics and Law: Overview* (2003).

Report on the 55th Session of the Economic and Social Council, Commission on the Status of Women (2011).

Resolution on the Integration of Women in Development CM/Res. 1215 (L), 1989.

S v Makwanyane (3) SA (391) (CC) 1995.

South Africa's Combined Fourth and Eighth Periodic Report to the Committee on CERD (2016).

South African CEDAW Report, 2008, *South African CEDAW Report, 'Progress Made on the Implementation of the Convention for the Period 1998 to 2008'*.

South African NGO Shadow Report on the South Africa State Report on the Banjul Charter and the Maputo Protocol (2016).

Southern African Catholic Bishop's Conference, 2006, 'Overview of the Implementation of the Refugee Act of 1998' *Briefing Paper* 167.

Special Rapporteur on the Right of Everyone to the Enjoyment of the Highest Attainable Standard of Physical and Mental Health, Paul Hunt, 'Promotion and Protection of all Human Rights, Civil, Political, Economic, Social and Cultural Rights' (2008).

Stephens Madue, 2015, 'South Africa's Foreign and Migration Policies Missteps: Fuels of Xenophobic Eruptions?' 11 *The Journal for Transdisciplinary Research in Southern Africa*.

Sustainable Development Goals of 2015 to Be Attained by 2030 as Enacted by the United Nations.

Sylvia Tamale, 2016, 'Controlling Women's Fertility in Uganda' 13 *International Journal on Human Rights*.

Tackson Makandwa and Jo Veary, 2017, 'Giving Birth in a Foreign Land: Exploring the Maternal Healthcare experiences of Zimbabwean Migrant Women Living in Johannesburg, South Africa' 28 *Urban Forum*.

The African Commission on Human and Peoples' Rights', *Concluding Observations and Recommendations on the 5th Periodic State Report of the Republic of Uganda* (2010–2012).

The Demographic and Health Surveys programme, *Maternal Health Services* (2004).

The EAC SRHR Bill, 2017, http://www.eala.org/documents/view/theeac-sexual-and-reproductive-health-rights-bill2017.

The Forced Migration Research Network, 2017, *The World's Biggest Minority? Refugee Women and Girls in the Global Compact on Refugees.*

The Maputo Plan of Action Review Report, 'The Reproductive Health and Rights of the African People: Looking Ahead (ST/EXP/HP/IV(I)' (2015).

The United Nations High Commissioner for Refugees, 2019, *Global Trends: Forced Displacement in 2019.*

Uganda Association of Women Lawyers & Others v Attorney General Constitutional Petition 2 of 2003 UGCC 1.

Ulrike Krause, 2020, 'Violence Against Women in Camps? Exploring Links between Refugee Camp Conditions and the Prevalence of Violence' *Health in Diversity—Diversity in Health.*

UNDESA, 2007, *The United Nations Development Agenda: Development for All*, https://www.un.org/esa/devagenda/UNDA_BW5_Final.pdf.

UNHCR, 2018, *Global Trends: Forced Displacement in 2018.*

UNHCR, *Women*, https://www.unhcr.org/women.html.

UNICEF, https://data.unicef.org/topic/maternal-health/maternal-mortality/#v.

United Nations Children's Emergency Fund, 2019, *Maternal Mortality*, https://data.unicef.org/topic/maternal-health/maternal-mortality/.

United Nations Development Programme, 2017, *Uganda's Contribution to Refugee Protection and Management.*

United Nations Fund for Population Activities, 2016, *Refugees' and Migrants' Reproductive Health Needs Overlooked*, https://www.unfpa.org/news/refugees'-and-migrants'-reproductive-health-needs-overlooked.

United Nations General Assembly, 2015, Resolution on Transforming Our World: The 2030 Agenda for Sustainable Development A/RES/70/1.

Varalakshmi Vemuru, 2016, *Engendering Hope: Uganda's Progressive Policies on Refugee Management*, http://blogs.worldbank.org/nasikiliza/engendering-hope-ugandas-progressivepolicies-on-refugee-management.

WHO https://www.who.int/sdg/targets/en/.

WHO, 2019, *Maternal Mortality*, https://www.who.int/news-room/fact-sheets/detail/maternal-mortality.

WHO, *Refugee and Migrant Health: Draft Global Action Plan Promoting the Health of Refugees and Migrants (2019–2023)*, https://www.who.int/migrants/en/.

WHO, *The Right to Health: Fact Sheet No. 31*, https://www.ohchr.org/Documents/Publications/Factsheet31.pdf.

Yvonne Munyaneza and Euphemia Mhlongo, 2019, 'Challenges of Women Refugees in Utilising Reproductive Health Services in Public Health Institutions in Durban, KwaZu-Natal, South Africa' *Journal of Interdisciplinary Health sciences.*

12

Access to Justice for Women in Eswatini: HIV-Positive Women as a Vulnerable Population

Simangele D. Mavundla, Ann Strode, and Zaynab Essack

1 Background

In 2020, 37.7 million people were estimated to be living with Human Immunodeficiency Virus (HIV) globally, with about 64% of all new infections occurring in sub-Saharan Africa, and 43% of those among

[1] Joint united nations programme on HIV/AIDS (UNAIDS), *Global HIV & AIDS Statistics—2021,* https://www.unaids.org/sites/default/files/media_asset/UNAIDS_FactSheet_en.pdf.

S. D. Mavundla (✉) · Z. Essack
College of Law and Management, University of KwaZulu-Natal, Pietermaritzburg, South Africa

Z. Essack
e-mail: Zessack@hsrc.ac.za

A. Strode
School of Law, University of KwaZulu-Natal, Durban, South Africa
e-mail: strodea@ukzn.ac.za

A. Budoo-Scholtz and E. C. Lubaale (eds.), *Violence Against Women and Criminal Justice in Africa: Volume II*, Sustainable Development Goals Series,
https://doi.org/10.1007/978-3-030-75953-7_12

women.[1] Violence against women (VAW) is a global problem and is regarded as one of the most widespread violations of women's rights.[2]Literature shows that women living with HIV are particularly vulnerable to violence, impacting on their ability to protect themselves from HIV reinfection and their ability to access care.[3]Studies have found that VAW is common in Southern African countries where HIV is prevalent.[4] Eswatini has the highest prevalence of HIV and acquired immunodeficiency syndrome (AIDS) in the world. The prevalence has continued to rise, climbing from 21% of the population in 2016 to over 27% in 2018 (20.4% males, 32.5% females).[5]

Heterosexual relations are the primary means of HIV infection spreads in Eswatini,[6] with gender power imbalances and socio-cultural factors strongly influencing heterosexual relations.[7] In 1999, the HIV epidemic was declared a national disaster; and it has continued to cause havoc. Ingrained traditions and customs are identified as significant challenges that the Eswatini leaders and the international health community face in attempting to curtail the rampant spread of HIV and AIDS.

VAW is a violation of women's human rights[8] and is often fuelled by outdated social and cultural norms that underpin VAW's acceptability and continuance in society.[9] For example, a Cape Town study found

---

[2] World Health Organisation (WHO), Violence against women key facts (2021), https://www.who.int/news-room/fact-sheets/detail/violence-against-women.

[3] Amita Basu, & Ratna Menon, *Violence Against Women, HIV/AIDS Vulnerability and the Law. Working Paper prepared for the Third Meeting of the Technical Advisory Group of the Global Commission on HIV and the Law, 7–9 July 2011* (2011): 1. See also Johanna Kehler et al., 'Gender and HIV violence: Perceptions and experience of violence and other rights abuses against women living with HIV in the Eastern Cape, KwaZulu-Natal and Western Cape, South Africa' (2012).

[4] Neil Andersson, Anne Cockcroft, & Bev Shea 'Gender-based violence and HIV: Relevance for HIV prevention in hyperendemic countries of Southern Africa' 74 *AIDS* (2008): 22.

[5] Government of the Kingdom of Eswatini. *Swaziland HIV Incidence Measurement Survey 2 (SHIMS2)*, 2016–2017, April 2019.

[6] The Swaziland health sector response to gender based violence guidelines march 2010.

[7] Ibid.

[8] Shazia Qureshi 'The recognition of violence against women as a violation of human rights in the United Nations system' 28 *A Research Journal of South Asian Studies* (2013): 187–198.

[9] Faith Kasiva, 'Robbed of choice forced and coerced sterilisation experiences of women living with HIV in Kenya' (2012), https://profiles.uonbi.ac.ke/kihara/files/report-on-robbed-of-choice-forced-and-coerced-sterilization-experiences-of-women-living-with-hiv-in-kenya.pdf.

that traditional attitudes on women's social status, gender roles, and rape myths persisted because they were endorsed by a minority of influential men and women.[10] Other studies posit that HIV and gender inequalities must be recognised as twin and intersecting challenges.[11]

Widespread violence among women uniquely intersects with HIV. On the one hand, violence or the threat thereof, increases women and girls' vulnerability to HIV by making it difficult for them to negotiate for safer sex, decide to abstain from sex or to persuade partners to be faithful.[12] On the other hand, physical violence or its threats from intimate partners present a barrier to women who wish to access HIV prevention options, treatment services, and care and support.[13] This was illustrated in a 2007 study by Lang and others, which found that VAW was prevalent among HIV-positive women accessing HIV services.[14] HIV-positive women in abusive relationships were found to be less likely to practise safe sex through the use of condoms; and thus, more likely to become pregnant.[15] These women were also more likely to experience physical abuse and threats of physical violence when requesting condom use.[16]

Basu and Menon argue that the relationship between VAW and HIV vulnerability exemplifies the 'HIV paradox', that is, preventing the spread of HIV infection among women could trigger intimate partner violence (IPV)[17]; and a woman's HIV-positive status often results in multiple layers of additional violence, and also certain forms of medical violence which only affect HIV-positive women. Basu and Menon advise that in order to promote a public health response, the rights of those vulnerable

---

[10] Seth Kalichman, 'Gender attitudes, sexual violence, and HIV/AIDS risks among men and women in Cape Town' 42 *Journal of Sex Research* (2005): 299.

[11] Johanna Bond, & Robin Phillips, 'Violence against women as a human rights violation: International institutional responses' in *Sourcebook on Violence Against Women* edited by Claire M. Renzetti et al., (2001): 481–499.

[12] Ibid.

[13] Human Rights Watch, *Just Die Quietly: Domestic Violence and Women's Vulnerability to HIV in Uganda*, (2003): 2–40.

[14] Delia Lang, & Laura Salazar, 'Associations between recent gender-based violence and pregnancy, sexually transmitted infections, condom use practices, and negotiation of sexual practices among HIV-positive women' 46 *Acquired Immune Deficiency Syndrome* (2007): 46.

[15] Ibid.

[16] Lang, & Salazar, *Supra*, Note 14.

[17] Basu, & Menon, *Supra*, Note 3.

to infection must be promoted, protected and fulfilled, in particular, the rights of women living with HIV (WLH).[18]

It is because of HIV stigma that women are often more susceptible to discrimination as a result of their HIV status. This element is coupled with their unequal position in society, which worsens their situation once they disclose their HIV status.[19] Fox reveals that men are more likely to become abusive to women after learning about the woman's HIV-positive status and often blame their own infection squarely on women.[20]

Some healthcare workers have resorted to sterilising WLH without informed consent just because they are HIV positive.[21] It is against this backdrop of abuse—domestic and systemic—that this study was undertaken. Discussed below are the following: Eswatini's response to HIV and VAW through the legal and policy framework; international norms on VAW and HIV, as well as the methodology employed in collecting and collating the data analysed in this article. Further discussed is the interlink between HIV and VAW through case studies on violence that perpetrated against HIV-positive (HIV+) women and medicalised violence. The article then addresses access to justice by WLH and lastly concludes by proposing recommendations.

2 Methodology

This study reports on research undertaken as part of a doctoral research titled 'Battered, dejected, ejected and rejected: the rights of HIV-positive women to be protected from violence – a critical analysis of the legal

---

[18] Ibid.

[19] Shirley Wang, 'Violence and HIV/AIDS: Violence against women and girls as a cause and consequence of HIV/AIDS' 17 *Duke Journal of Gender Law & Policy* (2010): 314.

[20] UNICEF, *Gender-Based Violence and HIV/AIDS in South Africa Organisational Responses* (2003): 15.

[21] Zaynab Essack, & Ann Strode, 'I feel like half a woman all the time': The impacts of coerced and forced sterilisations on HIV-positive women in South Africa' 26 *Empowering Women for Gender Equity* (2012): 24–34. See also, Open society foundations, *Against Her Will, Forced and Coerced Sterilization of Women Worldwide* (2011), http://www.soros.org/sites/default/files/against-her-will-20111003.pdf; Ann Strode et al., 'She made up a choice for me: 22 HIV-positive women's experiences of involuntary sterilisation in two South African provinces' 20 *Reproductive Health Matters* (2012): 1–9.

framework in Eswatini'.[22] The study adopted a qualitative methodology which entailed both empirical and desktop data collection. For the empirical data, 45 in-depth interviews were carried out in Eswatini during February and March 2016. 30 HIV + women were recruited from four HIV support groups in Manzini and Mbabane, comprising both rural and urban sites. There were also 15 key informants who were working in the field of women's health, human rights or HIV policy development in Eswatini. The recorded data was transcribed verbatim and analysed using Braun and Clarke's guide to thematic analysis.[23] A desktop review of literature on VAW and HIV and international laws and policies was also carried out. The findings of this study represent the views of the study participants and cannot be generalised beyond this context.

3 Eswatini's Response to HIV and VAW

Eswatini's laws do not expressly address the connection between VAW, and HIV and AIDS in parallel. Whilst there is no specific law aimed at protecting the rights of people living with HIV (PLH) in Eswatini, all government policies endorse the principle of medical confidentiality.[24] The Constitution outlaws discrimination and provides for equal rights for all.[25] The country does, however, have several discreet policies on HIV and AIDS. The chapter does an audit of the laws and policies on gender equality, VAW and HIV in the following sub-sections.

22 Simangele Mavundla, 'Battered, dejected, ejected, and rejected: The rights of HIV positive women to be protected from violence, a critical analysis of the legal framework in Eswatini' (Unpublished PhD Thesis UKZN July 2020).

23 Virginia Braun, & Victoria Clarke 'Using thematic analysis in psychology' 3 *Qualitative Research in Psychology* (2006): 16.

24 International Planned Parenthood Federation (IPPF) *Research Dossier on HIV Prevention for Girls and Young Women in Swaziland* (2007).

25 Ibid.

3.1 The Constitution of Eswatini

Section 20 of the Constitution of Eswatini[26] provides for equality before the law. It expressly states that 'all persons are equal before and under the law in all spheres of political, economic, social and cultural life and every other respect and shall enjoy equal protection of the law'. Further, Section 20(2) adds the following:

> ...for the avoidance of any doubt, a person shall not be discriminated against on the grounds of gender, race, colour, ethnic origin, tribe, birth, creed or religion, or social or economic standing, political opinion, age or disability.

The Constitution does not mention HIV/AIDS as a ground for non-discrimination. Section 28 of the Constitution provides for women's rights and freedoms as follows:

(1) Women have the right to equal treatment with men, and that right shall include equal opportunities in political, economic and social activities.
(2) Subject to the availability of resources, the Government shall provide facilities and opportunities necessary to enhance the welfare of women to enable them to realise their full potential and advancement.
(3) A woman shall not be compelled to undergo or uphold any custom to which she is in conscience opposed.

Whilst the promotion of women's rights provided for in Section 28 is commendable, it does not follow through with enforcement measures available to women in case of a breach.

[26] Eswatini Constitution, Section 20.

3.2 Sexual Offences and Domestic Violence Act of 2018

The Sexual Offences and Domestic Violence Act of 2018 (SODV Act) criminalises all forms of violence, such as domestic, IPV and sexual violence. The notable feature of this Act is that it reviews, and reforms earlier legislation, providing a normative framework that is aimed at curbing domestic violence and sexual offences holistically. The Act was enacted as a response to public outcry over the prevalence of domestic and sexual violence offences against women and children which was viewed as contributing to the high prevalence of HIV among adolescent girls and young women in the kingdom.[27] The SODV Act expands the definition of violence in line with international norms as 'any act that physically, sexually, emotionally, economically, verbally or psychologically abuses another person, including acts of intimidation, harassment, unlawful stalking or damage to property and controlling abusive behaviour'.[28] The Act is revolutionary in criminalising sexual harassment, stalking (acts which predominately lead to VAW) and by striking down the defence of implied consent available to married men in a charge of marital rape. It is the first law to provide for protection orders in cases of domestic violence,[29] and the establishment of domestic violence courts at the magistrate's court level.[30] It remains to be seen whether the Act will be interpreted holistically to afford appropriate protection to victims of violence. It has been shown in other countries, such as South Africa, that domestic violence legislation does not translate into action and fails to offer women the intended protection.[31]

---

[27] Zakhe Hlanze et al., *Customary Practices, the Laws and Risky Behaviours—A Concern for the Increased Prevalence and Vulnerability to HIV and AIDS Among Women and the Girl Child: A Rights-Based Approach* (2008): 155.

[28] SODV Act of 2018, Section 77(1).

[29] Ibid., Section 78–103.

[30] Ibid., Section 126.

[31] Ramadimetja S. Mogale, Kathy K. Burns, & Solina Richter, 'Violence against women in South Africa: Policy position and recommendation' 18 *SAGE* (2012): 580–594.; Gadinabokao Keaorata, 'Shortcomings of the South African domestic violence act 116 of 1998 in comparative perspective' (Unpublished LLM dissertation, University of Pretoria 2016).

3.3 International Law Norms on VAW and HIV and AIDS

Eswatini is a party to international, regional and sub-regional treaties responding to VAW and HIV. However, there are limited international law norms addressing the interlink between HIV and violence.

The state has a duty to respect, protect and fulfil all human rights and fundamental freedoms of women, regardless of the existing political, economic and cultural systems.[32] The protection of human rights in practice, however, is skewed towards the fulfilment of civil and political rights than the protection of economic, social and cultural rights.[33]

In 1993, the United Nations (UN) formally recognised VAW as a human rights abuse[34] through the adoption by the UN member states of the Declaration on the Elimination of Violence against Women.[35] Women's rights advocates had argued that VAW was the most pervasive violation of human rights experienced in families, workplaces and communities across the globe.[36]

In the context of HIV and human rights, the following human rights must be respected, promoted, protected and fulfilled: the right to confidentiality and privacy, human dignity, bodily integrity, equality and non-discrimination and the right to access healthcare.[37] These rights are provided by both international and national legal frameworks acceded to and put into effect by Eswatini as evident in the Constitution. WLH are afforded protection by the International Covenant on Civil and Political Rights of 1966 (ICCPR) and the International Covenant on Economic,

[32] The Vienna Declaration of 1993.

[33] General Assembly Resolution 32/130 of 1977 explicitly states that 'all human rights and fundamental freedoms are indivisible and interdependent; equal attention and urgent consideration should be given to the implementation, promotion and protection of both civil and political, and economic, social and cultural rights.

[34] Johanna Bond, & Robin Phillips 'Violence against women as a human rights violation: International institutional responses' in *Sourcebook on Violence Against Women* edited by, C. M. Renzetti, J. L. Edleson & R. K. Bergen (2001): 481.

[35] UN, *Declaration on the Elimination of Violence Against Women* of 1993.

[36] Bond, & Phillips, *Supra,* Note 32.

[37] UN *International Covenant on Civil and Political Rights* of 1966—See article 17 on privacy, article 10 on inherent dignity, article 26 on equality and non-discrimination and article 12 of international covenant on economic, social and cultural rights of 1966.

Social and Cultural Rights of 1966 (ICESCR).[38] Whilst the ICESCR does not expressly mention violence against women, the Committee on Economic, Social and Cultural Rights notes that in some countries, women still 'occupy a subordinate role in society' and that discrimination and VAW are serious social problems affecting women's enjoyment of their social, economic and cultural rights.[39]

Likewise, the Convention on the Elimination of All Forms of Racial Discrimination (CEARD) impliedly prohibits violence against women.[40] The ICCPR[41] was adopted in response to egregious human rights violations that continued to occur around the world, although violence against women is not expressly mentioned.[42] However, the Human Rights Committee (HRC) has remarked that state parties should adopt necessary measures to combat VAW, in particular marital rape, while ensuring that VAW is regarded as an offence and punishable under criminal law.[43] The HRC has pointed out that state parties should carry out awareness campaigns, ensuring that all forms of VAW are addressed, especially domestic violence, and that they fully comply with articles 3,[44] 6,[45] 7[46] and 26[47] of the Covenant.[48]

---

[38] Ibid.

[39] Audrey Chapman 'Violations Approach for monitoring the international covenant on economic, social and cultural' rights' 18 *Human Rights Quarterly* (1996): 23–66.

[40] UN convention against torture and other cruel inhuman or degrading treatment or punishment of 1984, ratified in 2004.

[41] International Covenant on Civil and Political Rights of 1966, ratified in 2004.

[42] Dina Bogecho 'Putting it to good use: The international covenant on civil and political rights and women's right to reproductive health' 13 *Southern California Review of Law and Women's Studies* (2004): 229–272.

[43] Ibid.

[44] ICCPR, article 3, provides that state parties undertake to ensure the equal right of men and women to the enjoyment of all civil and political rights.

[45] ICCPR, article 6, provides that every human being has the inherent right to life; that this right shall be protected by law and that no one shall be arbitrarily deprived of his life.

[46] ICCPR, article 7, provides that no one shall be subjected to torture or to cruel, inhuman or degrading treatment or punishment.

[47] ICCPR, article 26, provides that all persons are equal before the law and are entitled without any discrimination to the equal protection of the law and prohibits discrimination.

[48] Bogecho, *Supra*, Note 41.

Furthermore, article 16 of the Convention on the Elimination of All Forms of Discrimination against Women (CEDAW)[49] requires states to take appropriate measures to eliminate discrimination within the family.[50] Unfortunately, it has no specific provision on violence. The Committee on the Elimination of Discrimination Against Women (CEDAW Committee) in 1992 made up for the omission by including General Recommendation No. 19 dealing specifically with VAW, and requiring countries to include in periodic reports to the Committee the following:

> ...statistical data on the incidence of violence against women, information on the provision of services for victims and legislative and other measures taken to protect women against violence in their everyday lives, as well as harassment at the workplace, abuse in the family and sexual violence.[51]

It must be noted that this Recommendation has been updated by General Recommendation No. 35. In addition, the CEDAW Committee has over the years, actively engaged states on HIV/AIDS concerns, adopting and incorporating,[52] as a primary focus, a human rights framework for HIV prevention. Thus, the Committee has recommended that states accurately target the needs of affected populations through information and education strategies. Moreover, the CEDAW Committee recommended that states adopt strategies to ensure care and support for PLH by adopting steps to ameliorate the disease's social and economic impact.[53]

---

[49] UN convention on the elimination of all forms of discrimination against women (CEDAW) of 1979, ratified in 2004.

[50] Ibid., article 16 provides that states parties shall take all appropriate measures to eliminate discrimination against women in all matters relating to marriage and family relations.

[51] https://www.ohchr.org/EN/HRBodies/CEDAW/Pages/Recommendations.aspx.

[52] World Health Organisation, world health assembly, resolution 40.26, global strategy for the prevention and control of AIDS, Geneva, May 5, 1987. See also, Sofia Gruskin et al., 'Human rights and HIV/AIDS' (2002), http://hivinsite.ucsf.edu/InSite?page=kb-08-01-07.

[53] Ibid.

At the regional level, the African Charter on Human and Peoples' Rights,[54] and the Protocol to the African Charter on Human and Peoples' Rights on the Rights of Women in Africa (Maputo Protocol) protect and promote the rights of WLH and are binding on Eswatini.[55] In 2013 the African Commission on Human and Peoples' Rights (African Commission) adopted Resolution 260 on Involuntary Sterilisation and the Protection of Human Rights in Access to HIV Services.[56] The African Commission defined involuntary sterilisation as a procedure void of actual or informed consent or even against the wishes of the woman being sterilised. The African Commission asserted:

> [T]hat all forms of involuntary sterilisation violate in particular the right to equality and non-discrimination; dignity, liberty and security of person, freedom from torture, cruel, inhuman and degrading treatment, and the right to the best attainable state of physical and mental health; as enshrined in the regional and international human rights instruments, particularly the African Charter and the Maputo Protocol.

The above statement is significant in that it shines the light of equality on the practice of coerced sterilisation. The Resolution calls on states to ensure that their national legal and policy frameworks embody existing ethical and international medical principles on free and informed consent regarding all medical practices, in particular concerning sterilisation and access to healthcare services for WLH.[57] It obliges states to adopt measures that ensure that WLH are not unduly pressurised to be sterilised.[58] The Commission calls on states to investigate all claims of coerced or forced sterilisation of WLH by healthcare workers, hospitals

---

[54] African Charter on Human and Peoples' Rights of 1981, ratified in 1995.

[55] Protocol to the African charter on human and peoples' rights on the rights of women in Africa (Maputo protocol) of 2003, ratified in 2012.

[56] African commission, 260: Resolution on involuntary sterilisation and the protection of human rights in access to HIV services Banjul, The Gambia: Adopted during the 54th ordinary session of the African commission held from October 22, to November 5, (2013), https://www.achpr.org/sessions/resolutions?id=280.

[57] Paragraph ii of African commission, resolution 260 of 2013 (ACR).

[58] Ibid., Paragraph iii.

and policymakers.[59] It also calls on states to adopt institutional structures that allow for individual complaints by WLH who were subjected to forced and coerced sterilisation, with access to legal assistance.[60]

Significantly, explicit mention of HIV or the rights of persons infected or affected by HIV/AIDS is provided by only in the Maputo Protocol's text and at the African Union level. The African Commission gave guidance on how states may interpret article 14(1)(d) and (e) of the Maputo Protocol through this General Comment.[61] The Commission warned states to look into addressing the many forms of discrimination which were perceived to be responsible for preventing, and hindering women from protecting themselves and being protected by others individually and as a collective. The African Commission opined that African women had 'the right to the highest attainable standard of health, which includes sexual and reproductive health and rights'. Moreover, treaty bodies' Conclusion Observations as well as soft law such as the International Guidelines on HIV/AIDS and Human Rights of 2006[62] have further buttressed the health rights of women.

Eswatini has made commitments at international meetings such as the 1994 UN International Conference on Population and Development, held in Cairo, and the 1995 UN Fourth World Conference on Women, held in Beijing. These policy frameworks categorically pronounced governments' responsibility towards ensuring individuals' rights in the context of HIV/AIDS. Also, the UN General Assembly Special Session on HIV/AIDS (UNGASS) of 2001 is an essential document for advocacy and state accountability concerning HIV/AIDS and human rights.[63] International law, together with the 2030 Agenda for Sustainable Development, sets the basis for providing that every person has a right to health and access to HIV and other healthcare services.[64]

---

59 Ibid., Paragraph vii.

60 Ibid., Paragraph viii.

61 African Commission on Human and Peoples' Rights, *General Comments on Article 14 (1) (d) and (e) of the Protocol to the African Charter on Human and Peoples' Rights on the Rights of Women in Africa* (2012).

62 https://www.ohchr.org/Documents/Publications/HIVAIDSGuidelinesen.pdf.

63 UNAIDS, 'Declaration of commitment on HIV/AIDS: Global crisis—Global action,' United Nations General Assembly Special Session on HIV/AIDS, (2001).

64 Gruskin, *Supra*, Note 51.

People also have a right to equal treatment before the law and a right to dignity.

The 2006 International Guidelines on HIV and AIDS and Human Rights consolidated the HIV and AIDS guidelines adopted in 1996. The guidelines aim to help countries incorporate international human rights norms into their strategies in practice in the arena of HIV and AIDS.[65] There are 12 international guidelines, which consistently encourage countries to adopt frameworks that respond effectively to HIV and AIDS based on respect for and promotion, protection and fulfilment of human rights. All government departments have shared responsibility in executing such policies and programmes on HIV and AIDS.[66] Countries must ensure that communities are consulted in the design of the HIV and AIDS policy, the implementation of the programme, providing at the same time political and financial support.[67]

Countries are bound to address the HIV pandemic by reviewing and reforming public health laws.[68] They must also adapt their criminal laws and correctional systems to align them with international human rights law.[69] Countries are urged to enact and strengthen anti-discriminatory laws as well as pass laws to protect PLH and other vulnerable groups.[70] Guideline 8 of the International Guidelines on HIV and AIDS and Human Rights obligates states and communities to ensure that women and children live in an enabling environment by addressing inequality and prejudices through community dialogues.

The International Guidelines on HIV/AIDS and Human Rights are silent on violence against HIV-positive women. Reference is made to the CEDAW, which does not have a specific provision on violence. The omission has had serious ramifications for women's enjoyment and access to the other rights espoused in the Convention.[71] Thus,

---

[65] Ibid.

[66] *Supra*, Note 61, Guideline 1.

[67] *Supra*, Note 61, Guidelines 2.

[68] *Supra*, Note 61, Guideline 3.

[69] *Supra*, Note 61, Guideline 4.

[70] *Supra*, Note 61, Guideline 5.

[71] Christine Chinkin, 'Violence against women: The international legal response' 3 *Gender Development* (1995): 25.

the CEDAW Committee rectified the omission through Recommendation 19, in which it directed that countries should enact measures to eliminate violence and that discrimination included gender-based violence (GBV). The Committee made it clear that GBV is a form of discrimination that severely prevents women's ability to enjoy their rights. The issue for resolution in this chapter, however, is: In light of these well-established international standards as well national norms, are women living with HIV being afforded the required protection? Where violations are documented, are they able to access justice?

4 The Interlink Between HIV and VAW

Violence is a significant health issue that impacts an individual at both prevention and treatment stages of HIV. In the case of HIV-positive women, violence and fear of its occurrence prevent, and continue to encumber, women's access to healthcare leading to reduced life chances.[72] In order to illustrate the importance of having international norms on violence and its intersection with HIV, the chapter has extracted some perspective from the data in the thesis cited above. These extracts show the direct impact violence has on women living with HIV, in particular in accessing treatment.

4.1 Case Study: Violence That Interferes with WLH's Uptake of Antiretroviral Treatment

Women are disproportionately represented at healthcare facilities and are more likely than men to receive HIV treatment. However, a closer look at the findings of the study reveals that, although the right to access health and treatment is made available to all HIV-positive patients, women are often prevented from accessing and taking the life-saving drugs, such as antiretroviral treatment (ART) by violence, for example:

---

72 UNAIDS *Gender Matters: Overcoming Gender-Related Barriers to Prevent New HIV Infections Among Children and Keep Their Mothers Alive* (2014): 7.

> I am on ART. My boyfriend did not want me to take treatment, and we argued about it, and he chose to leave me for it. That hurt me emotionally. I decided that I would rather choose ART than him as it was time for me to start taking ART or risk dying.[73]
>
> Some women would even drop out of ART because her partner does not want her to take ART—this happened to me after I disclosed to my partner.[74]

The excerpts suggest that the gendered power imbalances and inequalities in relationships, coupled with the subordinate status of women, resulted in women's right to treatment being thwarted by their intimate partners.

Surprisingly, most of the key informants were aware that women's access to healthcare services, including enrolment for ART treatment programmes, were impeded.

> [. . .] some women have their ARVs treatment confiscated and thrown away by their partners.[75]
>
> [. . .] yesterday I had a client who is married and is afraid to take ARVs treatment because if her husband finds out about the treatment, he will beat her; when I asked her if her husband habitually beats her and she said yes, he does beat her frequently.[76]
>
> Again an HIV positive woman may be led to defaulting on ART due to fear that if she is discovered that she is taking ART, she might be chased, beaten or killed which often lead to the stage of AIDS.[77]
>
> Some women are being beaten for taking ART pills. One woman said her ART pills she keeps in the maize meal bag so that she can take them unsuspected by her husband as she cooks the maize meal because if her husband found out, she would be in trouble of beatings and being kicked out of the home.[78]

[73] Participant 7, WLH.

[74] Participant 30, WLH.

[75] Participant 39, KI.

[76] Participant 38, KI.

[77] Participant 36, KI.

[78] Participant 33, KI.

Uptake and adherence to treatment are critical in the AIDS treatment cascade and underscore the UNAIDS's 90-90-90 goals.[79] However, universal access to treatment is wrecked for women who are susceptible to extreme violence when endeavouring to access treatment. Policymakers must consider that WLH's attainment of the best health outcomes depends on protecting their human rights (to be free from violence).

4.2 Case Study: Medicalised Violence Against Women Living with HIV

The Eswatini study found coerced and forced sterilisation represented another form of violence perpetrated against WLH, this time in the healthcare sector. WLH linked their sterilisation as discriminatory violence as there were no reports of HIV-positive men being sterilised:

> I know of ###.[80] We were having a meeting comprising of HIV support groups from different regions; she had her womb removed without her consent at the hospital because she was HIV positive. She said her womb was removed, and as a result, her husband left her as time went by.[81]
>
> I know of three women who were forcefully sterilised. One of them was told that she was going to be sterilised as she was HIV positive and that they did not care if she consented or not; so, she did not sign any consent forms. One of the women really wants a child, and her husband is busy using the fact that she cannot have children against her.[82]

The above quotations from HIV-positive women demonstrates their involuntary sterilisation as a violation of their human right to reproduce. Women's rights advocates were aware of the malpractice carried

---

79 First 90: Percentage of people living with HIV who know their HIV status; Second 90: Percentage of people living with HIV who know their status and who are on treatment; and Third 90: Percentage of people living with HIV on treatment who have suppressed viral loads.

80 The name of the sterilised woman blocked, to ensure anonymity.

81 Participant 3, WLH.

82 Participant 26, WLH.

out by healthcare practitioners and it was not disputed by policymakers, for instance:

> Yes, I have been confronted by instances of coerced and forced sterilisation here at work; before that I was not aware that there is something called forced sterilisation. However, I have since learned that there are incidences of coerced sterilisation; there are women who say they have been coercively sterilised. For instance, there is a woman who tells her story that she was left to suffer labour pains for a long time whilst knowing very well that she can't give birth the natural way and because they wanted to sterilise her they coerced her; the health workers.[83]
>
> At that point in time because we didn't have treatment options and the PMTCT (prevention of mother-to-child transmission) was not there, there was no treatment, so it felt like it was a right thing to try and minimise; you know for a long time we have tried to promote family planning and trying to reduce unwanted births so, at that point in time instead of allowing people who are failing to use ordinary family planning methods to get maybe a permanent option, it looked like the best intervention than allowing them to get HIV positive children who were not going to live that much longer anyway; it looked like probably the best intervention to try and convince them that they needed it. So, it might sound very bad or unfair now or even atrocious now, but at that point in time, this is what most physicians were faced with.[84]

Forced or coerced sterilisations in Eswatini were performed by some physicians who thought this was an appropriate response to the HIV and AIDS pandemic, abrogating WLHs' human rights in the process. There is little official information about the victims seeking access to justice.[85]

---

[83] Participant 34, KI.

[84] Participant 37, KI.

[85] In 2016, the Southern Africa Litigation Centre (SALC) supported a case before the Swaziland High Court of a women who sued the government of Swaziland for being forcefully sterilised in a government hospital. The Government offered a confidential settlement of 50 thousand emalangeni (US$ 3 850).

5 Discussion

Women's heightened vulnerability to HIV infection due to cultural attitudes, gender inequality, violence and sexual domination by men has been well documented.[86] However, very few studies have looked at how these factors have impacted women's uptake of treatment after they are infected with HIV.[87]

5.1 Violence Prevents WLH from Accessing Treatment

Violence against HIV+ women is a public healthcare concern and a human rights violation. According to Mann, a champion of health and human rights, there is a meeting point between public health goals and human rights norms, as they are inextricably linked.[88] The interdependence has necessitated the adoption of a human rights approach in exploring the link between HIV and violence against WLH in the Eswatini context.

Globally, public healthcare and human rights interventions have chosen to deal with the twin epidemics of HIV and VAW.[89] Many studies

[86] Claudia Garcia-Moreno et al. *WHO Multi-Country Study on Women's Health and Domestic Violence Against Women: Initial Results on Prevalence, Health Outcomes and Women's Responses* (2005). See also, World Health Organisation (WHO) *World Report on Health and Violence: Sexual Violence* (2006). Also, Vikas Paudel, & Kedar Baral 'Women living with HIV/AIDS (WLHA), battling stigma, discrimination and denial and the role of support groups as a coping strategy: A review of the literature' 9 *Reproductive Health* (2015): 5. See also, Johanna Kehler, et al. *Gender and HVI Violence: Perceptions and Experience of Violence and Other Rights Abuses Against Women Living with HIV in the Eastern Cape, KwaZulu-Natal and Western Cape, South Africa* (2012).

[87] Chandreyee Roy, 'Human Rights and HIV/AIDS with Special Reference to Women' 35 *Indian Anthropologist*, (2005): 97–110.

[88] Jonathan Mann et al. 'Health and human rights' 1 *Health and Human. Rights* (1994): 7–23. See also Elizabeth Fee, & Manor Parry 'Jonathan Mann, HIV/AIDS, and Human Rights' 29(1) *Journal of Public Health Policy* (2008): 61.

[89] UNAIDS International Guidelines on HIV/AIDS and Human Rights of 2006 Consolidated Version, https://www.unaids.org/sites/default/files/media_asset/jc1252-internguidelines_en_0.pdf.

have already tackled the issue of violence hindering women's efforts to prevent acquiring HIV.[90]

At the treatment level, violence against HIV-positive women continues to be a critical health issue as it prevents women's access or adherence to ART programmes. Violence can delay or interrupt WLH's enrolment into HIV care.[91] In 2019 UNAIDS reported that the retention of PLH on the treatment was an increasing challenge.[92] The situation is worse for women attending antenatal services as fear of violence from intimate partners serves as a barrier to treatment, resulting in poor HIV outcomes for the women.[93] For instance, adherence rates of pregnant women who were initiated on antiretroviral treatment soon after confirmation of HIV-positive status, declined after delivery, particularly in women who had not disclosed their HIV status to their partners, thereby enhancing their risk of progressing to AIDS and dying.[94] The case of the woman who was quoted above as saying she was afraid that her husband would beat her if he found out that she was taking ART to protect her unborn baby illustrates the point.

There is no consensus on appropriate punishment for a person who disrupts an HIV-positive woman's uptake of ART: is it physical or psychological violence, or a blatant violation of the right to health and bodily integrity and right not to be subjected to inhumane and degrading punishment, or the right to life? Intimate partners throwing away ART and preventing WLH from their ART medication needs to be addressed as public health and human rights issues. Fortunately, some of the HIV-positive women, managed to keep their HIV status a secret from their abusive partners, enabling them to access care.

---

[90] Ying Li et al. 'Intimate partner violence and HIV infection among women: A systematic review and meta-analysis' 17 *Journal of the International AIDS Society* (2014): 4. See also Basu & Menon, *Supra*, Note 3.

[91] Anna Leddy et al. 'Gender-based violence and engagement in biomedical HIV prevention, care and treatment: A scoping review' 19 *BMC Public Health* (2019): 2.

[92] Joint United Nations Programme on HIV/AIDS (UNAIDS), Global and regional data 2019.

[93] Ibid. See also, Sally Field et al. 'Domestic and intimate partner violence among pregnant women in a low resource setting in South Africa: A facility-based, mixed methods study' 199 *BMC Women's Health* (2018): 18.

[94] Abdol Karim, & Cheryl Baxter 'The dual burden of gender-based violence and HIV in adolescent girls and young women in South Africa' 106 (12) *South African Medical Journal* (2016): 1151–1153.

Some of the women reported that their intimate partners rejected them for taking ART, leaving them destitute and without financial support. Other studies have alluded to sparse literature on the effects of GBV on treatment and the role fear of IPV plays as a barrier to treatment uptake and adherence for WLH.[95] Studies have also called for the integration of violence-related support within HIV prevention and clinical care, as essential for vulnerable groups such as women.[96] In the Eswatini study, WLH were blamed for bringing HIV into the home and were perceived as promiscuous by intimate partners, in-laws and family members. UNAIDS has also found that 'fear of being blamed for HIV and thus being physically or emotionally abused or abandoned sometimes led pregnant women to avoid disclosing their status and accessing treatment services'.[97]

All this underlines the impact of violence on the ability of WLH to access treatment, with women being afraid to inform their partners about their ARVs, consequently hampering adherence. This is a critical public health issue that requires urgent attention.

5.2 WLH Subjection to Medicalised Violence by Healthcare Workers

Forced and coerced sterilisations represent grave violations of women's human rights and medical ethics and should be perceived as 'acts of torture and cruel, inhuman, and degrading treatment'.[98] This is a form of structural violence, by which social institutions place individuals such as

---

[95] Ibid., 1151.

[96] Kristen Dunkle, & Michele Decker 'Gender-based violence and HIV: Reviewing the links and casual pathways in the general population and high-risk groups' 69(1) *American Journal of Reproductive Immunology* (2013): 20–26.

[97] UNAIDS *Gender Matters: Overcoming Gender-Related Barriers to Prevent New HIV Infections Among Children and Keep Their Mothers Alive* (2014): 7.

[98] Zaynab Essack, & Ann Strode 'I feel like half a woman all the time': The impacts of coerced and forced sterilisations on HIV-positive women in South Africa' 26 *Empowering Women for Gender Equity* (2012): 24–34. See also Open Society Foundation *Against Her Will, Forced and Coerced Sterilisation of Women Worldwide* (2011), http://www.soros.org/sites/default/files/against-her-will-20111003.pdf.

WLH in harm's way by stopping them from meeting their basic needs.[99] In the context of the HIV and AIDS epidemic, this resulted in HIV-positive women experiencing medicalised violence at the hand of the healthcare sector. Medicalised violence in Eswatini was experienced by only HIV-positive women through coerced sterilisation, which further undermined their standing in society. Coerced and forced sterilisation was also discriminatory, as no HIV-positive men were reported to have been sterilised.[100]

Despite advanced medication allowing HIV-infected women to live normally and have healthy children, many HIV-positive women are still told not to get pregnant.[101] Essack and Strode found that forced and coerced sterilisation of HIV-positive women happened worldwide.[102] Women's groups maintain that coerced sterilisations perpetuate stigma and discrimination suffered by WLH.[103]

Forced and coerced sterilisations should be perceived as 'acts of torture and cruel, inhuman, and degrading treatment'.[104] However, in Eswatini, no one takes responsibility for it; there have been no reports of justiciable compensation for the women who are alleged to have been coerced or forcefully sterilised.[105] In fact, it is reported that in 2000 the Swazi parliament attempted to table a Bill making mandatory sterilisation of HIV-positive people legal.[106] In other jurisdictions, legal claims have been filed against the relevant states, as in the case of 20 Namibian women whose sterilisations have been extensively documented.[107]

---

99 Paul Farmer et al. 'Structural violence and clinical medicine' 3(10) *PLoS Med* (2006): 1686.

100 Mduduzi Magagula, No babies for HIV + Women? Times of Swaziland November 17, 2013, www.times.co.sz/news/93328-no-babies-for-HIV-women.html.

101 Lydia Guterman, 'Women in Namibia fight back against forced sterilisation' (2010), https://www.opensocietyfoundations.org/voices/women-namibia-fight-back-against-forced-sterilization.

102 Essack, & Strode, *Supra*, Note 21.

103 Ibid.

104 Essack, & Strode, *Supra*, Note 21. See also, Open Society Foundations, *Supra*, Note 97.

105 *Supra*, Note 75.

106 Khabir Ahmad, 'Swaziland debates sterilisation of HIV patients' 356 *Lancet* (2000): 321.

107 Geofrey York 'HIV + women in Africa sterilised, stigmatised' May 2, 2018, The *Global Mail*, http://www.theglobeandmail.com/news/world/hiv-women-in-africasterilized-stigmatized/article4262581/.

the practical effect of 'driving these individuals underground, denying them access to public healthcare services and contributing to increased HIV/AIDS morbidity and mortality'.[115] Women also end up being the most affected by HIV specific criminal laws since in most cases they are likely to know of their HIV status before men do.[116] For all these reasons, this chapter calls for international consensus that violence against WLH that hinders and disrupts their access to treatment and ART be dealt with by ordinary laws of their respective countries.[117] Other countries have done this successfully. In South Africa, for example, an individual who deliberately puts a woman at risk of HIV infection is prosecuted under the common law offence of attempted murder.[118] In *Phiri v State*,[119] an HIV/AIDS counsellor who allegedly infected the complainant with HIV after twice refusing to use a condom when he knew that he was HIV + and the complainant HIV negative was prosecuted. The court ruled that Phiri was guilty of attempted murder as he had knowingly put the respondent at risk of contracting HIV.[120]

A similar approach is advisable for cases where WLH are maliciously hindered and prevented from accessing treatment, or their ART treatment is disrupted. The attempted murder offence could be preferred against perpetrators, upon proof of intention to harm WLH. However, others may argue that the crime of assault may be preferred.

This study found that most WLH did not rely on the legal and policy framework protecting women from VAW and HIV. Studies have found that focusing primarily on criminal intervention is limited by the fact[121]

---

[115] James Hodge et al., 'A global assessment of the role of law in the HIV/AIDS pandemic' 123(3) *Public Health* (2009): 260.

[116] UNAIDS *Action Linking Initiatives on Violence Against Women and HIV Everywhere*, ALIV(H)E framework (2017).

[117] Sophie Patterson et al. 'The impact of criminalisation of HIV non-disclosure on the healthcare engagement of women living with HIV in Canada: A comprehensive review of the evidence' 18 *Journal of the International AIDS Society* (2015): 1–15.

[118] Musara Lubombo 'Re-thinking HIV disclosure as ubuntu: Towards a social theory of communicative responses to the sub-Saharan epidemic' 15(3) *African Renaissance* (2018): 12.

[119] Phiri v S 2013 ZAGPPHC 279.

[120] Phiri v S 2013 ZAGPPHC 279 in Paragraph 15, the court found the fact that he worked in a clinic as an HIV counsellor an aggravating factor.

[121] Linda Mills, 'Empowering battered women transnationally: The case for postmodern interventions' 41 *Journal of Social Work* (1996): 261.

that women victims of violence are unwilling to report cases of VAW to the police and they may not seek any help, where help is available, or delay seeking help until long after the abuse began.[122]

HIV+ women will continue to suffer medicalised violence if the health institutions guilty of this practice are not called to account and ordered to compensate the victims. The notion of reparation was envisaged in the 1993 UN Declaration on the Elimination of Violence against Women, where it was enunciated as follows:

> Countries must develop penal, civil, labour and administrative sanctions in domestic legislation to punish and redress the wrongs caused to women who are subjected to violence; women who are subjected to violence should be provided with access to the mechanisms of justice and, as provided for by national legislation, to just and effective remedies for the harm that they have suffered; and that states should also inform women of their rights in seeking redress through such mechanisms.[123]

There is no jurisprudential guidance and clarity on whether a combination of criminal and civil remedies should be applied in the case of sterilisation without informed consent. Whatever the detail, such measures must ensure that informed consent is sought in the case of sterilisation of WLH. The failure of international guidelines to address violence against WLH prolongs the inadequacy of national laws to address this issue head-on. In the case of the complaint to the RSA Commission on Gender Equality (above), the Commission referred the matter to other bodies, risking the issue being bounced from one institution to another. Nations will continue to fail to deal with cases of coerced sterilisation unless guidance is given at international level. This is supported by the ease with which governments ignore their legal obligations under CEDAW. A provision in the International Guidelines to the effect that systemic institutional violence against WLH would attract punitive compensation to the victims would have settled the matter. Significantly, the African Commission addressed the link between VAW

---

[122] Ibid.

[123] UN declaration on the elimination of all forms violence against women of 1993 article 4, Paragraph (d).

and HIV through setting norms and standards on women's rights, HIV, including sterilisation.[124] Resolution 260, as discussed above, postulated that sterilisation should happen with WLH's full informed and free consent.[125]

The present study found that violence against WLH could be ameliorated through social, economic, and cultural rights interventions, in particular, women's economic empowerment. It is imperative in the fight against VAW and HIV that women do not entirely depend on their partners for financial support; a woman with her own income could respond more effectively to violence. Other studies have found that VAW and poverty are intimately connected and as such, 'measures to address this violence must tackle the social and economic factors that contribute to gender inequality'.[126] Also, studies have revealed that violence against women cannot be dealt with decisively in isolation from other social challenges such as poverty and poor education.[127]

Goldblatt opined that there is a need for the adoption of measures to address violence and social and economic factors that aid gender inequality in society.[128] Access to social and economic rights offers a rich possibility to find solutions beyond punitive criminal law responses to violence by providing more preventive measures that take cognisance of systemic inequality.[129] Allendorf opines that through empowerment and land ownership, women can decline men's power and authority over their lives to make decisions which can clear the pattern of IPV.[130]

---

124 Ebenezer Durojaye 'The role of the African commission on human and peoples' rights in developing norms and standards on HIV/AIDS and human rights' *Global Jurist* (2017): 4. See also Chantal Badul, The coerced and forced sterilisation of women living with HIV in South Africa: A critical review of existing legal remedies (unpublished PhD Thesis, UKZN, 2018): 7.

125 African Commission, Resolution 260 of 2013.

126 Beth Goldblatt 'Social and economic rights to challenge violence against women—Examining and extending strategies' *South African Journal on Human Rights* (2019): 169–193.

127 K. J. Amaka 'The girl child and gender-based violence: Implication on education performance and women empowerment' 3 *International Journal of the Forum for African Women Educationalists* (2015): 1–9.

128 Goldblatt, *supra*, Note 16.

129 Ibid.

130 Keera Allendorf 'Do women's land rights promote empowerment and child health in Nepal? 35 *World Development* (2007): 1975.

Women's empowerment is key to their enjoyment of their rights in Eswatini, entailing fulfilment of their socio-economic rights in an enabling environment that ensures their fair and active participation in the economy.[131]

6 Conclusion

Access to justice is necessary, especially for those marginalised in society and HIV-positive women are one such group. This study found that violence against WLH and HIV were interlinked and mutually reinforcing. It revealed that fear of violence by intimate partners interrupted and disrupted WLH's right to treatment and in particular uptake of ART. It was found that WLH were subjected to prejudice resulting in medicalised violence in the form of forced sterilisation. Also, the study found that WLH do not always report cases of violence. The omission of a provision addressing violence against HIV-positive women in the International Guidelines on HIV/AIDS and Human Rights has been criticised in this paper, because international human rights instruments profoundly influence states in the way they promote and protect women's rights and protect women from gender-based violence. The absence of such international norms to protect women from violence condemns women to be disproportionately affected by violence and vulnerability to HIV/AIDS. The use of criminal laws to redress violence against women was found to be not optimal and that the adoption of a mixed approach incorporating the fulfilment of socio-economic rights of women was advocated.

7 Recommendations

Given the finding of this study that in Eswatini violence is prevalent in the lives of HIV+ women, there is need for further quantitative research to look into the scale of the problem and propose new responses to

[131] Mills, *supra*, Note 107.

tackle violence as well as self-stigma in HIV + women. This study recommends that there should be clear cut guidance at international and regional level on the measures that countries must adopt to protect HIV + women from violence and as such, there is a need for the revision of the International Guidelines on HIV/AIDS and Human Rights of 2006 so it: 1. Expressly provides that states should condemn violence against women, in particular, HIV + women, and pursue by all appropriate means without delay a policy of eliminating violence against women; and 2. Expressly call upon states to prohibit all forms of institutionalised violence against HIV + women and in the case of medicalised violence, states must be ordered to ensure that institutions involved redress the harm done to women through access to justice and reparations.

The study further recommends that treaty bodies should require that countries enumerate in their state reports measures undertaken to eradicate violence against HIV + women and measures taken to target perpetrators, including those inhibiting them from accessing treatment.

The study further recommends that Eswatini implement domestic violence laws which invoke a combination of civil and criminal measures to protect women in line with international norms in such a manner that WLH can feel safe.

It is further recommended that Eswatini government addresses violence faced by women living with HIV and AIDS perpetrated by intimate partners, the family and healthcare workers through training of healthcare workers and community sensitisation on PLH's rights.

Lastly, the study recommends that HIV-positive women's experience of VAW should be taken into consideration when programmes and/or policies tackling HIV are being formulated.

References

A. M. Leddy et al., 2019, 'Gender-Based Violence and Engagement in Biomedical HIV Prevention, Care and Treatment: A Scoping Review' 19(1) *BMC Public Health*.

African Charter on Human and Peoples' Rights of 1981.

African Commission, 260: Resolution on Involuntary Sterilisation and the Protection of Human Rights in Access to HIV Services Banjul, The Gambia: Adopted During the 54th Ordinary Session of the African Commission Held from October 22, to November 5, 2013.

Amita Basu and Ratna Menon, 2011, *Violence Against Women, HIV/AIDS Vulnerability and the Law. Working Paper Prepared for the Third Meeting of the Technical Advisory Group of the Global Commission on HIV and the Law.*

Ann Strode, S. Mthembu and Z. Essack, 2012, 'She Made Up a Choice for Me': 22 HIV-Positive Women's Experiences of Involuntary Sterilisation in Two South African Provinces' 20 *Reproductive Health Matters.*

Audrey R. Chapman, 1996, 'Violations Approach' for Monitoring the International Covenant on Economic, Social and Cultural' Rights' 18 *Human Rights Quarterly.*

B. Goldblatt, 2019, 'Social and Economic Rights to Challenge Violence Against Women—Examining and Extending Strategies 35(2) *South African Journal on Human Rights.*

C. Garcia-Moreno et al., 2005, *WHO Multi-Country Study on Women's Health and Domestic Violence Against Women: Initial Results on Prevalence, Health Outcomes and Women's Responses.*

C. J. Badul, 2018, 'The Coerced and Forced Sterilisation of Women Living with HIV in South Africa: A Critical Review of Existing Legal Remedies' (Unpublished PhD Thesis, UKZN, 2018).

C. Roy, 2005, 'Human Rights and HIV/AIDS with Special Reference to Women' 35 *Indian Anthropologist.*

Christine Chinkin, 1995, 'Violence Against Women: The International Legal Response' 3(2) *Gender* and *Development.*

Dina Bogecho, 2004, 'Putting It To Good Use: The International Covenant on Civil and Political Rights and Women's Right to Reproductive Health' 13 *Southern California Review of Law and Women's Studies.*

E. Fee and M. Parry, 2008, 'Jonathan Mann, HIV/AIDS, and Human Rights' 29(1) *Journal of Public Health Policy.*

Ebenezer Durojaye, 2006, 'Advancing Gender Equity in Access to HIV Treatment Through the Protocol on the Rights of Women in Africa' 6 *African Human Rights Law Journal.*

Ebenezer Durojaye, 2017, 'The Role of the African Commission on Human and Peoples' Rights in Developing norms and Standards on HIV/AIDS and Human Rights' 17(3) *Global Jurist.*

F. Kasiva, 2012, *Robbed of Choice Forced and Coerced Sterilisation Experiences of Women Living with HIV in Kenya*, https://profiles.uonbi.ac.ke/kihara/files/

report-on-robbed-of-choice-forced-and-coerced-sterilisation-experiences-of-women-living-with-hiv-in-kenya.pdf.

G. York, May 2, 2018, 'HIV+ Women in Africa Sterilized, Stigmatized' *The Global Mail*, http://www.theglobeandmail.com/news/world/hiv-women-in-africasterilized-stigmatized/article4262581/.

General Assembly Resolution 32/130 of 1977.

Government of the Kingdom of Eswatini, Swaziland HIV Incidence Measurement Survey 2 (SHIMS2) 2016–2017.

International Covenant on Civil and Political Rights of 1966.

International Planned Parenthood Federation, 2007, Research Dossier on HIV Prevention for Girls and Young Women in Swaziland.

J. Kehler, et al., 2012, *Gender and HVI Violence: Perceptions and Experience of Violence and Other Rights Abuses Against Women Living with HIV in the Eastern Cape, KwaZulu Natal and Western Cape, South Africa.*

J. Mann et al., 1994, 'Health and Human Rights' 1(1) *Health and Human Rights.*

Johanna Bond and Phillips Robin, 2001, 'Violence Against Women as a Human Rights Violation: International Institutional Responses' in *Sourcebook on Violence Against Women* edited by C. M. Renzetti, J. L. Edleson & R. K. Bergen.

Joint United Nations Programme on HIV/AIDS (UNAIDS), 2019, Global HIV & AIDS Statistics, Fact Sheet, https://www.unaids.org/en/resources/fact-sheet.

K. J. Amaka, 2015, 'The Girl Child and Gender-Based Violence: Implication on Education Performance and Women Empowerment' 3 *International Journal of the Forum for African Women Educationalists.*

Keaorata Gadinabokao, 2016, 'Shortcomings of the South African Domestic Violence Act 116 of 1998 in Comparative Perspective', (Unreported LLM Dissertation University of Pretoria 2016).

Keera Allendorf, 2007, 'Do Women's Land Rights Promote Empowerment and Child Health in Nepal?' 35 *World Development.*

Kingdom of Eswatini Constitution Act 001 of 2005.

Kristine Dunkle and Michele Decker, 2013, 'Gender-Based Violence and HIV: Reviewing the Evidence for Links and Causal Pathways in the General Population and High-Risk Groups' 69 *American Journal of Reproductive Immunology.*

L. Gable et al., 2009, 'A Global Assessment of the Role of Law in the HIV/AIDS Pandemic' 123 *Public Health.*

L. Guterman, November 21, 2010, *Women in Namibia Fight Back Against Forced Sterilisation*, https://www.opensocietyfoundations.org/voices/women-namibia-fight-back-against-forced-sterilization.

L. Mills, 1996, 'Empowering Battered Women Transnationally: The Case for Postmodern Interventions' 41(3) *Journal of Social Work.*

Li Ying et al., 2014, 'Intimate Partner Violence and HIV Infection Among Women: A Systematic Review and Meta-Analysis' 17(1) *Journal of the International AIDS Society*.

M. Lubombo, 2018, 'Re-thinking HIV Disclosure as Ubuntu: Towards a Social Theory of Communicative Responses to the Sub-Saharan Epidemic' 15 *African Renaissance.*

M. Magagula, November 17, 2013, 'No Babies for HIV+ Women?' *Times of Swaziland*, www.times.co.sz/news/93328-no-babies-for-HIV-women.html.

Neil Andersson, Anne Cockcroft and Bev Shea, 2008, 'Gender-Based Violence and HIV: Relevance for HIV Prevention in Hyperendemic Countries of Southern Africa' 22 *AIDS.*

Open Society Foundations, (2011), Against Her Will, Forced and Coerced Sterilisation of Women Worldwide, http://www.soros.org/sites/default/files/against-her-will-20111003.pdf.

Paul Farmer et al., 2006, Structural Violence and Clinical Medicine *PLoS Med.*

Phiri v S 2013 ZAGPPHC 279 (August 8, 2013).

Protocol to the African Charter on Human and Peoples' Rights on the Rights of Women in Africa of 2003.

Q. A. Karim and C. Baxter, 2016, 'The Dual Burden of Gender-Based Violence and HIV in Adolescent Girls and Young Women in South Africa' 106(12) *South African Medical Journal.*

R. S. Mogale, K. K. Burns and S. Richter, 2012, 'Violence Against Women in South Africa: Policy Position and Recommendation' 18(5) *SAGE*.

S. C. Kalichman et al., 2005, 'Gender Attitudes, Sexual Violence, and HIV/AIDS Risks Among Men and Women in Cape Town' 42(4) *Journal of Sex Research.*

S. Field et al., 2018, 'Domestic and Intimate Partner Violence Among Pregnant Women in a Low Resource Setting in South Africa: A Facility-Based, Mixed Methods Study'.

S. Gruskin et al., 2002, Human Rights and HIV/AIDS, http://hivinsite.ucsf.edu/InSite?page=kb-08-01-07.

S. K. Wang, 2010, 'Violence and HIV/AIDS: Violence Against Women and Girls As a Cause and Consequence of HIV/AIDS' 17 *Duke Journal of Gender Law & Policy*.

S. Qureshi, 2013, 'The Recognition of Violence Against Women as a Violation of Human Rights in the United Nations System' 28(1) *A Research Journal of South Asian Studies*.

Sexual Offences and Domestic Act of 2018.

Susan Fox, 2003, *Gender-Based Violence and HIV/AIDS in South Africa Organisational Responses* (Centre for AIDS Development, Research and Evaluation, (CADRE).

The Swaziland Health Sector Response to Gender Based Violence Guidelines March 2010.

UN Convention Against Torture and Other Cruel Inhuman or Degrading Treatment or Punishment of 1984.

UN Convention on the Elimination of All Forms of Discrimination against Women (CEDAW) of 1979.

UN Declaration on the Elimination of all Forms Violence against Women of 1993.

UN International Covenant on Civil and Political Rights of 1966.

UN Vienna Declaration of 1993.

UNAIDS International Guidelines on HIV/AIDS and Human Rights of 2006.

UNAIDS, 2001, 'Declaration of Commitment on HIV/AIDS: Global Crisis—Global Action,' United Nations General Assembly Special Session on HIV/AIDS.

UNAIDS, 2014, *Gender Matters: Overcoming Gender-Related Barriers to Prevent New HIV Infections Among Children and Keep Their Mothers Alive*.

UNIFEM, 2010, *Ending Violence Against Women & Girls: Evidence. Data and Knowledge in the Pacific Island Countries Literature Review and Annotated Bibliography*, https://www.unicef.org/evaw.pdf.

V. Paudel and K. P. Baral, 2015, 'Women Living with HIV/AIDS (WLHA), Battling Stigma, Discrimination and Denial and the Role of Support Groups as a Coping Strategy: A Review of the Literature' 12(53) *Reproductive Health*.

Virginia Braun and Victoria Clarke, 2007, 'Using Thematic Analysis in Psychology' *Qualitative Research in Psychology*.

World Health Organisation, 2006, *World Report on Health and Violence: Sexual Violence*.

Zakhe Hlanze et al., 2008, *Customary Practices, the Laws and Risky Behaviours—A Concern for the Increased Prevalence and Vulnerability to HIV and AIDS Among Women and the Girl-Child: A Rights-Based Approach*.

Zaynab Essack and Ann Strode, 2012, 'I Feel Like Half a Woman All the Time': The Impacts of Coerced and Forced Sterilisations on HIV-Positive Women in South Africa' 26 *Agenda: Empowering Women for Gender Equity*.

13

Protection of Refugee Women and Girls from Sexual and Gender-Based Violence Under International Law

Charity O. Kaniye-Ebeku and Taiwo Odumosu

1 Introduction

Violence against refugee women and girls continues to attract more public attention because it refuses to abate. It is almost as if the world is getting nowhere to solving the problems faced by females in this category. Amongst other forms of attack exacerbated by armed conflicts on women and girls, violence on refugee female irrespective of their age has become a global issue which has attracted seminal studies as well as special consideration from the United Nations (UN) High Commission on Refugees (UNHCR). Obradovic noted that 'there are currently

C. O. Kaniye-Ebeku (✉) · T. Odumosu
University of Nicosia, Nicosia, Cyprus

C. O. Kaniye-Ebeku
University of Port Harcourt, River State, Port Harcourt, Nigeria

T. Odumosu
Olabisi Onabanjo University, Ago Iwoye, Nigeria

A. Budoo-Scholtz and E. C. Lubaale (eds.), *Violence Against Women and Criminal Justice in Africa: Volume II*, Sustainable Development Goals Series,
https://doi.org/10.1007/978-3-030-75953-7_13

59.5 million refugees worldwide'[1]; and within this zone of displacement, brutalisation of females has become a consistent and recurrent decimal. Violence against women and girls with refugee status has taken more sinister dimensions in recent times. During wars, conflicts and forced displacements, women and girls are put at great disadvantage and risks. The UN reported that amongst 258 million people who have crossed international borders fleeing from violence, almost half of them are women and girls.[2] The bleak future they face in such a sordid situation is captured more in this passage:

> During the journey women and girls are put in a number of dangerous situations including walking along roads in darkness and putting their faith in strangers. This leaves them highly vulnerable to violence and even rape.[3]

These women face further 'challenges and protection risks in transit such as family separation, psychosocial stress and trauma, health complications, particularly for pregnant women, physical harm and injury' and they are at 'risks of exploitation and gender-based violence'.[4] The Deputy UN Emergency Relief Coordinator, Kyung-Wha Kang for instance, asserts that militants 'from the Islamic State in Iraq and Levant (ISIL) have captured territories in Iraq and Syria, (and in jubilation)[5] they have used and punished women to demonstrate their power'.[6] The UNHCR noted that internal armed conflicts increased dramatically since early

---

[1] M. Obradovic, 'Protecting female refugees against sexual and gender-based violence in camps' (2015), ourworld.unu.edu.

[2] Volunteers Team, 'Violence against refugee women and girls' (2018), www.thecircle.ngo; See also the UN Report at The International Migration Report 2017 (Highlights) Multimedia Library—United Nations Department of Economic and Social Affairs, https://www.un.org/development/desa/publications/international-migration-report-2017.html.

[3] Ibid.

[4] UN Women (Europe and Central Asia), *Women Refugees and Migrants* (2020), www.eca.unwomen.org.

[5] Comment supplied.

[6] Our World, 'Scourge of sexual violence in armed conflict: Far from being rooted Out' (2015), www.ourworld.unu.edu.

1990.[7] The situation in 2020 has not mellowed as armed insurgence continues to ravage places like Africa. Curiously, civilian populations suffer more as they become targets of armed conflicts.[8] While internecine wars played a major part in the process of dislodging women and girls from their homes, internal displacement due to activities such as Boko Haram in Nigeria has increased the dangers of violence women and girls face.[9] The fallout of the violence has been itemised to include trafficking, rape, unwanted or undesired pregnancy, forced abortion, sexual slavery and sexually transmitted diseases like Human Immunodeficiency Virus/Acquired Immunodeficiency Syndrome (HIV/AIDs).[10] It has been estimated that the number of internally displaced persons (IDPs) has outnumbered asylum seekers and refugees put together.[11] In 2005, UNHCR worked with '6.6 million IDPs, a number that grew to about 15 million by 2010 and stood at more than 43.5 million at the end of 2019 – representing an almost 7-fold increase in only 15 years'.[12] In sub-Saharan Africa, there was nearly a three-fold increase in the number of refugees in the course of the decade, 'increasing from 2.2 to 6.3 million'. Conflict and violence in South Sudan, the Democratic Republic of Congo, Central African Republic, Somalia and Burundi 'forced millions of people to flee, but other crises contributed to the rise in refugees as well'.[13] Though UNHCR submits that 'recent armed conflicts have as their primary targets women and girls',[14] this may not necessarily be so. Rather the warmongers exploit the weakness of the

---

[7] T. Farrell and O. Schmitt, *The Causes, Character and Conduct of Armed Conflict, and the Effects on Civilian Populations*, 1990–2010 (2012).

[8] UNHCR, *Handbook for the Protection of Women and Girls* (2006): 7, https://cms.emergency.unhcr.org/documents/11982/57181/UNHCR+Handbook+for+the+Protection+of+Women+and+Girls.pdf/ed5b4707-337f-4275-86e7-3af5f81186ea.

[9] International Crisis Group, 'Fighting Boko Haram in Chad: Beyond Military Measures', March 8, 2017, https://d2071andvip0wj.cloudfront.net/24-fighting-Boko-Haram-in-Chad-Beyond-Military-Measures-l-Crisis-Group.

[10] Ibid.

[11] UNHCR Division of Operation Services. '2006 Global Trends: Refugees, Asylum Seekers, Returnees and Stateless Persons', July 16, 2007.

[12] UNCHR. Global trends Report (2019), https://www.unhcr.org/be/wp-content/uploads/sites/46/2020/07/Global-Trends-Report-2019.pdf.

[13] Ibid.

[14] Ibid.

women and girls whose husbands or fathers have been killed or escaped from the ravaging war. Allegations of rape and sale of girls in a Nigerian IDP camp was recently made and debunked by the Nigeria's National Emergency Management Agency (NEMA) as mere movement from one IDP camp to another.[15] Even when such allegations were made, the government agencies are not honest enough to say the truth.

While the insurgents gloat over their archaic egos on the exploitation and abuse of women and girls, the staff of humanitarian agencies have also been reported to sexually exploit these women and girls. Obradovic referencing a report writes that 'girls were sexually exploited by humanitarian agency staff and security forces in Guinea, Liberia, and Sierra Leone (and) yet this problem has still not been stamped out'.[16] Refugees, especially women and girls, have been victims of violence from police and border guards.[17] The smugglers who assist them often violate them while still asking for high prices to assist them entry into their border of arrivals.[18] Such experience often leaves indelible scars on the mind of the women and girl refugees for life. The humanitarian staff themselves should be monitored with the view to protecting the women and girl refugees.

This trend of violence against women and the girls who unfortunately found themselves either in IDP or refugees camps in other lands needs concerted efforts to halt. The apprehension that pushes them to move, rather than abating, merely continues even at the refugee camps.[19] We note strongly the efforts made at addressing the necessity to protect women in refugee camps and their equal participation in relief programmes. However, despite all the declarations, conventions and resolutions, the scourge persists.

To make sense of these experiences, as well as other less celebrated cases, various researchers have investigated the socio-legal consequences

---

[15] BBC, 'Nigeria to Investigate Alleged Abuses at Refugee Camps' (2015), www.bbc.co.uk.

[16] M. Obradovic, 'Protecting Female Refugees Against Sexual and Gender-Based Violence in Camps' (2015), ourworld.unu.edu.

[17] Jane Freedman, 'Sexual and Gender-Based Violence Against Refugee Women: A Hidden Aspect of the Refugee Crisis' 24(47), *Reproductive Health Matters* (2016): 18–26.

[18] Ibid.

[19] Volunteers Team (2018), *supra* note 2.

on women and girls, re-examined common challenges and developed new concepts and theoretical frameworks.[20] One of the results is that there is a need for a new dimension to ensure accessibility to justice by refugee women and girls. In view of the foregoing, this paper is divided into five sections. Section 1 of the chapter is introductory and gives a brief overview of the causes and the state of brutalisation facing females in the world today. Section 2 of the chapter dwells on the challenges that refugee women and girls who are survivors of violence face in accessing justice, most importantly when the staff of the agencies who are to guide them on the path to justice are actively engaged in the sexual abuse. In Sect. 3, we review the international laws concerning the protection of the right to access to justice of refugee women and girls with the view to determining its adequacy or otherwise. Section 4 then analyses the best practices across the continent while Sect. 5 provides a conclusion and recommendations.

2 Challenges that Refugee Women and Girls Who Are Survivors of Violence Face in Accessing Justice

At what point will the refugee women and girls qualify for access to justice, where does it becomes a challenge and what options are available to them? The UNHCR in a concept paper avers in general terms that the determination of the refugee status is an administrative or legal process and it is by this that a 'person seeking international protection is considered a refugee under international, regional or national law'.[21] This decision 'can be made on individual basis or through group-based'.[22] And where this is not immediately feasible, temporary protection can be provided.[23] This brings the status of the refugee women and girls

[20] Ibid., 26.

[21] UNHCR, 'The Refugee Concept Under International Law -Global Compact for Safe, Orderly and Regular Migration' (2018); B Nowrojee, 'Sexual Violence, Gender Roles and Displacement', in *Refugee Rights—Ethics, Advocacy and Africa*, edited by D. Hollenbach (2008).

[22] Ibid.

[23] Ibid.

within the ambit of the international law. They are thus entitled to have unrestricted access to all the legal paraphernalia available to sustain their extant circumstances. Literature analysis has shown that access to justice in this circumstance can be incredibly challenging, and sometimes unattainable. For instance, Nilsson states that 'refugee women are encouraged to primarily seek support from the community and not file a report to the police or seek assistance from humanitarian actors'.[24] This demonstrates how refugee women and girls are first subject to what we will term 'justicial self-denial'. Justicial self-denial is a situation where a distressed and suffering refugee women and girls are advised not to seek justice either because of tradition or empathy thereby inflicting themselves ingrained psychological trauma they may live with till the end of their lives. This seems to deprive the refugee women and girls the deployment of the rule of law to solve the predicaments they find themselves in. It strengthens the position of the UN Women in their perspective that 'the rule of law often rules women out'.[25] And for which they called 'on governments to show strong commitment, accelerate actions and policies to increase women's access to justice, and foster a responsive justice system that advances women's equal rights, opportunity and participation'.[26] Nevertheless, refugee women and girls are still grossly denied access to justice in the face of international law.

Under international law, we posit that municipal constitutions align with the age-old doctrine of access to justice. Access to justice is a significant aspect of human rights without which rule of law will be hard to observe.[27] States recognise that the right of access to justice extends to every person and must be available to all individuals 'irrespective of their nationality', statelessness, 'no matter their status either as asylum seekers, refugees, migrant workers, unaccompanied children or other persons who may find themselves in or subject to the jurisdiction of other

24 Helena Nilsson, 'Sudanese and South Sudanese Refugee Women's Sense of Security in Kakuma Refugee Camp' (2013): 29.

25 UN Women, 'Strengthening Women's Access to Justice', https://www.unwomen.org/en/news/in-focus/strengthening-womens-access-to-justice.

26 Ibid.

27 Declaration of the High-level meeting of the General Assembly on the Rule of Law at the National and International Levels, November 30, 2012, A/RES/67/1, paragraphs 14–16.

states'.[28] In practice however, it has been noted that refugees and stateless persons are denied access to justice systems in host states due to their administrative circumstances.[29] Usually upon arriving at refugee camps, host states often impose restrictions on the movement of the refugees and this deprives them of their right to access justice.[30] Donnelly and Muthiah noted that restriction on the movement of women and girls in refugee camps often has gender colouration.[31] This denial flies in the face of the commitment of the states under relevant international conventions and laws to eliminate discriminatory restrictions that can impair access to justice by women and girls in such circumstances.

International instruments are springboards where ideas could be tapped and measures adopted to protect the human rights, including access to justice, of refugees and asylum-seeking women and girls.[32] Studies have been conducted into the factors which constitute barriers to women having access to justice. In a study at the European Court of Human Rights on the low number of applications filed by women, the following are listed as causes of the low patronage of women to access justice:

> ...lack of awareness, confidence and resources, gender bias and cultural, social, and economic barriers. These barriers are particularly important in the case of women victims of violence who are in situations of vulnerability, such as women victims of various forms of discrimination.[33]

As a result, it can safely be deduced that inequalities between women and men, gender bias, stereotypes amongst other factors have resulted in unequal access of the women to justice.[34]

---

[28] Basic principles and guidelines on the right to a remedy and reparations for victims of gross violations of international human rights law and serious violence of international humanitarian law, VII, paragraph 12, A/RES/60/147, March 21, 2006.

[29] Rose Donnelly and Viknes Muthiah, 'Women and Girls in Refugee Camps States' Obligations Under International Law' (2019): 39.

[30] Ibid.

[31] Ibid., 39.

[32] Council of Europe, 'Migrant and Refugee Women and Girls', www.coe.int.

[33] Council of Europe, 'Guaranteeing Equals of Women to Justice', www.coe.int.

[34] Ibid.

Another area is funding. How much is available from government? Are there other sources of funding to assist refugee women to attain justice for the injustices meted on them? Are there legal aids aside what the government can provide within the available resources? In this sense, there might be need for the system to prioritise funding. Refugee women and girls should be encouraged with affirmative funding. That is, a funding policy that is deliberately skewed to help the refugee women and the girls for them to get access to justice and vent their grievances to the system.

Writing on the enthusiasm of the legal experts to find solution to every citizen (including refugee women and girls) accessing justice, Bock quoting Jenkins of Starbucks emphasised on 'the need for legal expertise to help citizens live their best lives' and that '[t]here's the need for people who do not have representation and aren't knowledgeable about the legal system to have someone assist them'.[35] Such legal expertise is not only limited to litigation but 'includes more universal legal needs'.

The Judicial Council on Cultural Diversity[36] also listed the challenges to access justice for refugee women and girls to include: 'the intimidating process of arriving at court'; 'concerns about safety while waiting at court'; 'lack of understanding of court processes'; 'difficulty understanding forms, charges, orders or judgements'; 'courtroom dynamics, including physical proximity of perpetrator to victim'; 'the impact of attitudes and actions of judicial officers, including lack of cultural sensitivity; lack of availability of men's behaviour change programs' and 'abuse of court processes by perpetrators'.

Although Jenkins' view is general, it can be said to be applicable to refugee women and girls. Other barriers to access justice is the lack of independence and inability to access employment.[37] Most often the refugee women and girls would not have the opportunity to work either

---

[35] S. Bock, 'Community, Legal & Industry Education, Professional Development Relativity' (November 8, 2018), https://www.relativity.com/blog/4-barriers-blocking-access-to-justice-and-how-to-break-them/.

[36] Judicial Council on Cultural Diversity, 'Barriers to Access to Justice for Migrant and Refugee Women', https://jccd.org.au/wp-content/uploads/2018/06/Migrant-Refugee-Women-FACTSHEET.pdf.

[37] Ibid., 31.

because of language barrier or lack of qualification. It is not expected that they will bring along any certificate in the circumstances of their leaving home. More so, some of them may also be uneducated and this will contribute to their inability to get employed in a better job.

Regrettably, in many countries such as Nigeria the criminal justice framework is being frustrated by many factors. These include the activities of the Boko Haram, lack of funding and lack of adequate institutional support, in places like Adamawa, Yobe and Borno States.[38] In these states, the incessant deadly Boko Haram attacks have affected the courts' work thereby denying women and girls access to justice. The courts and police stations have been the consistent target of the Boko Haram and this has weakened and paralysed access to justice. The judges, police and court staffs have therefore had to run for their lives. Enactment of anti-terrorism legislation, the Terrorism (Prevention) Act 2011 has not deterred the deadly operation of the organisation. The existing federal legislative framework has not been made functional because of the activities of the terrorists groups.[39] The difference here is that though there is opportunity to access justice in places where violence against women and girls are being carried out, yet the mere deadly attack of the Boko Haram on the institutions of justice has frustrated the road to access to justice.

3 International Law Concerning the Protection of the Rights of Refugee Women and Girls

Many instruments have been adopted at the international level to ensure the protection of refugee and asylum-seeking women and girls.[40] The main instrument is the UN Convention Relating to the Status

[38] Kubiat Umana, 'Effects of Boko Haram activities in Nigeria' (2019), http://researchcyber.com/effects-of-boko-haram-activities-in-Nigeria/.

[39] UNHCR, 'Access to Justice Project Report', June-December 2016, file:///C:/Users/user/AppData/Local/Temp/1483607913.pdf.

[40] The most recent of these instruments have been provided.

of Refugees and Exiles adopted in Geneva on July 28, 1951 (1951 Convention). The 1951 Convention defines refugee as:

> Any person who owing to a well-founded fear of persecution for reasons of race, religion, nationality, membership of a particular social group or political opinion, is outside the country of his nationality and is unable, or owing to such fear, is unwilling to avail himself of the protection of that country, or who, not having a nationality and being outside the country of his former habitual residence, is unable, or owing to such fear, is unwilling to return to it.[41]

The evident policy behind this article is based on the universal belief that an individual escaping from their country to another is running away from fear of persecution or any of the other causes listed in the convention and should be entitled to protection under international law. This seems to invest an individual with a natural right of entry. It is not entry however that makes it natural but the simple fact of the universality of the 1951 Convention and its applicability.

Article 1 of the 1969 Organisation of African Unity (OAU) Convention on Refugees also sets out, in addition to the criteria included in the 1951 Convention, the following:

> ...every person who, owing to external aggression, occupation, foreign domination or events seriously disturbing public order in either part or the whole of his country of origin or nationality, is compelled to leave his place of habitual residence in order to seek refuge in another place outside his country of origin or nationality.[42]

[41] Article 1A(2) of the 1951 Convention, as complemented by the 1967 Protocol.

[42] 1951 Refugee Convention and UN Protocol Relating to the Status of Refugees. Other instruments are listed below:

(1967) http://www.unhcr.org/3b66c2aa10.html; UN General Assembly International Covenant on Civil and Political Rights (1966), known as 'ICCPR', https://treaties.un.org/doc/Publication/UNTS/Volume%20999/volume-999-I-14668-English.pdf; UN General Assembly International Covenant on Economic, Social and Cultural Rights (1966), known as 'ICESCR', http://www.ohchr.org/EN/ProfessionalInterest/Pages/CESCR.aspx; UN General Assembly International Convention on the Elimination of All Forms of Racial Discrimination (1969), http://www.ohchr.org/EN/ProfessionalInterest/Pages/CERD.aspx; UN Convention on the elimination of All Forms of Discrimination against Women (1979) known as 'CEDAW', http://www.un.org/womenwatch/daw/cedaw/text/econvention.htm; UNHCR Policy on Refugee Women

This definition amplifies on the 1951 Convention and broadens the scope of causes that could make one become a refugee in another

---

(1990), http://www.refworld.org/docid/3bf1338f4.html; UN Convention on the Rights of the Child, known as 'CRC' (1990), http://www.ohchr.org/EN/ProfessionalInterest/Pages/CRC.aspx; UNHCR Guidelines on the Protection of Refugee Women (1991), http://www.unhcr.org/3d4f915e4.html; UN Declaration on the Elimination of Violence against Women, known 'DEVAW'(1993), http://www.refworld.org/docid/3b00f25d2c.html; UN Beijing Declaration and Platform of Action, Fourth World Conference on Women (1995), http://www.un.org/womenwatch/daw/beijing/pdf/BDPfA%20E.pdf; UNHCR Policy on Harmful Traditional Practices (1997), http://www.refworld.org/docid/3efc79f34.html; UN Optional Protocol to the Convention on the Elimination of All Forms of Discrimination against Women (1999), http://daccess-dds-ny.un.org/doc/UNDOC/GEN/N99/774/73/PDF/N9977473.pdf?OpenElement; UNHCR Policy on Older Refugees (2000), http://www.unhcr.org/4e857c279.html; UN Security Council Resolution No. 1325/2000 on Women and Peace and Security, http://www.europarl.europa.eu/sides/getDoc.do?pubRef=-%2f%2fEP%2f%2fNONSGML%2bCOMPARL%2bPE-571.702%2b01%2bDOC%2bPDF%2bV0%2f%2fEN; UNProtocol to Prevent, Suppress and Punish Trafficking in Persons, Especially Women and Children, Supplementing the UN Convention against Transnational Organized Crime, known as 'Palermo Trafficking Protocol' (2000), http://www.refworld.org/docid/4720706c0.html; UNHCR Five Commitments to Refugee Women (2001), http://www.refworld.org/docid/479f3b2a2.html; UNHCR Guidelines on International Protection: Gender-related Persecution within the Context of Article 1A(2) of the 1951 Convention and/or its 1967 Protocol relating to the Status of Refugees (2002), http://www.refworld.org/pdfid/3d36f1c64.pdf; UNHCR Sexual and Gender-based Violence against Refugees, Returnees and Internally Displaced Persons. Guidelines for Prevention and Response (2003), http; UN Economic and Social Council (ECOSOC) Resolution No. 31/2005 on Mainstreaming a Gender Perspective into All Policies and Programmes in the United Nations System, http://www.refworld.org/docid/463b3d652.html; United Nations Convention relating to the Status of Stateless Persons of 1954, https://www.coe.int/t/dghl/monitoring/trafficking/Source/PDF_Conv_197_Trafficking_Erev.pdf; Council of Europe Convention on Action against Trafficking in Human Beings (2005), https://www.coe.int/t/dghl/monitoring/trafficking/Source/PDF_Conv_197_Trafficking_Erev.pdf; UNHCR Guidelines on International Protection: the Application of article 1A(2) of the1951 Convention and/or its 1967 Protocol relating to the Status of Refugees to Victims of Trafficking and Persons at Risk of Being Trafficked (2006), http://www.refworld.org/pdfid/443679fa4.pdf; UN General Assembly In-depth Study on All Forms of Violence against Women (2006), http://daccess-dds-ny.un.org/doc/UNDOC/GEN/N06/419/74/PDF/N0641974.pdf?OpenElement; UN Security Council Resolution No. 1820/2008 on Acts of Sexual Violence against Civilians in Armed Conflicts (2008), http://www.refworld.org/docid/485bbca72.html; UNHCR Handbook for the Protection of Women and Girls (2008), http://www.refworld.org/docid/47cfc2962.html; Council of Europe Convention on preventing and combating violence against women and domestic violence (so called Istanbul Convention, 2011), https://www.coe.int/t/DGHL/STANDARDSETTING/EQUALITY/03themes/violence-againstwomen/Conv_VAW_en.pdf; UN General Recommendation No. 32/2014 of the Committee on the Elimination of Discrimination against Women on the Gender-related Dimensions of Refugee Status, Asylum, Nationality and Statelessness of Women, http://daccess-dds-ny.un.org/doc/UNDOC/GEN/N14/627/90/PDF/N1462790.pdf?OpenElement; UN Sustainable Development Goal (SDG) No. 5: Achieve Gender Equality and Empower All Women and Girls (2015). SDGs have been adopted through a UN General Assembly resolution in 2015, http://www.un.org/ga/search/view_doc.asp?symbol=A/RES/70/1&Lang=E.

country. This, it can be argued, amplifies and concretises the universality of the natural right as invested on an individual.

The European Union (EU) countries do not have any legislation having semblance to the 1951 Convention and the 1969 Convention of the African Union (AU).[43] Given the provisions of these conventions and fact that refugees have been maintained and assisted under them since 1951, could it be said that its contents are inadequate to deal with the modern refugee problems? Concerning refugee status, in Europe in 2019, the following were conferred:

> 109 000 persons were granted refugee status in the EU-27 (group) in 2019 at first instance, 52 000 were given subsidiary protection status, and 45 100 were given authorisation to stay for humanitarian reasons.[44]

To this extent, Sansonetti argues that though the EU may not possess competence in this regard, they must give effect to the international instruments in favour of the refugees.[45] Specifically, there is 'no EU legislation protecting refugee women and guaranteeing their integration into the host society'. This may explain one of the reasons why most refugee women and girls resort to prostitution, begging for alms and some other degrading vocations.[46] The benevolent treatment refugee women and girls enjoy therefore takes its root from the respect to international commitment which flows directly from those instruments and others to which the European countries are signatory to.[47]

In this sense, the Charter of Fundamental Rights of the EU enshrines the gender equality principle, which must 'be respected in all areas

[43] African Union is formerly the Organisation of African Unity.

[44] Euro stat Statistics Explained, 'Number of asylum applicants (non-EU-27 citizens), EU-27, 2008–2019' (2020), https://ec.europa.eu/eurostat/statistics-explained/index.php/Asylum_statistics.

[45] Silvia Sansonetti. *Female Refugees and Asylum Seekers: The Issue of Integration* (Policy Department for Citizen's Rights and Constitutional Affairs) (2016): 17, http://www.europarl.europa.eu/supporting-analyses.

[46] Al-Monitor, 'Syrian Refugee Girls Exploited by Prostitution Networks' (March 13, 2014) Syrian refugee girls exploited by prostitution networks (al-monitor.com).

[47] Ibid.

without preventing the adoption of measures providing specific advantages in favour of the more vulnerable sex'.[48] The EU has been supportive of not just refugee women and girls but others through integration. Most significantly, the EU's mandate to its constituents to ensure that 'victims should (are) provided (with) thorough information concerning their rights including the possibility to apply for international protection and the services they can have access to'.[49] Nonetheless, there are reports of refoulment[50] by some EU members which flagrantly disturbs their commitment under relevant instruments and directives.[51] The principle of non-refoulement, according to the UNHCR, 'constitutes the cornerstone of international refugee protection'.[52] It has become a normative issue in international law which all nations have subscribed to.[53] The 1951 Convention provides as follows:

> No Contracting State shall expel or return ('refouler') a refugee in any manner whatsoever to the frontiers of territories where his [or her] life or freedom would be threatened on account of his [or her] race, religion, nationality, membership of a particular social group or political opinion.[54]

The states are therefore bound by the terms of this provisions once an applicant falls within the definition of refugee as provided in the 1951

---

[48] Article 23.

[49] *Supra* note 36.

[50] Ibid.

[51] See Directive 2011/95/EU of the European Parliament and of the Council of 13 December 2011; The Directive mandates member states to consider the specific situation and needs of vulnerable groups including pregnant women, victims of trafficking, those who have been tortured, victims of rape, GBV especially at the time of implementation. They must also provide relevant help to pregnant refugees and gender-based violence (GBV) victims; see also the Directive 2011/36/EU of the European Parliament and of the Council of April 5, 2011.

[52] Advisory Opinion on the Extraterritorial Application of Non-Refoulement Obligations under the 1951 Convention relating to the Status of Refugees and its 1967 Protocol. https://www.unhcr.org/4d9486929.pdf.

[53] Shirley Llain Arenilla, 2015, 'Violations to the Principle of Non-Refoulement Under the Asylum Policy of the United States', 15(1) *Mexican Year Book of International Law* (2015): 283–322.

[54] Article 33 and 33(1) of the 1951 Convention. This Provision is Also Binding on States Party to the 1967 Protocol.

or 1969 Conventions. Signatories to the conventions are prohibited from refoulement because of the palpable danger that such victims may be subject to. Under international law, refugees are protected from any forcible removal including deportation, expulsion, extradition, informal transfers 'renditions', and non-admission at the border. Refugee women and girls must therefore not be returned[55] to their either place of habitual residence or country of transit to the present state. While it is not compulsory that they should be accommodated in the country they found themselves in, they must not be returned to the country of origin.[56]

It can be said from the foregoing that there are adequate protective instruments under international law that guarantee refugee women and girls their rights. However, how each of these instruments are complied with and implemented are serious issues that the UNHCR must constantly monitor. The African situation is pathetic. The UNHCR in its 2020 report on Africa observed the following:

> ...there were an estimated 24.2 million people of concern in the region at the beginning of 2018, including 6.3 million refugees and 14.5 million IDPs. By mid-2018, those numbers had risen again, with some 170,000 new refugees and more than 2 million new IDPs—mainly from the CAR, the DRC, Nigeria, Somalia and South Sudan.[57]

Arguably, the commitments to the provisions of the international instruments are observed and implemented more by global, regional and local non-governmental organisations (NGOs) than countries that are parties to the instruments. More needs to be done to ensure adequate response by those countries hosting refugee women and girl and all categories of refugees. Political will and commitment seem to be the essential factors to address the prevailing refugee issues affecting women and girls.

---

[55] It must be mentioned that this principle is not without an exception. Article 33(2) of the 1951 Convention states where a refugee has been convicted by a judgement on a serious crime, he can be returned to his country or country of origin.

[56] *Supra* note 42. We used the word *origin* not in the sense of place of birth, but in respect to any country where the refugee women or girls are coming from.

[57] UNHCR, UNHCR GLOBAL APPEAL 2019 UPDATE, 25, https://reporting.unhcr.org/sites/default/files/ga2019/pdf/Chapter_Africa.pdf.

4 Instances of Best Practices

Best practices are defined as:

> ...approaches, experiences or initiatives that are working well and can be replicated elsewhere, with techniques and methods that produce effects and results, considered to be effective in contributing to refugees welcoming and integration, and therefore deserving to be disseminated and proposed to other organisational contexts.[58]

The use of the term 'best practice' is flexible in its amplitude as it accommodates processes or interventions which could make life better for the refugees right from the time of their arrival till when they are integrated into the community they may find themselves in. Best practices in relation to refugee women and girls means the best effective 'procedures that are accepted or prescribed as being correct or most effective'[59] in the circumstances of the refugees. In terms of access to justice for refugee women and girls, it is expected that necessary attention will be accorded to them at the border of entry, including being informed of their rights under the law, and some collateral issues which could put them in the best frame of mind and relaxation from the gruesome experiences of the past. These collaterals include language training, housing, health, employment and managing relations with host communities.[60]

What amounts to best practices across the continents are peculiar to each region. However, it is not without a guidance. Each country is expected to afford refugee women and girls the best opportunity to present their cases and ensure that necessary supports are given to them. The Executive Committee (EXCOM) of the UNHCR explicates that each country has the duty to grant 'access to fair and effective procedures

[58] Sandra Mateus and Filipa Pinho, *'Welcome!' Collection of Good Practices Already Existing for Refugees' Welcoming and First Inclusion* (Asylum, Migration and Integration Fund, June 2018), http://www.pandpasproject.eu/wp-content/uploads/2018/10/Good_Practices.pdf.

[59] Cambridge Dictionary.org, https://dictionary.cambridge.org/dictionary/english/best-practice.

[60] UNHCR, *Refugee Resettlement: An International Handbook to Guide Reception and Integration*, United Nations High Commissioner for Refugees (UNHCR), October 1, 2002, https://www.unhcr.org/uk/protection/resettlement/4a2cfe336/refugee-resettlement-international-handbook-guide-reception-integration.html.

for determining status and protection needs'.[61] European countries seem to have the larger share of the refugees coming in from Africa and other parts of Asia.[62]

The 1951 Convention contains procedures countries may adopt for the purpose of assisting refugees generally. The best practices are developed with the view to maintain standards that could guarantee the observance and commitment to the 1951 and 1969 Conventions. To that extent, gaps have been identified between the UNCHR guidelines on refugees and the EU standards. The implication is that EU countries have been alleged to be paying 'insufficient attention' to the UNCHR guidelines which is capable of frustrating the efforts of the UNCHR.[63] It must be admitted that the guidelines are merely recommendatory and persuasive at best and are not binding stricto sensu on the countries. Consequently, officers at the border control must ensure the observance of the minimum standards. These include that the following are followed in cases of refugee women and girls:

> ...be referred to the competent authority; that their claims be heard by sufficiently qualified personnel; that guidance on the procedure as well as legal and linguistic assistance be provided; that access to UNCHR and relevant NGOs be ensured; and that authorisation to remain in the territory of the country concerned be guaranteed, pending a decision on the claim.[64]

To ensure best practices, countries are enjoined to use outstanding processes in circumstances that seem unfavourable to the refugee women

---

61 Elspeth Guild and Violeta Moreno-La, *Current Challenges Regarding the International Refugee Law, with Focus on EU Policies and EU Co-operation with UNHCR*, Directorate General for External Policies of the Union (DG EXPO), http://www.europarl.europa.eu/committees/en/studies.html.

62 European Parliament, 'Asylum and Migration in the EU: Facts and Figures'.

63 *Supra* note 61.

64 UNHCR EXCOM Conclusions No. 8 (1977), paragraph (e); and No. 30 (1983), paragraph (e)(i). The content of these have been reproduced in the Handbook, paragraphs 192 ff. See also UNHCR, Fair and Efficient Asylum Procedures: A NonExhaustive Overview of Applicable International Standards (Geneva: UNHCR, 2 September 2005), www.unhcr.org/refworld/pdfid/432ae9204.pdf as cited by Elspeth Guild and Violeta Moreno-La. See n. 47.

and girls.[65] This applies most importantly in cases involving 'third countries' nationals or cases that cannot manifestly be established through accelerated procedure. However, they must meet minimum guarantees to ensure compliance with the obligations of the countries willing to accept them. This will protect the refugee women and girls including other refugees from the scourge of refoulment. A good example is the case of *Ameh & Others v. UK*[66] where a Nigerian woman who had claimed asylum in the United Kingdom for herself and her daughters on grounds of fear of female genital mutilation/cutting, was refused such status under Article 3 of the European Convention on Human Rights. The complaint was held to be ill-founded and was rejected.[67] The implication is that the woman and her daughter risked being returned home to Nigeria to face the persecution she is running away from. The EU standard have been criticised to be relatively high and its member urged to comply with their international obligations.[68]

This is further contextualised by the UNHCR wherein it encourages EU members to relax unfavourable procedures which could easily hamper access to justice for refugee women and girls. Where refugees come across with fraudulent documents and for which the EU members have developed mechanisms to prevent abuse, they should still be given fair consideration. Nevertheless, they should not deny responsibility and should adopt fair procedural rules to deal with the situation. It is in this sense that procedural elements such as 'accelerated procedures; inadmissibility criteria; border procedures; and the "safe third country" concept' under which states may admit or withdraw persons from refugee status[69] become relevant.

Da Costa theorises the following since in a given context:

---

[65] *Supra* note 61.

[66] http://refugeelegalaidinformation.org/fgmc-case-law-and-other-legal-documents#main-content; Also in *Omeredo v. Austria* [2011] a Nigerian woman who had claimed asylum in Austria on grounds of fear of FGM/C, which was refused, invoked Article 3 of the European Convention on Human Rights. Her complaint was rejected, http://refugeelegalaidinformation.org/fgmc-case-law-and-other-legal-documents#main-content.

[67] Ibid.

[68] Council Directive 2005/85/EC of 1 December 2005 on minimum standards on procedures in Member States for granting and withdrawing refugee status [2005] OJ L 326/13.

[69] Ibid.

> ...government services and authorities may be decentralized in many countries, it is important that the moral obligation be also (considered in terms of) a legal obligation to assist refugees in their integration process.[70]

How far this thesis is acceptable depends on the personal commitments of each country and the level of their compliance with the extant instruments and guidelines. In places like Croatia, refugee women and girls are integrated through music diversity.[71] In Portugal and Czech Republic, families welcome other formerly unknown refugees' families and this goes a long way to integrating them into the host society.[72]

Addressing best practices issue of refugee women and girls in line with the 1969 Convention is important. Africa is an accommodating continent where non-indigenes can easily be integrated and be part of the community. Countries like Ethiopia, Kenya, Chad and Uganda host a large number of displaced persons in Africa.[73] Nigeria was host to the Liberian refugees during the war in that country between 1989 and 1998.[74] It behooves the AU to ensure that refugee women and girls in these places are given fair consideration. Carciotto and Ferraro emphasised on the enhancement of 'refugees' self-reliance and building resilience' as determinant goals that can assure success in African countries.[75] These African countries have been complying with Global Compact on Refugees. The efforts at integrating refugees including

---

70 Rosa Da Costa, *Rights of Refugees in the Context of Integration: Legal Standards and Recommendations*, https://www.refworld.org/pdfid/44bb9b684.pdf.

71 Sandra Mateus and Filipa Pinho, *'Welcome!' Collection of Good Practices Already Existing for Refugees' Welcoming and First Inclusion* (Asylum, Migration and Integration Fund, June 2018). http://www.pandpasproject.eu/wp-content/uploads/2018/10/Good_Practices.pdf.

72 Ibid., 10.

73 UN General Assembly, 'Assistance to Refugees, Returnees and Displaced Persons in Africa—Report of the Secretary-General (A/72/354) [EN/AR] < A/72/354 - E - A/72/354 -Desktop (undocs.org).

74 Gbenga Adeniji, 'Nigeria Tried for Us But We Need Help to Return Home -Oru Ex-refugee from Sierra Leone, Liberia', *The Punch*, January 28, 2018.

75 Sergio Carciotto and Filippo Ferraro, 'Building Blocks and Challenges for the Implementation of the Global Compact on Refugees in Africa', 8(1) *Journal on Migration and Human Security* (2020): 83–95.

women and girls in places like Rwanda is a good step.[76] The Directorate General of Immigration and Emigration (DGIE) and the Ministry of Disaster Management and Refugees (MIDIMAR) with the UNHCR in October 2018, began to issue machine readable travel documents for refugees. These documents have embedded in them the personal data and photos that are readable in conformity to International Civil Aviation Organization (ICAO) standards. It gives flexibility to the lives of the refugee women and girls as such document allows refugees to carry on productive business activities across borders, including business, study, medical treatment and family reunification.[77] Again, the Rwandan government integrated urban refugee students including girls in boarding schools in the National Community Based Health Insurance (CBHI) programme in 2019. These are best practices that should be replicated in other African countries where refugee women and girls are resident. The AU should make this a cardinal principle for all its members involved in refugee programmes.

5 Conclusion

Strengthening the framework which could ensure that refugee women and girls are protected from sexual and gender-based violence under international law is a task not just for the government and NGOs but for all who care about protecting women generally. We have demonstrated the reasons refugee women and girls are being traumatised and the reasons they often do not have access to justice. However, these issues can be well taken care of if parties to the 1951 Convention and its protocols as well as the 1969 Convention demonstrate functional commitments as prescribed under international law. By functional commitments we mean that parties should deliberately go out of their ways to create conditions that will be humane enough to accommodate the refugee women and girls and in fact all the refugees beyond the recommendatory prescriptions of the conventions and treaties parties

[76] Ibid.

[77] Ibid.

have subscribed to. The idea of best practices will be meaningful in this context if countries show both resilience and commitment to the ideals of humanity. When refugees including refugee women and girls are returned to their country of origin (in this case, the country where they escaped from), such country returning them violates not just the provisions of international law but offends against humanity. Needless to recount the suffering and psychological trauma that will be attendant to such returnee.

6 Recommendations

In view of the foregoing, below are the suggestions we offer to address some of the latent issues raised in the chapter.

- Women and girls should be encouraged to stand on their views and not give in to empathetic pleas based on cultural and traditional sentiments either of communal belonging or any other. At the border of entry, refugee women and girls are often persuaded to agree to terms that will either not assist them or those that will over-reach them in terms of future opportunities. Thinking that they are being assisted, such refugee women and girls could easily be lured into sexual deals.
- Most studies do not consider elderly women's accessibility to justice. They may be immobile and there may be lack of facility to move them to court. Under the principle of best practices, this issue should be considered, and provision should be made for elderly persons.
- Pro bono legal assistance should be intensified. In this case, legal firms should be given unimpeded access to the refugee women and girls. There should be confidential room where the refugee woman and girls will feel free to pour out their minds. In this sense, where there have been overtures from any of the staff of the organisation, the refugee women and girls will be encouraged to disclose this to their trusted legal representative or lawyers.
- Are refugee women and girls aware of the legal rights through which they could get access to justice? This is an important issue. As soon as they get to the border and their population counted, the refugee

women and girls should be informed of their rights under the relevant laws. Where the government officials would be preoccupied with other works, non-governmental organisations should be enlisted to assist in this instance.

- Countries that violate the concept of *non-refoulement* should be made to pay compensation. Relevant convention should be supplemented for this purpose. This will discourage refouling and ensure protection not just for the women and girls but all other classes of refugees.

References

1951 Refugee Convention and UN Protocol Relating to the Status of Refugees.

Adeniji Gbenga, January 28, 2018, 'Nigeria Tried for Us But We Need Help to Return Home -Oru Ex-refugee from Sierra Leone, Liberia', *The Punch*.

Advisory Opinion on the Extraterritorial Application of Non-Refoulement Obligations Under the 1951 Convention Relating to the Status of Refugees and Its 1967 Protocol. https://www.unhcr.org/4d9486929.pdf.

Al-Monitor, (2014), 'Syrian Refugee Girls Exploited by Prostitution Networks'.

Basic Principles and Guidelines on the Right to a Remedy and Reparations for Victims of Gross Violations of International Human Rights Law and Serious Violence of International Humanitarian Law, VII, para 12, A/RES/60/147, March 21, 2006.

BBC, (2015), 'Nigeria to Investigate Alleged Abuses at Refugee Camps', www.bbc.co.uk.

Cambridge Dictionary.org, https://dictionary.cambridge.org/dictionary/english/bestpractice.

CEDAW Committee, 2014, *General Recommendation No. 32 on the Gender-Related Dimensions of Refugee Status, Asylum, Nationality and Statelessness of Women*, http://daccess-dds-ny.un.org/doc/UNDOC/GEN/N14/627/90/PDF/N1462790.pdf?OpenElement.

Council Directive 2005/85/EC of December 1, 2005 on Minimum Standards on Procedures in Member States for Granting and Withdrawing Refugee Status, [2005] OJ L 326/13.

Council of Europe, 'Guaranteeing Equals of Women to Justice'.

Council of Europe, 'Migrant and Refugee Women and Girls', www.coe.int.
Council of Europe, 2005, Convention on Action Against Trafficking in Human Beings, https://www.coe.int/t/dghl/monitoring/trafficking/Source/PDF_Conv_197_Trafficking_Erev.pdf.
Council of Europe, Convention on Preventing and Combating Violence Against Women and Domestic Violence, https://www.coe.int/t/DGHL/STANDARDSETTING/EQUALITY/03themes/violence-againstwomen/Conv_VAW_en.pdf.
Declaration of the High-level meeting of the General Assembly on the Rule of Law at the National and International Levels, November 30, 2012, A/RES/67/1.
Elspeth Guild and Violeta Moreno-La. *Current Challenges regarding the International Refugee Law, with Focus on EU Policies and EU Co-operation with UNHCR*, http://www.europarl.europa.eu/committees/en/studies.html.
ER Donnelly and V Muthiah, 2020, 'Women and Girls in Refugee Camps-States' Obligations Under International Law', www.lse.ac.uk.
Eurostat Statistics Explained, (2020), 'Number of Asylum Applicants (Non-EU-27 Citizens), E-27, 2008–2019, https://ec.europa.eu/eurostat/statistics-explained/index.php/Asylum_statistics.
H. Nilsson, 2013, 'Sudanese and South Sudanese Refugee Women's Sense of Security in Kakuma Refugee Camp', http://www.diva-portal.org/smash/record.jsf?pid=diva2%3A636637&dswid=-4938.
http://www.un.org/ga/search/view_doc.asp?symbol=A/RES/70/1&Lang=E.
International Convention on the Elimination of All Forms of Racial Discrimination 1969.
International Crisis Group, March 8, 2017, 'Fighting Boko Haram in Chad: Beyond Military Measures', https://d2071andvip0wj.cloudfront.net/24-fighting-Boko-Haram-in-Chad-Beyond-Military-Measures-|-Crisis-Group.
Jane Freedman, 2016, 'Sexual and Gender-Based Violence Against Refugee Women: A Hidden Aspect of the Refugee 'Crisis'', 24(47) *Reproductive Health Matters*.
Judicial Council on Cultural Diversity, 'Barriers to Access to Justice for Migrant and Refugee Women', https://jccd.org.au/wp-content/uploads/2018/06/Migrant-Refugee-Women-FACTSHEET.pdf.
M Obradovic, 2015, 'Protecting Female Refugees Against Sexual and Gender-Based Violence in Camps'.
Our World, 2015, 'Scourge of Sexual Violence in Armed Conflict: Far from Being Rooted Out', www.ourworld.unu.edu.

Rosa Da Costa, 2006, *Rights of Refugees in the Context of Integration: Legal Standards and Recommendations*, https://www.refworld.org/pdfid/44bb9b684.pdf.

S. Bock, 2018, 'Community, Legal & Industry Education, Professional Development Relativity', https://www.relativity.com/blog/4-barriers-blocking-access-to-justice-and-how-to-break-them/

Sandra Mateus and Filipa Pinho, 2018, *'Welcome!' Collection of Good Practices Already Existing for Refugees' Welcoming and First Inclusion*, http://www.pandpasproject.eu/wp-content/uploads/2018/10/Good_Practices.pdf.

Sergio Carciotto and Filippo Ferraro, 2020, 'Building Blocks and Challenges for the Implementation of the Global Compact on Refugees in Africa', 8(1) *Journal on Migration and Human Security*.

Silvia Sansonetti, 2016, *Female Refugees and Asylum Seekers: The Issue of Integration* (Policy Department for Citizen's Rights and Constitutional Affairs) http://www.europarl.europa.eu/supporting-analyses.

T. Farrell and O. Schmitt, 2012, *The Causes, Character and Conduct of Armed Conflict, and the Effects on Civilian Populations, 1990–2010*.

UN Convention on the elimination of All Forms of Discrimination against Women 1979.

UN Convention on the Rights of the Child 1990.

UN Declaration on the Elimination of Violence against Women 1993.

UN Economic and Social Council (ECOSOC) Resolution No. 31/2005 on *Mainstreaming a Gender Perspective into All Policies and Programmes in the United Nations System*, http://www.refworld.org/docid/463b3d652.html.

UN General Assembly International Covenant on Civil and Political Rights 1966.

UN General Assembly, 2006, *In-depth Study on all Forms of Violence Against Women* (2006), http://daccess-dds-ny.un.org/doc/UNDOC/GEN/N06/419/74/PDF/N0641974.pdf?OpenElement.

UN Optional Protocol to the Convention on the Elimination of All Forms of Discrimination Against Women 1999.

UN Protocol to Prevent, Suppress and Punish Trafficking in Persons, Especially Women and Children, Supplementing the UN Convention Against Transnational Organized Crime 2000.

UN Security Council, 2000, Resolution No. 1325 on *Women and Peace and Security*, http://www.europarl.europa.eu/sides/getDoc.do?pubRef=%2f%2fEP%2f%2fNONSGML%2bCOMPARL%2bPE-.

UN Security Council, 2008, *Resolution on Acts of Sexual Violence Against Civilians in Armed Conflicts*, http://www.refworld.org/docid/485bbca72.html.

UN Women (Europe and Central Asia), 2020, Women Refugees and Migrants, ww.eca.unwomen.org.
UN Women. 'Strengthening Women's Access to Justice', https://www.unwomen.org/en/news/in-focus/strengthening-womens-access-to-justice.
UN, 1995, Beijing Declaration and Platform of Action, Fourth World Conference on Women, http://www.un.org/womenwatch/daw/beijing/pdf/BDPfA%20E.pdf.
UNCHR. *Global Trends Report 2019*, https://www.unhcr.org/be/wp-content/uploads/sites/46/2020/07/Global-Trends-Report-2019.pdf
UNHCR Division of Operation Services, 2007, '2006 Global Trends: Refugees, Asylum Seekers, Returnees and Stateless Persons'.
UNHCR EXCOM Conclusions No. 8 (1977), para (e); and No. 30 (1983), para (e)(i).
UNHCR, 1990, Policy on Refugee Women, http://www.refworld.org/docid/3bf1338f4.html.
UNHCR, 1991, Guidelines on the Protection of Refugee Women, http://www.unhcr.org/3d4f915e4.html.
UNHCR, 1997, Policy on Harmful Traditional Practices, http://www.refworld.org/docid/3efc79f34.html.
UNHCR, 2000, Policy on Older Refugees, http://www.unhcr.org/4e857c279.html.
UNHCR, 2001, Five Commitments to Refugee Women, http://www.refworld.org/docid/479f3b2a2.html.
UNHCR, 2002, Guidelines on International Protection: Gender-Related Persecution Within the Context of Article 1A(2) of the 1951 Convention and/or Its 1967 Protocol Relating to the Status of Refugees, http://www.refworld.org/pdfid/3d36f1c64.pdf.
UNHCR, 2002, *Refugee Resettlement: An International Handbook to Guide Reception and Integration*, https://www.unhcr.org/uk/protection/resettlement/4a2cfe336/refugee-resettlement-international-handbook-guide-reception-integration.html
UNHCR, 2003, Sexual and Gender-Based Violence Against Refugees, Returnees and Internally Displaced Persons. Guidelines for Prevention and Response, http://www.refworld.org/docid/3edcd0661.html.
UNHCR, 2008, 'The Refugee Concept Under International law -Global Compact for Safe, Orderly and Regular Migration'.
UNHCR, 2008, Handbook for the Protection of Women and Girls, http://www.refworld.org/docid/47cfc2962.html.

UNHCR, 2016, 'Access to Justice Project Report', https://www.data2.unhcr.org.
UNHCR, 2019, GLOBAL APPEAL, https://reporting.unhcr.org/sites/default/files/ga2019/pdf/Chapter_Africa.pdf
UNHCR, 2020, *Handbook for the Protection of Women and Girls*, www.unhcr.org.
United Nations Department of Economic and Social Affairs, 2017, https://www.un.org/development/desa/publications/international-migration-report-2017.html.
United Nations, Convention Relating to the Status of Stateless Persons of 1954.
Volunteers Team, 2018, 'Violence Against Refugee Women and Girls,' www.thecircle.ngo.

14

Margins Within the Marginalised: Violence and Access to Justice of Lesbians, Bisexual and Queer Women in Africa

Arudi Laurah

1 Introduction

1.1 Background

The category or label of 'woman' has taken a central position in various modern quests towards the realisation of rights and equity within society.[1] As asserted by Reanda, the International Bill of Rights and the subsequent conventions adopted prior to the Convention on the Elimination of All Forms of Discrimination against Women (CEDAW) did

[1] The Vienna Declaration (1993); cemented the place of women within the human rights framework. The linkage between women's rights and human rights was made and this expanded the discussion and integration of women's rights issues to the mainstream advocacy front. The slogan 'women's rights and human rights' resulted in the fusion and inclusion of women issues in many international human rights instruments.

A. Laurah (✉)
Network of African Human Rights Institutions (NANHRI), Nairobi, Kenya

A. Budoo-Scholtz and E. C. Lubaale (eds.), *Violence Against Women and Criminal Justice in Africa: Volume II*, Sustainable Development Goals Series,
https://doi.org/10.1007/978-3-030-75953-7_14

'not appear to deal specifically with violations of the human rights of women, except in a marginal way or within the framework of other human rights issues'.[2] History has proven that the implicit mention of women within the human rights instruments had minimal impact on the lived realities of women as, the 'scope of interpretation was limited and the instruments generally lacked the monitoring mechanisms that would evaluate progressive steps undertaken by different party'.[3] The CEDAW adopted in 1979 by the United Nations (UN) General Assembly was the first legal instrument that explicitly covered the rights of women.[4] The adoption of CEDAW augmented the principle of equality and its adoption brought with it notable developments within the women's movement and the recognition of the rights of women across the globe.[5] In Africa, the Protocol to the African Charter on Human and Peoples' on the Rights of Women in Africa (Maputo Protocol) has been a pivotal foundation in propelling and debunking social and cultural dynamics, which are specific to the African continent.[6] In matters of social, political, economic, health, cultural rights among others, the Maputo Protocol has proven to be a great catalyst in the domestication and recognition of the rights enshrined within it—in many African states.[7]

Despite the advancements that both global and regional legal frameworks have brought to the emancipation of a 'woman' in society, it can be noted that the homogenous outlook and perception behind the identity 'woman' in the interpretation and application of law has resulted in the marginalisation of womxn[8] whose sexual orientation, gender identity

---

[2] Laura Reanda, 'Human Rights and Women's Rights: The United Nations Approach', 3 *Human Rights Quarterly* (1981): 12.

[3] Ibid.

[4] Convention on the Elimination of All Forms of Discrimination Against Women, https://www.ohchr.org/en/professionalinterest/pages/cedaw.aspx.

[5] Reanda, *supra* 2.

[6] Protocol to the African Charter on Human and Peoples' Rights of Women in Africa (Maputo Protocol).

[7] 42 African states have thus far ratified the Maputo Protocol.

[8] Womxn in this paper is a term that encapsulates women whose sexual orientation, gender identity and expression does not conform to society's upheld perception of 'woman'.

and expression (SOGIE) are non-normative. The diversity and complexities that quantify the identity of woman within CEDAW have been critiqued of having a narrow and rigid category of woman and thus creating invisibility of intersecting issues surrounding race, religion and sexual orientation, gender identity and expression.[9] For the Maputo Protocol, the definition of a woman as 'persons of female gender' as opposed to female sex can be purposively interpreted to mean that transwomen are included.[10] However it has been argued that the 'existence of transgender women is often overlooked because transgender issues do not fit in within the dominant religious and/or heteronormative cultures' depicting a limitation in their enjoyment of rights.[11]

1.2 Problem Statement

In African countries, the law cannot be disregarded in its influence to propel the legality or illegality of the diverse forms of sexuality within the society.[12] As documented by Foucault, the seventeenth to nineteenth century brought a new dimension to how sex and sexuality was discussed in discourse and effectively how it translated into law.[13] The perpetuation of a single notion of sexuality through law caused an alteration in how people perceived, discussed, framed and socialised the society towards the embrace of non-conforming forms of sexuality (homophobia).[14] Despite this, in many African countries, the discussion surrounding diversity

---

[9] Lynn Kathleen Pasterny, 'The Subject of Women's Rights An Investigation of CEDAW's (Straight) Construction of Family-Related Human Rights' (Unpublished Master's Thesis, Lund University), http://lup.lub.lu.se/luur/download?func=downloadFile&recordOId=5467368&fileOId=5467372.

[10] Maputo Protocol, Article 1(k); Ashwanee Budoo 'The Maputo Protocol and Inclusivity' in Centre for Sexualities AIDS and Gender and Others 'TransMaputo: Conversations on the African human rights of Persons of Female Gender' (2018).

[11] Tegan Colleen Snyman 'The protection of African transgender women's rights to dignity, life and health through a teleological reading of the Maputo Protocol' (2019).

[12] Amnesty International UK, 'Mapping Anti-Gay Laws in Africa' 2018.

[13] Michel Foucault, 'The History of Sexuality: An Introduction', (1978) https://suplaney.files.wordpress.com/2010/09/foucault-the-history-of-sexuality-volume-1.pdf.

[14] Ibid.

of sexual and gender identities has and continues to be visible in the advocacy front through litigation, literature and within society.[15]

Although acknowledging the principle of equality and non-discrimination that emerges from the universality school of thought, the chapter is based on the intersectionality outlook—brought out by Kimberly who alludes that a human being's identity should not be constructed merely on natural or socially constructed aspects, as multi-disciplinary variables come to play in forming experiences.[16] The paper seeks to amplify the anti-essentialism feminist legal theory, which counters the outlook of women as a unified identity as, experiences in their natural or socially constructed realities are relative.[17]

The chapter contends that, the homogenous outlook on the identity of 'woman' has and continues to cause marginalisation of lesbians, bisexual and queer (LBQ) women especially around issues of violence be it physical, emotional, financial and social. In this light, the chapter attempts to demystify the upheld notion of woman as a homogenous unit to show the diversity that exists within gender. The chapter then highlights the African legal frameworks on women using a teleological outlook that views these frameworks as inclusive of LBQ women in application and interpretation. To conclude, the chapter highlights a few barriers that limit access to justice for LBQ women regarding cases of violence.

2 Diffusing the Margins

The paper echoes Butler who states that categorising 'woman as a universal presupposition of cultural experience which, in its universal

---

[15] Sylvia Tamale, 'Researching and Theorizing Sexualities in Africa', in *African Sexualities, a Reader* edited by Sylvia Tamale (2011).

[16] Crenshaw, Kimberly, 'Demarginalizing the Intersection of Race and Sex: A Black Feminist Critique of Anti-discrimination Doctrine, Feminist Theory, and Anti-racist Policies', 4 *University of Chicago Legal Forum*, (1989).

[17] Alison Stone, 'Essentialism and Anti-Essentialism in Feminist Philosophy', *Journal of Moral Foundation* (2004), https://www.researchgate.net/publication/233628032_Essentialism_and_Anti-Essentialism_in_Feminist_Philosophy.

status, provides a false ontological promise of eventual political solidarity'.[18] To put this in perspective, it can be noted that in Africa, LBQ relations and existence face the hurdle of legislation as laws that criminalise consensual relations 'either by express mention of female conduct'[19] or by using vague language result in criminalisation by interpretation and application.[20] Heteronormative notions are upheld while non-conforming identities, expressions and sexual orientations are vilified.[21] The validation of heteronormative narratives has resulted in the increased tolerance and legitimisation of violence towards those perceived to be non-conforming to the societal set of norms and standards, including LBQ women.[22] From the notions of upholding the moral values, religious beliefs and protection of the fabric of the young, cases of violence are either validated, not reported or at times sanctioned by state and influential people in society.[23]

In demystifying the identity of woman, the paper defines 'woman' as an identity that is heterogeneous in nature, embodying vastness in presentation, expression, sexual orientation, physical attributes and bodily autonomy. This richness in diversity is evident in literature, modern analysis of sexuality and gender studies and in the inclusion and explicit mention of the subject in some legal interpretations and frameworks across the world, and in Africa.[24] As Rich argues, existing literature can be seen to pay tribute to the heteronormative forms of

---

[18] Judy Butler, 'Performative Acts and Gender Constitution: An Essay in Phenomenology and Feminist Theory', 40 *Theatre Journal* (1988): 523.

[19] Human Dignity Trust, 'Breaking the Silence: Criminalisation of Lesbian and Bisexual Women and its Impacts' (2016).

[20] In Botswana, the case of *Kanane v The State* the court was seen to make the penal code provision gender neutral as they argued that it was discriminatory in terms of gender as it explicitly mentioned relations between men.

[21] Ashley Currier &Therese M. George, 'Lesbian'/Female Same-Sex Sexualities in Africa', 21 *Journal of Lesbian Studies* (2017): 133–150.

[22] Ibid.

[23] In Kenya for instance, police blackmail and extortion has been a major source of intimidation and source of violation of the rights of LGBTIQ person, KHRC 'The Outlawed Amongst Us' (2011).

[24] Ibid.

life and inevitably creating invisibility of the non-heterosexual women.[25] She further asserts that this is a falsified reality as those who identify as LBQ seem like they are the 'only ones' within their regions.[26] As echoed by a report on the status of women human rights defenders in Africa, heteronormativity has also created a hierarchy, where certain expressions are viewed as normal and others abnormal resulting in othering and consequently vast human rights violations.[27]

The lack of purposive interpretation of woman to cater for all types of diversities have resulted in less knowledge and limited laws that speak on protection with regards to SOGIE of LBQ women.[28] This limited outlook has also resulted in the lack of comprehensive information on violence as it relates to LBQ women as violations experienced by LBQ women are rarely captured as upheld prejudices and limited awareness hinder reporting and documenting.[29] As has been emphasised by various scholars, the significance of 'research and documentation is key in ensuring that lived realities and experiences are narrated with the intention of preserving culture, informing policy and monitoring the effectiveness of various programs and activities'.[30] This notwithstanding, research and intentional incorporation of the issues surrounding violence of LBQ women in Africa is limited.

The homogenous outlook of the identity of woman within the African continent can thus be deduced to limit the advocacy, legal application and the realisation of human rights of non-normative identities of women. In turn the visibility and quest for the inclusion of LBQ women

---

[25] Adrienne Rich, 'Compulsory Heterosexuality and Lesbian Existence', 5 *Women: Sex and Sexuality* (1980): 32, http://transasdocorpo.org.br/wp-content/uploads/2017/01/Compulsory-heterosexuality-and-lesbian-existence-2.pdf.

[26] Ibid.

[27] ACPHR, 'Report of the Study on the Situation of Women Human Rights Defenders in Africa', http://www.achpr.org/files/special-mechanisms/human-rights-defenders/report_of_the_study_on_the_situation_of_women_human_rights_defenders_in_africa.pdf.

[28] Federico Godoy, 'Mr & Ms X: The Rights of Transgender Persons Globally', *International Bar Association* (2014): 5.

[29] Mawethu Nkosana Nkolomba, 'A Case For Trans and Non-Binary Bodies' Inclusion in Gender-Based Violence Reporting' Huffington Post (2017), https://www.huffingtonpost.co.za/mawethu-nkosana-nkolomba/a-case-for-trans-and-non-binary-bodies-inclusion-in-gender-based-violence-reporting_a_23234880/.

[30] Ibid.

has been highly governed as the conflict with the dominant homogenousheteronomousoutlook towards the female identity is evident.[31]

3 Violence Against LBQ Women and Access to Justice

Violence against women is multifaceted as it evolves along different social legitimisation processes and varies in identification, culture, moral foundation, socialisation, interpretation, expression and naming.[32] As a social phenomenon, violence affects all persons in a society, disproportionately impacting on LBQ women in Africa.[33] Access to justice is a fundamental human right and a principle of the rule of law. The right to access justice enables constituents to exercise their rights and freedoms, air their grievances, challenge norms and discriminatory notions, attain appropriate remedies for their violations and increase accountability and transparency within a state.

African identifying LBQ women face multiple levels of discrimination and violence due to stringent laws, limited research, upheld morals and religious and political rhetoric.[34] It can be noted through various reports that non-normative women identities (LBQ), face multiple level of discrimination and violence. A report submitted to the Committee on the Elimination of Discrimination Against Women (CEDAW Committee) in 2010 highlighted that '(b)lack lesbians and transgender women have been raped, tortured and murdered simply because they refuse to conform to dominant heteronormative and patriarchal norms and values'.[35] In Cameroon and Togo, women who present

---

[31] 'Women and Sexual Minorities Denied a Seat at the Table by the African Commission on Human and Peoples' Rights', https://www.cal.org.za/2018/08/17/women-and-sexual-minorities-denied-a-seat-at-the-table-by-the-african-commission-on-human-and-peoples-rights/.

[32] William de Hann 'Violence as an Essentially Contested Concept', https://pdfs.semanticscholar.org/8fc4/96aded0ce49602c36174fb34424c9e38af50.pdf.

[33] Ibid.

[34] Ibid.

[35] Report prepared by Coalition of African Lesbians in collaboration with other women's organisation 'Criminal Injustice: Violence Against Women in South Africa' (2010).

masculine tendencies are viewed as emulating masculinity, resulting in violent attacks to 'correct' them.[36] In Zambia, reported cases of masculine presenting women are not taken seriously by the police as they perceive that the woman should have defended herself[37] and this shows the perpetuation of stereotypes by even state officials. In Kenya reports have indicated that violence faced by lesbians, gays, bisexuals, transgender, intersex and queer (LGBTIQ+) persons and, LBQ women in relation to this chapter, is high as multifaceted factors play a role in increasing the group's vulnerability towards violence.[38] In Uganda, reports of violence that range from police harassment to corrective rape of lesbian women have been documented.[39] As the law is key in ensuring that the right to access justice is realised, the paper will now analyse the African regional human rights framework with a focus on the Protocol to the African Charter on Human and Peoples' Rights on the Rights of Women in Africa (Maputo Protocol) and its provisions on violence and access to justice for all women in Africa.

4 African Regional Human Rights System

In contemporary Africa, the significance of the law and its impact on the sexuality discussion cannot be discounted. In most African states the law can be perceived as a major tool in affirming the legality of one form of sexual orientation while criminalising other forms of sexual orientations that do not necessarily carry the majoritarian support.[40] The formulation of laws on sexuality altered how people perceived, discussed, framed and

[36] T. Misi, 'Not Crossing the Line: Masculinities and Homophobic Violence in South Africa', *Agenda: Empowering Women for Gender Equity* (2009): 50–54; M. Armisen 'Between Us: The complexities of Lesbians, Bisexual and Queer Women's Organizing in Francophone Sub-Saharan Africa, Case Studies, Cameroon and Togo' (2013) Queer African Youth Networking.

[37] HIVOS, '*Responding to the Safety and Security Needs of LGBTI Communities and Organisations: A Situational Analysis of Malawi, South Africa, Zambia and Zimbabwe*' (2013): 11.

[38] L Arudi et al., '*Research on the Lived Realities of Lesbian, Bisexual and Queer Women in Kenya*' (2016); Human Rights Watch, '*The Issue is Violence: Attacks on LGBT People on Kenya's Coast*' (2015).

[39] Independent Advisory Group on Country Information 'Country Policy and Information Note Uganda: Sexual orientation and gender identity' (2017).

[40] Ibid.

socialised within the society. The classification of homosexuality in the Diagnostic and Statistical Manual of Mental Disorders acted as a catalyst to how laws were adopted, as constraining pathologies resulted in the legitimisation of sexuality through law.[41] However due to strategic litigation processes that many countries such as Kenya, Botswana, Gabon have attempted in decriminalising these punitive laws based on human rights principles, jurisprudence within the continent has increased.

The above notwithstanding, it is key to analyse the frameworks that exist within the African region in relation to violence and access of justice. The section that follows delves into recent developments made within the African region that can propel the conversation on the inclusion of LGBTIQ+ persons, and LBQ women specifically in the fight against violence and advocacy avenues.

4.1 Overview of African Regional Framework

The adoption of the Constitutive Act of the African Union in 2000[42] led to the smooth transition of the Organisation of African Unity (OAU) to the African Union (AU) in 2002 during the OAU summit in Durban.[43] The Constitutive Act established principles whose objective is to promote, protect and respect human and peoples' rights and ensure good governance and respect of the rule of law within its state parties.[44] The African Charter on Human and Peoples' Rights (African Charter/Banjul Charter) adopted in 1981 is the governing legal framework that recognises individual and peoples' rights[45] and establishes supervisory mechanisms that monitor and interpret its provisions.[46] A key feature within the African Charter is its notion of peoples' rights

41 Michel Foucault, 'The History of Sexuality: An Introduction' (1978), https://suplaney.files.wordpress.com/2010/09/foucault-the-history-of-sexuality-volume-1.pdf.

42 Constitutive Act of the African Union, https://au.int/sites/default/files/pages/32020-file-constitutiveact_en.pdf

43 Department of Foreign Affairs, Republic of South Africa 'Transition from the OAU to the African Union' (2002), https://www1.essex.ac.uk/armedcon/story_id/000528.pdf.

44 Preamble of the Constitutive Act of the AU.

45 Articles 1–29.

46 Articles 30–51.

which was not pitched by previous human rights instruments.[47] In relation to the LBQ women in Africa, it is important to point out that the African Charter recognises the rights of individuals to inherently enjoy the rights to equality and non-discrimination, dignity, liberty, security of persons among other rights.[48] Therefore the rights extend to LBQ women.

The African Commission on Human and Peoples' Rights (ACHPR) is a key mechanism within the AU. It is mandated among other things to ensure the protection and promotion of human and peoples' rights, to review state parties' periodic reports on the implementation of the African Charter, to receive communications concerning the violations of the provisions of the African Charter and to interpret the provisions within the African Charter.[49] The ACHPR has played a significant role in ensuring that discrimination and violence against LGBTIQ individuals in Africa are eliminated. In expanding the interpretation of the principle of equality and non-discrimination, the ACPHR in the case of *Zimbabwe Human Rights NGO forum v Zimbabwe* elaborated that equality and non-discrimination are central to the human rights movement and that Article 2 is 'an important entitlement as the availability or lack thereof affects the capacity of one to enjoy many other rights'.[50] Hence, the holdings in this case can be extended to protect the rights of LBQ women.

---

[47] Solomon A Dersso 'The jurisprudence of the African Commission (o)n Human and Peoples' Rights with respect to peoples' rights' *African Human Rights Journal (*2006), according to him the term peoples' within the African Charter has five interpretations; (1) A people that were once 'subject to colonial rule', (2) The number of people occupying a state or territory (Article 23(2)(b), (3) The people occupying and found in Africa, this can be found within the Preamble of the African Charter, (4) The definition can also be interpreted to mean the different ethnic or communal groups that are found within a particular territory, http://www.ahrlj.up.ac.za/dersso-s-a; Richard N. Kiwanuka 'The Meaning of 'People' in the African Charter on Human and Peoples' Rights', *American Journal of International Law* (1988).

[48] African Charter of Human and Peoples' Rights, Articles 2–17.

[49] Ibid., Article 45.

[50] *Zimbabwe Human Rights NGO forum v Zimbabwe* (2006) AHRLR Paragraph 169.

4.2 The Protocol to the African Charter on Human and Peoples' Rights on the Rights of Women

The increased visibility and advocacy of the women's movement in Africa strengthened the need and pushed for an instrument that was specifically geared towards the elevation of women human rights within the context of Africa.[51] In July 2003, the Maputo Protocol—alluding to the place of its adoption—was adopted by the AU Assembly of Heads of State and Government.[52] The Maputo Protocol then came into force in June 2005 after the minimum number of 15 states had ratified the instrument.[53] To date the Maputo Protocol has been ratified by 42 out of the 55 African states.[54] The Maputo Protocol which is a legally binding instrument geared towards the protection and realisation of the rights of women in Africa has been praised for its wide scope of rights covering civil, political, social, economic, cultural, reproductive and environmental rights.[55]

In providing guidance on the implementation of the provisions of the Maputo Protocol, the ACHPR has adopted three general comments under Article 45(1)(b) of the African Charter, two of which make mention of women forming part of sexual minorities.[56] These two general comments mention discrimination on the basis of sexual orientation when it concerns sexual and reproductive health rights. Hence, the general comments of the African Commission extend the scope of the provisions of the Maputo Protocol to LBQ women.

---

[51] Frans Viljoen 'An Introduction to the Protocol to the African Charter on Human and Peoples' Rights on the Rights of Women in Africa', *Washington and Lee Journal of Civil Rights and Social Justice* (2009): 18–31.

[52] Protocol to the African Charter on Human and Peoples' Rights on the Rights of Women in Africa http://www.achpr.org/instruments/women-protocol/

[53] The Maputo Protocol came into force after its ratification by 27 states who were also party to the African Charter http://maputoprotocol.com/the-countries-that-have-ratified-it.

[54] AU 'List of countries that have signed, ratified/acceded to the Protocol to the African Charter on Human and Peoples' Rights on the Rights of Women in Africa' (October 16, 2019), https://au.int/sites/default/files/treaties/37077-sl-PROTOCOL%20TO%20THE%20AFRICAN%20CHARTER%20ON%20HUMAN%20AND%20PEOPLE%27S%20RIGHTS%20ON%20THE%20RIGHTS%20OF%20WOMEN%20IN%20AFRICA.pdf.

[55] Victor Ayeni, *The impact of the African Charter and the Maputo Protocol in Selected African States* (2016).

[56] African Commission, General Comments on Articles 14(1)(d) and (e) Paragraph 4 and on Articles 14(1) a, (b), (c), and (f) and Articles 14(2) Paragraph 12.

4.2.1 The Maputo Protocol and Violence Against Women

Violence against women is defined within the Maputo Protocol as[57]:

> …acts perpetrated against women which causes or could cause them physical, sexual, psychological, and economic harm, including the threat to take such acts' as well as explored both public and private forms of violence.

The Maputo Protocol constitutes various provisions that protect women from violence, by both state and non-state actors.[58] In contemporary Africa, the forms of violence against women can be deduced to be caused by various intersecting factors for instance; economy, conflicts and unrest, patriarchy, religion, social and academic status, cultural and traditional practices and in the general formulation of policies and legislation that govern the society.[59] The Maputo Protocol is specific in tackling these manifestations of violence.

To ensure that preventive, legislative and affirmative measures are adopted and adhered to by state parties, the Maputo Protocol requires states to 'modify social and cultural patterns'[60] through awareness creation activities, education and use of vast media strategies.[61] It also calls for states to 'investigate, prosecute and punish the perpetrators of violence', and at the same time calls for remedial measures to be put up for the victims of violence.[62] Domestication of the Maputo Protocol is necessary for all the state parties that have ratified/signed it.

Sub-regional organisations also referred to as Regional Economic Communities (RECs) have been key in expanding the reach of human rights within their jurisdiction. One such instance is the 2018 decision of Court of the Economic Community of West African States (ECOWAS). It was the first sub-regional court to adjudicate on a case that invoked the

57 Maputo Protocol, Article 1.

58 Ibid., Articles 2, 5, 6, 8, 12, 13, 14, 20, 21, 22, 23 & 26.

59 Alberto Alesina et al., 'Violence Against Women: A Cross-Cultural Analysis for Africa' (2016).

60 Maputo Protocol, Article 2(2).

61 Ibid., Article 4(d).

62 Ibid., Article 4(e) & (f).

Maputo Protocol in a case that was on gender-based violence.[63] In their decision the court asked the Nigeria government to pay reparation to the victims for having their rights violated as guaranteed within the Maputo Protocol that the state had ratified.[64] Thus, the Maputo Protocol's provisions can be used to ensure that women are protected from violence and that their perpetrators are brought to justice.

4.2.2 The Maputo Protocol and Access to Justice

Article 8 of the Maputo Protocol provides for women's right to access justice and equal protection of the law.[65] The state has the duty and obligation to ensure that: women can easily and effectively access different forms of justice and legal aid services; that legal awareness is given priority to ensure that women are conversant with their rights; to train the state enforcement organs to necessitate their efficiency in ensuring a holistic interpretation and enforcement of the provisions to realise gender equality. Article 8 also goes further to expand on the necessity of adequate representation of women within the justice system and to ensure that discriminatory laws are repealed in order to enhance the rights of women.[66]

Research in various African countries highlight that legal aid provision is necessary to ensure that women whose resources are constrained are able to acquire effective justice.[67] The inadequate resources both financial and human have also been reflected to reduce the rate at which women are able to access justice.[68]

---

[63] *ECW/CCJ/APP/35/17 Aminata Diantou Diane (represented by APDF & IHRDA) v Mali.*

[64] IHRDA, APDF obtain another favourable judgement against Mali in gender-based violence case before ECOWAS Court, https://www.ihrda.org/2018/05/press-release-ihrda-apdf-obtain-another-favourable-judgment-against-mali-in-gender-based-violence-case-before-ecowas-court/.

[65] Maputo Protocol, Article 8.

[66] Ibid., Article 8.

[67] Center for Human Rights, 'The Impact of the Protocol on the Rights of Women in Africa on Violence Against Women in Six Selected Southern African Countries: An Advocacy tOol' (2009); The Lawyer's Circle, Oxfam, SOAWR and FIDA Kenya 'Implementing the Protocol on the Rights of Women in Africa: Analysing the Compliance of Kenya's Legal Framework' (2014) 50–52.

[68] Ibid.

4.3 Recent Developments in Relation to Sexual Orientation, Gender Identity and Expression

The African region has been making several progressive developments that seek to expand and improve the place of women in the society. Some of the key developments highlighted expand on the notion of inclusivity as they raise the visibility of groups of women that were neglected in other soft or hard laws. The recent developments also amplify the position of the women's movement as they raise the bar to which much advocacy, activities and empowerment on the autonomy of women hold in higher institutions in Africa.

4.3.1 Resolution 275 on the Protection Against Violence and Other Human Rights Violations Against Persons on the Basis of their Real or Imputed Sexual Orientation or Gender Identity

The ACPHR is an established organisation under the AU whose mandate is also to formulate principles and laws in form of soft law to create a better understanding of the provisions within the African Charter.[69] To highlight the issue around the persons of real or perceived SOGIE, the ACPHR adopted Resolution 275 in 2014. The Resolution is a recent development as it is the first document that has been adopted to highlight the plights of the LGBTIQ+ persons with a focus on discrimination, violence and stigma perpetuated against them by state and non-state actors. The resolution expands on Article 2 of the African Charter that calls for the prohibition against discrimination on any basis as well as sets out the duties and responsibility of the state on how to interact with the SOGIE persons.

---

[69] African Charter, Article 45(b).

4.3.2 Guidelines on Combating Sexual Violence and Its Consequences in Africa

The Guidelines on Combating Sexual Violence and its Consequences in Africa (Niamey Guidelines) were adopted in May 2017 by the ACPHR as a product of the Resolution 365. It was an initiative by the Special Rapporteur on Rights on Women in Africa to develop the guidelines as the issue of sexual violence was still on the rise in African society despite the legal provisions that had been adopted by various platforms.[70] The Niamey Guidelines can assist state parties in implementing, reforming, interpreting and combating sexual violence among young girls and women irrespective of their SOGIE, marital status among other factors. The Niamey Guidelines create an opportunity for civil society organisations, women's rights groups, judicial and quasi-judicial bodies and state actors to better tackle the issue of sexual violence against LBQ women in Africa.

5 Yogyakarta Principles

Following fragmented documentation of patterns of violations targeted and experienced by LGBTIQ+ persons across the globe, several distinguished human rights experts consolidated principles whose vision was to interpret international human rights law as it applies to persons of diverse SOGIESC.[71] It is worth stating that some of the main drafters were from Africa, namely, Kenya, South Africa and Botswana.

The Yogyakarta Principles drafted in 2006, contain 29 principles that establish the standards which states should follow in ensuring the realisation of human rights of all persons especially those of diverse SOGIE. The Yogyakarta Principles though a form of soft law expounds on the international standards set by other legally binding documents and go

[70] Resolution 365 on Developing Guidelines on Combating Sexual Violence and Its Consequences.

[71] Yogyakarta Principles.

further to give a roadmap on how each principle can and should be realised around the globe by both the state and non-state actors.[72]

On the issue of violence, Principle five speaks on the importance of the security of a person and outlines the obligations of the state in bringing this right to realisation. Some of the obligations include policy frameworks that prevent and protect against violence, awareness creation and emphasises the importance of proper investigations against reported incidences of violence.[73]

6 Mechanisms Available for LBQ Women to Access Justice in Africa

Women in society face several forms of discrimination, with women of diverse sexual orientation, gender identity and expression experiencing multifaceted levels of discrimination coming from the reality that their sexuality, gender expression and identity is not viewed with the same lenses as those that conform to the majority consensus.[74] As illustrated within the chapter, the LBQ women matters as pertaining to violence and access to justice have been neglected in the general advocacy initiatives by women's movement and in the interpretation of law that are to govern all women. There is need to re-evaluate and assess the legal frameworks and initiatives regarding violence so as to ensure the representation of women from diverse groups. For this, there is need for available, accessible and impartial justice systems that will ensure that remedies, redress and accountability to LBQ women grievances are efficiently addressed. To facilitate this, LBQ women within African states can seek for justice within various institutions mandated or advocate for this right to be realised. A brief overview of the available mechanisms for the LBQ women to access justice include the following.

---

[72] Human Rights Watch 'Yogyakarta Principles' a Milestone for Lesbian, Gay, Bisexual, and Transgender Rights, https://www.hrw.org/news/2007/03/26/yogyakarta-principles-milestone-lesbian-gay-bisexual-and-transgender-rights.

[73] Yogyakarta Principles, Principle 5, 9, 15 & 16.

[74] International Commission of Jurists, 'Women's Access to Justice for Gender-Based Violence' (2016).

6.1 Courts

Courts are part of the judicial arm of government that is mandated to preside in civil and criminal cases where they hear cases and pass judgements. Courts are constitutionally recognised and they seek to protect the constitutional rights of individuals within a state or within a region depending on the jurisdictions that they have. In Africa, there are three main types of courts that the LBQ women can access in a bid to have their grievances heard and to get redress and sometimes reparations from the violations of their rights.

6.1.1 Domestic Courts

These are the courts that are set up within the state and they function within the jurisdiction. In Africa, as both civil and common forms of law exist, victims and survivors of violence and other human rights violations can seek redress from courts. The Supreme Courts are mostly the highest courts that a person can seek justice. However as the chapter alludes, there is limited awareness of how courts are to treat cases that surround SOGIE.

6.1.2 Sub-Regional Courts

As Africa also constitutes of RECs as earlier mentioned in the chapter,[75] LBQ women can seek justice in these courts if domestic courts are delaying or failing to address the matters presented in a satisfactory manner. These courts have included the principles of human rights and LBQ women have the forum to ensure accountability for violations against their rights.

[75] Ibid.

6.1.3 African Court on Human and Peoples' Rights[76]

The African Court has jurisdiction over states that have accepted its jurisdiction[77] and have ratified the Protocol to the African Charter on the Establishment of an African Court on Human and Peoples' Rights.[78] The Court is mandated to adjudicate on cases brought by states, individuals, NGOs or referred to them by the ACPHR concerning the interpretation and application of the ACHPR and other relevant human rights instruments. The African Court has jurisdiction in two forms, contentious matters and advisory proceedings and their decisions are binding to the state.[79] Approach to this Court would also develop the African jurisprudence on matters related to LBQ.

6.2 The African Commission on Human and Peoples' Rights

The ACHPR is also mandated to receive communications concerning violations of the Maputo Protocol. Hence, LBQ can approach the ACHPR in the event their states are unable to protect them from violence. However, one may question the independence of the ACHPR in matters of LGBTIQ+ issues following the withdrawal of observer status granted to the Coalition of African Lesbians (CALs) due to a decision by the AU Executive Council.[80]

[76] African Court on Human and Peoples' Rights (African Court), http://www.african-court.org/en/.

[77] African Charter, Article 34(6).

[78] The Protocol to the African Charter on the Establishment of an African Court on Human and Peoples' Rights was adopted on 10 June 1998 and entered into force on January 25, 2004.

[79] Ibid.

[80] African Charter, Article 19: Withdrawing Coalition of African Lesbians' observer status threatens civil society participation' October 18, 2018, https://www.article19.org/resources/achpr-concern-with-decision-to-withdraw-coalition-of-african-lesbians-observer-status/.

7 Limitations to Access Justice for LBQ Women in Africa

7.1 Conflict of Penal Codes and the Constitution

As highlighted above, most African states have limited information regarding SOGIE. In instances where a transgender person is arrested due to breaking the law, if their identification does not reflect their gender identity, the police officers have been reported to violate the right to privacy and dignity of the individual in a bid to ascertain their genders. For instance, in Malawi, the case of *R v Soko and Another*,[81] highlights the conflict of the Penal Code and the Constitution, which provides that no person shall be discriminated. The violation of various substantive rights within the course of the arrest to the trial, depict various violations towards justice. The right to fair trial was seen to be violated as: the defence counsel appeared to be deprived of the chance to speak with the prosecution witnesses prior to the trial; the medical examinations that were conducted to the accused and submitted as evidence were a form of inhumane and degrading treatment[82] and the right to dignity and privacy of the accused was also violated as the transwoman was forced to undress in order for the police to ascertain her sex.[83] These claims were however not put into consideration before the Court and the conviction was seen to be passed as a form of upholding the moral compass that the society has on persons of diverse sexual orientation and gender identity.[84]

[81] *R v Soko and Another* 359 of 2009, https://malawilii.org/node/7142.

[82] *C O I & another v Chief Magistrate Ukunda Law Courts & 4 others;* In this case forced anal examinations were declared a form of torture and a violation to the right to dignity and privacy.

[83] L Price, 'The Treatment of Homosexuality in the Malawian Justice System*: R v Steven Monjeza Soko and Tiwonge Chimbalanga Kachepa*', 10 *African Human Rights Journal* (2010): 526–530.

[84] Mlenga Joe, 'How Sociology Enriches Human Rights: The Case Study of Malawi's First Openly-Gay Couple', in *Beyond the Law: Multi-disciplinary Perspectives on Human Rights*, edited by F. Viljoen (2012): 104.

7.2 Political Interference

Political leaders have diverted the attention towards LGBTIQ+ persons when corruption, economic crises and other leadership flaws are detected within their state. Countries like Nigeria, Ghana, Uganda, Zimbabwe, Cameroon and Kenya have been documented on this premise.[85]

One of recent significant set-back to access to justice for the LBQ movement was highlighted during the process of granting observer status to CALs.[86] Resolution 361 was adopted on 4 November 2016 to set up the criteria that would allow NGOs to acquire observer status with the ACPHR in accordance with the then Rule 68 of the Rules of Procedure of the Commission.[87] Following Resolution 361, CALs was granted observer status with the ACHPR. However, in August 2018, the observer status that had been granted to the CALs was revoked during the AU Summit in Mauritania. This decision attests the contradictions that the ACPHR and the AU Executive Council have towards the rights of LGBTIQ+ persons in Africa. As argued by Adrian, the inclusion of the word 'Lesbian' in the name could have been the unstated reason for the denial of the observer status by the ACPHR when the organisation first applied.[88] It is worth noting that the observer status for CALs was withdrawn on the basis that the CALs was imposing 'values contrary to the African values' as asserted by the AU Executive Council.

8 Conclusion

In conclusion, it is essential to state that the lack of holistic frameworks that explicitly include diverse groups results in alienation and the lack of protection. As much as the LBQ women in Africa are protected by

---

[85] David Smith 'Why Africa Is the Most Homophobic Continent', *The Guardian*, February 23, 2014; Rita Scafer & Eva Range, 'The Political Use of Homophobia Human Rights and Persecution of LGBTI Activists in Africa' 2015, http://library.fes.de/pdf-files/iez/10610.pdf.

[86] *Supra* note 78, Article 19.

[87] The ACHPR adopted new Rules of Procedure in 2020.

[88] Adrian Jjuuko, 'The Protection and Promotion of LGBTI Rights in the African Regional Human Rights System: Opportunities and Challenges', in Namwase S. & Jjuuko (eds) *Protecting the Human Rights of Sexual Minorities in Contemporary Africa* (2007) 298.

the human rights frameworks that most states have acceded to, there is room for more dialogue on meaningful and intentional inclusion. As the chapter has deduced, the homogenous outlook on the category of woman has led to limited room for participation for those deemed non-conforming. For an impactful change in addressing violence and access to justice for LBQ women in Africa, the women's movement has to be vigorous in ensuring the principle of equality and non-discrimination for LBQ women. As echoed by Offen, the relevance of the feminism concept is, 'to reclaim the power of difference, of womanliness as women define it; to reclaim its concern for broad social goals' with the view of seeking the 'principle of human freedom'.[89]

References

Adrienne Rich, 1980, *Compulsory Heterosexuality and Lesbian Existence Women: Sex and Sexuality*, http://transasdocorpo.org.br/wp-content/uploads/2017/01/Compulsory-heterosexuality-and-lesbian-existence-2.pdf.

African Charter of Human and Peoples' Rights 1981.

African Commission on Human and Peoples' Rights, *Report of the Study on the Situation of Women Human Rights Defenders in Africa*, http://www.achpr.org/files/special-mechanisms/human-rights-defenders/report_of_the_study_on_the_situation_of_women_human_rights_defenders_in_africa.pdf.

Alberto Alesina, Benedetta Brioschi and Eliana La Ferrara, 2016, *Violence Against Women: A Cross-Cultural Analysis for Africa.*

Alison Stone, 2004, *Essentialism and Anti-Essentialism in Feminist Philosophy Journal of Moral Foundation*, https://www.researchgate.net/publication/233628032_Essentialism_and_Anti-Essentialism_in_Feminist_Philosophy.

Ashley Currier &Therese Migrane George, 2017, 'Lesbian/Female Same-Sex Sexualities in Africa', *Journal of Lesbian Studies 21* (2017).

C O I & Another v Chief Magistrate Ukunda Law Courts & 4 Others.

Center for Human Rights, 2009, *The Impact of the Protocol on the Rights of Women in Africa on Violence Against Women in Six Selected Southern African Countries: An Advocacy Tool* (2009).

[89] Koen Offen, 'Defining Feminism: A Comparative Historical Approach' (1988) 156.

Coalition of African Lesbians, *Women and Sexual Minorities Denied a Seat at the Table by the African Commission on Human and Peoples' Rights*, https://www.cal.org.za/2018/08/17/women-and-sexual-minorities-denied-a-seat-at-the-table-by-the-african-commission-on-human-and-peoples-rights/.

Constitutive Act of the African Union, https://au.int/sites/default/files/pages/32020-file-constitutiveact_en.pdf

Convention on the Elimination of All Forms of Discrimination Against Women

Crenshaw Kimberly, 1989, 'Demarginalizing the Intersection of Race and Sex: A Black Feminist Critique of Anti-Discrimination Doctrine, Feminist Theory, and Anti-racist Policies' (1989).

ECW/CCJ/APP/35/17 Aminata Diantou Diane (Represented by APDF & IHRDA) v Mali

Frans Viljoen, 1999, 'The Realisation of Human Rights in Africa Through Sub-Regional Institutions', 7(1) *African Yearbook of International Law.*

Frans Viljoen, 2009, 'An Introduction to the Protocol to the African Charter on Human and Peoples' Rights on the Rights of Women in Africa' *Journal of Civil Rights and Social Justice.*

Gigi Louisa, Laurah Arudi et al., 2016, 'Research on the Lived Realities of Lesbian, Bisexual and Queer Women in Kenya'.

HIVOS, 2013, '*Responding to the Safety and Security Needs of LGBTI Communities and Organisations: A Situational Analysis of Malawi, South Africa, Zambia and Zimbabwe*'.

Human Dignity Trust, 2016, *Breaking the Silence: Criminalisation of Lesbian and Bisexual Women and its Impacts.*

Human Rights Watch, 2015, *The Issue Is Violence: Attacks on LGBT People on Kenya's Coast.*

International Commission of Jurists, 2016, *Women's Access to Justice for Gender-Based Violence.*

Judy Butler, 1988, 'Performative Acts and Gender Constitution: An Essay in Phenomenology and Feminist Theory', 40 *Theatre Journal.*

Koen Offen, 1988, 'Defining Feminism: A Comparative Historical Approach'.

Laura Reanda, 1981, 'Human Rights and Women's Rights: The United Nations', 12 *Human Rights Quarterly.*

Lynn Kathleen Pasterny, 'The Subject of Women's Rights an Investigation of CEDAW's (Straight) Construction of Family-Related Human Rights', Unpublished Master's Thesis, Lund University, http://lup.lub.lu.se/luur/download?func=downloadFile&recordOId=5467368&fileOId=5467372

Mariam Armisen, 2013, *Between Us: The Complexities of Lesbians, Bisexual and Queer Women's Organizing in Francophone Sub-Saharan Africa, Case Studies, Cameroon and Togo* Queer African Youth Networking.

Mawethu Nkosana Nkolomba, 2017, 'A Case for Trans and Non-Binary Bodies' Inclusion in Gender- Based Violence', https://www.huffingtonpost.co.za/mawethu-nkosana-nkolomba/a-case-for-trans-and-non-binary-bodies-inclusion-in-gender-based-violence-reporting_a_23234880/

Michel Foucault, 1978, *The History of Sexuality: An Introduction* (1978), https://suplaney.files.wordpress.com/2010/09/foucault-the-history-of-sexuality-volume-1.pdf

Protocol to the African Charter on Human and Peoples' Rights of Women in Africa 2003.

R v Soko and Another 359 of 2009, https://malawilii.org/node/7142

Resolution 365 on *Developing Guidelines on Combating Sexual Violence and Its Consequences*.

Rita Scafer & Eva Range, 2015, 'The Political Use of Homophobia Human Rights and Persecution of LGBTI Activists in Africa', http://library.fes.de/pdf-files/iez/10610.pdf.

Shadow report on The Human Rights Situation, Case Law, and Research on Protections on Grounds of Sexual Orientation, Gender Identity, and Expression in the Republic of Kenya 'Kenya Human Rights Commission & East Africa Trans Health and Advocacy Network' (2018) submitted to Office of the Independent Expert on protection against violence and discrimination based on sexual orientation and gender identity, https://www.khrc.or.ke/images/docs/KenyaSubmission.pdf.

Sylvia Tamale, 2011, *Researching and Theorizing Sexualities in Africa African Sexualities, a Reader*.

T. Misi, 2009, 'Not Crossing the Line: Masculinities and Homophobic Violence in South Africa', *Empowering Women for Gender Equity*.

Tegan Colleen Snyman, 2019, 'The protection of African Transgender Women's Rights to Dignity, Life and Health Through a Teleological Reading of the Maputo Protocol'.

The Lawyer's Circle, Oxfam, SOAWR and FIDA Kenya, 2014, *Implementing the Protocol on the Rights of Women in Africa: Analysing the Compliance of Kenya's Legal Framework*.

The Protocol to the African Charter on the Establishment of an African Court on Human and Peoples' Rights.

William de Hann, 2008, 'Violence as an Essentially Contested Concept', https://pdfs.semanticscholar.org/8fc4/96aded0ce49602c36174fb34424c9e38af50.pdf
Yogyakarta Principles
Zimbabwe Human Rights NGO Forum v Zimbabwe (2006) AHRLR.

Index

A. Budoo-Scholtz and E. C. Lubaale (eds.), *Violence Against Women and Criminal Justice in Africa: Volume II*, Sustainable Development Goals Series,
https://doi.org/10.1007/978-3-030-75953-7

The manufacturer's authorised representative in the EU is Springer Nature Customer Service Centre GmbH, Europaplatz 3, 69115 Heidelberg, Germany. If you have any concerns regarding our products, please contact ProductSafety@springernature.com

Printed and bound by CPI Group (UK) Ltd, Croydon, CR0 4YY
30/09/2026
02225700-0019